A RISING
OF COURAGE

Canada's Paratroops
in the Liberation
of Normandy

By Dan Hartigan

Published by:
Drop Zone Publishers
8 Hyler Place S. W., Calgary
AB, Canada, T2V 3G6

Distributed by:

Drop Zone Publishers   Bunker To Bunker Publishing
8 Hyler Place S. W.   1306, 333 – 7th. Ave. S. W.
Calgary, AB, T2V 3G6   Calgary, AB, T2P 2Z1

ISBN
1-894255-06-2

Canadian Cataloguing in Publication Data

Hartigan, Daniel Ronald, 1924 -
A Rising of Courage

Includes index.
ISBN 1-894255-06-2
1. Canada. Canadian Army – Airborne Troops – History.
2. World War, 1939-1945– Campaigns – France – Normandy.
3. World War, 1939-1945 – Aerial operations, Canadian. I. Title.
D756.5.N6M37 2000   940.54'49'71   COO – 910243 – 4

Book Production:
Bunker To Bunker Publishing.
Cover Design: Brian Hutchins Design.

Printed in Canada

ACKNOWLEDGMENTS

For map making, research and textual inputs: George Robertson.*
For MS perusal, critiques and encouragement: Brigadier James Hill, DSO,MC. (retd.).* Col. Fraser Eadie, DSO,CD. (retd.).* Lieut. Col. Ret J. Lynn Moffat, OMM, CD. George Robertson. * Syd Carignan. * R. F. Anderson (Past President, 1st Canadian Parachute Battalion Association). * Professor Emeritus Walter Romanow.* Dr. David Bercuson (Director of the Centre for Military Strategic Studies, University of Calgary. Author of *Maple Leaf Against the Axis, Significant Incident,* etc.). Anne Payne. Andy Charters. Stephen Mills. Hal Holden. Ken Crooks. Heidi Leury. Lillian Benham. James & Elizabeth Cox.
For research and confirmation of certain facts: Balfour Swim.* Richard MacLean.* Myles Saunders.*
For additional textual inputs, e.g. narrations of personal experiences as paratroopers: Dr. Colin Brebner MD.* Boyd Anderson.* Peter Braidwood.* Henry Churchill.* Marcel Cote.* Peter Griffin.* Richard Hilborn.* Howard Holloway.* Bert Isley.* Tom Jackson.* Jim MacPherson.* Esko Makela.* Bill Minard.* Harvey Minor.* Ray Newman.* Harold Miller.* Harry Reid,CD.* George Robertson.* Stan Shulist.* Norm Toseland.* R.Wyrostok.* Morris Zakaluk.*
For research help in Normandy: Col. Fraser Eadie, DSO,CD.* Myles Saunders (Former President, 1st Canadian Parachute Battalion Association).*
For document copies, photographs, and other valued inputs: Photographic Section, Department of National Defence. Col. (retd.) David Mallam, OBE. Jan de Vries (President, 1st Canadian Parachute Battalion Association). * David Galvin, son of Earl Galvin.* Jim Miklos.* Len Hellerud.* Geoffrey Todd.
For the editor: George Coulson, who in the course of a working relationship became a valued friend, colleague and supporter of my project of a lifetime.
For cover design and preproduction; also additional visual advice: Brian Hutchins Design.
For the support of our sons and daughter: Michael Hartigan. Patrick Hartigan. Colleen Goodman-Buker.
For short quotations from Colonel C.P.Stacey's *Offical History of the Canadian Army in the Second World War* (Ottawa: The Queen's Printer, 1960), Max Arthur's *Men of the Red Beret* (London: Hutchinson, 1990), Hans von Luck's *Panzer Commander* (NY: Praeger Publishers, 1989), John A. Willes' *Out of the Clouds* (2nd. Edition, 1995), General Sir Richard Gale's *Call to Arms* (London: Hutchinson, 1968).
For *making the history* related in this book: All who served in the Canadian Parachute Corps in the Second World War.*

*Comrades in arms

DEDICATION

Dedicated to my dear wife and ever supportive comrade

ROSALIE

with grateful thanks for the hard work and
long hours she has contributed to bring this book into being.

PREFACE

At the beginning of March 1942 Canadians had two and a half years of World War II behind them. The tremendous losses suffered by the Allies had led to the darkest period of the war.

Ours was a soldiering family. My brother David was a colonel in command of one of the large Royal Canadian Artillery fortresses set up on the Nova Scotia coast to protect our harbours against submarine attacks. Hugh was a sergeant in a similar fortress. Frank was a Royal Canadian Mounted Police constable protecting the high north. I was a corporal in the Canadian Dental Corps with nearly two years of soldiering under my belt and had recently celebrated my eighteenth birthday. (Yes, like many others I had lied about my age when enlisting.) Stationed in a fortress just outside our home town on Cape Breton Island, I was permitted to live at home.

Early in the morning on the last day of February, Hugh arrived home on two weeks' furlough, and for us the world promised to be a better place for a while. After breakfast all of us who were at home huddled around the radio waiting for the latest news. Suddenly the newscaster came on with a gripping announcement about a Major Frost, who on the night of 27 February dropped with his company of British paratroops behind the French coast near a small town named Bruneval. They invaded a huge estate occupied by the Germans, dismantled a radar station, carted off a heavy load of the latest enemy technology and made for the beaches, where they were picked up by the Royal Navy. This was a bright spot in an otherwise dismal war.

Hugh became excited about this new arm of the service and, a couple of days later, he told me that when his leave was over he would try to transfer to the British Army and volunteer for paratroop training. We parted company filled with respect for the British lads who demonstrated what a few paratroopers could achieve. Shortly, Hugh fell ill and nearly died. He recovered but had to return to civilian life.

I was transferred to Halifax and was about to be promoted to sergeant when a Part Two Orders call went out to all units of the Canadian Army. All unit commanders were ordered to release any soldiers who volunteered and could qualify for paratroop training. As an eighteen year-old sergeant with nearly two years' training as a dentist's chair assistant, I had a lot to lose (including my stripes!) by transferring out. But the lure of the unknown was too great; I had to go!

On 22 December 1942 I found myself, a private soldier, on a train bound for Fort Benning, Georgia, to begin parachute training. Seven months later I was on a ship embarking for the war in Europe. On my return to Canada in June 1945 I was a twenty-one year-old veteran with over four years' service, two and a half of which were in the 1st Canadian Parachute Battalion, which went into action with the British 6th Airborne Division.

Two years after that, during a class at university, I could hardly focus on what was going on around me. No matter how much I wanted to concentrate on the subject matter, I was cursed with a conglomeration of past patrols, vicious battles, lonely famished and thirsty and deadly-tired night watches and horrible scenes of war racing through my mind. To ease my frustration I began to scribble some distracting notes. They bore no relation to the class lecture on biochemistry. Instead, they included reminders of the fates of people like those whose names appear in the following pages.

It was then that I made up my mind to embark on intensive spare-time study of Canadian military history. This was with the hope that what I learned, combined with my own first-hand knowledge, would some day help me to write about the Canadian Airborne in the Second World War.

The story told here - somewhat disorganized, like the battle of Normandy which spawned it - is not an autobiography. It is true that now and then I do resort to the first person singular when relating events in which I was immediately caught up; but much more of the content describes the experiences of other Canadian paratroops - often in their own words - who dropped out of the clouds into France during the first minutes of D-Day, 6 June 1944. Some became casualties all too soon; others battled on alongside our allies from several nations until Europe was set free. Towards the end, in chapter fourteen, I try to let the reader know that in violent combat there may be two sides to most questions.

There are three sources for the information presented in this story:

1. Extensive reading and re-reading of histories and official documents that deal with events during the years leading up to World War II and during the war itself.

2. Copious inputs by battalion members who were there. The most prolific channels were taped interviews, detailed correspondence and written reports.

3. The piecing together of much circumstantial evidence, wrought by research, in an attempt to satisfy two sides of a question that has long remained an enigma for 6th Airborne veterans of the D-Day drop.

The story is not a dry history but a factual record of the 1st Canadian Parachute Battalion in the defeat of Adolf Hitler; its formation, its training for war, and the first crucial months of its fighting contribution to Victory in Europe.

TABLE OF CONTENTS

Chapter I	The Milieu and the Birth of the Battalion	1
Chapter II	Nazism Beyond its Peak	12
Chapter III	Company Commanders' Briefings	19
Chapter IV	Advance Party Briefings	36
Chapter V	"God Bless Canada"	51
Chapter VI	Battalion Flight into Normandy	73
Chapter VII	The Battalion Flight Continues	87
Chapter VIII	The Struggle to Rendezvous	99
Chapter IX	Seizing Varaville	108
Chapter X	The Men in the Plateau Country	133
Chapter XI	The Robehomme Bridge	146
Chapter XII	Consolidation of the Le Mesnil Crossroads	156
Chapter XIII	Paratroopers Still Loose in the Plateau Country	185
Chapter XIV	Enigmas Surrounding the D-Day Scattered Drop	195
Chapter XV	The Defence of the Le Mesnil Crossroads	216
Chapter XVI	The Return to Freedom	245
Chapter XVII	The Drive for the Seine	254
	Index	261

Portrait photos of a few of the soldiers killed whilst serving with the 1st Canadian Parachute Battalion introduce each chapter. R. I. P.

Chapter I
The Milieu and the
Birth of the Battalion

Gordon Davies

One afternoon during the final weeks of World War II, as the Western Allies advanced towards Victory in Europe, the 1st Canadian Parachute Battalion drove through a forested area of the Great North German Plain in what is now Lower Saxony. The overtly pleasant pine tree forest was not unlike those in which nearly all of us paratroopers had wandered during most of our young lives back in Canada, sung to by every gentle sough of the springtime winds and evergreen foliage. That day in northern Germany there was one great difference. New elements began to appear. Every now and then the truck and tank convoy we were riding stopped to let the appalled soldiers talk to numerous walking skeletons – incredibly emaciated people staggering or trying to crawl along the road and within the forest itself. We were now about forty kilometres northeast of Hanover and did not know our convoy would halt in front of a huge barbed wire enclosure about three or four kilometres farther along the road. There, we were told that we had arrived at the Bergen-Belsen concentration camp, newly liberated that same day, 15 April 1945. It was about ten months since the Allies had invaded Nazi-occupied Europe on D-Day, 6 June 1944.

In 1944-45 Canada was a powerful country in terms of military and industrial production. Yet, as an organized democratic nation born in 1867, Canada was only 78 years old. In World War I, with a population of under nine million, it produced an army of 600,000 and lost over sixty thousand killed in the great battles of France. Another one hundred and fifty thousand were maimed. The nation had fought hard.

On D-Day, of the one hundred thousand Allied soldiers landed by midnight, approximately twenty thousand were Canadian - from a population which then stood at eleven million. Out of such a small population - the size of London or New York at the time - Canada landed over twenty percent .of the D-Day soldiers that went over the beaches.

What was the milieu which produced this generation of Canadians, some of whom leapt from the skies over France and Germany to help put an end to the torturing and death-dealing system of Hitler's Thousand-Year Reich?

When Canada began absorbing significant numbers of Europeans into its population the Industrial Revolution was already in progress. By the end of the eighteenth century exploration by a small number of European and British adventurers, with a lot of help from numerous Canadian Native bands, had resulted in the crude mapping of waterways and land routes in the northern two-thirds of the North American continent.

1

The remarkable energy and know-how displayed by so few people from then until 1914 - a time span of less than two average lifetimes - to bring into being the Canadian political-cultural and industrial cohesiveness that generated a modern industrialized nation, was certainly unique. It probably stands alone as an example of human productive energy.

By then, though, the century of death having arrived, the growth of Canada was interrupted by Europe's Great War - August 1914 to November 1918. The severe casualties suffered by such a fledgling nation seemed catastrophic and Canada staggered in its development.

Following the conflict the ups and downs of world economics did not spare Canada. Eventually the rollercoaster of prosperity and hardship culminated in the worldwide financial collapse of late 1929. The Great Depression now held the world in its grip. The one real advantage Canada held during that oppressive period, which lasted into the middle of the 1930s, was that it was still largely a rural society in which a huge percentage of citizens lived off abundant natural resources: fish, cattle, wildlife, domestically grown berries and other fruits, plentiful vegetables and cereal grains. Dried codfish from the Maritime Provinces was traded for West Indian molasses.

But, as in other countries, money from wages was paltry and often unavailable, and the supply of certain foods was insufficient. Generally, though, thanks to parental ingenuity and family dedication, the population remained reasonably healthy and the decade prospered in the sense of technological adventure. Industrial progress in the world was probably at its most exciting by the fact of its acceleration alone. Modern flush-rivetted airplanes appeared; speed records were broken by land, sea and air; hydraulics and arc welding were perfected; railroads were reaching their zenith; new inventions were rampant; and with the advent of widespread radio communication we watched, without realizing it, the electronic revolution gearing up to challenge the Industrial Revolution.

Considering the thirties alone, with so much happening among so few people in such a huge country, it seemed that everyone lived their own private adventure. Hungry from depressed economic conditions or not, we could view the world as an oyster waiting to be plucked from its bed. Harsh changes of climate and remote situations subjected people to hazards that had to be faced with fortitude. But always, around the corner, opportunities for independent action or entrepreneurial initiative awaited development.

Boyd Anderson, from a ranching family in the Wood Mountain hills of southern Saskatchewan, was a youth in his early teens. He rode his horse more than twenty kilometres, round trip, to school every day. Sometimes, in a deluge of flash floods, Boyd and his brothers and sisters found nature's challenge to be fearsome and threatening, yet inspiring. On fine days the rolling hills, with their subtle multi-coloured variation of ground cover, made them feel the call of their ancestry, which went back through senior ranchers who had been neighbours and friends of the frontiersman Buffalo Bill Cody. On days when the temperature dropped to forty degrees or more below zero and strong winds endeavoured to slit the fragile lifelines of Boyd and his siblings and even their horses, or when frozen snow on the wildest of winds whited-out their world, he as the oldest one carried heavy responsibility. Often left alone to the resources of his own ingenuity and determination, he carried out the duties expected of him. In uncertain circumstances Boyd learned to overcome fear and danger. He assumed tasks that members of more protected urban families would think awesome and far beyond the scope of a teenaged boy.

In the warmer months, miles from home tending flocks of sheep or accounting for lost cattle alone, he ranged the prairies, always searching, searching, and in love with the magnificent countryside which had fostered him from birth. In stark contrast to the many times he had been threatened by his environment's severe elements he became one with the land.

It was as though he lived in two worlds, one violent but the other full of fantastic beauty and serenity. Yet even in the calm one he learned to risk the presence of howling bands of coyotes, face the fear of being lost and defy the possibility of being consumed by nature itself during violent prairie lightning storms. His two worlds turned him into a survivor as well as a productive range hand. Almost automatically he developed his inner strength in overcoming savage situations, and cultivated new ways to expedite the continuation of his own existence under the pressures of changing circumstances.

Meanwhile Boyd was oblivious to much of the political instability building up in the world. He could never imagine in his wildest expectations that in Berlin Adolf Hitler was creating armed forces which would, eventually, allow him to precipitate the greatest war in history. A war that Boyd, as a patriotic Canadian youth, would leap into as a paratrooper.

Another young Canadian, Jim MacPherson, was also from a thoroughly rural background. Similarly isolated by great distances, Jim spent his youth in the deep forests surrounding North Bay in central Ontario. He reached his teens in 1937, four years after Hitler came to power in Germany.

For Jim the legends of the region in which he lived, developed during the frontier period by his forefathers, sparked within him an awareness of his own unrestricted freedom. Talk of the adventurous years when the transcontinental railroads and the modern canals and locks of the Great Lakes were built imbued in him a sense of national pride, and an urge to participate in the natural advantages of his country. Canadian achievements during World War I gave him a sense of confidence in his country and homeland.

Like most other Canadian youths he came from robust stock, endowed with clear characteristics of personality and possessing principally Anglo-Saxon, French and Nordic values. His father, mother and grandparents, like many others, came to Canada for a variety of reasons and quickly learned an undying patriotism towards their new surroundings. Such was the heritage of Jim MacPherson, who in due course would be another volunteer for Canada's new "Canadian Parachute Corps."

3

By the winter of 1930/31 the crash of '29 left the farmers of the North American continent financially wrecked and scratching for a living. In central Saskatchewan, where temperatures dropped to forty below and winds howled unchecked by vegetation, the dried-out black earth filled the sky with choking dust and nothing could warm the farmhouses to any degree of solid comfort. Wheat farmers were in terrible shape. Often, there was no money to buy food. Even when the land had not dried out it was not satisfactory for growing vegetables or fruit, so money was needed to buy such commodities at the best of times. Fish was far from plentiful and winter storage of perishable goods was difficult to manage because of the extreme cold.

On one such cold grey night, with a bitter wind howling around the farmhouse far out on the prairies, eleven-year-old Bert Isley awoke to the roaring of fire and the smell of smoke as it filled his room on the second floor. For young Bert there was no way out; flames had already blocked the stairwell. His father, mother and a brother had escaped from the lower floor, and after a struggle young Bert managed to raise the frozen window sash of his bedroom. He was instantly terrified by his height above the ground. The urge to panic was overwhelming.

A galaxy of cruel thoughts raced through his mind: the prospect of bare feet in the frozen snow, the three-kilometre trek to the next farmhouse, and above all questions about the rest of his family. Had they escaped or not? At this point he didn't know. As for the horrible vertical chasm which lay between Bert and the ground, it was like an insuperable barrier to his chances for any future life.

All this tumbled in mass confusion through his mind in seconds, but to the terrified boy it was like forever. He considered again the depth of the fall and his almost certain death. But somehow he overcame his fear, summoned his courage and jumped.

He survived! Other members of his family were with him in a few seconds. But one sister, who had been cut off from him by the fierce blaze, was lost. The excruciating pain from the realization that she was gone was more than they could bear as they made it to the barn, surviving among their warm cattle until help came in the morning.

The Isleys rebuilt and went on, but the strength needed to deal with their great calamity and the ongoing Depression seemed endless and impossible to endure. Yet, they later realized, the character derived from facing such harsh times and such grief led to the development of courage and determination. "Never mind Bert," he told me one day that his mother often said. "Times will get better if we keep our courage up and say our prayers."

About 4,500 kilometres to the east, at Sydney on Cape Breton Island, lived another young Canadian destined to become a paratrooper: A. J. (Scotty) MacInnis.

Cape Breton Island, made up of the four most eastern counties of Nova Scotia, is a land of rolling hills, sharp bluffs, beautiful lakes and freshwater streams. Often shrouds of mist or fog, mixed with the smell of the sea on a slow breeze, create an environment that leaves an outdoors person feeling strong and favoured in the eyes of God. The southeastern quarter of the island settles into flatness between the Bras d'Or Lakes and the Gulf of St. Lawrence. From the towns of Sydney Mines and North Sydney the shore heads southeast past Sydney, New Waterford and New Aberdeen, then south to Glace Bay and onward through the treacherous waters of Scatari Island, passing Louisbourg to the open and often raging North Atlantic. The perimeter of that part of the island consists of rocky cliffs and stony beaches washed and rewashed by the ceaseless rhythm of the sea, sometimes gentle and at other times destructive. When raging at high tide, breakers roll up over the gravel and the rounded rocks and come to an abrupt halt against thirty-metre high sheer cliffs. From there they wash back to form more waves, which slam the island again and again.

Cape Breton Island's main industrial assets are its vast coal deposits. During the Dirty Thirties, when the miners' unions won the "Four-Dollar Day" for the coal miners of North America, the Cape Breton miner seemed fortunate by comparison with much of the world's working class. However, most miners had large families and markets for coal were slack. Men were lucky if they worked one-half day per week, so the "Four-Dollar Day" turned into a two-dollar week.

During the early thirties Scotty MacInnis was one of a family of twelve children. His father, on a half-shift every seven days, brought home fifteen cents a week for each member of the family. All too often the wind came off the Gulf of St. Lawrence, which in early spring was choked with drift-ice coming from Labrador on the North Stream. The wind off the icebergs, saturated with moisture, cut anyone who walked the beaches to the bone, but booty from the sea deposited on the beaches at high tide was left for those who were hardy enough to withstand the cold.

Clothing was scarce during the Depression years, especially for large families. Consequently most children wore hand-me-downs. By the age of twelve Scotty was accustomed to combing the shores after every big storm, searching for lumps of coal, usable lumber or any other flotsam which could be consumed at home or sold for a few pennies.

One April morning in 1933 Scotty went beachcombing with one of his brothers, who was a year or two younger. They rode the old tramway out towards Glace Bay and transferred to a bus which took them to the vicinity of some cliffs not far from Linghan Beach. It was early in the morning after a huge storm and they were buffeted by a high wind which made the weather feel more like February than April. The cold, in nearly a hundred percent humidity, was enough to penetrate the best of winter clothing. That day, the wind came off scattered drift-ice like a merciless scythe made of ice.

They turned up the collars of their flimsy second-hand suitcoats in a vain attempt to protect their ears. Leaning into the nor'easter until it seemed as though some unseen force were holding them up, they scudded along to the sounds of the seashore. The tide was nearly low by now, leaving the best condition for scrounging, but every few minutes they'd run to the face of the cliffs to avoid the splash of the bigger breakers curling towards them. Remnants of slush-ice, left behind by drift-ice gone down the coast and out to sea during the night, made their footing treacherous. Suddenly they spotted success. They came upon a pair of dory oars which had been lapped up onto the beach. They shouldered one each.

Scotty took the lead so that his body gave his younger brother some protection from the howling wind. Suddenly, to his rear, he heard a barely audible shout above the roar of the sea and the cry of the wind. When he turned to look he was horrified! His brother was being dragged from the shore by a receding wave. The boy had slipped on slush-ice and slid into the sea.

Already he was about thirty feet from shore and was about to be slammed by a huge incoming breaker. One thing allowed a glimmer of hope: the boy in the water still clung to his oar. The breaker engulfed him and washed him up towards the beach over the slippery slope, then dragged him out once more. Still, the boy tenaciously clung to his oar. Scotty had no time to think. He knew his brother had almost no chance of survival. Two or three more pummellings by the breakers, which were rolling broken ice and sea-rounded rocks up and down the beach, would wear him out and his numbing fingers would lose their grip. Even that hardly mattered, since the frigid water would kill him in a few minutes anyhow. Scotty knew that he himself would stand no chance if he went into the sea to help.

Time! Oh God, time! The experience that makes a lifetime flash by in a moment, or that makes an agonized moment last forever, was now so crucial. Scotty acted instantly. When the next wave withdrew he raced down the beach behind it. He rammed the hand-end of his oar down among the loose rolling rocks into the sand below and hung on doggedly. As the next curling breaker reached him he lashed out, grabbed blindly and caught his brother's coat. While the wave receded they made for the safety of a cleft in the cliff wall.

Scotty was proud of himself; he now knew that within him there was a fire, a strength of will, which would stand him in good stead no matter what the odds. Strangely enough, for fear of getting a licking for being too reckless, they never told the family the full details of their adventure. They simply explained their wet clothing away as a result of spume from the breakers, blowing on the howling nor'easter.

Their explanation was hardly heard anyhow, for it was suppertime when they got home and everyone was rivetted to the old radio in the kitchen, listening to a political commentary about Germany. In the turmoil of the day Reich President von Hindenburg had, some two months earlier, appointed a new Chancellor - Adolf Hitler. Since then, though not yet the official head of state, Hitler had already secured dictatorial clout. Undeterred by the aged President, he was now exerting his power with acts of terror and intimidation. Also, he suspended constitutional guarantees of individual and civil liberties.

Later broadcasts delivered even worse news. On 2 August 1934 Hindenburg died. Within the month Hitler was the legal head of Germany, with the positions of President and Chancellor combined in his own person. During the next few years, as Scotty MacInnis and his brothers and sisters grew up, the name Hitler came over the old radio more and more often. At first, some people in Canada gave him about the same consideration as they gave to politicians in any other distant country: practically none. In 1936, however, news about Hitler's refusal to shake hands with Afro-American Jesse Owens, the winner of four gold medals at the Berlin Olympics, made everyone sit up and take notice. The leader of one of the world's great nations suddenly turned out to be a racist "jerk." Now, in Cape Breton, that was something serious!

That's how it was in the Dirty Thirties. Throughout the vast reaches of our country things were tough. Winters seemed longer and colder, summers shorter, hotter and dryer, the wind more biting and full of frost, heat or dust. More than half the growing youth never reached high school. Of those who did few were able to go on to university or college. Even those who were studious enough or lucky enough not to have to leave school to help support their families often ended up walking the streets looking for menial jobs after they graduated. Commonly, boys in their early teens drowned with their fathers, fishing on the North Atlantic or on the Pacific off the Queen Charlotte Islands. Similarly, while mothers and fathers toiled for hours beyond reason to earn puny bits of cash they hoped would keep their families together, their teenage sons sometimes found it necessary to hit the road and beg for a living.
Economic conditions like those in Canada also blighted the entire Western World. Those who were rich lived away from it all, those who were not wallowed in poverty and hardship to the point where every country had its slums, hobos and starving classes. Strikes, protests, new political dogmas and petty crime created ever increasing waves of hardship, but two inexorable human entities were on a collision course. First, Hitler, who continued to slop around in the sewage of his own biases: hatred of Gypsies, Jews, Communists, real or imagined opposers of Nazism among his own people, and the perpetrators of the Treaty of Versailles. Second, the developing youth who would grow to form the future Allied forces and who became a designated generation: called by fate from the time of their birth to eradicate the monster who propagated and led the filth of Nazi thought and persecution.
It should have been easy to predict that a short lapse of time would bring hundreds of thousands of lads such as Boyd Anderson from the Wood Mountain hills of Saskatchewan, Jim MacPherson the Ontario lumberman's kid, Bert Isley the farm lad of Saskatchewan, and Cape Breton Island's intrepid beachcomber, Scotty MacInnis, to manhood from youth. It should also have been easy to see that, together with hundreds of thousands of other Canadian youths, they would voluntarily follow their older unemployed brothers into one of the three World War II services. Like their fathers in 1914-18, they would not let the challenge pass.
Hitler, together with what was frequently described in North America

as his hoard of goose-stepping automatons - the Gestapo, his Einsatz-SS and others – deserved to be wiped from the face of the earth. His political and nihilistic pogroms, accompanied by rhetorical speeches and lies perpetrated by him and his sycophants upon his own people as cover for their dastardly acts, were shameful in the extreme. All of it filled with revulsion the rest of the Western World, who now felt a compulsive need to obliterate Nazism.

So World War II in the eyes of the Allied world appeared totally just. The raw political power and hatefulness of Nazism exposed in the German homeland, especially on bookburning days and on *Kristallnacht*, had to be stopped.

In Canada the first ones to join up were the militiamen, who had trained the cadre of the new Army on weekends between the wars. These first volunteers were followed by a vast section of the population which was still unemployed following the Depression. They were, most frequently, the patriotic sons, nephews and cousins of the World War I Canadians of Flanders. Young boys who had not yet reached their teens in the mid-thirties were still too young for service in 1939; but by 1941 they had grown enough that, with a little stretching of the truth, they could pass for eighteen. Jim MacPherson, Boyd Anderson, Bert Isley, Scotty MacInnis and many thousands like them were all in the Army by 1941. When they joined up they could see only a vanquished enemy on the horizons of the future, and they knew they would emulate their fathers of the First World War: they'd fight and win. But they never imagined that their generation would be the critical one in winning the costly closing battles of the Second - having harnessed themselves to the race for leading technology to do it. And they were proud to be the sons of their victorious fathers.

New army camps, airports and naval establishments, along with new armaments production plants, shipyards and airplane factories, sprang up from Nova Scotia to British Columbia. Britain and its other allies, hard pressed to survive and contain the rampaging Nazi war machine, arranged lend-lease agreements with the United States to achieve logistical requirements. Canada built and paid cash for a modern tri-services establishment. It was comprised of a three-hundred ship Navy, five twenty-thousand soldier infantry and armoured fighting divisions, several independent armoured and infantry brigades and a Royal Canadian Air Force equivalent to thirty percent of the Royal Air Force.

To support these forces the necessary field hospitals, dental clinics, ordinance and mechanical services and engineering facilities had to be developed. Service-type electrical, signals and telephone communication units had to be established. The training facilities alone were unimaginable. In addition, many hundreds of millions of dollars were raised and sent overseas as gifts to augment the massive requirements of the British services expansion. Many wondered where all the money suddenly came from when only a few short years earlier everyone was so hard pressed for cash.

A close ally, morally as well as geographically, was Newfoundland-Labrador. It was then governed by a British-appointed commission but would become Canada's tenth province a few years after the war. Meanwhile it made an immense wartime contribution which included volunteers by the thousands in the British and Canadian Armies, Navies and Air Forces, and the servicing of naval and air bases which played key rolls in the Battle of the Atlantic and the Transatlantic Ferry Command. Interaction with Canada resulting from this alliance had a lot to do with Newfoundland-Labrador joining the Canadian Federation in 1949.

In the early years of the war a slide from optimism downward into darkness occurred for the Allied side. In 1939 Poland was overrun by the Nazis. In 1940 Belgium, Holland, Denmark and Norway collapsed and, most shocking of all, France surrendered, all at the hands of Germany alone. Then Italy, encouraged by the success of Germany and the ease with which she herself had previously grabbed her East African and North African empires at the expense of the Ethiopian and Arabian peoples, formed the Axis partnership with Germany and declared war on England and France when France was crumbling. The move was seen by the Commonwealth of Nations as a cowardly stab in the back.

The depth of bitter feeling throughout the British Empire and the Commonwealth, at the time the only world entities left fighting the Axis powers, was so intense that Roosevelt's "Day of Infamy Speech," made a year and a half later following Pearl Harbor, could have easily applied. Dark days turned even more morose for the balance of 1940, but the combined British ship of state sailed precipitously onward towards the abyss of 1941. That year, the highly organized and militarily motivated Germans overran Yugoslavia, Greece, Crete and most of European Russia. The dark night of World War II turned black!

But amid the blackness glowed a couple of bright spots. To begin with, a force of about four thousand soldiers from Britain, India, New Zealand and Australia gave the Italians, in their new-found empires, the shellacking of their lives. They put an entire Italian army of over a hundred and fifty thousand men into barbed wire enclosures. The perpetrators of "the great stab in the back" were seen as the proverbial buffoons of the battlefield, and their conquerors gloated.

The United States was still not in the war, but morale in Britain and its related allies soared. Then came the second bright spot: Hitler's folly led Germany towards its ultimate downfall. On 22 June 1941 he invaded Russia and picked up Hungary and Rumania as his allies along the way. Finally a cloud of infamy with a silver lining spread over the Pacific Ocean. The Japanese made an error. On 7 December they attacked and destroyed the United States' fleet at Pearl Harbor. Now the whole world was embroiled in insanity. The industrially developed, but socially retarded, nations of the world convulsed in a new firestorm. Even the degradation of World War I was exceeded. Of the industrialized Western nations only Sweden, Switzerland, Portugal, Turkey and Spain retained their neutrality - the last-named probably because it had so recently wallowed in its own revolutionary gore.

This was the state of affairs in the world of nations when Boyd Anderson, Jim MacPherson, Bert Isley and Scotty MacInnis were now private soldiers in the Canadian Army.

As part of the build-up of the new armed forces it was decided in early 1942 to copy Russia, Germany, Britain and the United States in chasing the newest technology of modern infantry warfare - the development of airborne forces.

Rapid planning led to the formation of the 1st and 2nd Canadian Parachute Battalions supported by two other units: a Parachute Training Centre at Camp Shilo, Manitoba, and a Parachute Infantry Training Company based in England.

By the summer of 1944 the Parachute Infantry Training Company had expanded to nearly battalion size in England. Together these units formed the Canadian Parachute Corps. Both the 1st and 2nd Canadian Parachute Battalions became famous when the 1st was attached to the 6th British Airborne Division and the 2nd joined with the Americans to form the 1st Special Service Force, nostalgically known as the Devil's Brigade.

The required organization for the development of the paratroop units began in 1942. Since there had been close co-operation between the United States and Canada, an agreement was reached to train Canadians at the U.S. School of Infantry at Fort Benning, Georgia, until the Shilo facilities in Manitoba were completed. An additional reason for getting training underway without delay was that some important strategists knew how Norway and the Aleutian Islands loomed large in the Allied collective mind. The Japanese were attacking throughout the South Pacific, the Central Pacific and along the Pacific Rim. They even shelled Dutch Harbor on Unalaska Island, one of the near islands of the United States' Aleutians. The new Canadian-American unit would train at Helena, Montana.

The 1st Canadian Parachute Battalion was originally meant for highly mobile home defence to meet threats to any of the Canadian coastlines. Savage shipping losses were suffered in the Gulf of St. Lawrence from enemy submarines, a short way off Sydney Harbour towards the Atlantic. It was therefore quite possible that accompanying enemy commando-type raids could well take place anywhere along the sparsely populated coastlines. In March 1943 the battalion returned from Fort Benning to Canada for advanced infantry training at the new Camp Shilo Paratroop Training Centre.

By then the raw manpower for the new units was partially assembled, but recruiting for the 1st Canadian Parachute Battalion was slow. Few who had the initiative to become paratroopers wanted to serve in a unit which at first was intended for home defence only. They wanted to get to England and help defeat Hitler's Nazis in the European theatre of war.

Many of these men already had from one to two and a half years of military service and had been through one of Canada's main advanced training camps such as Vernon and Nanaimo, B.C., Barrie and Camp Borden, Ontario, or Aldershot, Nova Scotia. It turned out that the collection of novice paratroopers was unique - mostly seasoned trainees and reverted non-commissioned officers from the regular army.

In June 1943 the 1st Canadian Parachute Battalion was issued with combat weapons at Camp Shilo and proceeded in July to Halifax, where they boarded the *Queen Elizabeth* - converted from a luxury ocean liner to a troopship - and in less than four days landed in Scotland. They immediately joined Brigadier James Hill's 3rd Brigade in General Richard Gale's 6th British Airborne Division. There, the Canadian unit not only trained hard for the next ten months but also did its share in the development and testing of new equipment, devising innovative techniques for the carrying and care of extra equipment on the person of the Airborne soldier. All the while the unit readied itself for warfare.

Chapter II

Nazism Beyond its Peak

G. Kroesing

When the 1st Canadian Parachute Battalion went into action in 1944 the Western Allies faced not the conquering enemy of the early and middle war years but an even more savage foe - a regime which knew that its very life was at stake and would fight with all the ferocity and cunning it could muster in a desperate bid for survival.

By the spring Nazism as a political force in world affairs had shot its bolt and was well beyond its peak. Great battles lay in the future but Hitler as Commander in Chief had run amok. By replacing the professionalism of the German General Staff with his own twisted Nazi doctrines and by issuing orders straight out of his own amateurism and intransigence, he had set his *Wehrmacht* on a definite path towards total destruction.

Between 1937, when he annexed Austria and Czechoslovakia, and the spring of 1944 his armies certainly did themselves proud. It was during this period that the designated generation born in the 1920s passed from boyhood to manhood and formed the cream of the armed forces of the Western Allies. Indeed, this same generation from most of the world was destined to bring the nearly six-year world slaughter to a close. By 1943-44-45, when the armed forces of the United States, Canada and Britain fought their really big battles, the Germans and Russians had already committed major portions of the same generation from their own people to the soil of the USSR and to the convalescence hospitals of Europe.

Although Hitler had completed his invasion of Poland in record time, and his occupation of that country was well organized in just two months, he allowed a full winter of political posturing to pass before he struck again. In the spring of 1940 he beat Britain and France to the punch, occupying Norway in the first half of April, then forcing the capitulation of Denmark, Holland, Belgium and France by the latter part of June. Early in 1941, before turning his massive armies loose against Russia, he found it necessary to complete the occupation of Greece, Yugoslavia and the Greek island of Crete in the eastern Mediterranean. While accomplishing all this he cajoled and bullied Bulgaria, Rumania and Hungary into joining forces with the German Reich.

At this time most political analysts would have expected the German Fuehrer to halt invasion plans for Russia in favour of a period of consolidation. Not Hitler. He barely left time to retrieve the forces he had committed to the Balkan campaign when, at dawn on 22 June 1941, he attacked Russia without warning. He made sweeping advances all the way to Leningrad, Moscow and, by Christmas, Stalingrad. Next, he moved on to the Caucasus by the summer of

1942.

Within the same months he had rescued the Italians from their difficulties in the North African countries south of the Mediterranean; by the autumn of 1942 General Rommel's *Afrika Korps* stood at El Alamein, the gateway to Cairo, the port of Alexandria and the Suez Canal. Further, between Hitler's September 1939 invasion of Poland and the spring of 1942, the Germans had fought the air Battle of Britain. This they lost, but established supremacy in the Battle of the Atlantic – by then reaching its crescendo. The Western Allies were fighting back with ever-increasing force and the economic power of North America was making itself felt.

To summarize the middle years of World War II: The summer and winter of 1941-42 were traumatic for Canada. The great turning point victories at El Alamein, Stalingrad and Midway in the Pacific had not yet happened. The stupefying successes of the Axis powers ground heavily on Allied morale. The Battle of the Atlantic was expanding but going badly; Hitler's submarine "wolf packs" dominated the oceans and carried their sea battle right into the Gulf of St. Lawrence. Around the southeastern shores of Cape Breton Island and the eastern and southern shores of the remainder of Nova Scotia, the U-boats took a heavy toll on huge convoys out of Sydney and Halifax. Allied shipping was being sunk within a hundred kilometres of Scatari Island, which lay about half way between the harbours of Glace Bay and Louisbourg.

Pearl Harbor had occurred on 7 December 1941. Singapore and Hong Kong fell not long afterwards. Then came the mentioned Japanese shelling of Dutch Harbor towards the Alaskan end of the Aleutian Islands chain. This last attack was significant to the North American continent and indicated that the British Columbia coast was also assailable. If the total war measures so far utilized by Canada and Britain are considered, including all the efforts of the convoy system, barely sufficient food to sustain the British in a healthy condition got through to them. It was a desperate time. Hope was never lost but the road ahead seemed almost too arduous.

It was during this dark period that powers in Ottawa, assessing our vast country's geography, realized the need for a means to rush defensive infantry to isolated and distant locations. To the logical minds of the military the answer was, as we have seen, Canadian Airborne Infantry.

Canada was already fathering an ultra-fast expansion of its armed forces. The country was under pressure from many sides. Britain needed more help. The Nazis had mopped up Europe. Japan had expanded its aggressive operations in the Pacific. And, almost incredibly to us, our shipping continued to be sunk in and just outside of the Gulf of St. Lawrence.

The main defences were our Coast Artillery, the Royal Canadian Air Force and the Royal Canadian Navy. There were infantry battalions in the many heavy artillery fortresses on the shores of the Canadian St. Lawrence estuary, the coastal harbours of the three Maritime Provinces and Newfoundland - but these fortresses were immobile. Obviously, infantry forces with a high capability for movement were required to support them - forces which could fly to the scene of any coastal attack and literally drop from the sky when needed.

But the focus was changing when the 1st Canadian Parachute Battalion returned from Fort Benning to Canada in March 1943 for advanced training at the newly constructed Camp Shilo Paratroop Training Centre. The period during which they were in Georgia had seen crucial shifts in the fortunes of war.

Such recent Allied initiatives as computers which broke enemy codes, their increased volume of shipbuilding (especially in the United States and Canada), their antisubmarine bombing at sea and the re-allocation of Allied forces in the Atlantic were causing the Germans to lose the Battle of the Atlantic. And in Russia and North Africa the enemy's formerly victorious armies had suffered crushing reversals. As for the Japanese, they had met some stunning defeats at the hands of the Americans and their Australian allies in the Pacific.

Prior to this, as we have noted, recruiting for the 1st Canadian Parachute Battalion had been slow. Few who had the initiative to volunteer as paratroopers wanted to serve in a unit which was not - at that time - intended for action in Europe. When word was passed that the 1st Canadian Parachute Battalion would join the British 6th Airborne Division, everyone knew its soldiers would probably face up to the Fuehrer's best forces in Europe. Enthusiasm escalated and new recruits poured into Camp Shilo.

Earlier, when I arrived at Fort Benning in Georgia on Christmas day 1942, about four hundred and fifty other volunteers had already qualified as parachutists under the agreement with the U.S.A. to cover the time it took to build the Camp Shilo Parachute Training Centre in Canada. They, like those to come, were from varied backgrounds. Bert Isley, Boyd Anderson, Jim MacPherson and Scotty MacInnis typified the thousands of 1920 kids who were now competing for acceptance into the new Canadian Parachute Corps. They came from towns, cities and villages; factories, farms and forests; offices, fishing fleets, mines, businesses and virtually every other endeavour. They had trained in branches of the military ranging all the way from infantry, artillery, and armoured tank units to the Medical, Dental or Pay Corps.

At Camp Shilo we trained hard and learned fast. In June 1943 we were given passes and went home to enjoy three weeks' embarkation leave before we were issued with the personal combat weapons we would carry "over there." After our disembarkation in Scotland we were transferred to Carter Barracks at Bulford in the south of England, near Stonehenge. There we met a tall, rather youngish brigadier with a firm jaw who looked like he meant business. He was Brigadier James Hill and our meeting turned into a great military relationship which became a lifelong friendship.

Although we had already earned our paratroopers' wings, and had slogged through advanced infantry schools, our training was far from over. Our first meeting with Brigadier Hill at the Bulford railway station set the tone for ten months of unusually tough infantry-commando-paratroop training.

As he welcomed us and sincerely told us how proud he was to com-

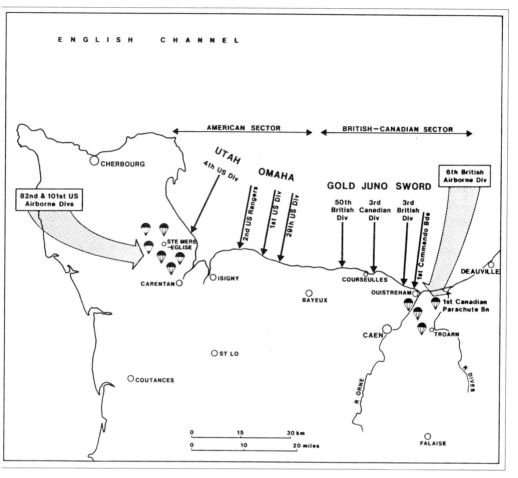

D-Day Invasion Map.

On D-Day, 6 June 1944, the Allied invasion forces landed along a 60-mile stretch of coast of northern France, extending from the Cherbourg Peninsula in the west to the Dives River in the east. The Airborne forces were the first to land, arriving shortly after midnight on their drop zones on the extreme east and west flanks of the invasion area.

mand a brigade with a Canadian battalion in it, he also informed us that he would brook no nonsense and had great expectations from us, as he had from his other two superb battalions already partially trained to the high standards he had set.

The next ten months were indeed filled with spectacular training experiences. The nature of paratroop training on a large scale was in itself dramatic. The Airborne of the infantry progressed in an unusually rapid way. Most of the Canadians in Hill's brigade had already participated in training exercises where three transport planes flying in V-formation put down three containers of equipment and thirty-six paratroops from a height of 1,500 feet - one container and twelve soldiers from each aircraft. This was called a mass drop. In the months before D-Day methods of transporting paratroops had advanced so far that these same men were now flying in aircraft blocks with four waves of nine aircraft flying wingtip to wingtip, three V's in each wave, each wave about ten seconds apart. The whole block of planes dropped between five hundred and six hundred soldiers in less than a minute. For Airborne brigade-size exercises the blocks or battalions flew only two minutes apart. Over two thousand soldiers would fall like a rain of confetti from the sky in six minutes.

The individual soldier didn't worry about separate containers of equipment any more. Parachuted containers were still used for extra equipment and supplies, especially ammunition, medical supplies, antitank mines and water. But each man's personal weapons, ammunition and other gear required for the immediate assault stages of an attack were carried either on his person or jammed into his parachute harness. Cigarettes and plastic explosive were often stuffed above the shock-harness inside his helmet. These and other items that would not be needed at once were also packed in a big kit-bag, modified so that he could strap it to one leg. A lot of the experiments which led to the many innovations used on and before D-Day had been done during the early months of 1944. They were worked in with the continuous training and added to the confidence of the individual soldier.

The kit-bag apparatus had a release mechanism so the soldier could lower it on a twenty-foot rope during his descent. The trooper and the bag hit the turf about one second apart. The release system often prevented the breaking of leg and foot bones.

Learning to beat new problems caused by the innovations created a competitive willingness in the ordinary soldier which was unsurpassed.

During the training period we met compulsory standards set down by Brigadier Hill. Five-mile runs four times a week before breakfast. Ten-mile runs with combat boots and light weapons in less than two hours. Twenty-mile run and walk marches in under four hours in full battle order every few weeks. And, toughest of all, fifty-mile marches in less than twenty hours in full battle order. This was over and above all the training tests imposed to measure stamina and the carrying of new or extra equipment by the Airborne soldier. We also made a series of night jumps with newly developed electronic Drop Zone finders. They were mainly Rebecca and Eureka - small radar sets, one of

A CHANGE OF CAPABILITY

A Mass Drop in February 1943.

A Mass Drop in February 1944.

which was stationed in the transport aircraft and the other placed at the beginning of the Drop Zone by a small party of pathfinders.

Finally the ultimate honour came our way - the assignment to the 1st Canadian Parachute Battalion of a great share in the crucial combat tasks to be carried out as part of the British 6th Airborne Division's role in the battles ahead. An explanation of these tasks, how they were executed and the results will follow. Meanwhile, the troops of the entire division felt complimented by their assignment between the Rivers Orne and Dives in Normandy. They knew that Generals Eisenhower and Montgomery would not have laid such obligations on any division that did not have their complete confidence.

We as Canadians felt a very close kinship with our French, British and American allies and longed to play our part in the liberation of France. As the preparations went forward our unit was increasingly proud of the assignments and orders we received. The average age of the 1st Canadian Parachute Battalion's soldiers at that time was 21 years, and that included the officers. So the average birth year of the unit's members was 1923, just five years from 1918. The sons of their fathers from World War I !

One day in the summer of 1937 Scotty MacInnis had skimmed an eastern Nova Scotia newspaper, the *Antigonish Casket*, while listening to the radio. The commentary was about Hitler and his twisted political philosophy. At the end of it, Scotty had tossed the paper on the floor beside his chair and said, "Jesus, Byes, that bastard Hitler's gonna have us Cape Bretoners over there fighting again before we know it!"

Chapter III
Company Commanders' Briefings

Andy McNally

Until 24 May 1944 the men of the 1st Canadian Parachute Battalion knew nothing of the exact plans laid down for them. When reveille sounded at Carter Barracks that new day the soldiers hit the deck expecting the usual five-mile run before breakfast. It came as a surprise when our sergeants arrived ahead of schedule and ordered us out to the mess hall early. Reveille had been moved ahead by one hour.

On our way back to our barrack rooms after breakfast it became obvious something was in the wind. There were guards posted every hundred feet or so around the camp. Each company hut had one or two heavily tarped-up trucks parked on the grass by the barracks' entrances. That really said something, for vehicles were never allowed to park on the neatly trimmed grass at Carter Barracks. It was regularly groomed in the evenings by soldiers who were confined to barracks for minor offences.

It was not long before our platoon lieutenants arrived with the news of an immediate move to a security transit camp. "You have three hours to be on parade in full battle order. All your spare kit is to be packed in your large kit-bags, fully labelled and placed on the foot of your beds, ready to be turned in to the Quartermaster's Stores until we get back from wherever we're going."

There was no need for any questions. We had been through the drill dozens of times in the previous ten months. Everything was automatic. We did not need to be told how to carry out the orders barked at us; we knew instinctively what was up and that this was the real thing. Subtle shades of difference today told us this was not exactly like the many other moves we had made. Our barrack rooms became beehives of activity and animated conversation: mostly smart-aleck jokes and bravado that masked inexplicable emotions and premonitions.

The 1st Canadian Parachute Battalion was by now a highly professional infantry outfit. Our Colonel, George Bradbrooke, had seen to that. He was a disciplinarian par excellence and a gentleman to boot. He had laid down a syllabus of physical, behavioural and infantry tactical training which was repeatedly rehearsed until the unit was as capable as the best in Canada's or any other country's army. Everything we did was executed with the dash and purpose which exemplify good military training. In view of the demanding struggles that would be required in the immediate future to finish off the Axis powers, strict discipline was vital. In addition, high standards would be essential to impress large numbers of reinforcements coming along to fill ranks dwindled by hard-fought battles ahead. No one can take Colonel Bradbrooke's

19

achievements in instilling all this away from him.

Now, an hour and a half after the lieutenants had given the orders, everyone had complied. The packed kit bags looked like they had been placed on the beds by a surveyor's transit, so straight were the lines they made up and down the barrack rooms. There was time left over for close friends to exchange ideas about what was happening. Cigarettes came out and were dragged deeply as we anticipated the arrival of the sergeants-major to move us out.

Further routines occurred automatically and with dispatch. Ammunition was issued from the trucks on the grass. The soldiers were paraded, inspected, and embarked onto large transport trucks which wheeled out of Carter Barracks and drove away past Stonehenge, taking a circuitous route to an unknown destination.

It was a memorable early summer day. Blue sky, white scattered clouds drifting on a fresh breeze, shadows coursing on the rolling countryside, gave life to the waving grass not yet turned to hay. The twisting highway ran through a myriad of quaint English villages full of thatched roofs, and small, deliberately designed nineteenth century bridges crossed freshwater streams and looped over railway tracks. Onwards through continuous tranquil scenery, suited more to pleasant living and humane endeavour than to the fighting of a violent war. Yet behind the beauty and benevolence, mental images of present reality left some kind of message for every soldier. Every man on the convoy knew that in his immediate future he must do what he must do and perform to the best of his ability. The assurances of homelife in Canada and England must somehow be rejected, and he must ram a new set of standards of conduct into his subconscious. Life would still be valued but with almost certain expectations of severe bodily deprivations. That was how the infantry was. Then again, the continuous threat of death would leave every individual life sustained by an ever more fragile thread, waiting to be slit by a thousand engines of man's ingenuity and devilry. That also was how the infantry was.

Before we left Carter Barracks, while the battalion was being inspected, a few thoughtful soldiers who remained behind as supply troops had quietly tossed an extra blanket aboard every transport truck, to be spread out on the floor to make the dice roll smooth. Crap games ran rampant throughout the route. Late in the afternoon the convoy turned off onto an unpaved track. It then crawled along at a snail's pace to a checkpoint at an opening in an ordinary page wire fence belonging to some English farmer.

After some sharp talk between the convoy commander and a guard, the convoy wormed forward again to a second checkpoint about a hundred metres beyond the first. There we saw a single strand of barbed wire, strung out about a metre above the ground and trailing off into the distance. We disembarked and marched into the largest canvas camp we had ever seen. When we were dressed off in formation a regimental sergeant-major spoke to us through a megaphone. He drew our attention to the strand of wire: "You are now in a place called a security transit camp. Here you are going to learn the best kept secrets in the world. Anyone who places a foot beyond that single strand of barbed wire will be shot without being challenged. Your best bet is not to go within a hundred feet of it."

That evening the unit personnel were paraded on a large open field within the canvas complex. We sat on the grass before a makeshift stage equipped with a loud-speaker system. Soon Colonel George Bradbrooke, accompanied by an entourage of battalion headquarters officers, took his place in front of a curtain-covered backdrop. Within minutes, when the curtain was removed, a great cheer went up. We were looking at a map showing the south coast of England and the north coast of France, towards the Atlantic end of the Channel. We had read and heard a stream of personal conjectures during the previous few months. Now finally we had the answer! Early on some men had guessed France, some Holland or Norway, and others even thought the strong Airborne forces in England might be used to cut off the Brenner Pass in northern Italy to trap the German Army to the south. At last the guessing was over. The facts were clear. It was to be France again as in the First World War. That was the decision most men favoured. France had a strong attraction for Canadians. After all, that's where their fathers had been successful twenty-five years earlier. If one were to fight and die there was no better place to do it than in France, especially beside the British. The bonds all round were strong and the rightness was evident - as right as rain!

Colonel Bradbrooke's briefing was merely an outline, but his sparse description of the invasion was enough to let the Airborne soldiers know that after our drop in France we'd soon have company. This would be an invasion force from the sea. "Later," he said, "I will give you an idea of its strength."

The general outline of the 6th Airborne's part in the whole scheme of things was left to Lieutenant R. D. J. Weathersbee, the battalion intelligence officer.

Weathersbee's revelations about the division's expected accomplishments were electrifying. Some bridges were to be captured intact, while others were to be destroyed. Certain communications installations were to be blown up and put out of business. German strong-points were to be assaulted and destroyed and their coastal defence battery, with its guns trained on British Sword Beach, was to be smashed. Although these briefings were short we were told that, beginning the next morning, they would continue in greater detail on a company-by-company basis. The men who were to carry out the many separate tasks would then learn about their own specific assignments. Where co-operation was to occur between separate units all the men involved would be briefed together.

Colonel Bradbrooke returned to the microphone and made some concluding remarks. He looked pleased and proud and his smile was a broad, confident grin.

"You're going to be surprised and happy," he said, "when you learn all the things you are going to do on this operation. Believe me, there will be a part for every individual soldier here. Get a good night's sleep and good luck! You'll begin your detailed briefings early in the morning," he repeated.

Next day everyone hit the deck on the first few notes as the bugler sounded reveille. Breakfast, served with greatly improved rations, was eaten with gusto. We rushed through it as though the quicker we ate the sooner we'd learn more about what we would soon have to do. With keen anticipation we marched off to the briefing points to hear what our company commanders had to say.

Major Clayton Fuller, commander of "B" Company, explained to his men how important were the tasks assigned to them. Following tracings on a map hanging in a briefing tent, he spelled out how his second-in-command, Captain Peter Griffin, would form and lead a "B" Company Bridge Party of two other ranks and two Royal Engineers. Griffin, immediately on landing, would gather in his party and head straight for two bridges near the village of Robehomme. His job was to reconnoitre the route to, and the area surrounding, these two bridges to expedite their destruction.

Then Lieutenant Norm Toseland would arrive with his Number 5 Platoon and part of a section of Royal Engineers under his command. Toseland's platoon would follow the route Griffin had reconnoitred, and would carry out the actual tasks of seizing and blowing the bridges with the help of demolition specialists from the attached Royal Engineers. The Canadian Airborne had no engineers of their own. So, since our unit was attached to the British 6th Airborne Division, we were supplied with British engineers as required.

The Griffin-Toseland bridge objectives were remarkably formidable. The bridges were about four kilometres from the centre of the Drop Zone. The drop was to take place in darkness and the route to the bridges was through territory studded with villages and farm buildings, any of which could cover enemy strong-points. Further, parts of the route were extensively flooded. This was bound to make for slow going because the submerged farm canals lurking beneath the surface of the floodwater were treacherous. In addition, the route would have to be examined for booby traps and tripwires, which would also be dangerous and time-consuming.

The actual route to be followed began at the battalion rendezvous and proceeded southwest to a T-junction made by the Varaville-Le Mesnil highway and a road running directly east to Petiville. It then proceeded through that village and on to a fork made by the Petiville-Varaville and Petiville-La Riviere roads. From there it was to continue east to a point on a narrow track half way between La Riviere and Les Champs, swinging south to the upper Divette canal. The route would then follow the Divette south to Bricqueville, south of Bavent. At Bricqueville, Toseland would meet Captain Griffin again. If the bridges were manned by enemy guards, which only Griffin would now know, the enemy would be disposed of silently. This brought up the unpleasant need for killing knives and unarmed combat. If the bridges were defended in force Toseland's troops would fight and capture them, then set up defensive positions until the Royal Engineers could place charges and destroy the bridges. This action would cut a link that ran west from Goustranville on the Dozule-Troarn highway, across the Dives at Robehomme and on through Bavent to the

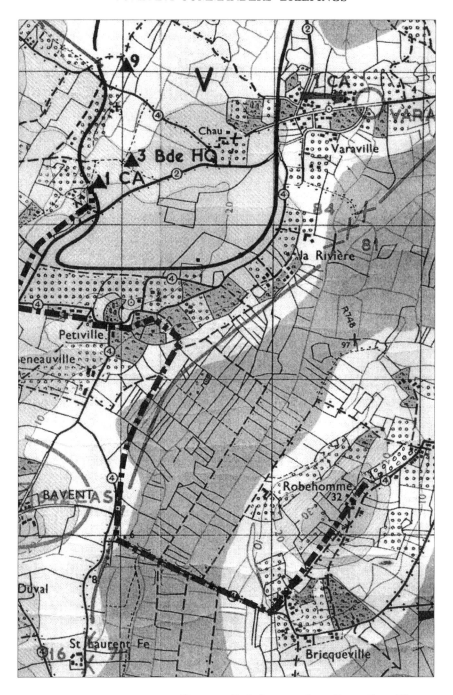

■ ▪ ■ ▪ ■ ▪ ■ ▪ ■ Route to Robehomme from Drop Zone V.

Cabourg-Caen highway. It would also destroy a second link that could progress south on a narrow track from a point on the Varaville–Periers-en-Auge road through a small farm village called Le Hoin, a kilometre north of Robehomme. This narrow road was carried across an old unused farm canal by a small bridge and could link up with Bavent via Bricqueville, making an alternate route onto the Cabourg-Caen highway at the same point as the road from Goustranville, just below the Le Mesnil crossroads position. Destruction of this link would help to keep the enemy out of one part of the Airborne lodgement area, supporting the 3rd Brigade's intention to interdict every route that led to the Cabourg-Caen highway.

"B" Company's Major Fuller reminded his troops at this point that they'd be wise to realize how even the small farm canals (less than two metres deep with soggy banks and bottoms) could make sudden-death traps for enemy tanks once canal and culvert crossings were destroyed. Here Fuller stopped to give his soldiers a chance to react and have a smoke. He was not disappointed. The briefing tent became a beehive of sizzling conversation. The officers and sergeants were besieged by men asking what their own particular parts would be. Those who were not in Lieutenant Toseland's platoon wanted to know the tasks of the other platoons. At this time the officers at company level knew no more than the men did, so the private soldiers would have to wait until after the break for more information.

When the briefing resumed Major Fuller assured his captive but eager audience that men not involved in the Griffin-Toseland objective had equally important tasks. True, the Griffin-Toseland mission seemed especially dramatic. For one thing, it would be one of the battalion's most remote initial actions, to be tackled at a precarious distance from the Airborne lodgement area. For another, the destruction of the two small bridges would rapidly interdict one of the enemy's three main highway routes from the east into the 6th Airborne Division's defensive perimeter. However, the other two "B" Company platoons - Number 4 under Lieutenant Rousseau and Number 6 under Lieutenant Arril - had been tasked with the most important of the battalion's aims in getting the perimeter established. First, they must seize the Le Mesnil crossroads. Then they must hold that critical position interdicting the main Normandy coastal highway running inland from Cabourg to Caen until the battalion consolidated its various sub-units and had scored their initial goals. Fuller himself would command the Le Mesnil phase of the operation. Again, his briefing tent became a focal point of excitement before he sent his troops off to other tents for their detailed platoon briefings.

Simultaneously with the other company briefings Major Don Wilkins, commander of "A" Company, led his entourage to the raised platform at the front of his company's briefing tent. Included were Captain D. S. MacLean; Lieutenants Russel Harrison, R. J. (Bob) Mitchell and John Clancy; Sergeant-Major G. W. Embree; the major's batman and the company runner.

His troops were already assembled. Bright lights illuminated maps on a backdrop behind the platform and reflected on the faces of the company rank and file. Perhaps it was the seriousness of the situation and the quizzical look on their faces that prompted Sergeant-Major Embree to look them over and remark to himself, "God, they're young!" He had heard statistics earlier in the month when someone at headquarters had taken the time to figure out the average age of the men in the battalion. Including the officers, it had come out close to twenty-one years of age; but it was only now, at this crucial time, that the point actually struck home to him. Embree was a powerfully built man. He stood straight and square of shoulder, and when standing to attention looked like he had been carved from stone. His only blemish was one half-closed eye, evidently from some kind of former injury.

"OK, men," Major Wilkins began, "you heard the colonel last night. This is it! The big one we've all been waiting for! How about that?"

As with "B" Company, the "A" Company briefing tent shook from the cheering. Sergeant-Major Embree jumped to his feet, swung his right fist about in a series of ardent gestures and, with his one fully open eye flashing over the scene, he shouted: "OK, men, cheer!"

"What did the sergeant-major say?" someone at the back shouted at the top of his voice to a platoon sergeant nearer the front. "What did he say?"

"He said, 'Cheer!' " the platoon sergeant hollered back, and the whole place burst into laughter.

"OK, men, settle down," Sergeant-Major Embree roared, and Major Wilkins continued with his briefing.

He stressed that Colonel Bradbrooke had given "A" Company important tasks to perform in the imminent invasion of Normandy. Especially serious was the job of protecting the approach of the British 9th Parachute Battalion as it moved from its rendezvous point to its jumping-off positions to attack the Merville Battery. The company would also provide left flank cover during the actual charge through the wire. This meant that "A" Company would have to move like greased lightning after its parachute descent. It would rendezvous close to the 9th Parachute Battalion at a point just south of a right-angle bend in the Varaville - Gonneville-sur-Merville road, on the northwest side of the Drop Zone. That would be some distance away from the main Canadian rendezvous on the southeast side. The company would then set up a firm firebase right in Gonneville-sur-Merville, between the 9th Battalion rendezvous and the Merville Battery fortifications, so when the 9th moved north towards the battery its route would already be secured.

Simultaneously, standing patrols would be sent by "A" Company to points northwest of Gonneville-sur-Merville to block several footpaths leading up from the area Sallenelles-Les Marmiers on the right shoulder of the Orne River estuary. These villages were southwest by west of the battery, and the "A" Company patrol positions would block any German interference with the 9th Parachute Battalion from that direction. Further, the combination of the firm firebase in Gonneville and the standing patrols would secure the 9th Battalion's rear from the south once it reached its jumping-off positions to attack.

Many soldiers in "A" Company felt they would rather join the actual storming of the gun battery along with the 9th Battalion. Their job on the flank seemed to them a lesser task than they were capable of. Had they really understood the big picture they would have felt differently. The truth was that Brigadier Hill had worried about the vulnerability of the 9th Parachute Battalion's rear and left flank ever since he had done a "top secret" appreciation of the 3rd Parachute Brigade's likely problems in the Battle of Normandy for General Gale back in April 1944. Especially with regard to the 9th Battalion's rearward safety.

He thought the enemy might have some forces somewhere that they could redeploy to take the 9th in the rear as it carried out its attack. It was a sixth-sense appreciation on his part, for it soon became known that the first and second battalions of Colonel von Luck's 125th Regiment, of 21st Panzer Division, which were fully up to strength, were only six or seven kilometres south of Gonneville-sur-Merville - as far forward as Escoville. A twenty-minute ride on half-tracks or tanks could have brought his armoured forces to the 9th Battalion's rendezvous or "A" Company's firm firebase.

Looking at the whole picture, although the seizing of the battery by the 9th Parachute Battalion was dramatic, who did what didn't really matter. The important thing was to get the gun battery out of action and so assist the seaborne forces - the British 3rd Infantry Division with troops under command - coming over Sword Beach in the morning. In that light "A" Company's job was crucial.

Major Wilkins ended his briefing by re-emphasizing the momentous nature of "A" Company's objectives. His comments sounded something like this:

"I could tell you about Brigadier Hill's 14th of April appreciation paper, in which he shows a deep concern about the vulnerability of the 9th Parachute Battalion's rear in relation to enemy units he senses might attack Colonel Otway's battalion while it is seizing the Merville Battery. That would let you know how critical your flank protection assignment will be. But I'm not going to do that. You already know how much depends on you. I have every confidence in you."

In short, he had decided to let his soldiers meet the enemy where they would, knowing they'd take reality in stride and handle their situations in the most determined way they knew how. He also told them that a dominant concern of the division's senior commanders was to avoid unnecessary losses during the separate assaults on the initial objectives, so that there would be sufficient troops to carry out the main task later. This task, to be done together with the 5th Parachute Brigade and the 6th Airlanding (Glider) Brigade, was to form and defend a sound, behind-enemy-lines perimeter, which would protect the left flank of the Allied invasion bridgehead and the 6th Airlanding Brigade's already captured River Orne and Canal de Caen Bridges.

In the action soon to come Brigadier James Hill's brigade assaulted more difficult objectives with alacrity, captured more territory and prisoners, and destroyed more enemy soldiers and equipment than might be expected of any parachute brigade in one operation. He was an exceptional commander. He knew how to make decisions that achieved goals well beyond reasonable expectations. Also, at the same time, he husbanded the lives of his troops.

By the time the rifle company commanders had briefed their men on their individual company objectives it was close to noon on the second day in the security transit camp. What was left of the morning was free.

As they strolled around the open areas of the huge camp the men gathered into groups to talk. The atmosphere definitely remained electric and almost seemed unreal. It was difficult to believe that the Second Front was finally going to be established and that every soldier being briefed was going to be individually involved in a special way. The western world's largest newspapers had published screaming headlines throughout the spring, dramatizing the need to get onto the continent soon to take the heat off the Russians. The same cry had been heard since early 1942. Allied leaders had found it difficult to preserve faith in their performance when they had postponed the event for 1942 and again for 1943. During that time the public could not be told that the Allies were building the world's biggest invasion armada ever, one that could not fail to lumber up onto the fields of France. Now, it was actually about to happen and the paratroops and glider-men of the 6th Airborne Division - young Britons and Canadians excitedly discussing the latest revelations near Down Ampney in England - were among the first people in the world to know. What was more, they would be the first to participate in the land fighting.

Lunches in the security transit camp were an even bigger surprise than the breakfasts had been. The food was so unusually good that satirical jokes flew through the camp, all related to fattening the proverbial calves before the slaughter. After lunch there was an hour of compulsory rest. Yes, the troops were actually ordered to rest in their beds for one hour after lunch every day until they left the camp and flew away to war.

The afternoon saw the beginning of the platoon briefings. This is where the down-to-earth details of the plans were formed and solidified in the soldiers' minds. The colonel's broad briefing on the first evening, and the briefings by the company commanders, were all informative but did not get down to the nitty-gritty of the varied small but significant jobs that had to be done.

The platoon briefings, on the other hand, would be tactical. They would give actual directives of what was to be done - and how - by the platoons, by their sub-units and by individual soldiers. They would deal with the actual why and how of the seizure of all the initial objectives. They would detail how the securing of the highways and the ground between the Rivers Orne and Dives were to be achieved "by you, the guys we're talking to right now," the briefing officers said.

Before the small-unit briefings, since rivalry between companies was not only natural but was often fostered, the men of the rifle companies tended to look down their noses at some of the Headquarters Company platoons. And of all the platoons so disparaged the one considered most useless, next to the Provost Section, was the Intelligence Section. It was natural enough for a rifle company soldier to feel that way. He slogged the countryside day after day, learning how to face and kill an enemy. In contrast, he saw the Intelligence Section soldier as a guy with a cushy job who only had to attend lectures, play with paper cut-outs and make toy symbols month in and month out. But now the "mighty riflemen" were to be taught a sharp lesson about the pecking order of importance. On the second afternoon of the briefings there began a process that nearly staggered them and began to change their image of the Good Time Charlies of the Intelligence Section.

By now we knew that in a few days time, in the middle of the night, the battalion would not only jump into a foreign country, but would land on a field within the defended coastal belt of the German Army's vaunted Atlantic Wall. Once there, we would be expected to march as much as six kilometres in darkness to find some of our widely scattered objectives. The only aids would be maps which were hard to read at night. And all this in an area not only filled with obstacles but also totally unfamiliar to us - or so we paratroopers thought until the next stage of the briefing process.

We were marched off by platoons to heavily guarded tents. In the first tent was a well-lit topographical model of the 6th Airborne Division's lodgement area in Normandy. The model covered about thirty-five square metres. Within its boundaries we saw, shown to scale on the west side, the Canal de Caen and the River Orne. On the east side, about twelve kilometres away, was the River Dives. Between them the Divette canal, seen running in close association with the River Dives, followed a varied run along the model. About half way between the two rivers ran the Le Mesnil Ridge, angling off to the southeast from Hauger, above Les Marmiers and Sallenelles, through Amfreville, Breville and Le Mesnil, then descending to Herouvillette. A sort of extension to the ridge, after it sloped down to Herouvillette-Escoville, was a long rising, sparsely forested series of meadows which rose gradually all the way past Troarn to Verriers Ridge, several kilometres southeast of Caen.

On the west side of the Le Mesnil Ridge lay great open fields and small forests like those at Le Bas de Breville, Le Bas de Ranville and St. Côme which would later become important. Here, beyond the open fields, several main objectives were also shown in place: the Canal de Caen and the River Orne bridges, Ranville, Benouville, Sallenelles, Les Marmiers and the Merville Battery. On the east side, between the ridge and the Dives, flooded countryside lay ominously on the model. In the flooding were the four bridges on the River Dives system together with the one on the Divette canal at Varaville. Those on the Dives were: one at Troarn, two at Bures and one at Robehomme. Also to be targeted was a culvert at Le Hoin and a farm irrigation canal a kilometre north at Robehomme, towards the sea.

Other objectives such as the defensive positions at Varaville, enemy radio signals facilities, telephone installations and the signals station that controlled communications for the artillery along that part of the French coast were displayed to scale. Villages, power lines, highways, pillboxes, trails, tracks, houses, barns, quarries, churches, orchards, hedges and fortifications were all shown in place. These were the fantastically realistic models produced by the Intelligence Section.

"Holy Jesus!" someone said, turning towards a couple of men from the section. "You mean to tell me you jerks did this? It's remarkable. How in hell did you get all that information?"

The answer was drowned out by the babble of excited voices which filled the tent and became so animated that it soon had to be controlled. Every question had become so tangled with successive ones that nothing was being achieved. But confidence was growing by leaps and bounds and admiration for the Intelligence Section reached a level that would once have seemed impossible. It is probable that morale hit an all time high during the sessions at the briefing models.

Lieutenant R. D. J. Weathersbee, the battalion intelligence officer, explained the details of the model. He used a long pointer to highlight special features as they pertained to the 6th Airborne Division, the 3rd Brigade, and especially the 1st Canadian Parachute Battalion. He showed how the Le Mesnil Ridge, the flooded Dives and the destroyed bridges could be used against the enemy. Particularly obstructive to enemy movement would be the myriad of over-flooded farm canals of the lower Dives. Now the German defence plans of 1942 would be reversed, the tables turned. The enemy, forced to keep their tanks on the roads in the Airborne lodgement area, would be cut off by blown bridges as they approached. This wide interdicted area, laced with numerous hedges and hedge mounds, would be ideal for our short-range PIAT antitank weapons. Ordinary soldiers were about to make the enemy tanks suffer.

"But be mindful," Lieutenant Weathersbee continued, "that in the first few hours of D-Day, before the men of the 8th and 9th Battalions and the 1st Canadian Parachute Battalion can make their way through the Le Mesnil Ridge, this flooded area might prevent us all from moving across country and, at times, confine us to the highways too."

When the intelligence officer finished a smoke break was called. Out in the sunshine they feverishly talked over what they had seen and heard. After the break they formed up again and marched to another tent, which contained a battalion model. Here the objectives and other features of specific concern to the 1st Canadian Parachute Battalion were shown in larger detail.

So far, on the second day of briefings, Majors Wilkins ("A" Company) and Fuller ("B" Company) had given their soldiers an impressive overview of each company's objectives, and had seen the excited troopers through the division and battalion models. Collectively "A" Company and "B" Company, together with "C" Company, were known as the 1st Canadian Parachute Battalion's rifle companies. With attached troops from PIATs and signals, they made up about three hundred and fifty lightly armed soldiers who would seek and confront the enemy on a semi-continuous basis as long as they could survive.

Headquarters Company was different. Its role was one of support, both for offensive and defensive operations. It included an antitank platoon, separate mortar and medium machine-gun platoons, medical and intelligence sections, signals and transport platoons. Headquarters Company was nearly as large as the three rifle companies put together. Its commander, who was also the colonel's second-in-command, was Major Jeff Nicklin.

Nicklin was a former defensive end with the Winnipeg Blue Bombers football team. When he gave orders or informative talks to his soldiers he sounded like a football coach. As he addressed his Headquarters Company that day he came across something like this:

"OK, men, listen up! Now we're getting ready to get in there and slam them Krauts around. I want every man on his toes and totally up to scratch. No slackers, ya hear? We're going to get in there and steam-roller right over those guys, and we're not going to quit till it's all over. You know the drill. Antitank platoon, medics and signals will be split up between all four companies, including our own. Vickers machine gun, mortar platoon and the transport section will be held at Battalion Headquarters to be used as needed for the individual support of rifle companies or battalion endeavours. You'll get detailed briefings from your platoon commanders. For those of you who are not farmed out to the other companies I can tell you this right now, when you hit the turf go like hell for the rendezvous near the Varaville-Le Mesnil road and get your platoons organized for defence.

"And another thing," Nicklin snarled. " 'C' Company will be attacking the enemy defences at Varaville while two platoons of 'B' Company, Battalion Headquarters and Brigade Headquarters will move to seize the Le Mesnil Ridge at the Le Mesnil crossroads. It will be your job as Headquarters Company to keep open the highway from Varaville to Le Mesnil until you're called forward to Le Mesnil when Colonel Bradbrooke sees fit. Now don't forget, if you don't play hardball you can't win. So right up Jerry's arse, eh?"

The company commanders broke their men off in mid-afternoon. As already indicated, the idea was to not rush things but rather to begin with an outline of the tasks ahead, as Colonel Bradbrooke had done on the first evening, then become more detailed as the days went by. These briefings were going to be the most thorough ever given to any troops anywhere. The reasoning was that if the men were given fairly long stretches of recreation time, during which they could hash over what they had been told so far, their learning would take place in creative stages and could be tied together near the end.

When we were back in our own tents most men began to sew extra pockets on their camouflaged smocks to carry more ammunition and smoke grenades. That act in itself told a story. We already had as much ammunition on our persons as the army thought we would need for an initial fight. Now, though, the briefing information told us to form our own opinions. We might be in for a prolonged dogfight and were not about to get caught short of ammo or smoke.

Men got into small groups for discussion and there was little doubt about the subject. It was the same all over the camp. There were no loners.

Then some groups strolled off to the NAAFI for a beer. Others collected around crap games. Still others stuck with their recently acquired aerial photographs and made personal plans pertaining to what they would do if things went wrong when they got to France.

There was much speculation about how tough the enemy would be to beat, or how heavy the expected fighting might be. But few were very outspoken about what every man thought about most, the prospect of losing one's life. This topic demanded near-silence but was always present in the soldiers' minds. They knew they'd have to accept the worst for invading German territory. Casualties would be high and for many of them that would mean death. During a conversation with Lieutenant McGowan, Sergeant Mac-Phee and a few others, Private Bill Chaddock brought the rarely discussed subject up.

"Hey listen Lieutenant, how come nobody ain't saying nothin' about Ole Deadly?"

"Who do you mean, Chaddock?" the officer replied, tongue in cheek. "Who the hell is Ole Deadly?"

"Aw c'mon Lieutenant, you're kidding me! Everybody knows who Ole Deadly is. He's that old devil in the back of everyone's mind that decides whether or not to slit the little thread. We might as well face up to it. Why don't somebody give us an estimate of what the top brass thinks of our chances?"

"OK, Chaddock, I'll speak to the Colonel and some other officers tonight. Perhaps tomorrow we'll have some ideas for you. Maybe it would help us all to understand the plans better if we were to talk a bit about what we might expect in the way of casualties."

After dinner the soldiers found themselves mentally tired from excitement, from trying to keep up with all they had learned and from pondering the possibilities of their situation. They turned in early. Sleep came as a release from the reality of what lay ahead turning over and over in their minds. Already it was possible to imagine, in quite vivid imagery, the close combat necessary to destroy fixed enemy positions at night, especially within the Atlantic Wall, or to silently remove German guards from bridges and other installations.

They awoke on the third day looking forward to their additional briefings. They already knew what they were supposed to do on D-Day. Now they would get the latest dope about exactly how they were going to do it.

Lieutenant Toseland's Number 5 Platoon was already seated in the briefing tent when the young officer strode in to take his place in front of the map. At this point his four sergeants were issued military maps of the district of Troarn. The map scale was 1 inch to 0.79 miles. Toseland found it easy to keep the attention of his men as he showed them how, once they arrived at the battalion rendezvous, they'd immediately organize into sections and set out in single file, with standard spacing, along the Varaville-Le Mesnil road until they came to a T-junction that led to Petiville. Sergeant Tom Pasquill's Number 1 Section would lead off, followed by Platoon Headquarters which included Toseland, his batman, his platoon runner and Platoon Sergeant Joe Lacasse.

Behind Platoon Headquarters would come Sergeant Larry Irving's Number 2 Section followed by a detachment of Airborne Royal Engineers. Sergeant John Kemp's Number 3 Section would bring up the rear.

On the advance to the Robehomme Bridge Toseland's force would move fast, following the route Captain Griffin's Trowbridge party had reconnoitred. They would avoid action with the enemy as much as possible, except for Sergeant Kemp's Number 3 Section, which would engage any enemy interference, allowing the main part of Toseland's force to maintain the speed of its advance. Once Kemp had dealt with any such incidents he was to disengage as soon as possible and catch up on the double. Beyond Petiville, at a fork made by the roads to Varaville and La Riviere, they would hurry on to the midpoint on the road connecting La Riviere and Les Champs. Then they'd proceed through three additional reference points listed in Operations Order Number 1, reach Bricqueville and rendezvous with Griffin's Trowbridge party. Once there, no time would be lost. Captain Griffin would lead his Trowbridge party, including a squad of Royal Engineers' demolition experts, onward to the culvert crossing the farm canal at Le Hoin. Toseland with his main bridge party would proceed to the bridge crossing the River Dives below Robehomme. This bridge was the first crossing of the Dives behind the coast after the bridge at Periers-en-Auge. The destruction of the Robehomme Bridge would create one of the main interdictions of the highways leading from the River Seine estuary below Paris into the left flank of the Allied invasion bridgehead.

When the demolition was completed the Royal Engineers would return to their section position at Brigade Headquarters near Le Mesnil, escorted by Sergeant Tom Pasquill's section. The remainder of Number 5 Platoon would deploy as follows:

Sergeant John Kemp would organize his section in positions on an exposed levee south of the demolished Robehomme Bridge. His field of fire would now include a long slope up the highway east of the blown bridge. This road formed a T-junction with the Dozule-Troarn highway which would be used by any counterattacking enemy troops east of the Dives. Kemp had his orders. The rebuilding of the bridge by the enemy must be delayed for as long as possible.

The whole area below the high ground at Robehomme was flooded, and the narrow approach-road to the levee was fully exposed to view by the enemy on the east side of the river. Kemp and his men would be prime targets, vulnerable to accurate artillery and mortar fire from the high ground in the direction of Goustranville, east of the river.

To partially remedy this, Sergeant Larry Irving and his section would dig in on the fairly steep slope, covered by an apple orchard, in front of Platoon Headquarters. Irving's section would be above and behind Kemp's, overlooking the destroyed bridge and the levee as well, and could cover Kemp and his men if they had to withdraw.

The plans allowed for Sergeant Pasquill and his men, when they returned from their escort duty with the engineers - a three kilometre journey to and from Le Mesnil - to dig in a defensive position facing west on the Robe-homme-Bricqueville road. This would consolidate the two villages into a single position and would tend to make the enemy assemble a larger force than would otherwise be necessary if they should think of trying to recover the area by counterattack. That way the enemy would be delayed in any reaction they might make against the Canadian intruders. It might sound like nonsense to encourage the enemy to assemble larger forces against one's own positions, but as a delaying tactic the plan would provide what was needed most - time!

In these positions Number 5 Platoon and Griffin's Trowbridge party would prepare to stand and fight until called back to Le Mesnil to take part in the defence of the crossroads - probably as much as thirty-six hours after the destruction of the bridges. This was a tough assignment and Toseland's briefing stressed the need for readiness and prolonged, dogged determination in the attitude of his men.

Lieutenant Philippe Rousseau, Commander of "B" Company's Number 4 Platoon, was a French-speaking Canadian who spoke no English when he came to the battalion a few months earlier. When he arrived he brought his brother Maurice, also a lieutenant, with him. But Maurice was recruited away to the Special Air Service a few weeks before D-Day because he was eager to come to grips with the enemy and had no way of knowing when D-Day would be. Now, a few days before the Normandy battle began, Philippe spoke reasonably good English and talked in passionate tones. His remarks are well remembered by the survivors of his platoon. He said:

"Number 4 Platoon is to join with Number 6 Platoon to carry out operations against the most important objective assigned to the 1st Canadian Parachute Battalion - the occupation and consolidation for defence of the Le Mesnil crossroads position. It is about half way between Breville and Herouvillette in the central part of the Le Mesnil Ridge. To help us in this, our own Battalion Headquarters and the 3rd Brigade Headquarters, which of course are both substantial units, will move with us. The order of march of the Le Mesnil force will be as follows: Our platoon will be in the lead followed by Battalion Headquarters, then Number 6 Platoon followed by the 3rd Brigade Headquarters. The route will be from the battalion rendezvous, southwesterly and roughly parallel to the Varaville-Le Mesnil highway. It will then pass along the south side of a farm canal, through the corner of a nearly rectangular wood situated between the highway and Le Bas de Breville, below Breville itself.

"From there we'll go directly into the slightly acute angle formed by the northeast quadrant of the Le Mesnil crossroads. Altogether it will be a distance of about a mile and a half. We'll then march through the fringe of the forest around Manoir St. Côme on the eastern side of Breville. Breville is an important point since it has the highest elevation on the Le Mesnil Ridge and overlooks the Orne bridges. Number 4 Platoon will clear a pottery works south of the crossroads so our Battalion Headquarters can establish its position there. Our Number 4 Platoon will then rejoin 6 Platoon at the crossroads itself. Together we'll deny the use of the Le Mesnil feature to the enemy until the troops of 'C' and 'A' Companies return from the seizures of Varaville and Gonneville-sur-Merville later in the day. While this is happening the 3rd Brigade Headquarters will have passed to the south and will dig in around the Manoir du Mont just off the Varaville-Troarn highway across the road from the Le Mesnil pottery plant, the Canadian Battalion Headquarters.

"At the same time the British 8th Parachute Battalion will seize Herouvillette and establish defensive positions there, just as the 9th Parachute Battalion will do later at the Château St.Côme in Le Fôret St. Côme south of Breville. Once these positions are established, each bringing the Varaville-Caen highway within range of its fire, this highway will be interdicted in depth from Varaville to Herouvillette, some three miles of its length thick with our field fortifications. Come what may, our lightly armed force will not let go of these defences and are expected to defeat any counterattacks the enemy can muster, including attacks with tanks. At the crossroads we will continue to do so alone, until the soldiers of our 'A' Company return from the Gonneville-sur-Merville area and 'C' Company arrives from Varaville in the late morning or afternoon of D-Day."

As the days passed the briefings, as predicted, became more intricate. Yet they also became more clear. For the Canadians a vivid picture emerged of a battalion charged with far ranging tasks that, only a year or so earlier, would have seemed far too much for a single battalion to accomplish in the type of close country that would be our battleground.

Now, with a year of active training completed, the battalion had developed a new perspective and had built up confidence in the senior commanders of the 6th Airborne Division. There was a heightened sense of "Whatever it is, we'll get it done!" Our own Colonel Bradbrooke appeared increasingly enthusiastic and astute. The youngish Brigadier, James Hill, who had met us at the Bulford railway station ten months previously - the day we joined the division - had gained our trust with actions that spoke even louder than his words.Chance meetings during military exercises in rural England had occurred with the 6th Airborne Division's two other brigadiers: Nigel Poett of the 5th Parachute Brigade and the Hon. Hugh Kindersley of the glider-borne 6th Airlanding Brigade. Though short and incidental, the meetings had given the Canadians a liking and respect for these two battle-proven officers. Our forthright and fair divisional commander, General Sir Richard Gale, was well known to all his troops and was held in high regard. In addition he was trusted by James Hill, and that was good enough for us.

By the fourth day in the security transit camp large parts of the Headquarters Company signals and PIAT antitank platoons were split off and attached to the rifle companies. Naturally they participated in the remainder of the company briefings. Mortar and medium machine-gun (Vickers) platoons, having been given a common task on D-Day, were briefed as a separate unit.

Both the 3-inch mortars and the Vickers machine guns were of relatively long range and could cover targets from Le Mesnil to Varaville, to

Gonneville-sur-Merville, and up to the Le Plein-Breville positions. Therefore the briefings conducted by Lieutenant Marcel Cote, commander of the mortar platoon, and Lieutenant Richard Hilborn, commander of the Vickers platoon, became more complicated and intensive because of their weapons' versatility.

As Scotty MacInnis walked back to his tent after the day's briefings he said to a friend, "If we carry out all them plans, we'll be known as the parachuting Wizards of Cause."

Chapter IV

Advance Party Briefings

L. Sauder

Flashback (An explosive interlude!): One sunny morning in late April 1944, Major Murray MacLeod ordered Captain John Hanson to parade "C" Company near some training trenches by a large spruce copse on a rise west of Carter Barracks. The troops were, as ordered, in place at 09:00 hours. Major MacLeod arrived with a jeep pulling a trailer loaded with every kind of ammunition used by the company's weapons, including the right stuff for Corporal W. E. Oikle and his PIAT antitank gun section crew, attached from Headquarters Company. In a matter of minutes the major designed an exercise the like of which the men had never seen.

A short distance out in the field was a scruffy zigzag trench about fifty metres long. It was simply hollowed out turf left in the ground from an old backfilled training trench, probably from World War I. MacLeod had some men place an empty forty-five gallon oil drum to the left of the trench and another to the right, where the soldiers were seated on the grass. Captain Hanson saw to it that "C" Company Platoon Lieutenants McGowan, Walker and Madden issued a plentiful supply of live ammunition to every soldier. Platoon Sergeants MacPhee, Rice and Davies now concentrated the troops opposite the full length of the trench, but back about seventy-five metres from it. Section corporals, nine of them with their 2-inch mortars, were located another twenty-five metres to the rear of the main body, but at the five o'clock position on the left flank facing the trench. Corporal Oikle's PIATs on the right flank were somewhat closer to the barrels.

The major gave a signal and the corporals laid down a few mortar smoke bombs on the trench position. But while the first smoke projectiles were in flight the two drums disappeared in smoke and flame as the PIAT men blew them to smithereens with antitank rockets. The drums had each been charged with a primed seventy-five Hawkins antitank grenade to make them explode. The PIAT men withdrew rapidly and the 2-inch mortars switched to high explosive shrapnel type ammunition. Shoulder to shoulder, the line of soldiers walked forward. The moment the mortars stopped firing they began to run, shooting from the hip. Nine Bren machine guns, twelve submachine guns and approximately seventy-five rifles made a solid din which swept over the zigzag trench.

This was an entirely new occurrence in total contrast to all the doglegging, crawling and hugging of ground cover during the previous year. The troops wondered why there had been no explanation before the exercise, and none was given after it was over. It was as though it had just happened spontaneously and that was that! However, the concentration of men and weapons of a full Airborne infantry company impressed the power of co-ordinated firing upon our minds. More importantly, we would always carry with us an unforgettable image of its impact upon enemy soldiers who might try to defend such a trench position.

Sergeant-Major Johnston had the unused ammunition packed on the jeep trailer. Then the major gathered the troops in for a talk. There was no mention of the exercise but the gist of his talk was:

"I can tell you now that sometime in the future there is going to be a special night operation in enemy territory. Our company has been given a chance to get the job, but we are not the only Airborne company so notified. We have to train for it, carry it out in practice, compete with the other companies and qualify for it. I'm going to see to it that when our turn to practice comes up it will be a very black night. Black as ink! We'll jump from Albemarle bombers and our tasks will be to jump, rendezvous, set up on an assault start-line, and within twenty-eight minutes of the time the last bomber drops its men we'll make a mock assault on a small village. Of the companies competing, the one which finishes the exercise the quickest and in the best organized way will get the job. Just know that, as of now, we are going to practice the needed skills out of trucks on enough dark nights so there will be no mistake about it. Believe me, we're going to get that assignment!"

From then on the company took on a new attitude with a unique meaning. Every soldier knew he was part of something special. Morale went up like a kite. The troops were dropped off trucks in sections, in threes, in pairs or alone all over Salisbury Plain on dark nights. We learned how to get orientated and find our way to certain points as though blindfolded. We practiced rendezvousing in the dark until we were more than good at it - it almost became second nature.

On 30 April a commanding officers' conference presided over by Brigadier Hill ordered that companies be dropped by night from Albemarle aircraft, for special training for a purpose as yet undisclosed.

Soon, on a black cloudy night in May, in a wind unsuitable for parachuting, our drop was made. Although the wind caused painful injuries, none were reported. No soldier was going to miss the real jump. On the mock exercise the start-line was gained within the prescribed twenty-eight minutes. Major MacLeod was pleased. Later that month he was awarded the operation. So far, nobody else below the rank of colonel knew what it was.

On the first morning in the security transit camp Major MacLeod began his address in the briefing tent to "C" Company. Smiling from ear to ear he said, "Listen! Remember that night exercise, out of Albemarles, where we'd get a special assignment if we won a contest? Well, hang onto your hats or maybe I should say your helmets. Our company is going to be the first fighting unit from the entire Allied invasion force to land in France. What do you think of that?" The roar of approval that went up nearly blew the roof off the briefing tent.

Facing the non-commissioned officers and other soldiers who sat on chairs arranged in theatre fashion were his Company Headquarters personnel. They included Major Macleod himself with Captain John Hanson and their two batmen, Privates P. I. Bismutka and E. J. Delamere. Company Sergeant-Major R. F. Johnston was there too, together with Company Runner Private Reginald Walker, Company Administrative Clerk Corporal Alex Flexer, Radio Signals Corporal John W. Ross and his assistant Private L. C. Grenier, as well as Corporal Oikle and his number 2 PIAT–gunner, Private L. A. Neufeld.

The Lieutenants, Sam McGowan of Number 7 Platoon, Chuck Walker of 8 Platoon and John Madden of 9 Platoon, seemed as pleased as their Platoon Sergeants Mosher MacPhee, Earl Rice and Gordon Davies. And all of them looked only slightly less elated than Captain John Hanson, "C" Company's second-in-command.

To them it was a coup and the soldiers participated in the elation without a second thought as to what it was they might be called upon to do. Their attitude was, as usual, to hell with it, every infantryman knows he faces the worst - the possibility of dying or being wounded or, even worse, captured. But when the elation subsided curiosity was natural.

"So what are the tasks going to be," Sergeant G. H. Morgan shouted. "What do we have to do?"

"OK, Morgan," Major MacLeod replied, "here's what we're going to do. First of all, this is going to be a clandestine operation. In other words, the enemy is not going to know we are even in France when we hit 'em out of the night at the village called Varaville."

He went to the map and continued, "Lieutenant Madden's 9 Platoon will seize and destroy a bridge over a canal called the Divette at Varaville. Lieutenant Walker's 8 Platoon will seize and destroy a fairly large concrete enemy pillbox, and Number 7 Platoon will do a direct assault into an enemy trench position and the trench's antitank gun position. All three objectives are in the village of Varaville. Captain Hanson, with a few hand-picked men, will see to the destruction of a signals station near Le Bas de Breville, and Sergeant Larry Bray will lead a small party to recover His Worship the Mayor of the village, whom he will bring to my headquarters."

"How do we carry out all those tasks," Sergeant R.O. MacLean asked in a mildly disbelieving tone.

"We're going to fly there in Albemarle bombers, like we did on the practice night jump last month, and will be inserted into a bombing raid which will hit the Merville Battery. Then, to increase the noise and allow us to get into Varaville without being detected by the enemy, a Mosquito fighter-bomber night-strafing raid will blanket the area at the same time we're landing and getting up to the wire. That will keep the enemy's heads down. It's believed, with these measures in place, the enemy will write the whole thing off as another nightly bomber raid along the coast. The plan is this: we'll jump, rendezvous, form up on our start-lines, do the other more menial things we need to do and then charge the positions without the enemy even knowing we're there until we blow the barbed wire surrounding their positions. The assault, after that, should take only a minute or two. They won't know what hit them."

As enthusiastic as the troops were, Major MacLeod could see he had given them quite a bit to think about. Every man knew the Germans were smart and were first-class soldiers. And although the plan was imaginative and exciting, it was obvious right from the start that if one section of it failed a helluva mess could ensue. The major therefore continued with the idea of getting more details into their heads which they could mesh with what they had already learned.

"Now look here," he said, going back to the map. "This little village, Varaville, is situated right here, on the southeast side of the Drop Zone V, on which the 9th British Battalion, the 1st Canadian Parachute Battalion and the 3rd Parachute Brigade Headquarters are going to land. They will begin landing forty minutes after we, 'C' Company, get down. Following them by approximately one hour there will be a stream of over seventy Horsa gliders landing there during the remainder of the night. They'll be loaded with the 3rd Brigade's heavy equipment and the 224 Field Ambulance's Advance Party; not to forget truck tanker trailers of drinking water and purified water for medical uses.

"The strong enemy positions at Varaville include all of the 3rd Brigade's main Drop Zone in their fields of fire. The reason I say fields of fire instead of field of fire is that the defensive elements of all the enemy positions are established within the village. The two-storey concrete pillbox, the sizeable roofed-over dugout at the end of a well defended trench system, and the anti-tank gun position about thirty yards from its western end are all mutually supporting. They can cover the joined fields of the Drop Zone and can lay down commanding fire over the several road junctions within the village, and over at least all the company objectives so far disclosed to you. In turn, all the defensive weapons of all the various enemy positions, wherever they are located, can act independently over the same areas. So any of our activities can make us their targets. It's an exceptionally flexible position with its main defensive features well sited close to two of the village's highway intersections. We believe the pillbox and the trench system will be each equipped with several machine guns and some mortars.

"So I can't repeat too often that the various elements within the village are capable of all-round defence and can therefore change their fields of fire or sustain several fields of fire at the same time. The positions are also favoured with an undersized antitank ditch, between a row of Lombardy poplars and Le Grand Château de Varaville. What's more, the positions are wired in with barbed wire. And, as you will see when you go through the detailed maps and aerial photographs in the next few days, there is reason to believe mines are sown within parts of the wired in perimeter. Every feature must be engaged or neutralized before the main 3rd Brigade drop begins. But we're going to make sure the enemy at Varaville is out of business before that!"

By the beginning of the fourth day in the security transit camp all the platoons were well into the detailed briefings. "C" Company had been given its special first task: to drop early and secure Drop Zone V for the pathfinders. These would set up special lighting to guide in twenty-one hundred paratroops plus the more than seventy gliders which would land on Drop Zone V during the remaining hours of darkness in what we knew would become a famous night.

"B" Company had its orders to seize and destroy the bridge at Robe-homme, and to occupy the crossroads at Le Mesnil and the culvert at Le Hoin.

"A" Company had its orders to establish standing patrol positions west of Gonneville-sur-Merville. Plus a further objective, the destruction of a sentry position west of the perimeter-wire of the Merville Battery. This was in addition to its important task of giving the 9th Parachute Battalion left flank protection and safety from rearward attack during the 9th's charge into the Merville Battery itself.

"C" Company's orders were to be carried out in five phases. They were well laid out in Operation Order Number 1 for D-Day.

To summarize:
First Phase:
    (a) Drop and rendezvous.
Second Phase:
    (a) Neutralize or destroy signals post in buildings at Map Refer-rence 167753 [southwest side of Drop Zone] with one section [ten men].
    (b) Destroy ENEMY FORCES in defensive position at Varaville including buildings at Map Reference 177756 [Le Grand Château and its outbuildings], both tasks to be completed 30 minutes from time last bomber makes its drop.
Third Phase:
    (a) Seize bridge and cover Royal Engineers' destruction of same on the Divette Canal at Varaville. Map Reference 186758. Demolition to be completed by "H" plus two hours or about 09:30 hours D-Day.
    (b) Send a section to meet Royal Engineers 500 yards northeast of Le Grand Château at two hours thirty minutes before dawn.
    (c) "C" Company Headquarters B Party will escort one section Royal Engineers and one section 224 Field Ambulance from Battalion Rendezvous to Junction made by Gonneville-sur-Merville road with the Varaville to Le Mesnil road.
Fourth Phase:
    (a) Cover demolitions and deny enemy the use of the roads through Varaville until relieved by a cycle troop of Number 6 Commando not sooner than 5 hours after they'll come over the beaches at Ouistreham.
    (b) Provide covering party to escort two sections Royal Engineers and

one section 224 Field Ambulance and any casualties to Le Mesnil Crossroads Position.

Fifth Phase:

(a) When relieved by Cycle Troop Number 6 Commando, withdraw "C" Company to take up defensive position at Le Mesnil Crossroads.

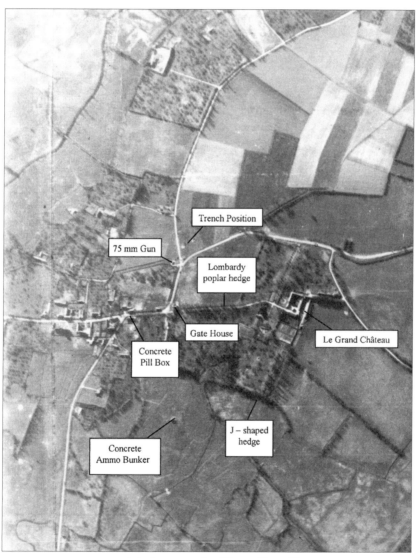

Aerial photograph of Drop Zone V
and several of the battalion's initial objectives.

These operations were meant to frustrate the movement of the enemy on the highways in the area, and to contribute to the safety and free movement of the balance of the 1st Canadian Parachute Battalion, the British 9th Parachute Battalion and the 3rd Parachute Brigade Headquarters when their landings began forty-five minutes later - a little more than the required time for "C" Company to lay down their intended fire and destruction over the enemy positions.

The "C" Company objectives, other than the bridge on the Divette, were to be completed ten minutes before the main 3rd Brigade drop was to begin. Also, the destruction of the signals station would interfere with telephone communications in a substantial portion of enemy installations along the Dives-Orne section of the enemy's defences on the Channel coast. This particular benefit was not a part of the 6th Airborne's objectives, but simply showed up as a bonus. Best of all, the destruction of the signals exchange would spoil the enemy's chances to communicate from position to position within their own defences relative to any counterattack that the presence of the 6th Airborne's paratroops might provoke from them. It would also help to prevent the enemy from organizing counterattacks against the 9th Battalion, reinforced by the Canadian "A" Company, during the 9th's attack on the Merville Battery, or against the Canadians at Varaville.

In a nutshell, the German positions in Varaville consisted of two concrete and stone-masonry blockhouses, a defended trench system, a large chateau (Le Grand Château) with its gatehouse, which were used as German living quarters, and an antitank gun. But at the time of the briefings it was not known that this was a 75-mm field gun able to fire shrapnel-type or armour-piercing ammunition. The trench system included a secure underground dugout for ammunition and weapons storage at its eastern end. The dugout's log cribwork reinforced walls and roof also gave some protection from shelling, bombing and strafing.

The trench portion of the defensive strongpoint was about 50 metres long and had a good parapet with earthen machine-gun pits. It was situated on the west side of an intersection which divided roads to Cabourg and Petiville and began about fifty metres down the Petiville branch, which ran southwest towards a point between Bavent and Le Mesnil.

The enemy antitank gun, acquired from France by the Germans, was well located about thirty metres away from the Petiville-Le Mesnil junction. It was most likely recovered from the huge Hotchkiss factory near Paris, where massive amounts of France's 1940 guns and armoured tank components were modified by *Wehrmacht* engineers for use by the German Army. The 75-mm gun at Varaville, whether from Hotchkiss or not, was a modified French 75-mm field gun and covered the roads leading from Varaville to Le Mesnil, to Merville, to Cabourg, to La Riviere and Petiville, and to Periers-en-Auge. Because of its range it also covered roads well beyond all those points.

As Major Murray MacLeod warned his men, the entire position was surrounded by coiled barbed wire, and included the fork made by the Petiville road with the main trunk road which led out of the village to the junction of the Le Mesnil and Gonneville-sur-Merville roads. The German position, bristling with small arms and supported by the field gun, produced a formidable capability for defence.

"C" Company was to complete its drop by 00:20 minutes on 5 June. And with only thirty minutes to rendezvous, form up and charge the positions, it was sorely hard pressed for time. The remaining objectives, other than the demolition of the bridge, were to be achieved in quick succession.

Looking at the sheer number of objectives one by one puts the Varaville details of the assignment into focus.

First Phase:

To drop and rendezvous would be taken for granted on any other paratroop drop. But in this case it was both special and problematic. The Drop Zone was short, considering the extent of the water hazards, and was criss-crossed by hedges. These conditions were bound to make loss of direction commonplace as the paratroops headed for their rendezvous at a high J-shaped hedge. The shortage of time was critical. We were to move fast to cover the distance from our landing points to the rendezvous - so fast that there would be time to spare to move through the village, past Le Grand Château de Varaville to the start-line near the gatehouse, examine the ground from there to the wire for mines, set Bangalore torpedoes to blow gaps in the wire and let the assault parties through in a hurry. All this had to be done during the twenty-eight minutes from the time the last man came out of the last bomber. On first exami-nation it seemed nearly impossible, but in terms of the attitudes fostered by the Airborne mystique it was readily accepted as something which would be done.

The written orders stipulated that the bridge at the village was to be destroyed by "H" plus two hours. That meant by two hours after the seaborne forces came over the beaches. But the other objectives at Varaville were crucial to the success of the main 3rd Parachute Brigade landings, which was why the objectives had to be achieved by thirty minutes after "C" Company was on the ground. In the military milieu of the time it was imaginative and exciting stuff. Varaville was not only an important telecommunications exchange in the German coastal defence system; it was also a defended highway communica-tions junction behind Cabourg and Dives-sur-Mer. It was also well connected to Ouistreham (British Sword Beach) by way of Ranville, and possibly by sea through Cabourg - Dives-sur-Mer at high tide. Further, it was easily accessed from the main coastal highway through Deauville, or from Periers-en-Auge using the Villers-sur-Mer - Pont l'Evêque lateral for connections to the main east-west highways. It was connected to Pont l'Evêque through Bavent and to Breville, Herouvillete, Troarn and Caen by the highway leading through the Le Mesnil crossroads.

"C" Company's rendezvous point was the loose end of the tall J-shaped hedge, northeast by north of Le Grand Château de Varaville, about three hundred metres from the main enemy positions.

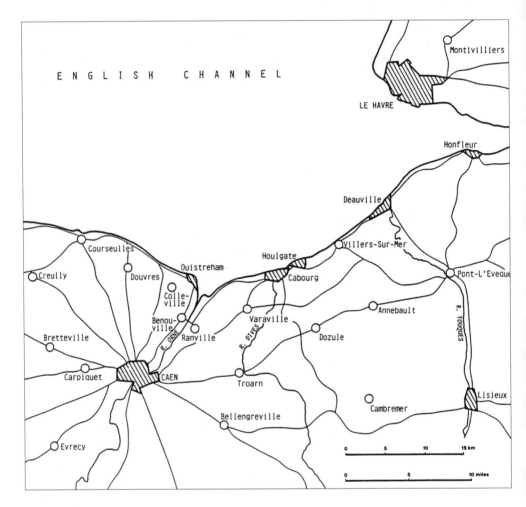

Feeder Routes from Seine estuary to Varaville coast road.

Note how the main highways converge on Caen like spokes of a wheel. When the highway bridges from Troarn to the Channel were destroyed, the enemy was forced to repel the invasion from the sea by frontal attack. This was not their favourite manoeuvre. The collector routes feed into the main coastal highway from Honfleur. This leads into the Airborne Lodgement Area by way of the Cabourg to Caen highway.

During the briefings plans were made and practiced. Take-off time for eleven Albemarles carrying "C" Company was to be 22:40 hours on 4 June. The delay due to foul weather changed it to the same time on 5 June. Major Murray MacLeod was worried about shortage of time and the planned twenty-eight minute span from the completed drop to the firing of the Bangalore torpedoes under the wire at Varaville. Nobody seems to know how he did it, but it became evident that he lobbied the RAF aircrews at every opportunity on the afternoon of 5 June. He was looking for ten extra minutes. And sure enough "C" Company did begin its takeoff at 22:30 hours, ten minutes earlier than planned.

The bombers were to fly line-astern at forty-five second intervals. This meant it should take nine to ten minutes to put "C" Company on the ground and, since the estimated flying time to the Varaville Drop Zone from Harwell airport was estimated at one hour and twenty-three minutes, Number One Bomber should cross the French Channel coast at 23:53, 5 June. The eleventh bomber should discharge its paratroops at two or three minutes after midnight on 6 June. All the timing was estimated that minutely.

The necessary directional orientation for finding their way to the "C" Company rendezvous was to begin with their arrival over Drop Zone V. From 450 feet altitude, in a nearly half moon with a clear sky, the ground would be somewhat visible. We were to fly at five hundred feet crossing the beaches. On the approach, though, we would descend to jumping height. From the beaches onward the first two soldiers in each stick would be able to look down through the exit to spot one or two features on the Drop Zone when they arrived there a minute later. From these observations they could confirm their relative prox-imity to the rendezvous and pass the information back to the other members in their stick in a sort of two or three word fast broadcast. There were only seconds in which to do it. For when they saw a hedge shaped like a jackboot they were already at the centre of the Drop Zone. During the previous minute, the two minute warning light would have been casting its red glare throughout the aircraft. The red, also known as the two minutes to green, allowed the long-est two minutes in the history of the world to tick away. The features the first two men in each stick were to look for were: The J-shaped hedge and the outline of "Jackboot hedge," with its sole up against a village. The top front corner of this "German jackboot," just below the kneecap, was slightly beyond the beginning of Drop Zone V. The village at its sole would be Gon-neville-sur- Merville. Varaville was about nine hundred metres southeast by south from there. Any of the Number One or Number Two jumpers, on identi-fying any of these special orientation markers, were to confirm for the remain-der of their stick that they were being dropped right on the money and would be able to orient themselves on their way to the ground. The descent, the paratroops knew from experience, would last approximately fourteen seconds.

After hitting the ground the next thing to do was to check the north star. Failing these three chances to determine the location, the fourth thing to do was to listen for the bombers bringing the remainder of "C" Company. They would be flying nearly from north to south. This fourth check, of course, would not work for the paratroops jumping out of the last two bombers, numbers ten and eleven. But by the time these men landed they should automatically get caught up in the scurrying for the rendezvous.

If the weather obscured the moon, making the night completely dark, the paratroops would have to put their already trained senses to work to find the J-shaped hedge - their rendezvous. There was one caution: if somehow one became disoriented and absolutely could not find his way, he should lie low until the main force came in. Then there would be three more sets of transports flying approximately forty-five seconds apart, carrying the British 9th Parachute Battalion, the balance of the 1st Canadian Parachute Battalion and 3rd Brigade Headquarters - all flying from north to south. So any soldier who was completely lost could get his direction from them. There was no doubt at all that, wherever he found himself, Varaville would be somewhere southeast, south or southwest of him and only about 1.5 kilometres away. So accurate was the RAF that we needn't even bother to think about being anywhere except where we were supposed to be. In addition, the roads in the area were memorized for curves, nearby buildings, treed features and a big powerline on high steel towers - all orientation markers. The floodwater itself could be a help. If a soldier walked a straight line off the Drop Zone in any direction there was a two-thirds chance he would strike floodwater. From there all he needed to do was follow the water's edge to come to Varaville.

Finally, several additional aids were handed out to help reach the rendezvous in the dark. They were a series of "toys." Put to proper military use they were good. Small tin noisemakers mimicked crickets, bird chirps and frogs. They indicated the rough distance and direction the soldier was from anyone who used them on the ground. Even if paratroops had tried to jump on the backs of the men in front them as they slipped through the exits of the bombers, they could have wound up about ninety metres apart when their parachutes opened and be spaced in a similar way when they hit the ground. The "toy" noisemakers, if used wisely and not too repetitively, did make useful aids. But if the soldiers were edgy or nervous and used them without discretion the "toys" would make a mockery of their inventors. If used for two-way communication they were a dead giveaway. The thing to do when you heard a single distant bird, cricket or frog was not to reply to it, but to move cautiously towards it. That way you would probably find a fellow soldier. If not you might find an enemy soldier who had accidentally found a "toy," and who could be challenged and taken prisoner, or killed if he resisted. It was paramount on this type of military enterprise to keep a cool head, make the best of every available aid and try not to screw up. You were behind enemy lines and must never forget that the slightest mistake could cause sudden death or capture for you or your comrades. In the 6th Airborne Division the use of the aids was planned and practiced intensively while in the security transit camp.

Second Phase:

In this phase "C" Company operation commands at all levels were always duplicated. For instance, the company commander flew in one aircraft while his second-in-command flew in another. Lieutenants who were platoon commanders flew separately from their platoon sergeants. In the case of section sergeants and their corporals, the most senior was the last man out of the aircraft while the more junior was first man out. This separated them by the length of their stick. From the colonel to the corporals, if someone in command were lost there was a good chance that the next in rank would be able to take over his duties.

One of the early essentials in the second phase of "C" Company's role in Operation Order Number 1 was to "neutralize or destroy the signals post in buildings at Map Reference 167753," a short way from Le Bas de Breville. The way to find it was to draw on a map a straight line from Petiville to Merville. Then, by following a southward extension of that line, the signals post would be ninety metres south of the Varaville-Le Mesnil highway.

Captain John Hanson with part of one section of Number 9 Platoon - Company Administrative Clerk Corporal Alex Flexer, Batman Private E. J. Delamere and Runner Private Reginald Walker - would seize and destroy the signals station, while Major MacLeod would lead the remainder of the company in the attack on the trench and gun positions and the concrete bunker. The other tasks were broken down as follows:

Number 7 Platoon, Lieutenant McGowan's, was to cut the wire and charge the gun and the trench position, leaving the occupants dead about two minutes after the Bangalore torpedoes went up under the wire. Lieutenant Chuck Walker's Number 8 Platoon, less Sergeant Willard Minard's section attached to 7 Platoon, was to form a firm firebase for the assault on the trench position by seizing the château gatehouse. Lieutenant John Madden's Number 9 Platoon-less part of one section split between Captain Hanson (signals station) and Sergeant Larry Bray (who would go and get the village mayor) - would seize and defend the bridge on the Divette for later destruction by the Airborne Royal Engineers.

A concrete promenade ran back from the gatehouse to the château, a distance of about two hundred and seventy-five metres. Six metres south of and parallel to the promenade, running half way up from the gatehouse, was a row of huge deciduous trees with trunks about sixty centimetres in diameter. When Major MacLeod called them Lombardy poplars he was probably right. Along this line of trees was an antitank ditch about 1.5 metres deep. In the ditch Sergeant Willard Minard's section, together with two of Number 7 Platoon's machine guns and three 2-inch mortars, would establish a firm firebase in support of that platoon.

Sergeant R. O. MacLean and Private H. B. Swim, working about six metres apart from each other, were to start crawling for the wire, laying down narrow white tape to indicate a corridor as they went along. Each of them would also drag along a Bangalore torpedo and clear any mines. As they proceeded away from the firm firebase trench, Corporal A. M. Saunders and Private Eddie Mallon were to lock on additional Bangalore torpedo sections, to

47

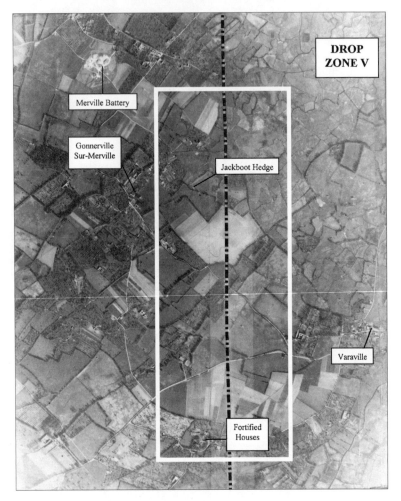

Drop Zone V *(Flight Path* ▪ ▬ ▪ ▬ ▪ *)*

make torpedoes that would reach the full distance under the wire. Eventually, as they progressed, MacLean and Swim would each trail about five metres of Bangalore. At the same time Privates R.E. Mokelki and A.J. McNally were to move forward between MacLean and Swim to clear the centre of the narrow corridor of mines which the two torpedo-men could not reach as they laid the tape to the wire.

While all this was happening Lieutenant McGowan and Sergeant MacPhee would organize the remaining twenty-four men of 7 Platoon on a start line parallel to a hedge which ran from the château end of the Lombardy poplars to the main Varaville-Le Mesnil highway. Sergeant Minard would organize the machine guns in the firm firebase end of the antitank ditch.

Lieutenant Chuck Walker, with his two remaining platoon sergeants, was to lead an assault on the main pillbox. Sergeant Tom Keel would work with Lieutenant Walker while Sergeant W. R. Kelly formed a covering-firebase, seventy metres from the main concrete bunker. Keel was to form up his section on a start-line amid scattered shrubbery in the immediate vicinity of the carriage house portion of the gatehouse.

Lieutenant Madden and Platoon Sergeant Gordon Davies, with one section of Number 9 Platoon, would seize the bridge on the Divette. The other two sections of 9 Platoon were to be away on special assignments. As mentioned, Sergeant Larry Bray was to get the mayor of Varaville. His objective was to bring the mayor to meet Major MacLeod, to smooth relations with the civil authority. The other section with a special objective was Sergeant R. Trepanier's to provide escort for the Royal Engineers and the 224 Field Ambulance personnel, bringing them from the 1st Canadian Parachute Battalion's rendezvous to the intersection of the roads that led from Varaville to Merville and Le Mesnil.

Number 9 Platoon's soldiers would have been on the ground for three quarters of an hour before the engineers dropped with the main parachute units and the Canadians would have already done reconnaissance work on all the routes through the village including the way to the bridge at Varaville - simply to expedite what Brigadier Hill called "speed in thought and action."

At the point in the "C" Company operation where MacLean and Swim would complete the placement of the Bangalore torpedoes under the wire, the troops for all the company's varied tasks would be in place. Sergeant Bray would be waiting to enter the mayor's house. The Number 7 Platoon assault party would be ready to take out the trench system and the antitank gun. Lieutenant Walker's troops going for the concrete bunker and the gatehouse would be in position to jump off and destroy the enemy soldiers. Lieutenant Madden would have his soldiers lined up opposite the bridge on the Divette canal and would be ready to pounce. Finally Captain Hanson with his ad hoc group, poised to strike the signals station, would complete the readiness.

There were two main intentions:

1. Up to this point all should have been completed in silence. The blast of the Bangalore torpedoes under the wire would be the common signal to attack.

2. Within two minutes of the gap being blown in the wire everything should be in "C" Company's hands. An unsuspecting enemy should be dead without having known what hit them. Such were the possibilities in the new technological war.

According to the original orders "C" Company had to be on the ground by 00:20 minutes on D-Day, and must be in their rendezvous somewhere close to ten minutes after that to have time to move on to the antitank ditch by the gatehouse, lay tapes for a final approach corridor, clear mines and place the Bangalore torpedoes by 00:48 minutes. So a definite diversion was needed to make time for their immediate urgent tasks and provide noise-cover for covert activity. Major MacCloud had already told us how the cover would be provided in co-ordination with the Air Force. Now more details were given.

The beginning of Drop Zone V was little more than a kilometre from the Merville Battery and it had been decided that softening up by heavy bombers was needed for the British 9th Parachute Battalion, which would assault the battery a short time later. A bombing raid was therefore laid on, timed to begin with the latter part of the "C" Company drop. While the paratroops were moving up to their rendezvous another violent diversion would be created. Thirty-six Mark VI Mosquito night fighter-bombers would strafe the whole area of the 6th Airborne's objectives from 23:50 hours on 4 June until 00:50 minutes on D-Day. This would be during the time the Advance Party would move up to the rendezvous and to the barbed wire and set the torpedoes. This was exceptionally heartening news and the troops felt a certain degree of invincibility.

The bombing and strafing by the Air Force, besides shaking up the battery, was also intended to create a confusing picture in the minds of the enemy, especially their troops near Varaville, Cabourg, Dives-sur-Mer and along the east shoulder of the Orne estuary. It was thought the German defenders all along the coast had grown so accustomed to being bombed almost nightly during the preceding winter and spring that heavy bombing and widespread strafing one more time would not surprise them. They'd write the whole thing off as a regular occurrence. The throttled-back Albemarle troop-carrying bombers which would enter this violent night scene, slipping in over the coast at five hundred feet altitude, would make hardly more than a low purr even if there were no other noises in the vicinity. One hundred bombers carrying full loads - each reputed to be two four-thousand pounders, or 400 tons in total weight for the raid - would take up the enemy's full attention and let the paratroops, mostly a kilometre or so away, escape notice by the enemy.

The bombing was to occur at "P" (pre-dawn) minus 4 hours 50 minutes to "P" minus 4 hours 40 minutes (or from ten minutes after midnight until twenty minutes after midnight). The Mosquito fighter-bomber strafing would be from "P" minus 5 hours 20 minutes to "P" minus 4 hours 40 minutes (or from ten minutes to midnight until ten minutes after midnight). The "C" Company drop would be from midnight until twenty minutes after. In brief, because of Major MacLeod's lobbying for the extra ten minute departure time, the Advance Party drop would take place entirely during the bust-up created by the Air Force.

The little bridge on the Divette was only five or six metres wide. Hardly a bridge worth the name, but the canal beneath it was deep, about five metres of water with an ancient soggy bottom that would suck any mechanized vehicle completely out of reach. With the bridge gone the canal would be a bulwark, totally impassable to mechanized traffic. The main road through the Le Mesnil Ridge and inland to Caen would be out of business one or two minutes after the first angry shot was fired in the ground war on D-Day. So went a single Airborne infantry company's plan in the grand strategy of the Allies' re-entry into Europe.

Chapter V

"God Bless Canada"

Murray MacLeod

In England, a few minutes before the 1st Canadian Parachute Battalion moved out of the security transit camp to head for its airports, there had been a short period of mingling of the whole battalion. Many good wishes and exhortations passed both ways between friends from all the companies. The main part of the battalion would head for an airport near Down Ampney but the Advance Party, "C" Company, would go on to the more distant Harwell airport.

Although "C" Company would be in Normandy only forty-five minutes before the other main Airborne landings, it seemed like a long time for a single infantry company to be within the defences of Rommel's "impregnable" Atlantic Wall, supposedly able and poised to rebuff a massive invasion from the sea. Everybody knew the invasion would consist of hundreds of thousands of Allied soldiers. Meanwhile we faced a serious moment in airborne military experience which stressed the perils of the night ahead, yet also expressed the confidence and willingness in the paratroops to give their lives if necessary to see the beginning of the end of the disgusting Nazi historical period. It seemed almost certain that Hitler's Thousand-Year Reich was about to be cut down to a ten or eleven-year Reich.

When "C" Company's transports were moving out of the security transit camp it was not a case of, "Well, we'll see you again in an hour or two," but of certain knowledge that some close friends would never see each other again. Here is how the departure, as well as the previous one from Carter Barracks, was described by Henry Churchill of the mortar platoon from Headquarters Company:

"As I try to write about my experiences, the first one I think of is the one we all shared when departing Carter Barracks for the security transit camp, a week or so before D-Day. As we bade farewell to those we left behind, I can see them yet as they stood there, and I know they thought the same as I did... well, there go a lot of them that we will never see again... and I guess it turned out that it was so.

"I know everyone's desire was like mine, to see action, and we did. And another time I often think about was when 'C' Company left the security transit camp for France on the evening before D-Day: I can still see your company as you went on ahead - those charcoal blackened faces - as we wished you luck and said a little prayer. That scene will be in my mind forever."

By the fifth full day in the security transit camp the soldiers of the 1st Canadian Parachute Battalion had been given most of the information about the enemy, the countryside we were about to attack, and what we were expected to do. The concentrated pouring-over of aerial photographs, intelligence reports and maps, all related to every detail of the expected activity in France, had largely ended. We had memorized it all. Every possible point related to the information we had been given, and every landmark we had learned about to help speedy orientation in our new surroundings, was fixed in our minds. We were ready to go. The whole idea of soldiering had changed from one of mock-up and practice to one of purpose and reality. The enemy were about to feel a sting of retribution for the hell they had raised in Europe and the world.

There was now a little time for personal feelings, for thought and for recreation. The unusual foodfare continued, as did reasonable allowances of cigarettes and beer. Mail deliveries seemed to increase and the news from home was welcomed by all. The contents of parcels from Canada were shared, as were thoughts about our families at home: personal thoughts of how loved ones left behind would take it when informed of inevitable deaths in the weeks ahead.

Materially, the Canadian citizenry were exceptionally well off compared to the peoples of Europe but large increases in casualty lists after the invasion began would be bound to affect them deeply. They were accustomed to long casualty lists after some of the big battles in Italy and from the huge air battles over Germany in 1943 and '44, but this was the showdown and the casualties were about to expand in a big way. It seemed to the soldiers that the coming invasion would be the beginning of putting the world back on a more even footing. To them, D-Day would be the final great turning point that would not only signal the beginning of the end of Adolf Hitler and his Nazis, but of all the Axis powers. The thinking was: when Germany goes Japan will follow, and the last remnants of the fascists of Italy will simply fade away. The soldiers knew what their part in the invasion was to be and what was expected of them. Throughout the Allied world the public looked to the soldiers of the Second Front, combined with all the other armed services, to bring World War II to a close. It made us feel good, knowing we could handle it.

In the evenings, from the second day of June onwards, movies were shown and gambling flourished, although the most enjoyed entertainments were the concerts worked up by the troops themselves. The 1st Canadian Parachute Battalion had a surprising number of soldiers who were good performers. Medical Corporal Bill Ducker was a baritone vocalist, while Sergeant George Capraru was an equally good tenor soloist. It was hard to beat Corporal T. A. (Doc) Dodd and his friends on their guitars, and Private J.P. Thomas of Number 8 Platoon could break your heart with his nostalgic piano renditions.

Some of the spontaneous concerts and sing-alongs these men and their friends - every one a top rated soldier - put on during the week before D- Day will always be remembered by the war veterans who heard them. It was impossible to imagine, during these performances, some of the things that would happen to many participants and members of the audience, beginning in just a few days. With so much life in the camp, it seemed incredible that many would be dead or maimed within a week. They knew it would have to be that way but it still seemed unreal.

The morning of 2 June was free. That afternoon the companies embarked on trucks, closed-in with tarpaulins so their division could not be identified in transit. They were transported to a large estate where a deep natural swimming pond in an abandoned quarry awaited them. The water was cold and refreshing. There were good banks for competitive diving and stunting and the perennial comedians did their stuff. After the swim the evening was spent writing letters. One, especially designated by each soldier, would be held for a week after D-Day and then sent out uncensored. In that letter the soldier was free to write anything he wished. All other mail would be subjected to the usual censorship.

The early morning of 3 June, the day before the eve of planned D-Day, was one of the most interesting of the transit period. For a start, the officers and platoon sergeants brought around a maze of new P. O. W. escape aids. New shirts were issued which had special buttons. They were cloth-covered buttons with stiffeners inside. In one button, with a barely perceptible longer shank, the stiffener was an efficient miniature compass. There were small hacksaw blades of especially hardened steel, about ten centimetres long, which could be slipped between the layers in the sole of a boot. Another escape aid was a double layered triangular yellow silk scarf which had a dual purpose. In combination with others, it could be used as an identification panel to warn friendly fighter aircraft not to strafe. Slit open and laid down inside out, each scarf displayed a map of France plus generous portions of bordering countries.

Another thing distributed that morning caused embarrassment for some soldiers who were later taken prisoner and searched. It was a generous issue of rather thick condoms. The men called them inner tubes, so little did their thickness suggest sensitivity. Still, they were carried with an eye to the future when some survivors might have a leave in continental Europe and actually meet up with Ma'moiselle from Armenteers, or Lilli Marlene - up against a barrack gate but, as everyone knew having grown accustomed to the European blackout, not "underneath the lamplight."

Later in the morning the troops were transported to an airport where in a hangar they were addressed by General Sir Richard Gale, Divisional Commander. He made a beneficial and lasting impression upon them. He was a "fine figure of a man" to begin with - big, tall, straight and square of shoulder. He was always impeccably turned out - high brown boots polished like a fine mirror, fawn corduroy breeches with khaki tunic pressed to a T, Sam Browne belt to match his boots and just as highly polished. His bearing and manner combined with his even white teeth and thick, carefully groomed moustache. But almost certainly it was the quizzical expression in his penetrating eyes and the way he wore his red beret that gave him his charismatic quality. He would brook no slackness, but he exuded an empathetic feeling for those he ordered to do his bidding. You could tell he felt the agony of combat for his soldiers. His influence was infectious.

His address was as penetrating as it was reassuring and informative.

The German Army had flooded the Dives Valley to keep invading tanks on the highways, so they'd be easy targets in the event the invasion of Europe came through that part of France. They did this in 1941.

"Now it's three years later," General Gale continued with a gleeful gleam in his eyes. His 6th Airborne Division was about to drop from the sky and seize the Dives territory, and so turn the tables on the enemy. This would be a considerably different kettle of fish than what the clever Germans had anticipated. The men of his 6th Airborne would bring their six-pounder and seventeen-pounder antitank guns with them in huge Horsa and Hamilcar gliders.

They'd tow their guns throughout the Airborne lodgement area with jeeps and trucks which they'd fly to France in the same manner. Now it would be our turn. Now it would be us who'd blast the enemy tanks off the roads into the flooded, soggy-bottomed Dives marshes, canals and ditches. Already the tables would be partly turned, but that was not the end of it. To complete the reversal, approximately one hundred PIAT rocket-guns, carried on the persons of the Airborne soldiers themselves, with a good supply of ammunition packed into kit-bags strapped to the legs of other parachutists, would complete the anti-tank armaments that would face the enemy. And, glory of all glories, it would be the first time in modern warfare that individual infantry soldiers went into combat seeking monstrously huge monolithic tanks as their prey.

The Germans would not know what to make of this. They had never even thought of such a scenario. It would be the first time they would meet lightly armed infantry who were prepared to fight their tanks. "Besides," he said, "you superb soldiers standing in front of me know as well as I do there are approximately fifty medium and three hundred light machine guns in our division to add to the other armaments I've spoken about, and it is with the combination of all of this that we will smite the enemy."

General Gale conjured up a clear picture which warmed the hearts of his soldiers, a picture calculated to back up his actual intentions. When a significant number of his men, individually armed with PIATs, combined with the large number of individuals armed with personal machine guns and the heavy, glider-borne antitank guns, were ensconced under camouflage in the hedges along the highways through the territory of the flooded lower Dives, a few hours before the invasion forces from the sea would come ashore, there would be a different kind of shooting party. The German tanks would be brewing up, burning their ammunition uselessly - or falling off the shoulders of the roads into the mucky-bottomed floodwaters. The soggy valley of the Dives would become the enemy's bloody nemesis.

To cap it off, he ended with a superb statement: "The Germans know only a damn fool would drop a division of lightly armed airborne troops into the quagmire that is the flooded Dives. But! What they do not know is that I'm just the damned fool who is going do it. Besides, my decision is going to allow my soldiers to win the battle for me. So good hunting!" he said, "and, go to it!" He was treated to the usual resounding cheers.

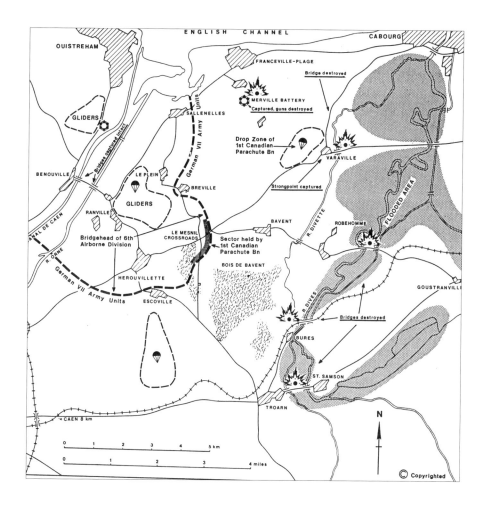

Explosion Map.

Map depicts Drop Zones and Objectives of the 6th Airborne Division.
Destruction of Merville Battery.
Destruction of the Bridges on the River Dives system.

The men of the 6th Airborne Division had complete faith in Gale and his brigade commanders. As far as the Canadians were concerned they would make it happen just the way the general laid it out. The tank regiments of the German 21st Panzer Division, less than ten minutes away from one of the 3rd Brigade's Drop Zones, were certainly not the main concern of the 6th Airborne's rank and file two nights later when they took to their transport planes and gliders.

The Canadians' first and most pressing needs were to take their initial objectives, which were all within a circle with a five-kilometre radius or less from the centre of Drop Zone V:

- Block the roads and pathways leading to the Merville Battery from the south and to the west towards the Orne estuary where it exits into the Channel.
- Destroy the bridges at Robehomme on the Dives and on the farm canal at Le Hoin.
- Seize and destroy the bridge and the enemy defensive positions at the village of Varaville.
- Seize and set up defensive positions at the Le Mesnil crossroads. Also seize and control the three-kilometre stretch of highway from Varaville to Le Mesnil.

They had it all in their heads and it could run through their minds so fast that they didn't even have to think about it.

Following the meeting with General Gale the troops were re-embarked in the trucks and rolled off to other airports to fit their parachutes, and to talk to the aircrews who would be flying them to combat. Once introduced to them, there seemed little to talk about. The aircrews knew their job, the paratroops knew theirs and there was not enough time or a meaningful way to explain it to each other. But to both the other man's job seemed deadly.

One predominant question was on the paratroopers' minds. Would the aircrews be able to put them on the Drop Zone accurately, the way they had done during training? The typical reply was, "We're going to drop you on a sixpence, Mate," or "We'll put you down exactly, Old Boy, right where you'll want to be."

The paratroops were full of confidence anyhow. But these assurances, coupled with what we knew from the almost daily newspaper reports during the last few years about the renowned accuracy of the RAF on bombing raids, made us feel completely reassured. We were trained to operate as definite teams: sections, platoons, companies and battalions. To know in advance that the drop was going to be on target was more than gratifying; it gave us positive assurance that we would have a definite point from which to start towards our rendezvous.

Most of the paratroops would fly in C-47 aircraft. Twenty numbered parachutes, already placed in each aircraft, were now brought out, fitted for each trooper's size and checked for careful packing. The parachutes were then returned to the aircraft in the seating sequence in which the troopers would

*General Sir
Richard Gale.*

*A clever and
innovative Division
Commander.*

*Brigadier
S. James Hill.*

A soldier's soldier.

Padre G. A. Harris.
A brave and holy man. Killed on D – Day.

Major H. D. Proctor.
(Forceful, killed.)

Lieut. – Col. G. P. Bradbrooke.
(Organizer, promoted.)

Major J. A. Nicklin.
(Disciplinarian, killed.)

Lieut. – Col. G. Fraser Eadie.
(Expediter.)

The Four Battalion Commanders.

Captain C. F. Hyndman.

Captain C. N. Brebner.

Lieutenant Robert Begg.

Captain P. G. Costigan.

The four Medical Officers of the Battalion.

They did their best to repair human carnage and to save lives in the field.

A sample of the Battalion soldiers. Training break before D – Day. A picture says a thousand words.

jump. Tomorrow, in the late afternoon of 4 June, the men of the main battalion would return to reclaim their property, harness up, and be ready to jump into Normandy beginning shortly after midnight: at 00:50 minutes 5 June, D-Day. That was the way things stood on the evening of 3 June 1944.

Returning to the security transit camp that evening was a special event in itself. Everyone knew this would be our last night on British soil until our part in the Battle for Normandy was over. But we did not know when that would be. Once in the camp we went straight to our tents, examined our weapons and other equipment once more to make certain everything was in place. We then settled down for the night. The excitement and anticipation which had filled our day began to subside. We were ready for sleep.

How we would seize our objectives was clear in our minds. Risks were understood and accepted. The record of the German Army too? We could not forget that the same army had conquered most of Europe from the French Atlantic coast to Baku in the Caucasus. Now, left with our private thoughts and our memories of home, knowing the fourth of June would be a long day, the night of the fourth and fifth even longer, and the fifth, D-Day, longer still, we absolutely needed sleep. Sleep though, with such momentous happenings racing through our minds, wanted to avoid us. Soon, as darkness fell on the slack canvas of our tents, a foot or two above our heads a light rain began to tap out a rhythmic alternating tattoo of life and death. Mercifully, young minds full of personal prayer slipped into restful sleep.

Reveille was a shock. We opened our eyes to a windy, cloudy June morning. Tent canvas was now taut but flapped and snapped in the late spring wind. Foliage rustled and whispered a portent of bad weather. By 09:00 the news came down the line of tents: General Eisenhower had cancelled the operation indefinitely. The nightmare every soldier feared had happened. The super security system that had been in place to keep such a colossal enterprise secret might now break down. We all knew that all kinds of communications would have to occur to stop the day's original plans. Would the security system hold? Everyone down to the youngest private soldier held his breath. We, as Canadians, knew too well the damage which had been done by the cancellation, then the remounting more than a week later, of the Dieppe assault in 1942.

By mid-afternoon a wind-driven inundation swept over the camp. The soldiers worked feverishly to create deeper ditches around their tents and to dig miniature canals to drain the water away. But their equipment and personal ammunition was exposed to a lot of water despite all the special efforts made to protect them.

It seemed as if the hand of fate had intervened to destroy much of the preparatory work we had done during the previous five or six days. But by 18:00 hours it was a hot sunny afternoon and everything went out to dry. The evening was spent cleaning weapons and ammunition. At lights out the thinking and the trip to sleep were repeated, but this time there was no rain-dance of the gods of war on the canvas tents.

5 June dawned with uncertainty. A general clean-up and breakfast

parade, quickly over, left the men with no reassurance that the operation had been rescheduled. Everyone was apprehensive. Speculation was rife again until about 09:00, at which time the platoon commanders arrived to give the word. The operation was on again. D-Day would be 6 June.

Things now happened fast. The troops were soon dressed in full battle order. The senior non-commissioned officers again checked every man for equipment, ammunition and readiness. Big transports rolled up to the security wire and the men embarked. The officers took up-to-date reports from their subordinates and the truck convoy rolled away. Most of the battalion went on to Down Ampney, while "C" Company, the coup de main Advance Party for the Varaville operation, drove on to Harwell airport. There they linked up with the group of RAF crews who were to fly the Albemarle bombers to Drop Zone V in Normandy. Although the reinforced "C" Company of the 1st Canadian Parachute Battalion required only eleven bombers the flight was somewhat larger, for attached were the pathfinders of the 22nd Independent Parachute Company - six more bombers - plus another one for a ten-man section to do a British 9th Parachute Battalion reconnaissance patrol round the Merville Battery barbed wire.

The late morning was clear and warm. The countryside of southern England, still drenched from the previous evening's downpour, fairly teemed with early summer growth. By mid-afternoon the transports rolled into Harwell airport and a delicious meal was served courtesy of the RAF. But the troops were looking skyward again. Light scattered cloud was beginning to form once more. The day became ominous.

Things seemed strange that day. We might almost have entered a different world. The highways and the airports were a continuous mass of mechanical activity. Great mobile equipment convoys had rumbled down the highways towards the South Coast for many days and nights and the continuing din of them could be heard through 5 June. The concentration of motor vehicles was so huge and dense, you would have to be totally insensitive to change not to see that the coming enterprise was massive.

The airports were no different. They were crammed with glider troops, parachutists, C-47 transport planes, Albemarle, Halifax and Sterling bombers (paratroop and glider tug aircraft), Mosquito night fighter-bombers and Lancaster bombers for raids along the Channel coast (Operation Flashlamp), which included the Merville Battery bombing. All this seemed to swamp the airport at Harwell.

Service organizations to handle the needs of the combat personnel and equipment were everywhere. Everything worked like a finely-tuned machine. The service personnel acted in a curiously stand-offish way, painfully trying to keep the correct form when they spoke to the Airborne soldiers. "Really, we don't know a thing about what's going on" made it seem that a charade existed somewhere in the social atmosphere of the airport. These same service personnel had catered to British and Canadian paratroops during the previous winter training period. They had always appeared friendly and conversational. Today, though, it was as if something was being left unsaid. Small talk was the order of the day. They were not supposed to know what was about to take place, but it was pretty darned evident that the push was on. But as many civilians did in southern England, the thing to do was to act as though you didn't know.

During the mid-afternoon lunch break each paratrooper was also served two huge, super-nutritious sandwiches wrapped and ready to go. These would serve as a late dinner at about 21:00 hours. It would be their last meal in England for some time.

At Down Ampney airport, close to 18:00 hours, the troops were resting on the warm grass beside their Dakota transports. At this time the final preparations were made. The company commanders gathered their troops and gave them a final talk. They ran through the objectives yet again and reiterated the need for speed in thought and action. Major Clayton Fuller emphasized the critical importance of completing the destruction of the "Lieutenant Toseland" bridge at Robehomme and of the little bridge on the farm canal at Le Hoin. He also stressed the equal importance of Lieutenants Philippe Rousseau and Ken Arril's assignment of seizing the crossroads on the Le Mesnil ridge. The order of the day for "B" Company was: "Do it fast, do it smart, and do it all!"

Major Jeff Nicklin acted out the old football scenario as he addressed his Headquarters Company platoons. "One more time," he snarled, "I want everybody on their toes. Head for the rendezvous as soon as you hit the deck. Don't waste time. Get in there and get things done! You don't need to hunker down if you find it necessary to challenge somebody with the password, just find out the best way you can who the other son-of-a-bitch is, whether he's one of ours or not, and if he ain't, just lay it on 'em. Forget the crap. Just get it done. The order of the day is: Hit the deck, run like hell for your rendezvous and get it done! Clear?"

Major Don Wilkins gave his "A" Company a less rhetorical talk. He stressed the importance of blocking the roads south of the Merville Battery and the byways and pathways up from the coast road which curved along the River Orne estuary through Sallenelles, Les Marmiers and Le Grand Homme. "I know, you know, that this includes the seizure of the intersections within the town of Gonneville-sur-Merville itself, and the destruction of an enemy post by the Gonneville-Merville road immediately to the west and right up against the wire of the Merville Battery. These jobs," the major reminded them once more, "require finesse and silent warfare. There will be no room for squeamishness tonight. If a guard gets in your way take him out silently and fast! When you get in that kind of a situation just say to yourselves, 'Piss on 'em, tough luck for him, we gotta get the job done.' No squeamishness, understand?"

When Major Murray MacLeod addressed "C" Company his firm and truthful personality came to the fore. The general thrust of his short address was: "Gentlemen, this is a momentous moment in history and is a tremendous honour for me as well as you. The Allies are going back to France, and I'm going to lead one of the first two organized fighting units to land in this entire invasion force. That has to be a military man's dream! We've worked together for nearly two years now, and you know what my expectations are. I can truthfully tell you I know you will do your best, and I know that will be good enough to give us everything we want. I know you're as proud of Canada as I am and to have this chance is more than we could have ever expected. You might wonder how much Brigadier James Hill and General Sir Richard Gale know about us and what they think of our abilities. Well, I can tell you it's both of them who've pondered hard and long to make the decisions that have brought us to this point. We can be proud and thankful to them for their favourable insight.

"Tonight, we should not forget the tremendous sacrifices our Air Force units have made over Europe and our Navy in the North Atlantic, while the Army has been building for this day. From Dunkirk to D-Day has been a long road. Our countrymen's selflessness at Dieppe and Hong Kong are already legend. The sixty-thousand man 1st Canadian Corps in Italy has fought shoulder to shoulder with the Allies' best armies and yesterday Rome fell. It's time for us to do our part to defeat the Nazi scourge.

"I'll now give you the password for our first day. New ones will be issued in due time. The challenge during D-Day will be 'Punch' and the identification will be 'Judy.' Punch and Judy, easy to remember, eh! Let us pray for success on this venture, and from the bottom of our hearts say: 'God Bless Canada!'"

The soldiers heaved their gear-ladened bodies up into the waiting Albemarle bombers. They were so overloaded with equipment they could barely walk. It would be a relief to get on the ground again after the flight. Once in the bombers they had to check each other again for errors in clearances between primed explosives such as Bangalore torpedoes, antitank mines and different types of grenades which might easily get hooked to a detonator pin ring or to their web equipment. One accidental error and an explosion could destroy the bomber and everyone in it. "No accidents please!" Sergeant Morgan would say in a high pitched, frivolous voice, "no accidents with ammunition or static line entanglements. Do your checks thoroughly. The last thing we need after coming this far is an accident." Then he'd roar in an army sergeant's voice, "Get it fucking done and be fucking careful too."

Everything done, the overloaded Albemarle bombers roared to full throttle and scooted down the runways three quarters of a minute apart. The first signs of oncoming darkness permeated Harwell airport. Corporal Saunders looked at his synchronized wrist watch: "22:31 hours at lift-off," he said. "I guess the major got his extra ten minutes. He's the greatest, ain't he?"

The aircraft engines seemed to strain for a long time as the bombers lifted off into a gradual climb to a few hundred feet altitude. Soon they began to ease when the captain pilot levelled off and coaxed the aircraft into cruising mode. Suddenly the atmosphere became one of tense expectation.

The men who flew in the first four bombers were:

Bomber One: Sergeant R. O. MacLean and Privates R. Mokelki, Don Carver, Peter Bismutka, L. Sauder, H. B. (Sinkor) Swim, H. E. Guenther,

Andrew McNally, W. Yurkowski and Fred Russell.

Bomber Two: Sergeant Harvey Morgan, Corporals Myles Saunders and Dan Hartigan, Privates William Middleton, Eddie Mallon, M. M. (Pop) Clark, William Chaddock, Gilbert Comeau, Colin Morrison and Cliff Douglas.

Bomber Three: Sergeants Mosher MacPhee and Harry Wright with Privates Andy Hogarth, E. J. Pinay, E. Damstrom, W. D. Murray, H.R. Croft, J. A. Anderson, S.R. Woodward and J. G. Sloan.

Bomber Four: Lieutenant Sam McGowan and his batman G. A. Thompson, Private R. E. Pilon, Signalmen Corporal John W. Ross and Private L. C. Grenier, together with PIAT antitank men Corporal W. E. Oikle and Privates L. A. Neufeld, J.T. Church and Bob Carlton.

Lieutenant McGowan and Sergeants Wright, MacLean and Morgan each occupied the tenth position in their respective ten-man sticks and sat with their backs against the bulkheads between the troop cabin and the pilots' cabin in each of their bombers. They wore headphones and could hear the conversations between the pilots. Occasionally they reported what little information there was to the paratroops in their sticks.

Corporal Hartigan in Bomber Two made his way to the Plexiglas tail section of the aircraft as soon as it was up and trimmed off. From there he was able to give a running commentary on what could be seen as the flight progressed.

As last light began to turn the rich green landscape of southern England to charcoal-grey, Bomber Two passed over a fairly large town. Hartigan reported that the streets were filled with people promenading on the sidewalks. He was surprised how crowded the open spaces of the town were and added the thought, "The pubs or movie theatres must have just closed down for the night." Nobody commented on what he had just said, so he knew that in their hearts all the guys were thinking the same thing he was: some men from the stick, or maybe all of them for that matter, would never have the chance to go to a pub or a movie again. Ever! That was a truly lonely moment.

As the Albemarles came out over the South Coast no one needed to be told, since the familiar sinking bump during the transition from land to water told its own story. It was now a half-moonlit night and those who could look out were treated to a great surprise. Right out there, as though you could reach out and touch them, were the startling white faces of the great cliffs along the South Coast of England. The bombers had come down close to the surface of the Channel to frustrate efforts by enemy ships' radar to detect them. The radar waves bouncing off the cliffs would make the bombers indistinguishable from the cliffs themselves. The paratroops, none of whom had ever seen the white cliffs from the seaward side, were now to their astonishment actually looking up at them.

Hartigan was by now well sprawled on the floor of the bomber, enjoying a complete panoramic view, and because of his favourable location was the most amazed person on board. Immediately, his mind began to experience the strong clear voice of Vera Lynn singing her magnificent wartime

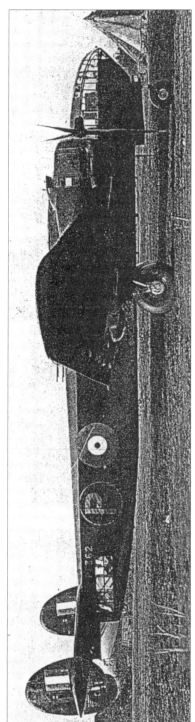

ALBEMARLES
(Obsolete Bombers used as Airborne transports.)

Above:

Model with windows forward of tail.

Left:

Off into a stormy evening sky.
June 5th., 1944.

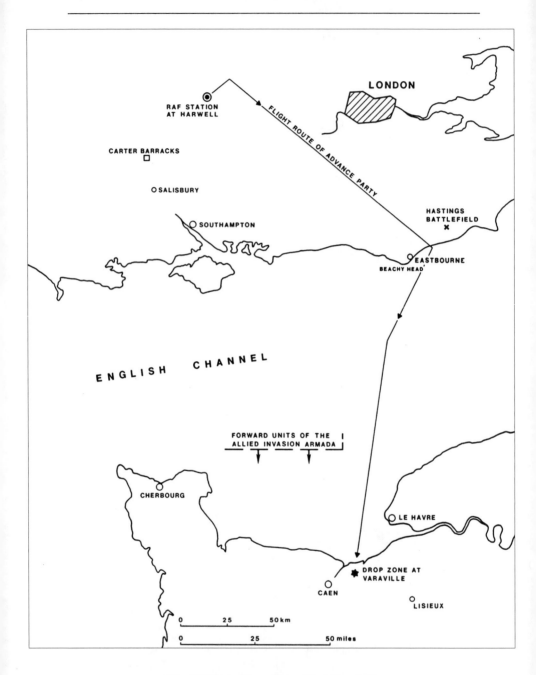

The Flight to Drop Zone V at Varaville.

songs "The White Cliffs of Dover" and "We'll Meet Again." A lot of nostalgia related to wartime history since 1940 came rushing in: the Battle of Britain, Dieppe, the Battle of the Atlantic, battles won and lost in the Western Desert, Italy, the Mediterranean islands and East Africa. The scene, with the deep blue of the nighttime sky matched by the colour of the Channel's surface contrasting with the white cliffs lit up by the moon, made a fleeting mind-rendering moment; powerful, never to be forgotten, a definite drifting-in-space sensation - a world completely without orientation when one looked away from the cliffs.

In the historical milieu of the time the flight experience instantly imposed a thick collage of military success and failure on the viewer's thoughts. It was full of historic glory: Celtic, Roman, Norman and other historic and fearful melodramas attuned to the present situation.

"Leap down! There is nothing to be terrified about," a Roman tribune had exhorted his men who showed concern about the depth of these opaque, greyish Channel waters on a cloudy day nearly two thousand years before. Disciplined, the Roman soldiers leapt down from their boats brandishing their swords and charged ashore during Caesar's invasion of Britain. After that on and on it came, the surreal review of nation after nation, battle after battle, war after war, until at last the most successful invaders, the Normans, nearly a thousand years ago landed close to cliffs like these near Beachy Head. Now, in about an hour's time, highly disciplined paratroops would leap down, harbouring concerns and fears like those the soldiers of Rome's long ago legions had felt. This time the fearful water would not be the Channel but the water of the flooded Dives in Normandy: the territory from which the most powerful of all the Normans - William the Conqueror - had come with his fighting men.

Soon there was another view. When the bomber left the land behind and now flew close to the water, strangely the sky and the surface of the Channel continued to meld into a common colour - a uniformly deep midnight blue. When one looked away from the moon in the southeast, he felt a heightened sensation of having left the planet and of cruising in space.

Time seemed to pass quickly, and suddenly everyone felt a sharp adjustment to the right. They knew they were more than half way across the wide part of the Channel. The bomber's planned course had been explained during the briefings; it was flying from the vicinity of Chichester straight on to Le Havre. But about fifteen kilometres before reaching Le Havre it would make a right turn and fly southwest by south directly over Drop Zone V. The course adjustment was expected. Ten to fifteen minutes later, while describing the beauty of the racing moon's path dancing on the Channel's surface, Hartigan reported that one part of the night horizon appeared darker than the rest of it, and offered his opinion that the cause was the greater distance to land up the Bay of the Seine and the famous river's estuary.

The coast of France was getting closer and stormclouds were being watched closely. There were huge scattered, cumulo-nimbus thunderclouds which possessed brilliant silver edges as a result of the half-full moon to the southeast. The clouds coming in from the Western Approaches were ominously drifting towards the bomber-stream's flightpath. The bombers, after the adjustment to the right, were flying southwest by south, at a right angle to the thirty mile an hour northwest-by-west wind blowing across their bows. The scattered thunderheads leapt skyward far into the stratosphere, making the night look like fiction. At times the moon lit up their eastern billows in a way which made them seem like huge towers of ethereal silver, reaching forever into an unknown chasm. A chasm like the one the paratroops would jump into in a few minutes!

A stormy battlefield loomed. Wills were hardened and set. Fears were suppressed by determination. Tempers rose in anticipation of fighting. The paratroops took on the mood of the night; furious! angry! Knowing that, as it would always be in the 6th Airborne's warfare, battles would be fought to unconditional decisions. Only one side could win. In the paratroopers' minds, the enemy must lose.

No soldier likes to be surrounded by the enemy. But for the next few days that was going to be the name of the game for these invaders.

Private Gilbert Comeau said to Sergeant Morgan, "I hope everyone here feels like I do, Serg. Think of it. I'm going to be one of the very first Allied soldiers to land in the third battle for France in the twentieth century. One of the very first to do his part in such a great effort. No kidding! If my folks could know where I am right now they'd be so damn proud they wouldn't know which way to turn. They'd worry like hell, but they'd be proud just the same. Don't you get some kind of feeling like that?"

Sergeant Harvey Morgan was also a proud man, not only for himself but for his country. He wanted Canada to be right up there with the bigger Allied nations. He knew he was from one of the most favoured lands in the world, and nothing suited him better than having his homeland out front in all its endeavours. For himself? Well, he was just like everybody else, a little guy, right there riding the vanguard of history. As he himself said: "My fifteen minutes of glory, my one day in the sun, or whatever it is they say." One unbridled night with no limits to its adventure. For the first time in his life he saw the world as something few men had the opportunity to see in a lifetime, and it suited him just fine. "Maybe," he said, "that's the way the world is, a life and death struggle." He was an ordinary joe who had some special understanding of the extraordinary events ahead, and he knew that intimate death might be waiting for him. Neither he nor his buddies showed any doubt about their ability to carry out their tasks. Regardless of what the enemy at Varaville might do, he knew he and his friends would give all they had.

Comeau knew that their commitment, reinforced by the irrevocable nature of its combative beginnings - landing on a field within the defences of the Atlantic Wall - made anything other than victory unthinkable. The die was cast.

The earth passed into darkness again as thunderclouds obscured the moon's light. Conversation in the bomber faded into sombre pensiveness.

Everyone felt the Drop Zone and the enemy at Varaville coming closer. Tension mounted. The men squirmed to get the cramps out of their muscles. One could feel the charged atmosphere within the bomber's fuselage. Morgan heard his headphones crackle, followed by the voice of the first pilot. Morgan immediately called out, "Pilot says ten minutes to go. Don't forget, when you hit the ground fix bayonets."

Corporal Hartigan, as number two jumper, worked his way forward to the bathtub-shaped exit hatch and hooked up his static line. He could see the outline of the men in silhouette as number one jumper, Corporal Myles Saunders, began working at the hatches to get them opened up and latched back. "OK," Saunders shouted, "they're up and locked. Ready for exit!"

"OK, good! Only eight minutes to go," Morgan reminded them. "You all know that means we're only about fifteen miles from Varaville. Is everybody happy?" A roar of assent filled the fuselage; it soon faded into a tailed-off effort, but for a short moment the noise of the bomber's engines had been drowned out. Again, everyone began to stretch and shift positions in their futile effort to rid themselves of muscle cramps. For an hour and twenty-three minutes they had squatted on the floor of a fuselage too low to stand up, while controlling about a hundred pounds of equipment. Their legs and backs cried out for relief, but they knew it wouldn't come until their parachutes opened up.

The co-pilot gave a five-minute warning to drop time. The men checked their static lines hooked to a cable running along the left wall of the fuselage, and settled down to wait for the two-minute red light warning to come on above the exit. It would stay red for two minutes, then switch to green. There would be about twenty seconds of pandemonium, then the bomber would have shed the last of its paratroops.

"Jesus! Gimme a cigarette Middy," Comeau said to Bill Middleton.

"You nuts? You know you can't smoke here. You could blow this damn old crate sky high."

"Stow the cigarettes till after Varaville," Sergeant Morgan growled.

"I don't mean for now, but I'm crackin' and I want it for the first chance I get when we're on the ground." In the tension of getting through this whole ordeal Comeau had simply forgotten his cigarettes.

"OK," Middleton replied. He took his helmet off, fished a package of Sweet Caps from above the webbing inside and said, "Here, take the whole damn package for good luck. You might need it. And if you live long enough to smoke 'em all, you might stand a chance of coming back."

As the bomber came close to the French coast the moon shone through again and the Channel showed up with moderate clarity below. The pilot began to climb and soon levelled off at five hundred feet, with only about two kilometres to the beaches. The two-minute red light was now on. It was only slightly larger than an ordinary flashlight lens, but it seemed like the biggest and brightest traffic light anyone had ever seen.

In Bomber Two it was possible for Corporals Saunders and Hartigan to get a complete view below through the exit. As we came in over the beaches there was another surprise. What we now saw should have been expected, but it wasn't. It had been imagined that a nighttime silhouette of a three dimensional coastal beach would be down there, but no! What was there, so close, five hundred feet below, was a two-dimensional wet surface that looked like a charcoal-grey, dimly visible map of the coast of France. Apart from its wetness it was featureless except for the estuary of the River Dives about a hundred yards to the east. Behind the beach was another wet-looking expanse. We were looking at a wet beach and flooded land.

The Channel tide was less than half full. The Dives estuary showed up on the flat "map" as a conglomeration of small islands where geological time had allowed the continually running water to cut several deep rivulets into the shale beach, leaving the islands between them. Over a fairly wide area ahead and to the right, rising above the surface of the flooding, black lines formed squares which appeared to enclose land areas about the size of small fields. It became obvious that they were made by hedges and fences protruding above the surface of the floodwater and that they ran away to the west towards the Merville Battery.

It was now known that when the bomber made a slight adjustment to the right the flight was dead on for Drop Zone V northwest of Varaville, less than a minute away. All of this was reported to the stick as Bomber Two came in over the beach near Cabourg - Dives-sur-Mer. The RAF aircrew was performing one hundred percent. Suddenly, with another adjustment to the left, the unmistakable features of "Jackboot hedge" came dimly into view, with the boot's sole touching the southeast side of Gonneville-sur-Merville. The large field of fall stubble, where the top front of the boot made a slight acute angle near the middle of the Drop Zone, was ahead and to the right.

At this point the corporal's report ended. The whole stick now knew that the aircrew was right on the money. The paratroops, although waiting for the green light to flash on within a second or two, were relieved as they looked forward to meeting the remainder of the company at the J-shaped hedge northeast of Le Grand Château de Varaville.

It was reasonable to conclude that the other bomber crews were as accurate as was the crew of Bomber Two. No thought was given to any other possibility.

In Bomber One carrying Sergeant R.O. MacLean's stick, forty-five seconds ahead, Privates Peter Bismutka and H.B. (Sinkor) Swim were to jump the one and two positions. The glaring red light switched to green and the two men leaped out together, one from the front of the exit, the other from its rear. It was six minutes to midnight on 5 June. They were the first soldiers from the Allied assault forces to land in Normandy.

In England, shortly before leaving for the airports, A. J. (Scotty) MacInnis overheard Major Murray MacLeod mention to another officer that he was going to end his remarks to "C" Company with "God Bless Canada." Scotty quietly said to a friend, "Especially for us Cape Bretoners, Bye."

W. S. Ducker

Chapter VI
Battalion Flight into Normandy

G. A. Comeau

Once "C" Company departed for its airport at Harwell, the remainder of the battalion moved to Down Ampney airport and went through much the same experience as the Advance Party. They brought their previously fitted parachutes out of the C-47 transports, parked them beside the runways they would take off from and checked each other's equipment. A further inspection of ammunition and supplies made sure nothing was missing. They ate the huge sandwiches received at lunch time and smoked cigarettes or drank tea delivered by a canteen or NAAFI wagon. Charcoal touchup was applied to any exposed skin. In the early going their battle would be one of rapid movement, without the benefit of slit trenches, so camouflage would be a must. The remaining free time before takeoff was spent talking to the aircrews.

As an example of what took place let us eavesdrop on Lieutenant Rousseau's stick, which included the former lads Boyd Anderson from the Wood Mountain hills of southern Saskatchewan, Bert Isley from the open prairie just about a hundred and sixty kilometres to the north, Jim MacPherson from North Bay, Ontario, and the former intrepid beachcomber A.J. (Scotty) MacInnis from Sydney in Nova Scotia. In the late afternoon they sat around on the grass with a fifth soldier, Joseph Moffatt. This relative newcomer to the 1st Canadian Parachute Battalion had recently passed through the parachute training school at Ringway near Manchester. He had come to the paratroops as a highly trained infantry soldier from Le Regiment de la Chaudiere.

They talked about how Moffatt viewed the prospects for the seaborne infantry that would come over the beaches in the morning, D-Day, and were reassured by his enthusiastic pride in the 3rd Canadian Infantry Division, and other famous units within it, that he had come to know during his three years of training in England. Like most of the soldiers in Lieutenant Rousseau's stick, he now subconsciously relied on the tests of courage he had faced while a youngster to overcome fear. They remembered the formative years that had led them into some of the best regiments of the Canadian Army, and finally to the 1st Canadian Parachute Battalion. Within hours they would be meeting the enemy on his own ground. It was time to stand tall and put what they had learned in the detailed briefings into practice.

After their equipment was fully checked there was another waiting period before boarding. The paratroopers' greatest concern was still whether or not the aircrews could drop them accurately on the chosen Drop Zones in Normandy. There was no reason to believe that they could not. All through training there never had been a mistake. Night jumps, day jumps, jumps when it had been too windy - one thing the paratroopers could always count on was the accuracy and punctuality of the aircrews. They were always right on the Drop Zones, always right on time. But something kept nagging at the paratroopers' minds which made them seek further reassurance.

When George Robertson asked the question being put to aircrews by paratroopers all over southern England that evening, he received a reply much like the one given everywhere else. "We're going to drop you on a sixpence, Mate," the first pilot replied and was quickly backed up by his co-pilot. "That's right, we're going to put you down exactly where you want to be."

"That's all we need to know," Robertson replied with a broad smile on his face.

"I'll say! Its music to our ears," Boyd Anderson cut in. "If you guys were dropping troops back where I come from in southern Saskatchewan, you could kick 'em out anywhere you pleased and your parachutists would land on open ground. But around the Varaville Drop Zone, now that's different. The Merville Battery troops on one side, the village of Varaville with its defensive positions on the other. The land around it is flooded for three fifths of its perimeter, and a big power line on steel towers runs right through the middle. I'll say we'd better be right on!"

"Like I said, Mate, on a bloody sixpence!"

It was the same as it had been for the soldiers of "C" Company. Everyone knew that for nearly two years the enemy had flaunted their Atlantic Wall as unassailable. Nazi propaganda bragged that their great concrete fortifications, special weapons and beach obstacles made their coastal defences attack proof. The Airborne troops, like the soldiers of the seaborne assault forces, didn't believe it. But they had to admit the enemy was formidable and produced soldiers who established themselves as troops who were not to be sneezed at. There was no doubt the German Army would give a first rate account of itself, it always did. These factors created a definite possibility - although it seemed unthinkable - that after the Airborne assault troops dropped behind the German coastal defences the seaborne forces might not be able to get ashore. But with the massive Allied preparations, and with General Montgomery as battle commander, failure seemed inconceivable. Yet the nagging persisted. All knew that if things went wrong the Airborne would be in a desperate situation. It was great to be confident, but wise to be aware that reality can be vicious. A letter written by George Robertson justifies the atmosphere as it existed that night:

"Before takeoff, I went under the C-47's wings to inspect the load that had been attached there. I saw four parachute equipment containers and four three-bomb anti-personnel bomb canisters, a total of twelve twenty-pound anti-personnel bombs. The aircraft appeared so loaded I wondered how it could fly, especially considering that twenty heavily loaded parachutists were yet to go aboard. At twilight Padre Harris was with us briefly. It was a charged moment, but a time to ponder and a time to be humble. Our loads were so heavy we were able to get up into the plane only with great difficulty. Soon we were at full throttle, and as it seemed to us, skimming the last stretches of smooth runway. I'm sure, like me, other members of my stick had feelings of apprehension too. As we approached the south coast of England the pilots let us know that Worthing was directly ahead. In the gloom I was able to look down and see vehicles in convoy on their way to board ships. I thought of my many friends, ones I made during my years with the Highland Light Infantry of Canada, knowing they were probably out on the Channel on their way to Normandy too. Without question, many of us were aware this was an important historic moment. There was a feeling of adventure amid feelings of self-assurance, fear, and determination as one rode the vanguard of history for one important night.

"As we proceeded across the Channel most men were taken up with their own thoughts. Occasionally some kibitzing broke the tension. From England's coast to about half way across the Channel we became aware of a throttling up and down of the C-47's engines. We soon figured out the need for that was to remain on station relative to other aircraft in the transport stream. About mid-Channel the flightstream was supposed to make a fairly abrupt adjustment to the right.

"Up to this point the outward leg of the journey kept us as far as possible to the east of the seaborne flotillas heading for France. Now it would change to the right to keep us out of range of heavy anti-aircraft concentrations, expected off the shores of Le Havre as we headed in for the French coast and then two minutes onward to the Varaville Drop Zone.

"I was jumper number fifteen in Lieutenant Philippe Rousseau's stick. Suddenly we ran into a lot of anti-aircraft fire from the defences along the Atlantic Wall and our aircraft was jinkin and dodging all over the place. As we crossed the coast the aircraft suddenly lurched upward, jolting many of us to our knees. A brilliant white flash below lit up our aircraft's cabin. Since we were only about four hundred feet up, we took this to be the flashes from our own exploding bombs, which we knew were to be dropped as we crossed the beaches in the hope it would fool the enemy into thinking we were only another bombing raid crossing into France. Those of us who were able to remain on our feet through the period of evasive action fought fiercely to deal with a nearly disastrous situation. The extra heavy loads carried by a number of men in the stick were thrown around by the movement of the aircraft and the men carrying them needed help to wrench their big kit-bags back into position. Some men were falling down and had to untangle themselves from each other's equipment before they could right things again. The worst of all possible events was happening: the stick's exit from the transport was being slowed down. Time, crucial to the success of battle, was being lost, and the stick was being spread out on the ground over much too long a distance.

"The RAF dispatcher was screaming, 'Get out! Get out!' At one point, in the dim shadows I saw him raise a foot at a man exiting the door. This angered me as I knew there wasn't a man there who would not get out as fast as possible. Years later, I learned he was only trying to help Bert Isley up the grade to the door. The aircraft was banking in an evasive turn to starboard, while the exit was on the port side, and Bert was in danger of toppling over backwards because of his top-heavy load.

"As I went through the door I was faced with a column of anti-aircraft tracer fire in close proximity - between the exit and the tip of the port wing - that was horrible. There were red, yellow, and blue tracers in the firestorm. In half a second I had fallen away from the tracers and was thankful I was not hit. Nor was our C-47, I believe. It seemed to me like a miracle. During my descent I was close to an enemy four barrel anti-aircraft gun, probably the one which spewed the column of fire past my aircraft as I came through the door. In the soft moonlight I could make out the silhouette of the parachute canopy of Mel Oxtoby who jumped next to me. It was obvious right away that when we'd hit the turf our stick would be split in two by the enemy gun. I was going to be on one side of it while Mel was going to be on the other. Worse still, there was probably enemy infantry protecting the gun's crew. As soon as I did hit the ground, and got out of my parachute harness, I knew we were in country which had no resemblance to Drop Zone V at Varaville. Disaster! What the hell had gone wrong?"

Boyd Anderson, who jumped a few positions ahead of Robertson, had a somewhat different experience. That in itself demonstrates the pace of change in an airborne assault. As fifth man, ten seats ahead of Robertson, Anderson would get out about ten seconds ahead of him under usual jumping conditions. Now, because of an interrupted drop, they would be a minimum of one hundred and fifty metres apart when they hit the ground. That meant the whole stick would take about three kilometres to get out. Such a rate of exit might even stretch the length of the stick out from three kilometres to five or six - depending on how long the interruptions were. A four minute stick could see the men separated by as much as two hundred and fifty metres from each other. An intolerable distance for soldiers trying to rendezvous on each other in the dark.

Boyd Anderson reports in a letter:
"A few days prior to the invasion, Sergeant Beaudoin ordered me to report to Lieutenant Rousseau. As sort of an afterthought he added: 'I've recommended you, specifically, for a particular task. Mr. Rousseau will brief you on it.'

"When I met Lieutenant Rousseau I was surprised at the difficulty of the assignment. It had to do with a patrol to Dozule, twelve kilometres from the Drop Zone at Varaville. Dozule is a fair-sized town located on a main highway which runs southwest from the Seine estuary through Beuzeville, Pont l'Evêque, and Dozule to the city of Caen. The plan was for Mr. Rousseau, with his batman, Private Broadfoot, and myself to split off from our 'B' Company immediately after we made it to the rendezvous on the Drop Zone at Varaville. We were to light out with all haste and by whatever means possible to Dozule across the Dives River to the east. Once there, we were to apprehend the Mayor of the town, whose name was also Rousseau, with a view to getting accurate information on the enemy troop concentrations east of the Dives. Lieutenant Rousseau was excited about his assignment and was pleased to have been selected for such an important and dangerous mission."

Anderson continues: "On 3 June, while behind barbed wire in the Security Transit Camp, we had a chance to meet our aircrew which would fly us into France. The first pilot's name was Frank Cuer. Cuer and his crew were highly experienced, having served with 271 Squadron RAF on many bombing raids over Germany. He assured us we would be put right on the Drop Zone, and since I had spent quite a lot of time talking to him during our two meetings, he asked me to write to him care of RAF Down Ampney to let him know just how accurate he had been on the drop. I never saw him again, for he and his navigator Andy Anderson were killed on a re-supply drop on the fifth day of the Arnhem operation the next September.

"The risks on the Normandy drop were tremendous. The Atlantic Wall was an unknown factor and the 6th Airborne Division was going to be off to the east of the main Invasion Forces for several days, or maybe for weeks. I think my feelings were mixed. We were committed to going. We wanted to go or we wouldn't have been in that camp. Joining the paratroops had been a voluntary matter and, although we knew the risks, we also knew we had the stuff in us to do the job. I felt it was similar to when I rode broncos in rodeos as a kid. If the bronco you drew was known to be an extremely dangerous hard bucker you went through with it, because you were committed to do the job by the time the draw was made, and you wouldn't be caught dead chickening out. The idea then became, what the hell, let's get in there and get it over with in a hurry. Another analogy might be that it was like riding the range as a young boy and suddenly having to face a nearly vertical bluff on a coulee or river. When you looked down from the top, and it seemed the horse would never make it without slipping into a roll, your heart came up in your mouth, but when you started down and you were committed, you got ready for the dangerous spill.

"On the flight to Normandy," Anderson continues, "I started to think about what took place when we arrived at the airport at Down Ampney earlier that evening. We arrived a little ahead of time and, when everything was ready, we had a few minutes to lie there on the beautiful soft grass rainy old England is famous for. I was lying square on my back looking up at scattered clouds drifting on a fresh breeze from the northwest by west. My past life was coursing through my mind. The Wood Mountain hills, and the rangelands I had roamed from the time I was a preschooler, slid along in my mind beside the drifting clouds. The way we'd been battered by furious blizzards in winter, and sweltered under the blistering sun and dusty wind in summer, made me long to be alone and at home. Vast distances and the searching for predators which might have harmed our newborn calves and lambs had sharpened my wits. I was not afraid to pit my capabilities against any of Jerry's good soldiers. I wondered what lay ahead for all of us. We all knew some of us would die this night - maybe most of us for that matter - but the risks had to be taken. The Western world was pretty well convinced that freedom and liberty were threatened. Certainly nobody anywhere had experienced freedom to such a degree as I had, on the great open range, in a country untroubled by hatred, unreasonable restrictions, class society or violent prejudice. I could only wonder what might be ahead for all of us, and why Germany was the way it was at that time."

Anderson has talked about his experiences several times in the last few years. The flight into action that night was a momentous experience for him and every other soldier involved. It was obvious to every man that, whether the massive invasion succeeded or failed, the historical consequences for the whole world would be mind boggling. Every soldier meant to deal with what was ahead of him - but just what would that be? The previous five years of reading the newspapers, listening to the radio and watching combat news-reels had formed clear ideas in their minds about the violence to be expected. From conversations with their parents' generation about the First Great War, they knew about the sounds, suffering and stench of the battlefield. But, despite the realism of their training, what would it be like to experience the terrors and horrors of war?"

At this point in Anderson's letter it seemed impossible to read on without trying to find a colourful description of the Airborne soldier's feelings on his flight into combat, especially at night and at such dangerous odds to himself. His letter says: "On the way across the Channel everyone seemed submerged in their own thoughts." The thoughts of many during their flight into combat might be expressed like this:

Airborne soldiers flying to battle,
heads crammed full of death's mean rattle.
A prayer in their hearts for courage, steeled
against "the searing mutter of the battlefield."
Wing through the night, family left behind,
into circumstances remote, unkind.
No more the fast steed, sword or shield,
but a ranging trooper on night's battlefield.
Remember the briefings clear and thorough,
prepare to defend from digging's burrow.
Mind set? Attack the enemy's best,
stand every trial, pass every test.
Remember the wise things - Be brave! Be bold!
Follow your orders, do what you're told.
Find your rendezvous though it be dark.
Aircrews will drop you right on the mark.
The red light's on two minutes to green,
it's the damndest thing you've ever seen -
strangest starter to a savage fight,
a monstrous glaring traffic light.
Get out! Get out! Green light's too late!
Be quick before it seals your fate.

78

Never mind the sweat on black face's soot,
you're swinging free on your parachute!

Dan Hartigan

"When we had been flying for quite a while," Anderson continues, "I could see what looked like a shoreline with high bluffs in the semi-moonlight. I asked the RAF dispatcher what it was and he replied: 'The headlands northeast of Le Havre.' He was also the navigator and he was not surprised by this. He certainly gave no sign that his aircraft was off course, but I didn't think we should be that close to Le Havre - probably a kilometre off the cliffs. Within seconds all hell broke loose. Looking out the exit, I saw the sky lit up *with anti-aircraft fire*. First Pilot Cuer took violent evasive action - down, banking left and right, upward and repeating. I thought it was the end, but Cuer straightened her out and we had to climb since we'd been down near the surface of the sea. We got over the beaches all right, still at low altitude. By the time the two-minute red warning light came on we must have been over what Cuer and his co-pilot thought was the Drop Zone. Things were going wrong though, for the red light switched to green as soon as the red came on, instead of remaining red for two minutes as it was supposed to have done. We were on our feet through all of this except for those who had fallen down.

"The pilots had gained some altitude over the land, and when descending in my parachute I was surprised at how quiet it was - all the noise had suddenly stopped. I knew that 'C' Company would already be in combat at Varaville, and also that we were supposed to be quite close to where some of the planned bombing, other than at the Merville Battery, was to take place. Yet all was quiet. What the hell was going wrong? There was some scattered cloud and a bit of moonlight. I was more than relieved to get out of the plane alive. On the descent my rifle was dangling below me, secured to my person with a light rope. I had made a special pouch which I had tied to my chest, with over twenty-five pounds of extra Bren machine-gun ammunition. The ground came up fast and on a forward swing, bowled along by the fresh breeze, my feet just missed the surface of the earth. I came down on the backswing and crashed flat on my back. I thought the heavy ammunition pouch on my chest had caved me right in. Right then I cared very little whether I lived or died. My training took over. I unhooked my harness and crawled away to a hedge where I could get the lay of the land."

Jim MacPherson jumped between Anderson and Robertson. The enemy flak, combined with the rocking of the C-47 and the darkness, made it almost impossible for him to wrench and twist his heavy load towards the exit. Once out, though, he was suddenly surprised that in the semi-moonlight he was able to see features and structures on the ground. During the last moments of his descent he was certain they were the same ones he had memorized throughout the briefings back in England. He was encouraged because he thought he was smack on the Drop Zone. Then came an agonizing landing as he slashed through the limbs of a huge tree which caused him to tumble, and then bump from limb to limb until he blacked out. When he came to he stirred painfully and wormed out of his equipment. He had skin burns on much of his arms and legs but no broken bones.

In a letter he writes: "When I found I was able to walk I knew it would be deadly for me not to get out of there. I had no idea of the length of time I had been unconscious. It turned out the landscape did not match the one we had memorized in England after all. I had no idea where I was. I was woozy and so began to wander. I became the victim of some bombing and was burned by a chunk of shrapnel which sliced through my right leg behind the knee and nicked one of the big cords there. I swore at the German air force, not knowing that it was our friends in the RAF who had given us the gears. Near daybreak, while crossing an ancient sunken road with a fence blocking it off, I was challenged. 'Halt,' the other man called in a low voice. 'Who goes there?' 'Punch,' I replied. 'Judy,' he said, and I knew it was a friend. It was Jim Broadfoot I found - Mr. Rousseau's batman. What a relief to finally get together with one of our own men. In a way, though, we were no better off, for Broadfoot had no idea where we were either, but we were aware the landscape was not the one we had trained for - disaster! Something had gone very wrong."

Stanley Shulist, number fourteen jumper in the stick, came down in an open field close to a road. Now that the anti-aircraft guns had stopped firing it was quiet as sin. He got out of his harness and began to follow the line of flight of his aircraft, which led to the other side of a highway. Suddenly he felt lucky that he had not been wounded by flak on the way in, or on his way down, but he did not know that he was not on the Drop Zone. A few minutes later he heard what he took to be some rustling in the hedge across the road. He thought it was made by some of his fellow paratroopers from his own stick but as he crossed over, in the semi-moonlight, someone let loose at him with a submachine gun.

Because of the nighttime operation he never knew who shot him, but he felt like he had been hit by a freight train. The bullets, though fired in the darkness, came from short range and reached their target with remarkable accuracy and impact. They went through both legs, one arm and one side of his body. He went down in a heap and prayed that one of his friends would find him. He was in the defences of the Atlantic Wall and knew that if he called for help he would call in sudden death, or summon enemies who might subject him to interrogation. So he just lay there in agony and waited.

Meanwhile, Lieutenant Rousseau's stick was now in deep trouble. It was divided on the ground by an enemy force in the middle of the night.

Members of both halves of the stick, not realizing they had been dropped in a curve, thought that if they moved off the planned flight line - which they would have to do in order for both halves to link up - their situation might get even worse. They would have to make a fairly wide detour to avoid the crew of the German anti-aircraft gun. And one party might try to bypass the enemy on the east side while the other might try on the west side. In that case they would never meet.

It appears that most of them made a similar decision: to stay on what they thought was the flight line until the two sergeants, who jumped as numbers one and two and Rousseau, who jumped last, could roll up the stick from both ends towards the gun. And that's the way it happened.

Slowly, most jumpers from numbers one to fourteen rolled up to George Robertson, while those from numbers sixteen to twenty were gathered in by Lieutenant Rousseau as he rolled his part of the stick to Mel Oxtoby. These directions would have been strange had the flight path been - as intended - from north to south. However, there is strong agreement among the survivors that the plane had nearly completed its exit from what the aircrews thought was the lodgement area turn, and was actually flying a zigzag course (generally on a northeast heading) by the time the soldiers jumped.

George Robertson had been on the ground only a minute or two when he heard a single rifle shot, and later thought it might have been the gunfire that wounded Shulist. He then heard a stampede of sound coming towards him. This turned out to be a herd of cattle running away from the shot. He moved a short way off the flight line to get some protection from a hedge, and hunkered down to wait for Sergeants Beaudoin and Trenholm to roll up on him with the other twelve men in his part of the stick. He waited for an hour or more, by which time he figured that he had been missed by the other rendezvousing soldiers. He moved off for some distance, stopped on a small rise and did a three hundred and sixty degree search of his moonlit surroundings. While he peered into the night he saw a glint of the moon flicker on a helmet just down the slight slope from him.

"Halt. Who goes there?" he demanded in a hoarse whisper. "Friend," came the reply. "Punch," Robertson tested further. "Judy," the intruder said, "and am I glad to find you!" With that his friend Gordon Conneghan came forward.

After a short conversation the two men decided to stay close to the original flight line. Soon they learned they had made the correct decision, for Sergeant Beaudoin did show up with a number of men. They included Sergeant Jack Trenholm, Corporal Gordon McWilliams and Privates Arthur Schillemore, K.M. Pledger, V. S. Willsey, Joseph Moffatt and Bert Isley. Eight men of the stick were now together. But there was no sign of Corporal Anderson, Privates Ellefson, Broadfoot, MacPherson, Oxtoby, MacInnis and MacKenzie or of Lieutenant Rousseau.

Sergeant Beaudoin reported to Robertson and Conneghan that number fourteen from their stick, Stanley Shulist, had been found shot through the knees and elsewhere. He had been drugged with morphine from Shulists' own emergency medical kit, covered with a groundsheet and left to his own devices. It was a tough, heart-rending decision, but that's the way it had to be.

After discussing their situation and the shocking implications of the fact that no other C-47 aircraft passed overhead, the rendezvoused soldiers all agreed that none of them had any idea where they were. They could not tell whether they were east, west or south of the Drop Zone, but they knew they were in countryside quite different from the landscape they had expected. This told them they were probably a long way from Varaville, but in which direction?

Soon, a vicious bombing took place to the west and slightly north of them. They thought this must have something to do with the Merville Battery. They were wrong, for the bombing of the battery had already taken place while the battalion flight was little more than half way across the Channel. That error caused them to head west. After proceeding a mile they found that they were no better off.

There was still no recognizable feature to suggest where they were. They agreed it would be foolhardy to trust the occupants of just any house to tell them their location. They needed an indication that the occupants would be friendly. Sergeant Beaudoin decided to lay low until the seaborne invasion came ashore after daybreak. They'd get their bearings from that. As time passed it became more certain, because of the utter silence, that their suspicions were correct. They were a long way from the Drop Zone at Varaville. Shocked by this devastating disappointment, they took up an all around defensive position to wait out the darkness.

Lieutenant Norm Toseland flew confidently to France. He knew the little bridge at Robehomme on the Dives was a key objective. The second main east-west highway, a mile or two south of the coastal highway, came west from Beuzeville near the River Seine below Rouen. It then progressed further west through Pont l'Evêque, Dozule, Troarn and onward into Caen.

Toseland knew the same highway would be cut by the 8th Battalion at Troarn before it reached Caen. This would cause the Germans to swing west at Goustranville, to try to get into the Airborne lodgement area by that route. This was an oblique lateral, which after splitting off from the main Pont l'Evêque road at Goustranville proceeds across the Dives bridge at Robehomme and drives straight west through a village called Bavent to connect with the main Cabourg-Varaville-Le Mesnil-Caen highway a half a kilometre from Le Mesnil. If he should fail to destroy the bridge at Robehomme, he would nullify the effects of destroying the road junctions at Varaville and would also leave an easy route into the Le Mesnil Ridge position open to the enemy.

If, in turn, the enemy could eliminate the 1st Canadian Parachute Battalion's positions at Le Mesnil, they would effectively cut through the middle of the 3rd Parachute Brigade and leave the Germans with several routes open to the Orne bridges, where Brigadier Nigel Poett's 5th Parachute Brigade was in defence. There was no question that the little bridge at Robehomme was critically important, especially in the early going.

The flight was going smoothly as Toseland mulled all this over in his mind for the umpteenth time. That it was his responsibility was beyond doubt. The 6th Airborne Division's orders through Operations Order Number 1 had specifically named Toseland to the task.

The knowledge that there was an enemy battalion at Dozule, about two kilometres from his bridge, gnawed at his mind. However, his confidence soared because he knew he was leading a platoon of determined soldiers, all with one idea in mind - to achieve their objective of blowing the bridge. Suddenly, the two minute red warning light was glaring above the exit of the blacked-out C-47. Apart from a little roughness caused by enemy flak, everything seemed normal.

The red glare switched to green and his twenty paratroopers, already jammed up against one another for a quick exit, stampeded into the night.

Swinging free on his parachute, Toseland was surprised at the serenity of the night. The enemy anti-aircraft guns had stopped firing, the moon was obscured and the light wind from northwest by west seemed warm and almost friendly.

He landed softly on open ground in an apple orchard. Everything was going like clockwork. As he extricated himself from his parachute harness another C-47 passed overhead, and since he had jumped as number one man in his stick he simply followed its flight path thinking he would pick up his nineteen soldiers. It was not to be.

As he left his landing point Toseland could not help feeling lucky. He noticed he had just missed landing in water to the north of him so figured he was on the east side of the Drop Zone. He would simply have to go southwest and would be in his battalion rendezvous in two or three minutes.

He walked south for about a minute when he came upon C.H. Nickerson, one of his corporals. A minute or two farther south they met water again. He was perplexed and decided to skirt the water. They no sooner veered east than they met Platoon Sergeant Tom Pasquill. They continued by swinging back onto the line of the original flight but found no more soldiers from their stick.

The water became deeper so they moved on a more westerly path again and came out on dry land, probably a little way northeast of Bavent. They now knew they had been on a small island in the floodwaters north of Bavent. Not beside the Drop Zone at all! They wasted no time and lit out on a bearing which they thought would take them to the River Dives at Robehomme.

Soon, on a narrow lane, they halted a twenty-one year old French girl on a bicycle who said she was out for the night air. Having an intimate knowledge of paths and byways where she was certain that there were no enemy soldiers, she cast her bicycle into some bushes and led Toseland to Robehomme - above his objective bridge!

Dr. Colin Brebner, one of the troops' favourite officers in the battalion, had sent two medical corporals, R.C. Hall and Bill Ducker, on ahead with "C" Company. It was pretty certain there would be casualties at Varaville,

83

since the company's plans included charging right into the enemy trench position there. For that reason Dr. Brebner would make Varaville his first call. Once the casualties had been attended to, he and his medics would remove them to the main objective at Le Mesnil and set up his medical aid station in Major MacLeod's temporary headquarters position. But, for him as for so many others, a share of misfortune lay ahead. He writes in his letter:

"Flight over the Channel uneventful, except for flak over the coast of France. Our excellent pilot had to abort the drop at number fifteen jumper and left five of us in the aircraft to go round again. The second approach was good and we got out without trouble. Jumpers that night were busy people and I was no exception. During the fifteen-second descent, I had to lower my kit-bag and prepare for my landing. The big bag was loaded with important medication and other essential life-saving material including minimum surgical instruments, disinfectants and gauze bandaging supplies. To get a good landing was an absolute necessity. Well, with all this worry and other business, I did not check behind me and nudged into the lower parts of the outer limbs of a giant elm-like tree. The trouble with elm trees is that the ends of the outer limbs are still a long way off the ground and far out from the tree trunk. When my parachute harness on the end of the twenty-two foot suspension lines brought me up short, I was swinging free twenty to thirty feet out from the trunk of the tree, and was still from thirty to fifty feet off the ground. Unable to pull the chute out of the limbs by climbing my rigging lines, or by swinging them to enable me to reach a solid branch, I was sweating profusely as exertion plus the weight of my equipment eventually wore me down. Since I was unable to jettison my equipment, the seat strap of my parachute harness worked its way up to the small of my back and caught over the holster of my forty-five calibre pistol, which in reality I was not supposed to be carrying. The jig was up. I was like a puppet on a string with no puppeteer to activate my body parts. It was now impossible for me to make any further attempt.

"I took the only course open to me. I hit the quick release box on my chest, slipped out of my entanglements and went for the long free fall to mother earth. It was a desperate move and I knew my chances of surviving in a healthy condition were not good; but the whole purpose of my life's work was at stake and I could not stay where I was. I was needed where my men were dying.

"I attempted the drill for a hard landing, but only remember a stupefying wrenching of my existence before I lost consciousness. When I came to I checked my legs and found I could move them. Then came the shock that I had smashed the bones in my left wrist. A one-handed doctor was going to be severely handicapped but could still be valuable. I then rolled over on my stomach, pushed myself up on my knees with my one good hand, and finally stood up. I took one step and fell hard - flat on my back. As a doctor, I realized I had broken my pelvis and that my active war was over. But one overriding and recurring torment crowded my mind. I would be of no use to the wounded this night. My only solace was the knowledge that I had trained my paramedics well and knew they would do a superb job of performing their duties. I hoped better luck had befallen them than had befallen me."

Colonel George Bradbrooke was surprised when he landed up to his knees in water. He had been privy to the D-Day plans for the 1st Canadian Parachute Battalion for much longer than any of his subordinates. He not only knew the territory close to Drop Zone V and around his battalion's initial objectives, but was familiar with the wider territory as well. So it didn't take him long to realize he was only a short way east of the Drop Zone. He quickly located his batman and was one of the first to make it to the assigned rendezvous near Le Bas de Breville southwest of the Varaville-Le Mesnil road. Once there he was pleased to find that his intelligence officer Lieutenant R. D. J. Weathersbee, his second-in-command Major Jeff Nicklin, and Lieutenant John Simpson, the signals platoon officer, had already arrived. But obviously there had been an unqualified screwup on the drop. Instead of being able to muster his battalion (less "C" Company and Norm Toseland's platoon), nearly four hundred men, he was only able to account for a mixed bag of troops totalling less than seventy-five. Even worse, that small force was made up of not only scattered elements of his own support platoons and rifle company personnel, but a few men from other battalions and divisional troops who had been dropped on the wrong Drop Zone.

The magnitude of the disaster Bradbrooke faced, and the mental anguish imposed on him by circumstances, might well have incapacitated a lesser man. Two full years of organizing, training and moulding a thousand trainees into a first-class infantry battalion, supported by a competent reinforcement battalion, seemed to have disappeared at the culmination point of its ultimate purpose. He had no way of knowing whether his missing troops had gone down in the Channel, were scattered hither and yon, had been shot down as they came in over the enemy defences of the Atlantic Wall or were drowned in the wastes of the flooded Dives.

Whatever the reasons for the mess the colonel now faced several dilemmas. The installation of his troops on the Le Mesnil crossroads was crucial to the retention of the ridge as a barrier defence position for the River Orne and Canal de Caen bridges. General Montgomery's orders made it mandatory that those bridges be held for future use.

Whether the Le Mesnil crossroads position was actually defended by the enemy nobody knew for certain. If it was and he approached it with too weak a force, he might suffer a serious rebuff and not be able to take it at all. If it was not presently defended by the enemy and he waited too long to approach it, they might seize it before he did. So he had to decide how much time he could allot to gathering up more of his troops - if in fact they were even in the immediate area. It was also crucial for him to know what had happened to his "C" Company at Varaville.

It should be remembered that the parts of "B" Company not meant to be at Robehomme - Lieutenants Rousseau's and Arril's platoons - were primarily responsible for occupying the Le Mesnil crossroads. Also that Lieutenant

Dick Hilborn's Vickers machine gun platoon, together with Lieutenant Cote's mortar platoon, were to keep open the section of the Cabourg-Caen highway between Varaville and Le Mesnil until they were called forward to Battalion Headquarters later on D-Day.

But the scattered dropping of the paratroopers now forced a change in all these plans. Colonel Bradbrooke ordered Lieutenant Weathersbee to take two men and reach Varaville, then report back about the status of the battle at that village, the din of which could be heard from their present location. He also informed Major Nicklin that the plan to protect the highway would be abandoned. The major was to organize all those in the rendezvous into an effective echelon so they could advance on the Le Mesnil position. Private Andy McNally from "C" Company, who had rendezvoused with Major Niklin immediately after the main drop and was supposed to be at Varaville anyhow, volunteered to scout the route to the village for Lieutenant Weathersbee. An initial recovery from an unmitigated disaster, as feeble as it was, had been put into motion.

Chapter VII
The Battalion
Flight Continues

Andy Hogarth

Lieutenant Marcel Cote had been in the army since 1940 and could rightly boast about his background with the Royal 22nd (Vingt-Deux) infantry regiment of Montreal. He had worked his way up to lieutenant from private and now, after his transfer to the 1st Canadian Parachute Battalion, was proud to be standing near the three C-47 transports that would carry his mortar platoon across the Channel to play its part in the liberation of France.

The mortar platoon consisted of forty soldiers, making it twenty-five percent larger than most other platoons. It was made up of four sections of nine men, plus Platoon Headquarters which included the lieutenant, his batman, the platoon sergeant and a runner. Because the platoon included some signals radio men and medical personnel, three C-47s that could carry up to sixty men were needed. Fate played a major role in the eventual well-being of the platoon members. Right from the beginning, when Lieutenant Cote assigned them to their positions in their aircraft, chance played its part. The platoon runner Private W. Paterson, for instance, was assigned to Platoon Sergeant B.T. Blagborne's aircraft, while the officer kept his batman Private W. H. Kendry with him. That act alone made a great difference to Kendry, for he became a prisoner of war. Paterson was wounded on 10 June 1944 but escaped any further injuries.

Similar differences affected many other soldiers of the platoon. Now, though, as they stood around their aircraft it was too soon to foresee how minor decisions would shape the fates of the participants.

Besides W.H. Kendry, Lieutenant Cote's stick included Sergeant G.M. Breen's section made up of Corporal Harold Miller and seven regular mortar men. As they waited for embarkation time, 23:05 hours, they lived with their own thoughts, their memories of home and the families they had left behind. The knowledge that many other Canadians were dying every day to put the Nazis out of business was not lost on them.

Cote thought about his young wife and children at home in Montreal and wished he could be with them, but knew he was where he had to be and was eager to play his part in the great battle ahead. He watched the remnants of the previous day's storm make the sky look uncertain and thought of the men now at sea who would go over the beaches in the morning. When embarkation time came he ordered his sticks on board. Also flying with Cote were Headquarters Company Signalman Joseph Nigh and some British personnel: a captain, a lieutenant and two other ranks who brought aboard a large radio transmitter.

For some time the flight to France seemed to be a precise operation. They were still about fifteen kilometres off the coast when one of the pilots came on the intercom to give the "five minutes to red light" warning to be followed by "two minutes to green," when the paratroopers would be gone into the night. But there was a jarring interruption. Heavy anti-aircraft fire from batteries on shore plastered the sky with high-explosive shells. This seemed out of line because intelligence had not reported heavy ack-ack batteries in the area of the River Dives. During the three or four minutes it took to fly to the coast it seemed the aircraft would never make it. The pilots put evasive flight manoeuvres to the test and bedlam reigned as the troops struggled, cursed, righted themselves and jammed up to the exit. From the French coast onward, for the last half minute of the paratroops' flight, the gutsy pilots flew straight and level. Under these circumstances the jumpers were able to get into good exit positions and heave themselves and their heavy loads out into the chaos of the night.

Lieutenant Cote does not remember much except thinking the enemy had been warned of their arrival. When out of the C-47 he saw not only anti-aircraft fire chasing his receding transport, but machine-gun and rifle fire coming from the ground directly below. At his landing point everything went blank. When he came to he found the left side of his helmet had been smashed in by the blow that had stunned him. As he struggled to regain some sort of equilibrium he dimly saw that three German soldiers were standing over him. One was pointing a rifle directly at his brain.

Corporal Harold Miller, second-in-command of Sergeant Breen's mortar section, landed at the main gate of an important enemy installation and was taken prisoner by the guards almost immediately upon getting out of his harness. Neither he nor Cote had any idea where they were but they knew it was nowhere close to Varaville.

Sergeants Jack Hetherington and Hiram Smith of the Medium Machine-Gun Platoon experienced conditions similar to Lieutenant Cote's: heavy enemy anti aircraft fire, troubling evasive action and interruption of the stick's exit. The aircraft actually came in close to the correct flight path but missed the Drop Zone, due perhaps to cloud and dust from the bombing of the Merville Battery that temporarily obscured the area. When the aircraft made its turn to the east to exit from the vicinity of the Dives the stick was still on board. When the green light did come on the aircrew had throttled up to full speed to get the hell out of there. Faced with air traffic congestion, they manoeuvred violently. The paratroopers, each carrying a Vickers machine-gun barrel or base tripod, a heavy load of mortar ammunition or other equipment - from eighty to a hundred and twenty pounds - were knocked down and tangled up while still in their aircraft. By sheer determination they got back on their feet and made their exits into a savage slipstream while their plane flew up to eighty kilometres an hour faster than it should have. With every interruption of their exit, time was their enemy. Adrenalin pumped at full thrust. They knew they would be hours getting together on the ground, if they ever did.

When they did come down they found no similarity between the ground they found themselves on and the ground they had studied in the briefings back in England. The first jumpers from the stick were smack in the southeast corner of "Satan's Quadrangle," an area about nine kilometres south of Dozule and roughly the same distance east of Troarn, a short way south of Hutot. From there they were spread out until the last man, Colin Lewis, landed close to Honfleur on the left shoulder of the Seine estuary, nearly fifty kilometres from the Drop Zone!

Private Morris Zakaluk was observant and astute. He took his surroundings in with interest as his C-47 roared down the runway at Down Ampney airport in the blacked-out night conditions of 5 June 1944. The mild turbulence that made his aircraft rise and fall perceptibly drove home to him how far he had come since his childhood days in Poland.

He remembered how his bones ached from the bruises he suffered at the hands of his childhood friends as rock-throwing mock battles were fought in the fields outside his family's rural village. Tonight it would not be stone missiles he'd have to contend with, but hot steel ripped into jagged chunks screaming through his environment, which were meant to dismember his body. His imagination worked overtime wondering what the battle would be like. He did not have long to wait. He writes:

"As we approached the French coast in the half moonlight you could hear and see exploding shells in the sky, and streams of tracers arching their way towards us. It was scary - but almost hypnotizing. The enemy is awake to our presence. How many of them will be waiting for us on the ground? Will we land on the correct Drop Zone or amongst those big coastal artillery guns and their defending troops? Will I have a chance to get my weapon out of the big bag I have strapped to my leg, or will the enemy be upon me before I can get out of my parachute harness?

"We are crossing the beaches now and there are searchlights playing on the scattered clouds of the night. Shells continue to explode and I think I hear shrapnel cutting through the aircraft's thin skin. We are still OK, though - she's still flying. It's all happening so fast, but it feels like forever. We know the Drop Zone is only a minute or two from the beaches. We're on our feet and hooked up for the jump, but the red light is staying on too long. When in hell are we going to get the green light? Finally it comes on. 'Go! Go!' someone shouts. There's heaving of kit bags in the darkness of the inner fuselage along with swearing and the usual stampede of the steel-clad boots on the metal ridges along the aircraft floor.

"I'm out and feel the great jerk of my parachute as it slows me and my eighty-pound kitbag to what feels like a complete stop. But I'm not stopped and catastrophe is at hand. Somehow, which never happened before in training, my kitbag and its attachments slip down around my ankles, strapping my feet together in a tight knot. The quick release that is supposed to play the bag out on twenty feet of rope, so it will hit the ground a split second before I do, won't work. Within seconds my feet are going to be jammed between my heavy load of equipment and the hard ground while travelling at thirty miles an hour. Before the thought of it is complete I hit the ground like a freight train. I know, right away, I've either broken or sprained my right ankle. I'm by a hedge in an apple orchard. It's quite dark. I'm alone. I have no idea of direction now. The pain in my ankle is excruciating - overpowering! I'm in France. Will my friends find me before our enemies do?

"I get to my feet but I cannot walk - my ankle is too painful. It is a relief to know, although it might be cracked, it is not totally broken because it will allow me to hobble on it with great pain and difficulty. Using my rifle as a cane I drag my kit-bag and make my way to a thick hedge a short distance from an orchard farmer's house. Once inside the hedge, it turns out it is actually a double hedge with a fairly deep ditch between the rows of trees. Although I have been unfortunate and am now crippled and have a much greater potential of becoming a victim of the enemy's counteraction to the airborne landings, I am ready to make the best of my circumstances and know I have found a perfect place to wait out the arrival of other members of my stick. My greatest worry is the thought that if the enemy finds me I might be shot while I am alone, and nobody will ever know what's happened to me. My ankle is swelling up - throbbing! With my rifle by my side, my mobility almost nil, I have a short sup of water from my bottle. I give my mental attitude a sharp talking to about courage and prepare myself for the worst, if it comes. I am now playing the waiting game."

Regimental Sergeant-Major W. J. (Knobby) Clark's transport came in through flak, too, and took erratic evasive action. When the first fourteen men were out the dispatcher stopped the jump. Private Harvey Minor, one of the soldiers under his command, writes:

"When my time to exit came they stopped the jump and told us to unhook and sit down. There were six of us left in the C-47 including RSM Clark.... When we came round again and jumped, I landed in the lower limbs of a tree and somersaulted into water. I was tangled in my parachute lines but cut myself free. I was alone, but after a while found Clark and the other four. We were in terrible country - crisscrossed by canals but not flooded - nothing like the flooded canals around the Drop Zone."

Battalion Headquarters Medical Corporal Ernie Jeans and another man were jumpers nineteen and twenty in their stick. They had a jump similar to Clark's stick - concentrated ack-ack, evasive action, and an order from the dispatcher to unhook and sit down after the first eighteen men had gone. They went around, did it all over again and jumped into the black night in an area they could not recognize.

All companies of the 1st Canadian Parachute Battalion were now on the ground in France. But except for about a hundred men out of the five hundred and twenty-seven who jumped, they were scattered widely. Only slightly over half were within four miles of where they should have been and, considering the terrain and the enemy dispositions, they might just as well have been a million miles away as far as the taking of their initial objectives was concerned. Almost as damaging, though they didn't know it at the time, was the fact that three-fifths of the equipment needed for the initial stages of the battle was lost.

Another crucial factor was the fact that, in the first hour after the drop, the troops knew nothing of the magnitude of the disaster. After that the situation unfolded only gradually, and by daylight there was utter disbelief and rage. During the night the one thing over eighty percent of them knew for sure was that they could not recognize a single thing. Because their exits had been interrupted, they were having an appalling time rendezvousing on each other. Everyone was so certain the RAF could not make a collective error that each stick thought it was the only one dropped off the mark. Many felt abandoned and lonely.

When Boyd Anderson crash-landed flat on his back, following a forward oscillation, he crawled away from his parachute into a hedge and lay writhing with pain. It was as though the whack from the twenty-five pound pack of machine-gun ammunition he had strapped over his chest had crushed his lungs. Gradually, during the next half hour, the pain subsided and his breathing returned to normal. Suddenly he became aware of the utter silence of the night - no airplanes, no bombs, no weapons firing or tanks harshly rumbling but total serenity. He realized he had probably missed the roll-up of his stick and began a 360-degree search of his locality. Peering into the night, he became aware that someone was out there. Drawing a bead in that direction:

"Halt," he demanded

"Punch," someone replied.

"Judy," Anderson answered. "Advance with caution."

"Hi, Boyd!" O. M. Ellefson, his Bren gunner, said in a spirited whisper. "Where the hell are the five men who jumped between us?"

Neither of them had seen or heard of anyone since they came through the door of the C-47. The only thing they had heard was a single burst of small-arms fire somewhere in the distance. It might have been the weapon that nailed Shulist but they knew nothing about his situation at that time.

Anderson writes: "Ellefson and I spent the rest of the night searching for a direction to the planned Drop Zone, and for other men from our stick, but no luck. We found nothing. The only significant events experienced were when the ground shook from a nearby bombing raid, and some time later when we heard a group of marching men on a highway. We assumed the latter to be enemy. Towards dawn we found a high knoll with tall trees, with shrubbery beneath them, so we decided to hole up there until it got bright. We still couldn't understand why we could not hear any battle noises since we still had not come to the realization that we were such a long way from the Drop Zone at Varaville. The sun came up bright and clear, and nature taking its course under the most dire of circumstances, I suddenly realized I needed to go to the bathroom - which would have to be a small clear patch among the shrubbery. As I completed the job, and was getting my pants up, I heard voices. I grabbed my rifle and moved away for a view in the appropriate direction as Ellefson had already done with his machine gun, and there not a hundred feet from us was a German patrol, consisting of ten or twelve men, passing by. I gave the quiet sign to Ellefson and we let them go. They were talking a lot and were loud. This confirmed what we had been told in training - German soldiers were noisy. When the crisis passed I wished I could tell someone at home about my first good close-up look at the enemy, and how they literally almost caught me with my pants down.

"This near miss gave pause for sober thought. Even with all the quiet, in a beautiful country setting, we now knew this was no exercise. We were now at war, deep in enemy territory, and had no way of knowing how many enemy were right over the next hill. However we did know, since dawn had turned to daylight, that we should be now hearing the great naval artillery barrages and the bombing and strafing by the air forces, as the seaborne assault troops would be coming ashore.

"The calm and silence of the morning told us we were a long way from Varaville. There was still absolutely nothing - complete silence! I climbed the tallest tree on the top of the knoll and, even from there, capable of seeing far into the distance, I could see no airplanes, no battleships, no invasion signs at all, only some kind of an indefinite dark object - like a ship - in a distant haze. I could not even be certain it was the ocean I was observing - simply a light haze with a smudge upon it. Then again, I was now overtired. With all the stressful experiences we had endured over a continuous twenty-four hour period, I wanted to see ships and ocean. So to this day I'm convinced I never really saw either."

Anderson and his Bren machine gunner Ellefson moved cautiously for most of D-Day - one man taking a firing position to cover the other, who scouted along hedges and depressions in the terrain until he could find a favourable firing position for himself. The second man would then catch up and go ahead by repeating the process. Anderson believes they covered a few miles in this manner. He says they lost some time scouting out locations where they thought they saw movement, only to find that their eyes had been playing tricks on them. He is very frank about this. He is certain that, with his eyesight better than twenty-twenty at the time, and with his experience in searching for predators while tending young lambs and calves on his family's Wood Mountain rangelands, he could compete with the best when it came to sighting movement in the distance. Yet he was being fooled. With machine-gunner Ellefson covering him he would investigate suspicious persons in the distance and find that he had been duped by mirage activity.

He readily admits: "With my good eyesight and my experience with mirages on the prairie while watching for predators, my imagination was still playing tricks on me." Anderson wasn't the only man so deceived. Today it is common military knowledge, learned from World War II, that a combination of lack of sleep, severe stress, dehydration and hunger can produce severe hallucinatory activity in a soldier's sight and interpretive mechanisms. Some soldiers, having chosen to shuck off their ration packs as one method of lightening their loads when in trouble, were suffering from all four by the late afternoon of D-day.

Nevertheless, it was no hallucination when, late in the afternoon, Anderson and Ellefson came across a dirt road that looked like it was being used. They decided to parallel it at a safe distance. Anderson says: "We had been told, in England, that a lot of French people who were thought to be sympathetic to our cause had been moved away from the coast. So we were wary."

In an hour or so someone appeared on a bicycle. The two Canadians made for the road and stopped a middle-aged man whom they suspected might be a farmer or farm labourer. Seeing the two paratroopers in drab camouflage uniforms not common at the time - rags tied up in the netting over their helmets, their faces and hands blackened with charcoal, and weapons, ammunition and grenades hanging from every nook and cranny of their equipment - the Frenchman was understandably nervous. He quickly pointed east and kept repeating something like "La mere" or "La mer." Neither of the men spoke French so they assumed he was passing the buck and was pointing in the direction of the mayor's house. It was now getting on towards the early evening of D-Day and all they had seen was one man on a bicycle and a German army patrol of a dozen men or so. Still no vehicles, bombers, fighters or battle noises.

By dinner time they came upon a farm and saw a man walking towards his barn. When they approached him he turned out to be friendly. He knew the invasion had started some miles to the west and was able to tell the Canadians there were no enemy in the immediate vicinity. It was now some hours since their close encounter with a German patrol.

Anderson's account continues: "At great risk to his family, the farmer put us up in a loft in his barn. We just lay down side by side, with our equipment on. The farmer then buried us by forking wheat sheaves on top of us. I don't know how Ellefson slept, but I had a very fitful night. I was uneasy about trusting the farmer. I worried about Lieutenant Rousseau and Jim Broadfoot, with whom I was supposed to have done the patrol to Dozule. I knew there was no chance of that now. The jig was up as far as our patrol was concerned.

"Shortly after daylight the farmer came to the barn and made us understand many of our soldiers had been captured by the Germans - and the way we understood it, their hands had been tied behind their backs, and they had been shot. Right from the start I was convinced, if we were caught, that's what would happen to us. A lunatic order Hitler had given, putting what amounted to a bounty on our heads as paratroopers, left us uncertain and concerned. A few weeks earlier General Eisenhower had gone on radio and warned the German High Command not to carry out such illegal orders. Yet, once such an order had been issued, everyone knew it was difficult to turn those who are in a position to carry it out away from it. Later we were able to find out that the part

93

about our friends having been shot was a misinterpretation of the French farmer's sign language. Ellefson and I were certainly relieved by this knowledge, but followed the learning of it with a discussion between ourselves about our predicament. We decided to get away from the farm and into the forested country we could see to the south. Once there, we would move by night and hunker down by day. We would go deep into France and then move west to meet the Allied invasion troops."

Returning to Jim MacPherson and Jim Broadfoot after they rendezvoused on the ancient sunken road that had been blocked off by the barbed wire fence: They took time to dress the shrapnel wound MacPherson had received behind his knee. He was in great pain, both from the slash and from the bruising he had received while bumping from limb to limb in the huge deadwood tree during his parachute landing. They both knew he would be in great risk of infection. All Airborne soldiers knew that to use their one shell dressing for a minor wound might leave them helpless in the event of a more serious wound later, but they had to make the decision. It would be different when they linked up with their unit and could rely on resupply from battalion medical stores brought in by the big Horsa gliders. Now, although the suffering MacPherson was reluctant, Broadfoot insisted, for he could get a better look at the condition of MacPherson's leg than MacPherson could. He got out his own sulpha powder, shell dressing and bandage, and did the best he could under such conditions.

Jim MacPherson describes their situation like this:

"It was now a sunny morning on D-Day. We were in beautiful upland country that consisted of hedged-in small fields with medium-sized deciduous trees spotted along the hedges, and small spruce copses here and there. The thing that nagged us most was the lack of battle evidence, either audible or visual, and the astounding fact that we were unable to find other soldiers from our own stick or even from the battalion."

Under such exasperating conditions they began another search. The going was slow since they knew they would not survive unless they took advantage of ground cover. In the bright daylight, to move at all could bring instant death. They searched all day, sticking to an area they thought would have been covered by their own aircraft's flight path. They saw nothing of their own or the enemy's side until, at twilight on the evening of D-Day, they came upon a parachute. When darkness came they stepped up the pace of their search until close to midnight. It was now some thirty-six hours since they had awakened in the security camp in England on 5 June, and they were well into the beginning phases of exhaustion. They found a patch of low shrubbery and flaked out.

In the morning they were awakened by the firing of what they assumed to be a German field gun. Having begun their search again, they saw from a hedge a farmer milking a cow in the middle of a small field. They talked to him but could learn nothing of consequence because of the language barrier. As they moved back to their hedge they observed a low-flying Spitfire that came directly over them and rolled up on one wing. The pilot was clearly visible.

MacPherson writes: "Broadfoot pulled out his yellow celanese triangle and waved it as the airplane came round again. The pilot recognized us as friendly and waved back before he flew away to the west. The impunity with which the Spitfire pilot cruised the area gave us our first substantial clue that we were indeed a long, long way from the Drop Zone at Varaville.

"Coincidentally, within a few minutes I spotted a camouflaged jacket. On investigation we moved up on the area and challenged from a concealed position.

" 'Halt,' I called out. 'Who goes there?'

" 'Friend,' came the reply.

" 'Punch,' I tested farther.

" 'Judy,' he said.

"Then I got up and motioned him forward. To my surprise a number of English soldiers came forward. Soon afterwards the French farmer who had been milking the cow came to us and led us to a long trench by a hedge. It was the same trench where George Robertson, and seven others, had hunkered down after Sergeants Beaudoin and Trenholm had disappeared on the patrol along a railroad track. We progressed along this long trench and eventually connected up with Robertson and his group.

"They were as happy to see us a we were to see them, and Robertson quickly filled us in about what had happened to most of the men who had landed southwest of the four-barrelled enemy flak gun. We now knew that Shulist, badly wounded, was lying out there somewhere. The two sergeants were missing, Lieutenant Rousseau and the other men who had landed on the northeast side of the enemy four-barrelled gun were nowhere to be found, and the number of us in the ditch by the hedge was now increased to ten again - all Canadians from our stick, together with approximately an equal number of English soldiers out of a Horsa glider."

Things looked bleak, but Jim MacPherson and Jim Broadfoot felt more secure with a group than they had been when they were alone.

Stan Shulist was still lying on the middle of the dirt road where he had been shot shortly after the drop. He was quite clear in his mind that Sergeant Beaudoin and some other men had tried to make him comfortable. It was then that he realized he had been shot through both knees. He remembered a soldier he thought was Mel Oxtoby helping Sergeant Beaudoin stuff the machine-gun magazines, grenades, mortar shells and bandoliers of ammunition he had suggested they take with them into their already festooned camouflaged equipment.

Shulist reports his first hours alone as follows:

"Beaudoin had used his own ampoule of morphine to comfort me and covered me over with a parachute to try to keep me warm. I wondered what he would do for morphine should he be wounded himself later. He then wished me well and apologized for having to leave me behind, and headed out.

"I remained on the road throughout the night. Nobody came near me. I eventually began to get cold and my injuries pained unmercifully when the morphine wore off. I prayed some friends would return to help me. The night began to stretch into eternity while my body shivered and weakened. I thought about my family back in Timmins, Ontario. I wondered how many of them had gone to work in the gold mines this day, and would now be far beneath the earth's surface where it was warm. God! Will the morning sun never come?"

Eventually the world began to turn grey and sullen. A light cloud covered the sky. Time passed and the countryside remained as quiet as pastoral Canada. It perplexed him. He felt as though he had been parachuted into a fictional land of tranquillity crammed with pain. Eventually a young peasant girl came walking up the road. She knelt beside him and, through the blur of his impaired vision, he recognized a countenance of sorrow and compassion. In halting English she said, "There is nothing I can do but I will try to get help. Try to live with your pain."

Shulist pleaded: "Thank you Angel, I can make it for a while but not too long. Bring help soon." He made her understand that he desperately needed a doctor and that if he didn't get medical attention soon infection would do him in. The girl, trying to reassure him, promised she would return as soon as she could. When she was gone Shulist cringed as he tried to stifle his pain, but decided that come hell or high water he would survive his ordeal.

Sergeants Beaudoin and Trenholm experienced vastly different fates. Although they had been simultaneously separated from the original ten-man rendezvoused group, they were not captured at the same time. George Robertson had heard the Germans noisily carting Beaudoin away as a wounded prisoner of war after the sergeant had been cut down on the railway track. Of Jack Trenholm, however, he heard nothing. In fact the latter, having inadvertently gone right down the embankment to a location virtually under the enemy's noses, was not seen by them.

When the action was over he had no way of extricating himself from his position without attracting their attention. Therefore he did the wise thing - remained motionless until they turned away and vacated the locality. By that time, however, his group had moved off a kilometre or so to the west, where they ran into a line of enemy machine guns and were forced to find a position of concealment. Consequently Trenholm could not contact them and was left to fend for himself. For him, as for many in similar straits, D-Day had turned into a nightmare.

After Dr. Colin Brebner took the long fall from the elm tree near Varaville, smashing his left wrist, he found that he had also fractured his pelvis. He just lay there praying to God he would be found by his friends rather than by the enemy. Sure enough, it was his batman Private Bill Adams who found him about a half hour later.

Dr. Brebner writes: "I was able to direct him on a line that would lead him to our original intended rendezvous. He loaded up with all the medical supplies and equipment he could carry. He didn't want to abandon me to my fate, so I ordered him to get going, thinking I could manage to give myself a shot of morphine that would carry me through for a while. It turned out, though, I couldn't break the seal in the syringette because of my useless wrist. I needed two hands to do it. So I waited out the night knowing the British 224 Field Ambulance was going to set up a temporary hospital nearby and that I would be found eventually.

"Shortly after four or five of the longest hours I had ever endured, dawn had cracked, and I saw a red beret nearby. I called out and several red berets cautiously came forward. Sure enough, they were the British medics I had hoped to meet. They carried me to the northwest corner of the Drop Zone where they had set up their temporary medical facilities under command of a Captain Nelson, whom I knew quite well. They whomped me with a shot of morphine as they were busy with other wounded, and I dozed off.

"Suddenly, I was awakened by a great noise and commotion - we were being bombed and were showered with settling earth but no one was injured. Then, at about 07:30, an enemy patrol retreating from the coast came across us and the whole darn works were taken prisoner. They started us off across country, four German soldiers carrying me. After a while, at about 11:00 hours on D-Day, we came upon an equipment container dropped by one of our transport planes, so the enemy soldiers carrying me stopped and opened it. What do you suppose was in it? Among other things, there were stretchers and a two-wheeled collapsible cart for wheeling a stretcher. They gave me an injection of Pentothal anaesthetic from the container. Afterwards they splinted my broken wrist, and off we went with me slumbering on my new mode of transportation.

"I awoke as we entered the small town of Troarn. Soon the uninjured captured soldiers of the 224 Field Ambulance were lined up along the walls of a huge storehouse with we injured on the opposite side of the room. After a while Captain Nelson and another doctor from 224 Field Ambulance, a major, came in to attend to our injuries.

"When they came to me they were worried I might have injured my urinary tract in my stupefying collision with the ground. They continued to worry and constantly checked on me until, at about 03:00 hours on the morning of 7 June, some twenty-eight hours after I had last urinated in England, I joyfully flooded my trousers and everything on the floor around me for three or four feet. After they found a complete change of clothing for me, I was put on notice that I would be going to a hospital in the city of Caen at about 07:30 on Wednesday morning. We had dropped at midnight the night of Monday-Tuesday."

Stanley Shulist suffered his excruciating pain all through the afternoon of D-Day. His vision became blurry as he checked to see if the French girl was returning. There was no sign of her or any helpers. Maybe she would not come down the same route as she had used before, and this thought made him try to survey the land around him; but to twist his body was absolutely out of the question. All he could do was pray she'd come soon and reassure himself that, no matter what it took, he would survive.

After the sun went down that night he became unbearably cold, shivering and shaking. "Oh God, let them come soon. " There were no stars, only interminable hours of what felt like icy rain, and complete darkness - no dogs, no cows, no horses, no humans - only fear, loneliness, thirst and darkness, but most of all rain and pain. He now wanted to die.

When the sun rose up in the sky again he was no longer able to keep track of time. He could only imagine nobody ever coming with help. As the day passed, no matter how hot the sun became, he could not get warm. His mind told him he would never be warm again and time was monstrous. Somehow he continued to live on but knew it could not be for much longer. Yet he still dreamed in his wakeful sleep that he would survive!

As the day turned to darkness on the evening of Wednesday 7 June, it didn't mean much to Shulist. The difference between day and night was almost cancelled by hopelessness. He knew, now, there was little chance he'd be found in the near future. It had been the night of the 5th when he consumed the huge sandwich at Down Ampney. Even if his water bottle and ration pack were still with him they might as well be on another planet. He was still freezing, but one can only get so cold. The night of the 7th/8th was simply more of the same. Every exaggerated sensory torture possible tried to destroy his being; but time, the dimension that makes a life go by in a wink, continued to be his torturer. A little bit of time was now forever. How could that be?

On the afternoon of 8 June, at about the same time as the remnants of his "B" Company were consolidating after a brave attack down the Varaville highway, Shulist, through his blurred eyes, saw five figures approaching from the direction the French girl had taken an eternity ago. Four of them were dressed in black: SS soldiers, not pall-bearers, which to him they might as well have been. The fifth person was the angel who had gone for help in the first place. Three of the black figures carried submachine guns, the other a stretcher.

Chapter VIII
The Struggle
to Rendezvous

Peter Bismutka

By 01:15 hours on 6 June 1944 five hundred and twenty-seven men of the 1st Canadian Parachute Battalion were on the ground in France. The D-Day landing for 6th British Airborne Division was in full swing. To say the 1st Canadian Parachute Battalion drop was a disaster is to understate the situation.

Over a hundred and forty soldiers were spread out close to the coast of France from near Colleville-sur-Orne, sixteen kilometres west of the Drop Zone at Varaville, to Octeville-Montivilliers, fourteen kilometres northeast of Le Havre. It was a distance of over ninety kilometres of coastline as the crow flies and over one hundred by road.

Most of the soldiers were in the department of Calvados; a few were in Eure, and a few more were farther away in Seine Maritime around the Seine estuary below Paris. Another group of about two hundred and twenty were wallowing in "Satan's Quadrangle." Of the remaining hundred and seventy only eighty to a hundred had been put on or near the Drop Zone. The remainder were scattered throughout the Bois de Bavent and St. Côme Forest.

They had been briefed, trained and prepared to recognize landmarks that would set them off on specific routes from Drop Zone V to accomplish their several special tasks. Now, eighty-five percent could recognize absolutely nothing! The unfamiliar territory and unplanned obstructions made linking up with each other difficult and in many cases impossible. Men from individual sticks ran into widely varied troubles when they came up against flooded canals, thick forests, thicker hedgerows, widespread flooding and ground elevation shifts from low to high or vice versa. Not to mention enemy patrols which were out to locate and liquidate them. Most of the elements in their surroundings caused them to change their directions or activities and made them lose their way. They tried to relate where they were now to the directions of their individual flightpaths, hoping to find one another along equivalent paths on the ground. In the darkness they frequently missed one another and remained alone or fragmented in small groups. The worst possible situation! Despite Brigadier Hill's warning to expect chaos, in an address he gave to the brigade before it left England, the results of the scattering were devastating.

Its effect on the soldiers might have been even worse had they known how widespread the scattering was. They had so much faith in the aircrews that chaos to them meant the chaos of battle, not error by the flyers. So much faith, indeed, that men from every stick could swear it was only their own stick that had been misplaced. Confidence in the accuracy of the RAF crews had been ingrained in us by their precision during our training drops and by reports in the wartime press. It seemed impossible that this misadventure could have happened to more than one or two sticks.

For many, feelings of despair began to intrude and with good reason! The objectives laid out in the briefings in England had been numerous when related to the number of men in these particular Airborne units. True, this made the forthcoming adventure all the more exciting, and willingness to get a grip on the enemy, even at unfavourable odds, went without saying. But those odds also convinced the troops that they must have a complete quota of their own comrades in order to achieve so many objectives.

When they found themselves misplaced - and even worse as they continued to find others who were also misplaced - uncertainty about the battalion's ability to achieve its tasks crept in. Some also felt that if they could not reach their objectives on time they would be letting their friends down - contributing to their failure to achieve their goals. Above all they needed time, but there was no time. Time had run out. Everyone knew it was essential to be close to their objectives immediately, but they also knew that this was now impossible. That knowledge tortured them. It drummed through their brains that the bridges at Robehomme, both on the Dives and on the farm canal at Le Hoin, had to be blown up. The bridge on the Divette at Varaville and the signals telephone exchange in the vicinity of the Drop Zone also had to be destroyed. The left flank of the British 9th Parachute Battalion had to be protected from enemy interference at points above the River Orne estuary and directly south of the Merville Battery.

The direction of the drive inland by the Allied invasion force when it came ashore in the morning would be opposite to the Airborne thrust, which would drive towards the coast and to the battery overlooking the Channel.

The 9th would need the protection as it attacked and seized the enemy coastal artillery installation. The pillboxes, the trench position and the antitank gun at Varaville must be destroyed. It was essential for Headquarters Company to secure the highway from Varaville to Le Mesnil. Most urgently the Le Mesnil crossroads had to be occupied and semipermanent defences set up there. The latter was crucial because the Le Mesnil crossroads location was certain to become a key point in the defence of the Le Mesnil Ridge - an important bulwark in the outer defence system protecting the relatively larger bridges on the River Orne and its parallel Orne canal. These were the main initial objectives. Consequently, they constituted the paratroopers' major worries. But there were more:

Lieutenant Rousseau's patrol to Dozule. The taking of the Mayor of Varaville. A patrol to the "Y" in the road running east from Escoville, where the 8th Battalion would set up defences later. The destruction of a sentry post at the barbed wire on the western edge of the Merville Battery. Plus escort patrols to protect British Field Ambulance sections who would be unarmed, and to guide Airborne Royal Engineers to objectives already seized for destruction. Execution of all these tasks was mandatory. But all were now problematical in the scattered soldiers' minds.

Lost in the unfamiliar, German-dominated territory, many were plagued by the fear that failure to complete their assignments would jeopardize or even abort the entire operation and make their enemies their masters. Yet even an hour or two after the drop none of them knew the full gravity of the disaster at hand. Nor would they until weeks later! Even some senior officers, also struggling with the night far from where they should have been dropped, were in a similar state of ignorance. Had some supernatural god of war been able to inform them of the true state of their troops' dispersal, many of them might have concluded that the 1st Canadian Parachute Battalion had suffered a deathblow by default.

Yet, when we look back now, it is apparent that shortly after the drop the scattering of the Battalion produced a positive phenomenon. The very traits of character which motivated the men to volunteer for parachute training to begin with - which saw them through the severity, rigours and fears of their period in the "Frying Pan" at Fort Benning, Camp Shilo and Salisbury Plain - now impelled them to respond to new adversity with added resources of resolution, determination and just plain guts. The very threat of defeat evidently summoned from the distant reaches of their collective being an escalation of fortitude - "a rising of courage."

Moreover, the knowledge they gained at the security transit camp briefings - in a depth normally reserved only for more senior ranks - now meshed with their fearful predicament to make every man his own general for that one terrible night. Having accepted the early shock of the separate plights they had literally dropped into, they reset their wills. Individually and in small groups they began to fight with the night and the circumstances which surrounded them. "Reach my bloody objective, come hell or high water!" sums up the silent, internal battle cry that drove them. The night, the enemy, the submerged farm canals, the unknown topography, the growing realization that they had been dropped 'way off target, created "hell and high water" in abundance.

The remedies they employed varied widely from man to man and from group to group. There were small collections of soldiers who had no ranked leader, and others who were made up of officers or NCOs without private soldiers, like generals without an army. Many had no one to turn to for ideas or support. Yet they made their own way by their own rules and time schedules. Utterly confused by every possible impediment, they struggled against the odds, sweltering from exertion and constantly worrying about their personal lack of contribution to the battle. Regardless of uncertainty they pushed on. While some succeeded, some played out. Some were wounded, others drowned or died of other causes.

In the groups that were dropped farthest away, some kept going until confronted by overwhelming enemy opposition and were killed, wounded or trapped and taken as prisoners of war. A few evaded the enemy until the Allied advance overtook them nearly three months later after the breakout at Falaise.

Before sundown on D-Day Sergeant Earl Rice and Lieutenant John Madden successfully led their sticks eastward from Colleville-sur-Orne and

Hermanville, respectively, safely into the Airborne lodgement area near the 6th Airborne Division's headquarters at Ranville. Sergeant Willard Minard, having turned back across the Channel to get a stuck jumper out of his Albemarle's exit, brought his section back from England in a Horsa glider on the evening of D-Day. And hundreds of other jumpers still spread out from Octeville airport to Montivilliers and northeast of the Seine estuary to the River Dives had not lost heart.

When Lieutenant Marcel Cote regained consciousness, close to an enemy guardhouse entrance, he was in severe pain from the blow which stove in the side of his helmet. His first reaction was one of intense anger. "Furious as hell!" he told me. "Jeez! Four years of military combat training had just gone down the drain." Immediately, the Germans marched him around the wired-in perimeter of the military installation to the main gate. There they met some other men from his own stick - Sergeant George Breen and his second-in-command Corporal Harold Miller, along with Private Doug Mearow. They waited under guard for an hour or so in the custody of what they identified as Luftwaffe personnel. Then more Luftwaffe brought in Privates W.J. Summerhays, Mike Warwick, Don Waddell, Clyde Dunphy and Jean Dumas. Still missing were Privates John Coburn, W.H. Kendry and Joseph Nigh. Also missing was the signals platoon radioman attached to Cote's mortar platoon, and there was no sign of the strangers who flew in Cote's transport - the unrecognized officers and their companions with a big radio.

From dawn onward the captives heard airplane engines revving up and dying down, over and over again. It reminded them of the many times they sat around airports in England, waiting to take off on practice jumps as mechanics worked on and tested engines. Occasionally a German plane would take off and they now knew they had landed outside the security fence of an airport. The only airport mentioned in their briefings was the one at Carpiquet, five or six kilometres west of Caen. They simply could not believe it, for that was some twenty kilometres from the Varaville Drop Zone! Some of them assumed that they were now at Carpiquet. But how could they be so far off their mark?

"Impossible! Impossible!" some soldiers argued.

Time passed quickly while a lot of enemy Air Force people came and looked the situation over with great curiosity. Photographers arrived and took pictures which were splashed all over Germany's national newspapers the following day.

In the early afternoon Lieutenant Cote and Sergeant Breen were separated from the others and were taken away. The remaining Canadian prisoners were marched off to a prison in Le Havre. They were flabbergasted. They now knew for sure they were far from Varaville. As they departed from the airport they could hear concentrated enemy machine-gun fire in huge wheat fields off to their left, to the south. Coburn, Kendry and Nigh were still on the loose.

Lieutenant Cote and Sergeant Breen had been driven away in a truck. A few minutes after their departure Cote got a glimpse of a road sign which read, "Octeville 4 Km." He had been allowed to keep his cigarettes and had managed to hide a stub of pencil in the package, so he wrote the information down. He and Breen now knew they had been dropped at Octeville airport, namely the Le Havre airport some twenty kilometres northeast of the Seine River estuary. It was half way to Dieppe from Varaville.

Cote now asked himself the first question the Luftwaffe interrogation officer would later ask him, and which other interrogation officers would ask him over and over again in the months to come. "What were you and your men doing at Octeville? Why were you dropped there in the first place?" It was easy for Cote to tell them the truth. He had no idea why he was there. But the Gestapo interrogators could not believe him. Typical Nazi personnel, victims of direct-line thinking, incapable of interpreting peripheral input, they followed the same line day after day.

"Why were you dropped at the Octeville airport?"

"I have no idea," Cote kept replying.

On the evening of their capture he and Breen were taken as far south as the city of Rouen amid bombing and strafing by the Allied Air Forces. There, they found themselves locked up in one of the great cathedrals of Europe. Their Gestapo interrogators were determined to find out why Canadian paratroops were dropped into the area of Le Havre. They lived out the remaining hours of D-Day without giving any real answers. It was here that the possibility of their having been dropped as decoys first crossed their minds. They had suddenly become aware that they were off the Drop Zone at Varaville by more than sixty kilometres.

In Lieutenant Rousseau's stick, during the early hours after the drop, other soldiers faced equal uncertainty. When D. N. J. Beaudoin, Rousseau's platoon sergeant, made the decision to take up an all-round defensive position with the nine men he had collected from the southwest portion of his stick, he was quite confident that dawn and the incoming invasion would solve his orientation problems. But such a solution never happened.

Dawn came and went with no evidence of enemy fighters or bombers flying east or west to combat the invasion. Impossibly, there was absolutely nothing to indicate that the invasion was taking place at all. Not a sign of any Allied planes or ships. Not a sound of bombing, machine-gun fire or naval gun fire.

After some puzzled thinking on their part the situation told them they were a long way east or south of their Drop Zone. They knew that if they were west of the British beaches they would be in front of the Canadian or American beaches. It was truly mystifying. They had come to be part of the largest assault armada ever to leave the shores of any land. Where the devil had all the attendant noise and military activity gone? How could it be? Nothing, absolutely nothing, except a totally serene rural, early summer morning in the lush countryside of Normandy. They hoped!

Suddenly came a long, loud burst from an unmistakable enemy MG-

42 medium machine gun about a hundred metres away. Sergeant Beaudoin knew that the firing, out of a thick underbrush, was not aimed at his group but probably at some of the missing men from his own stick. Maybe at A. J. (Scotty) MacInnis, whom nobody had yet met up with.

Beaudoin ordered some of his troops to keep an eye on the area of the enemy fire while he studied the situation. The enemy machine gun was only a minor detail. His main problem was still to find out where he was. He organized a three-man reconnaissance patrol which he himself would lead. Strangely, he chose the only other sergeant in the group, Jack Trenholm, as the second man, but wisely selected a competent rifleman, Private George Robertson, as the third.

Without delay, making a slight detour to avoid the Germans who had fired the machine gun, he headed northwest. He hoped he would find high ground from which he could see the Channel. They had gone only a short distance when he struck a deep ravine with a railroad coursing through its bottom. He posted Robertson near the top of its embankment and Trenholm closer to the railroad to provide covering fire for his intended reconnaissance of the tracks ahead. He had advanced only a few yards when he was cut down by another enemy machine gun.

Robertson waited for Trenholm to return, responsibility now weighing heavily upon him. If he tried to rescue Beaudoin, or made too much commotion trying to locate Trenholm, all three of them would likely become casualties and the patrol would be useless. After futile attempts to quietly contact Trenholm, his duty clearly became to report what had happened to the remainder of his group. He had heard German soldiers shouting as they receded into the distance with the wounded Beaudoin and, he assumed, with Jack Trenholm too.

Robertson's position was truly precarious. He knew he was between two groups of enemy soldiers, both of which had machine guns. And, since he and the two sergeants had not come far to begin with, the distance between the machine guns was not very great. With a heavy heart, burdened by the events which had overtaken both his sergeants, he managed to evade the German positions, return to his group and report the loss of Beaudoin and Trenholm, as well as his impression of the enemy strength.

He and the others took advantage of some hedge cover to move into a long ditch by a hedged-in sunken wagon track on slightly higher ground. Here they hoped to defend themselves and survive to reach their objective - now the Le Mesnil crossroads.

Meanwhile Lieutenant Rousseau, when he landed a few minutes before 01:00, waited only a short time after rendezvousing with Privates Colin MacKenzie, Mel Oxtoby and another soldier - possibly Scotty MacInnis - to take decisive action and decide whether to roll up the remainder of his stick or not.

He was an exceptionally dedicated officer and gave reaching his objective absolute priority. Thinking they were all not far from Varaville, he

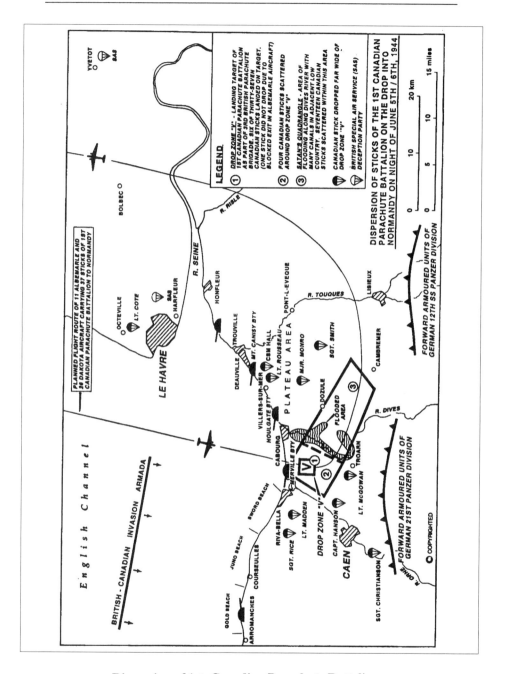

Dispersion of 1st. Canadian Parachute Battalion.
Map illustrating planned flight route to Varaville Drop Zone "V", and scattering of sticks of the 1st Canadian Parachute Battalion on D-Day, June 6, 1944.

reasoned that to try to link up with the other part of his stick would be a waste of time. To get involved in an overlong process would destroy any chance of reaching the Drop Zone in time to carry out his patrol to Dozule. So he changed his strategy.

He was satisfied that Sergeants Beaudoin and Trenholm and the rest of his stick would reach the rendezvous. He ordered the few men he had with him to follow him in open order. This meant three paces apart, with every second man on an opposite side of the road. Once the rendezvous was reached he would meet his two Dozule patrol members - his batman Jim Broadfoot and Corporal Boyd Anderson. Immediately he set out on a course he thought would solve his problems.

He soon found a house and woke the occupants. Since he spoke French fluently he found out in short order where he was. He was thunderstruck to learn that he was between Villers-sur-Mer and the River Touques, about twenty kilometres east of the Drop Zone. In an instant he realized that an ill wind had blown some good! He was now within easier reach of the town of Dozule than he would have been if he had dropped in the correct place, because he was on the Dozule side of the River Dives. Instead of being deterred by his "bad news" he saw it as an opportunity.

He was advised not to take the coastal road or the Rouen-Pont l'Evêque highway. Instead, he should take a zigzag series of insignificant roads, as directed by the French farmer he had awakened, and head for Dozule about six kilometres distant. As they moved on he told his men that his sergeants would have to take care of the other part of the stick. The thing to do was get on with the job at hand.

The final part of his route to Dozule included more than a kilometre of cross-country marching to cut off some of the angles and switchbacks in the zigzag tertiary road system he followed. This improvisation kept his route as short as possible. But when they broke out of the fields onto a narrow sunken and paved road, only about a kilometre from Dozule, he and Private Melvin Oxtoby were cut down by an enemy machine gun fired from almost point-blank range.

Colin MacKenzie escaped the enemy's grasp but was shot through the shoulder by a machine gun or rifle bullet. He tried to continue on toward the Dives in the hope he would eventually reach the Drop Zone, but was forced by loss of blood to lay up with a French family.

Now, in the early hours of the lovely Norman morning, Lieutenant Rousseau and Mel Oxtoby were dead. Rousseau's platoon sergeant, D. N. J. Beaudoin, and Private Stanley Shulist had their legs shot out from under them. Scotty MacInnis and Sergeant Trenholm were missing. The remaining fourteen men of the twenty-man stick were split into three groups still fighting with the Germans and trying to figure where in hell they were.

Another stick in deep trouble was that of Regimental Sergeant-Major W. J. Clark. Leaving England it had included Padre George Harris, Private T.

O'Connell, "C" Company Headquarters Administrative Clerk Alex Flexer, Paymaster Major E. T. Munro, Battalion Headquarters medical NCOs Corporal Earnie Jeans and Sergeant D. F. Wright, Corporal R.R. Brooks - Colonel Bradbrooke's jeep driver - and Privates H.D. Braumberger, W. L. Sweder, J. S. Sinclair, Harvey Minor and eight other antitank platoon soldiers. Minor's brief description of the stick's disrupted jump is quoted in the previous chapter. He also writes:

"I was with the antitank platoon and left England with the rest of the battalion to fly to France on the night of 5 June.

"When we crossed the French coast we were in anti-aircraft fire. Apparently our plane was damaged. I saw one hit on the left motor as we were waiting to jump.

"After the first fourteen men got out they stopped us (instead of continuing the green light) and told us to sit down again. The motors were revving up and I thought we would be in England for breakfast, but after some time the dispatcher just yelled out: 'Red on, green on, hook up, Go,' all in succession. We must have been very low as I was not long in the air after my parachute opened, and I somersaulted through some low trees and landed in water. What a jolt! Alone, I began to search around and soon heard someone coughing. It turned out to be our Regimental Sergeant-Major W. J. (Knobby) Clark.

"We soon found Braumberger, Brooks, Sinclair and Sweder, but never found any of the others. We could get no idea of where we were, but moved towards some noise and commotion we could hear in the distance. When we got to where we thought the noise had come from we found nothing there.

"After daylight we came in contact with a small boy and a French woman. She directed us towards the Robehomme bridge. We were smack in the worst part of Satan's Quadrangle - down around Hutot seven or eight miles east of Troarn."

It was now 09:00 hours on D-Day. Clark and his small party wondered where the remainder of his stick were and what had gone wrong with the drop. Weighed down by their concern about the impossibility of now tackling the important tasks they were supposed to achieve, they bent their wills to reality and strove to reach Robehomme. There they hoped to join up with Lieutenant Norm Toseland's platoon near the blown bridge.

RSM Clark had guessed he was east of the Dives, but whatever his location it was impossible to move bathed in daylight; the German 15th Army 711th Infantry Division's patrols were thick on the ground, far outnumbering and out-gunning him and his few misplaced paratroopers. Since movement meant sudden death he organized his men, hunkered down in some forested ground and waited out the day.

H. S. Mohring

Chapter IX

Seizing Varaville

When we last looked at "C" Company, the 3rd Parachute Brigade Advance Party, their two-engined Albemarle bombers had just come in over Drop Zone V. Some of the paratroopers recognized "Jackboot hedge" in the half moonlight from the four to five hundred feet altitude at which they were flying, so knew they were right on the money for an accurate drop.

In Bomber One the green "Go" light flashed on above the paratrooper exit. The first to leap were Privates H. B. Swim and Peter Bismutka.

As noted in the briefings, it was "C" Company's job to secure Drop Zone V by attacking one of the first two objectives in the battle for France, namely:

(1) The destruction of the German defensive positions at Varaville by the British 3rd Parachute Brigade's Advance Party, "C" Company, 1st Canadian Parachute Battalion, led by Major Murray MacLeod.

2) The capture of the Orne bridges at Benouville and Ranville by the British 5th Brigade Advance Party (Ox and Bucks Glider Party), led by Major John Howard.

The Albemarle bombers in which "C" Company flew came in over the beaches at Franceville-Plage in line-astern formation, forty-five seconds apart. It should have taken ten minutes to drop the entire company if things had gone according to plan. However, increasingly heavy anti-aircraft fire from the ground slowed the drop as the fly-in progressed. And for those who did land within the prescribed time there were big surprises ahead.

On the way across the Channel the hundred Halifax and Lancaster bombers which were to blast the Merville Battery with about 400 tons of high explosive bombs must have overtaken the slower paratroopers' two-engined bombers. The heavy bombs began to drop as the last three or four Albemarles were coming in over Drop Zone V at Varaville. The result was horrific. Several of the bombers had overshot the Merville Battery target and scattered their big bombs around the Drop Zone. But that was not all. During the Advance Party drop the thirty-six Mosquito night fighter-bombers of 418 and 605 Squadrons carried out their planned ground strafing attacks on the assault areas. These fighter-bomber sorties included strafing of the Drop Zone. In certain ways the raids on the rise above the Drop Zone, where the battery was located, were effective and helpful: it is believed that they gave essential noise cover, and they did convince the enemy that this was simply another of the almost nightly bombing raids along the coast. Even so the perils and terrifying din were scarcely a comfort to the paratroops from the first few Albemarles, newly dropped in the night and already traversing the Drop Zone amid the blasts of the scattered bombs and the strafing from the Mosquito fighter-bombers. But at least these men had touched down at or near their Drop Zone. Many other "C" Company paratroopers were not so lucky and were put well off their targets.

Sergeant Earl Rice and his stick were dropped the farthest away. They landed on the west side of Colleville-sur-Orne, about twelve kilometres west of the Varaville Drop Zone, well on the wrong side of the River Orne and dangerously close to the German 736 Grenadier Regiment's 2nd Battalion Headquarters at Tailleville. Lieutenant John Madden and his stick landed between Colleville-sur-Orne and Hermanville, about ten kilometres west of Drop Zone V.

This put Rice and Madden in front of the British invasion beach "Sword." They were roughly on the centre and the left wing, respectively, of the British 3rd Infantry Division's seaborne invasion at Ouistreham, with all its attendant pre-attack softening up violence by the Royal Navy, Royal Air Force and Royal Canadian Air Force. In short, the two sticks had landed in extremely perilous places. The planned weight and depth of the artillery and naval support bombardments, let alone the violence from both the tactical and heavy bomber forces which would accompany the seaborne troops, was horrendous.

It is believed that Lieutenant Sam McGowan's stick landed eight kilometres southeast of the Drop Zone, below Troarn on the west bank of the Dives - the western edge of "Satan's Quadrangle."

Sergeant G. Kroesing's stick from 9 Platoon landed ten kilometres to the east, far across the River Dives. They dropped right into the upland territory of the German 15th Army, where they were either killed or captured. It is believed the location of this stick was near Heuland.

As mentioned earlier, Sergeant Willard Minard's stick had to turn about. His number one jumper slipped and brought down one of the exit doors in his bomber. The doors in normal flight formed part of the floor of the bomber. For the jump the doors had to be hinged up and latched against the sides of the fuselage. The man who slipped and brought down one door became jammed in the open half of the hole. Caught by his parachute pack in the back and by his web equipment in the front, he could not be freed from the exit. After going out to sea and flying around for half an hour, while the troops and aircrew tried to get him loose, the bomber was forced to return to England with all on board. The Albemarles were equipped with tricycle landing gear, so the aircraft was able to land with the trooper still stuck in the exit but with his feet well above the landing strip. The men were glider-borne back to Normandy the same day, but hours after they were needed for the Varaville assault.

Captain John Hanson's stick formed the "C" Company Alternate Headquarters, which had been made up for any such emergency as was now happening. He landed about six kilometres away from Drop Zone V, south of Ranville, where the British Ox and Bucks Glider Party was about to land and seize the two large bridges over the River Orne and Canal de Caen.

Due to the dropping misplacements and mishaps, sixty of the hundred and ten "C" Company soldiers who left England were out of action from the very start, as far as securing the Drop Zone and assaulting the enemy positions at Varaville were concerned. Such conditions seemed enough to assure a complete failure of the company's plans.

But there was more. In the cases of the four sticks of Sergeants Dick MacLean, Harvey Morgan, Tom Keel and W.R. Kelly, the shortness of the Drop Zone in relation to the flooding came into play. The only explanation is that, when through the belt of coastal anti-aircraft fire, the bomber crews switched from the red light to the green a few seconds too late. The first few men in each stick landed on a finger of dry land running northeast from Varaville to Les Boursiers. But in all four cases, from the third or fourth man onward, the paratroops went into the flood.

Overall, the misplacement of jumpers meant that only seventeen men from the "C" Company Advance Party reached the rendezvous, at the end of the J-shaped hedge close to Le Grand Château de Varaville, within the prescribed time limit. The first to reach it were Privates "Sinkor" Swim, Peter Bismutka, E. J. Pinay and five others.

By the time Albemarle Bomber Seven reached the beaches the big bombs out of the Halifax and Lancaster bombers were crashing down on the Merville Battery and were encroaching southward over Drop Zone V - a few of them half way to the Varaville-Les Boursiers line.

Two or three minutes after Swim and his friends arrived at the rendezvous they were joined by Major Murray MacLeod, his batman G. A. Thompson, Signals Radioman Corporal John Ross and one or two others.

Despite arriving with such a pathetically small force, Major MacLeod saw his vital objectives as virtually unchanged so he made it his first concern to make sure that the enemy in the Varaville positions could not interfere with the drop of the twenty-two hundred men who would jump from one hundred and twenty C-47 transports three quarters of an hour later. In short, the remainder of the 1st Canadian Parachute Battalion, plus the British 9th Parachute Battalion and the headquarters of Brigadier James Hill's 3rd Parachute Brigade. This would include attached Royal Engineers, parachute medics and service troop units.

Behind them, an hour or two later, would arrive an echelon of the 6th Airlanding Brigade's Horsa gliders carrying the 6th Airborne Division's 4th Antitank Battery, plus Royal Artillery and 224 Field Ambulance equipment and personnel. These gliders would also bring heavier Airborne equipment than the parachutists could carry or could be dropped from the C-47 troop transports by equipment parachutes. There would be jeeps hitched to ammunition trailers, water-tank trailers, medical supplies trailers, six-pounder and seventeen-pounder antitank guns, to mention only some of the heavy stores that were all essential to sustain the battle on D-Day. Resupply and non-emergency rations would come later.

Meantime, Major MacLeod took stock of the greatly reduced number of Advance Party soldiers available and the massive loss of equipment. After a short consultation with Lieutenant Chuck Walker - the only other officer present - the major ordered Sergeant Gordon Davies to take one man to reconnoitre the bridge on the Divette. Lieutenant Walker with his batman and two other troopers would rush the houses on the Petiville end of the Drop Zone. There, the enemy were expected to be covering the Drop Zone with machine guns supplementary to the ones in the village itself. Next, MacLeod immediately deployed his remaining few soldiers as a harassment party to keep the enemy in the fortified positions "heads down."

The crux of these decisions was to scrap the original plan for silence. MacLeod knew that his plan had probably been given away by the scattering of the troops anyhow. He also figured that, whatever had kept over eighty percent of his men from showing up at the rendezvous, some of them were bound by now to have become casualties or fallen into enemy hands. His decision, even with the few men he had, was to discard the silent approach and shift to open warfare. He'd make as much noise as possible and drive well-aimed selective fire onto the enemy positions. This, he hoped, would convince the enemy to keep their heads down and stay in the positions they had taken up when they were rudely aroused from their warm beds by the misplaced bombs from the raid on the Merville Battery.

Major MacLeod's new plan - noise and all - kept the enemy fully occupied for the next hour. Namely, during the main drop of the 3rd Parachute Brigade which, as we have seen, included the main body of the 1st Canadian Parachute Battalion.

But during that hour Major MacLeod was still faced with the problem of finding ways to penetrate the wired-in portion of the village positions and seizing the enemy bunker, the trench position and the antitank weapon emplacement.

Had things gone right, he now would have had over one hundred men in position, armed with nine light machine guns, sixteen submachine guns, one PIAT antitank gun, nine two-inch mortars and a dozen Bangalore torpedo lengths - in addition to ninety riflemen. Instead, having dispatched the small reconnaissance patrols to Petiville and to the little bridge on the Divette, he began his assault on the village with only eleven men. They were Sergeants Mosher MacPhee, Dick MacLean and Harry Wright, together with Corporals A. M. Saunders and W. E. Oikle, and Privates H. B. (Sinkor) Swim, Peter Bismutka, Ralph Mokelki, Jack Church, Andy McNally and Bill Chaddock.

The major deployed them in a thin, spread-out line and began a sweep into the village. The distance between individuals made it difficult to keep contact with one another, but all were able to recognize silhouettes of village features thanks to the effective detail of their briefings in England, and so were able to converge on Le Grand Château de Varaville. Half way to that objective MacLeod and Bismutka came across Private Fred Rudko leading Mike Ball and five other somewhat shocked soldiers from 9 Platoon. This made up the small force to seventeen men carrying one PIAT antitank gun, three Sten submachine guns, twelve rifles and one pistol.

When they reached the château he ordered an all-round defence and sent Sergeant Mosher MacPhee and Privates Swim and Bismutka to search, by standard procedure, the edifice and its outbuildings. They found that part of the main building had been converted into a barracks. It was clear of enemy personnel but many of the bunk beds were still warm!

Major MacLeod continued to press forward down the promenade towards the château gatehouse with its attached wagon house arching over the driveway, which ran parallel to the promenade. Privates Swim and Rudko led as scouts and quickly moved into the antitank trench between the promenade and the row of Lombardy poplars, where Sergeant Minard's covering-fire group would now be setting up had the action gone according to the original plan. Swim and Rudko entered the ground floor of the gatehouse by the standard house clearing method. No sound came from the upper floor so they mounted the stairway with a rush and found that storey clear except for some more warm bunk beds! It was later calculated that the Great Château and its gatehouse provided accommodation for over eighty enemy soldiers at Varaville. That number coincided with intelligence reports from France during the briefings in England. Other men, possibly Corporal John Ross and Private L. G. Grenier, the company's signallers, cleared the wagon house.

By this time heavy scattered clouds drifted southeast by east low over the area, alternately turning the night from half-moonlit to dark. At times it was still possible to see the silhouettes of structures for about a hundred metres. When the gatehouse position was consolidated Swim guarded the west door facing the street while Rudko kept watch over the door by which they had entered the building. Rudko's position also kept contact with the personnel in the antitank ditch, where the remainder of Major MacLeod's men took up firing positions covering the trench system and the antitank gun. These positions accounted for everybody in the initial assault upon the village except the signallers, Corporal Ross and Private Grenier, who located their Signals Headquarters in an abandoned enemy ditch-type trench at the opposite end of the wagon house. In these early minutes of the operation Ross, Grenier and Swim were the only soldiers with a view towards the large stone and concrete bunker about seventy metres west of the gatehouse.

MacLeod kept the remainder of his small force facing the enemy trench positions and the antitank weapon until Lieutenant Walker returned from the houses at the end of the Drop Zone. He reported that they had also been recently evacuated by the Germans. It appeared that all enemy soldiers in the vicinity of Varaville were now ensconced in the bunker or the trench system, or were patrolling the area of the Drop Zone.

It was now 01:00 hours on 6 June. "C" Company had been on the ground for about an hour when fifteen more of its soldiers arrived from the flooded ground. A picture of what had happened to the missing men began to take shape.

Sergeant Dick MacLean and others from the sticks that landed partially dry and partially dunked had various experiences in finding their way. First, many had to get out of entanglements caused by their parachute suspension lines snarling up with underwater objects such as old fences, tree roots and other assorted obstructions. They had landed in water varying from about knee-deep to deeper than they could stand up in.

As some dunked soldiers progressed they heard groaning and frantic splashing. Upon investigation, one man found Sergeant W.R. Kelly hanging upside down, with his head in the water, from a huge deadwood tree. His parachute suspension lines were knotted around his legs and feet. The canopy had caught on a limb and suspended Kelly so he was submerged from the top of his head to his neck.

Kelly was a hardrock miner from Red Lake, Ontario, and was exceptionally strong and wiry. Otherwise he would have already drowned. His sixty to eighty pounds of equipment, which normally hung on his body gravitating towards his feet during his parachute descent, was now bundled up around his chest. It took a massive effort to keep lifting his face above the water for gulps of air. He was nearly exhausted when the soldier found him, cut him loose and assisted him to dry land.

Once there, the soldier who had saved him helped him get his equipment off, then pleaded that he had a higher duty. He told Kelly that he was forced to leave him and go on to fight at Varaville. When finally able to function and make his own way there, Kelly caught up to his rescuer and most of his section of men.

There were now just over thirty of "C" Company's men on the Varaville position. So Major MacLeod was a little better off, even though in size his small force was equivalent to a platoon, not a company.

The unmistakable sound of throttled-back C-47 transports began to pass over the area. The main Airborne force was now exiting its transports. But something had gone wrong. There were too few transports over the Drop Zone and they were not all flying in the same direction. Men already on the ground were beginning to sense a screwup. They had been told in England: "If any of you happen to lose your way, wait for the incoming main force. It will be flying from north to south, and you can get orientation from that." Now here were transports flying in several directions! The men could only ask themselves, "What the hell went wrong?"

Peter Bismutka had come into Varaville from the Drop Zone with "Sinkor" Swim and together they were posted to the upper floor of the château gatehouse. Fred Rudko, Jack Church and Ralph Mokelki held the lower floor. Lieutenant Chuck Walker and a few of his men made a valiant effort to roust the enemy out of the stone and concrete bunker but were repulsed by an overpowering blaze of small arms fire. It was then decided to keep the bunker area masked off with a few soldiers from 8 Platoon, whose objective it originally was, until the antitank gun and the trench system could be dealt with.

Major MacLeod and Lieutenant Walker proceeded to the upper floor of the gatehouse with Private G.A. Thompson. They quietly took the sashes out of a window facing the trench position and the antitank weapon. Peering into the sporadic moonlight, they made out the silhouettes of the gun emplacement and some machine-gun bays on the long trench's parapet. As is common at night, the more they studied the silhouettes the clearer they became. It surprised both officers that the emplacement for what they thought was an infantry anti-tank weapon was so large. Anyhow, it would have to be destroyed in the assault on the trench system when more paratroopers showed up from the flooding.

As Major MacLeod continued to survey the night scene to the front, Swim, now on the upper floor as a lookout, watched towards the antitank weapon position. Rudko also scanned the shadows towards the antitank ditch. Since there was a second window facing the gun emplacement, Swim was soon moved there to make better use of his good fieldcraft judgment and sharp eyes. Sure enough, he gave the major some estimates of distance to the gun which later were found to be absolutely accurate. But suddenly a great crash and turmoil engulfed the lower floor of the gatehouse.

Major MacLeod and his men were flabbergasted. From the supposed "antitank rifle" position had come a great white flash followed by the crash beneath the major's feet. He now knew there was actually a weapon of field artillery calibre out there in the enemy gun emplacement. The Germans had determined that the gatehouse was occupied by their enemies and had fired an armour-piercing shell right through the building. It had entered just below the level of the first floor ceiling and went out through the wall at the carriage house end on a south-north axis. The soldiers on the upper floor, to say the least, experienced one hell of a surprise but Rudko, Church and Mokelki, on the ground floor, were smothered in a choking atmosphere of pulverized masonry which nearly suffocated them.

Scratched and bruised, they were forced to retreat through the door facing the château. Exiting through the other door into the street would have left them exposed to open fire from both the bunker and the trench system, which were mutually supporting.

MacLeod sent his runner down to bring up the only destructive weapon he now possessed, the PIAT antitank gun. Its crew commander, Corporal Oikle, took Private Neufeld with him, and Swim and Bismutka were now posted to the upper floor as taskmen. That meant to take on any ultrahazardous job that needed doing. Private Bob Carlton was stationed as first lookout in the antitank ditch by the Lombardy poplars to keep liaison with the remaining riflemen, who were in the Airborne battalions also the ammunition carriers. Oikle studied the situation from the open window and said he thought he would have a good chance of hitting the German gun in its emplacement.

Oikle positioned his PIAT gun, took aim and fired. As so often happens in estimating range at night, the projectile fell a few feet short. It caused a great blast against the enemy position but left the enemy gun unscathed. Before Corporal Oikle could reload, the enemy gun replied with a high-explosive shrapnel shell that penetrated the wall of the room Major Mac-Leod and his men occupied. The explosive force not only opened up the brick wall of the room, but ignited Oikle's remaining PIAT bombs and caused a disaster. Major MacLeod and Private Bismutka were fatally wounded. Lieutenant Walker, Corporal Oikle and Private Neufeld were instantly killed and scattered amongst a pile of masonry rubble. Private G.A.Thompson had the part of his hand wrapped around the stock of his rifle completely severed. "Sinkor" Swim was blown clear out into the upper hallway, the only man in the room to escape serious injury or death. Shattered furniture and bunk beds lay strewn around the wrecked room. The gatehouse tragedy and the scattered drop were a heavy blow to the remnants of what was a well organized and efficient Airborne infantry company.

The Gate House at the Château, Varaville.

Prospects for the company now looked even grimmer. It had lost the initiative, a criterion vital to any battle big or small. The fight for the village became a stalemate, and during a brief interval of quiet the enemy captured three Canadians from the main battalion drop who landed within their wired-in positions. Sergeant Joe Middleton was one so for him the gig was up before he got started. Lieutenant Ken Arril, badly wounded, was picked up by the Germans and hauled into the stone and concrete bunker near the gatehouse. Middleton was held in the bombproof dugout attached to the south end of the trench system and, in addition to having his hands tied behind his back, was blindfolded.

The most severe problem for "C" Company was that there were now no commissioned officers present for combat in the village. Lieutenants McGowan and Madden, as well as Captain Hanson, had been dropped far off target. Major MacLeod was dying, Lieutenant Walker was dead and Lieutenant Arril was a prisoner. The top-ranking active soldier on the site was Sergeant

Mosher MacPhee. Sergeant Gordon Davies of 9 Platoon was fully occupied with the bridge on the Divette. Sergeants Earl Rice, Willard Minard, Tom Keel, Larry Bray, G. Kroesing, R. E. Trepanier and Harvey Morgan were all missing. Sergeants Harry Wright and Dick MacLean were present but were junior to MacPhee.

In character Sergeant Mosher MacPhee was as similar to Major Mac-Leod as anyone could be. He had a strong personality - disciplined, clean living, upright in his principles, courageous, stable and resolute. He never has been given any official credit for his handling of the situation during the period between MacLeod's fatal wounds and the arrival of Captain John Hanson.

During that time MacPhee kept the situation under control by affirm-ing the positions of the troops who were there. He re-invigorated his men by making certain they took every opportunity to direct well-aimed fire onto the enemy positions. These chances were sporadic and sometimes quite far apart due to the darkness and because the enemy simply went to ground in their well-defended positions. They were impossible to see and were able to husband their good supply of machine guns, ammunition and, of course, the field artillery gun that had caused such deadly havoc in the gatehouse. MacPhee's aim was to keep them tied down until dawn, when heavier equipment might come in from the gliders or when paratroopers with 3-inch mortars might show up. He was successful, although the hoped-for reinforcements and equipment did not come to help.

Finally, just before dawn, Captain Hanson arrived from the area south of Longueval on the River Orne just in time to support Major MacLeod's upper body across his lap as the major died. It was a sad interlude in the frivolousness of war - two valorous friends together for the last time in the grey dawn of the first dull sky of a most vicious battle.

Had he survived Major MacLeod might have told us someday what was in his mind during his short-lived role in the action, while his half-hour time limit to reach strategic positions for effective assault on the enemy ticked away. Knowing his situation and his temperament, we can at least speculate.

Topmost in his thoughts would be his determination to gain his objec-tives. But it must have been mental agony to wonder what had happened to the missing eighty percent of his men - both because he needed them desperately and because he cared about them.

It probably crossed his mind that several of "C" Company's eleven bombers used as air transports might have been brought down by enemy fight-ers, or by accurate fire from the ground as the transports slowly flew just five hundred feet above the muzzles of the coastal anti-aircraft guns.

He might have thought it possible that his missing paratroopers had dropped a few seconds too soon and were now buried in the huge craters from the Allied bombing meant for the Merville Battery. Or again, in the night's confusion, could one transport pilot have strayed slightly off the narrow flight-path - in which case a string of others, following his dimmed tail-light, could have been led astray and dropped their paratroopers just a kilometre or so away? If so, would the troopers soon show up with their equipment and add their weight to the major's pint-sized force?

Meanwhile, as he and his remnant of soldiers stubbornly did what they could, Major MacLeod might already have been physically injured. He had mentioned, almost offhandedly, that on the Drop Zone he had been severely jarred by a close bomb blast. He had no visible wounds; but troopers who entered the village with him have said the major did not seem in good shape and was almost certainly suffering from some internal injury as he battled on.

His successor, Captain John Hanson, was unlike Murray MacLeod except in bravery and purpose. Rough, tough and blustery, he definitely lacked the major's even temperament. He could be ruthless or kind, fair or unfair, but always gung ho! He couldn't see the sense in being an officer and a gentleman all the time. For him an officer's attitude should be: "Well piss on it, let's get in there and get it done by slamming somebody around. This is what we're faced with so let's take the right course and clobber the sons-a-bitches." But worry about being a "gentleman" in the middle of a goddam war? In Hanson's estimation: ridiculous! But if you asked "C" Company's men how they rated him as an officer, it's a fair guess that they'd all say the same thing: "One of the best!"

Hanson sized up the situation and continued with the tactics Sergeant MacPhee had carried out. But now it was daylight, so he was able to increase the pressure on the enemy by sniping at them more often and more accurately. One Mademoiselle Laura Hiervieux, a robust lady of about thirty years of age, somehow made her way to Hanson's headquarters. Laura and her brother Rene had a French father and an English mother. Although they lived in Varaville both Laura and Rene were educated in England.

Their family came to live in Varaville in 1933, the year Hitler came to power. Although they had come to like some of the German soldiers who were stationed in Varaville during the two or three years before D-Day, they loathed the Nazis. The Gestapo had reason to hate Rene too, for he worked actively against them. Up until two or three evenings before we invaded, his good friend, a *Wehrmacht* sergeant, was his lookout while Rene milked his cow in his back pasture. As Rene pulled the cow's teats and the milk foamed in the pail, his friend came running into the pasture to warn him the Gestapo were coming. Rene stopped for a moment to pat his cow and shake his German friend's hand, then headed for the Bavent Forest. From there he went into hiding farther away, beyond what was to become the main battle area. His sister Laura was now on her own for the first time in her life.

When Laura realized the Canadians had come she made herself known to Captain John Hanson. She told him bluntly that she knew a number of the German soldiers now in action against him and that she could give him valuable information about them and their positions. She added that the enemy numbered about eighty with plentiful weapons and ammunition. The village positions were the responsibility of an Austrian major whose German non-commissioned officers led a mixed bag of German and Eastern troops - Poles, Russians, Rumanians. Hanson now knew there was no way he could assault the enemy positions unless he found substantial reinforcements of both men and equipment. He was satisfied, however, that he could rely on Laura Hiervieux for help based on her personal knowledge of the enemy soldiers.

Without delay he installed Sergeant Dick MacLean as an observer in the village church tower, a most precarious place to be with the enemy machine guns and the field gun at point-blank range. From there, MacLean could see much of the enemy activity that was taking place in the trench position. He passed the information to Private Andy McNally, below in the choir box, who in turn sent it by runners to the riflemen on the firing positions. With this make-shift "intelligence network" MacLean was able to increase the hurt inflicted upon the enemy. Improvisations like this became a pattern in the 6th Airborne Division as they fought through the rest of the war, which took them to the Baltic Sea north of Berlin.

Hanson's next move was to set up some kind of communication with the enemy in the trench system, who in turn were in telephone contact with the two-storey bunker. It is thought that Laura Hiervieux was instrumental in effecting dialogue between Hanson and the Germans.

Immediately upon taking command Hanson decided to keep the enemy busy, continue to hurt them as much as possible, convince them that their situation was hopeless and persuade them to save their own lives by sur-rendering before it was too late. Despite the odds in the enemy's favour, Hanson felt he was going to win. He was a perennial optimist, spurred on by his confidence as a paratrooper. With MacLean's observations from the church tower, Hanson began to make progress.

The events just described took place before this writer reached Varaville. My arrival was delayed by a curious episode which took me away in the wrong direction. First, however, my parachute drop at least put me down on dry land - the narrow strip from Varaville to Les Boursiers. In contrast, seven members of our ten-man stick had to extricate themselves from the floodwaters. The trooper who jumped behind me was Private Middleton. His last words to me when the green light flashed above our bomber's exit were: "OK, Hartigan, I'm right on your back, see you on the lower deck!" That was the last I heard of Middleton until the war ended. He slashed into a large deciduous tree, jamming a foot hard into a crotch between the trunk and a limb. His parachute snagged on a higher limb. He hung there helplessly in an almost horizontal position through the night, with his ankle twisted at a ninety-degree angle to his leg and swelling bigger by the hour. To this was added the cruel knowledge that even should his fellow paratroopers find him, they would be duty-bound to press on and leave him to his fate. Getting to their objectives had to take priority over their personal feelings - that was the order of the night. At last, on the next day, some Germans saw him and laboriously extracted his foot from its trap.

When Middleton was freed from enemy imprisonment in May 1945 he weighed forty-five kilograms. They had given him a rough time, incarcerated in what they called a prison for "bad guys." These included former escaped prisoners of war and those the enemy thought were cantankerous and likely to

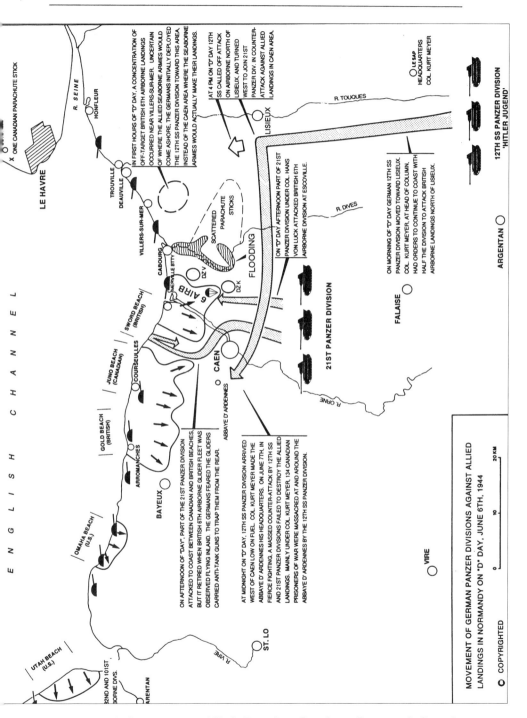

Response of Germans to Allied Invasion Beaches, Juno and Sword.

try an escape: paratroopers, commandos, and aircrews forced to parachute from shot-down planes.

To put it mildly my own parachute descent was eventful - never to be forgotten. There was a feeling of absolute, irrevocable commitment when the parachute first opened - no going back! We had all made many jumps, but this was my first leap into actual, no-pretense combat. There was a moment of giddiness or exhilaration as I contemplated this, saying to myself: "Oh My God, what have I done?" I began to whisper the Lord's Prayer during my descent to the hedged-in Normandy countryside, all the time getting the lay of the land below. In the subdued moonlight it was clear which way we should head for the rendezvous at the end of the J-shaped hedge, slightly northeast by north of the Grand Château de Varaville.

Slashing through the outer limbs of an apple tree, I slammed into the plank back door of a Frenchman's house, landing flat on my buttocks on his stoop. Surprise was complete. In the half moonlight one could still see quite well for about sixty metres before being cut off by the hedges. All was quiet, no enemy in sight.

The property had a thick hedge along a paved road. A high gate was visible across a little field. I felt really conspicuous climbing those poles, awkwardly because of my heavy load. Once I was out on the road things began to happen fast. Having moved only a short distance towards the rendezvous, I heard heavy boots pounding the pavement and advancing closer. I felt totally trapped. There was no way to get off the road. To get through the dense hedges was impossible. Nor was there time to retreat back to the gate. Training took over. Instantly, I was lying doggo on the earth shoulder of the road, tautly waiting for an enemy bayonet or a bullet in the back. I knew some of them would clomp by only three or four feet away.

As they began to pass me I had an almost compulsive urge to jump up and bolt or scream. But any move meant capture or death. My only hope was that they would not see me lying there in the shadows. The big question: Would my camouflage and blackened hands, face and neck do the job in the dim shadows?

While they were still approaching I had unscrewed and removed the cap from my powerful Gammon bomb. The cloth tape which would pull the firing pin loose was held in place by my right thumb. All this was done automatically with the bomb down by my right hip. The plan was to throw it into their midst as soon as they were at a safe distance and call for their surrender - and, if they did not, bolt for cover. This might have given me time to escape. But such ideas were born out of necessity, not reason.

When they actually did pass by I could have reached out with my left hand and tripped some of them. Then, rising up to do the job with the Gammon bomb, I saw they were not soldiers at all but peasants wearing wooden boots. I picked up the detonator cap and rescrewed it onto the Gammon bomb, with a prayer of thanks that I had not thrown it without taking time to look. To this day I don't know whether the Norman farmers saw me or not.

It was now ten minutes or so after our drop and the bombing raid on the Merville Battery, which was now supposed to begin, was actually ending. It tailed off from the earsplitting thunderclaps of the concentrated noise-storm into sporadic impositions of hell. Then it ended - but not quite. A last lone four-engine bomber with high-pitched Merlin engines came in over the coast. It kept on coming too long, and then the increasing whine of its single bomb fell to earth as though it was going to strike one directly on the back of the head.

As trained, I was down against the built-up base of the hedgerow by the road. There was a fifty-fifty chance the bomb would land on the opposite side of the mound, and it did. The earth-shattering blast left me half stunned and only conscious enough to feel the soft chunks of Normandy earth building up and seeming to bury me alive. When the earth-rain stopped I guessed that the interment had built up to about an inch or two above the body. What I remember clearly is the awful weight of the small amount of earth which had piled up on my back when I first attempted to get up, and my utter disbelief at being alive. My joints had taken such a beating that, because of the jerking of my limbs whenever I went anywhere for the next few days, my jovial buddies honoured me with a new nickname: "Hopalong."

Some time after the blast I sensed that blood was dribbling from my nose and mouth, and my state of half-consciousness directed me to walk away from the bomb crater towards the rendezvous in the direction of the J-shaped hedge. Enough savvy remained to tell me to get off the road and into the fields and I began a weak climb over another gate. When onc leg was eventually lifted over the top pole a sharp jab in my right buttock from a bayonet, followed by the word "Punch," let it be known that the intruder was a friend. It was Eddie Mallon. "Judy," I said, "you dumb bastard!" Mallon laughed like a fool as though nothing serious was going on.

He was somewhat shocked too, but still physically healthy. We travelled in what we thought was the right direction but eventually realized we were going in circles. We rested for a short while then set out again. Mallon and I felt better now but were still rattled. Eventually we became aware of people approaching as we came to another paved road. We crouched on opposite shoulders and called in a low voice:

"Halt! Who goes there?"

"Friend," came a hoarsely whispered reply.

"Punch," Mallon challenged, again in a low voice.

"Judy," came the voice from the night. Louder this time.

"Advance to be recognized with your hands raised."

A lieutenant from the British 9th Parachute Battalion came forward and we identified each other. He told us that he had six of his own men with him and that he was lost. "Do you know where you are?" Our reply was sarcastic, something about being in France, which let him know we were lost too, and "pissed off" about the bombing. He could not believe the RAF could drop a bomb anywhere but on target, and would not credit that we had been treated to a blast by of one of our own four-thousand pounders. He then said something about the drop being a disaster, and told us we must go to the Merville Battery with him. We objected strenuously, but he insisted and told me that, although we were in different battalions, we were in the same brigade. "Corporal," he said, "I'm an officer of His Majesty's bloody army and you'll do as you're damn well told!"

I tried to impress on him how important it was for us to get to Varaville, but he'd have none of it. "Seven men is too few to go mucking about in Hitler's Atlantic Wall. You'll come with me as I've said."

We worked together and decided that, because of the few C-47s flying over, it was difficult to get direction from them. It did seem, though, that most were going in one particular direction, so we assumed that stream to be north-south. We went that way on the paved road for what seemed to be a long time. Eventually we became aware that someone was approaching from the front. Instead of moving quickly to the shoulders of the road and crouching down his six men, all in a bunch, headed for what looked like an opening in a hedge. They ran smack into a page wire fence across the gap and made the damnedest squeaking, squawking ruckus ever heard. If the oncoming intruder had been an enemy officer ahead of a patrol we would have been the victims of a turkey shoot.

Luckily for us he turned out to be a French civilian. The lieutenant called Mallon and me forward, having found out Mallon could speak French. As we went up I put his men in an all-round defensive position which they quickly took up. When the Frenchman guessed we were part of the Allied invasion he threw his arms around Mallon and began to kiss him. We both began to laugh because we had never seen a man kiss another one.

Uncertain whether the stranger could be trusted, I began to prod him in one side with my bayonet, at the same time warning Mallon: "Don't trust him." Leaving me as a lookout on the road, the lieutenant took Mallon and the Frenchman down into a depression. There, the officer shone his flashlight on his map of the district and got all his directions straightened out. When they came up on the road again the Lieutenant said his goodbye in French, and the Frenchman started off into the night. Enraged, I abruptly halted him. The Lieutenant got angry and we were at odds again.

I said, "Sir, did you show that stranger your battalion's rendezvous?" He admitted that he had. When I asked how the hell he knew the civilian would not bring the whole German Army down on his battalion while it was still vulnerable in its rendezvous position, he lit into me once more. "Listen here Corporal, I've had it just about up to here with you!" This time he really laid into me about who was in charge. By now I was pulling at straws to protect myself and pointed out the way his men had behaved at the gap in the hedge and raised bedlam when there was no need to do so. I was gratified when he answered in effect: "You're right Corporal. Look, you're the only NCO here. I want to put you in charge of the men back there to keep them properly spread out." From then on everything was fine between us and we made good progress through the darkness of the night.

At 02:30 hours we joined up with Colonel Terence Otway's jumping-off position for his attack on the Merville Battery. We found that only a little more than the equivalent of a company strength of the 9th Parachute Battalion had shown up at his rendezvous. Otway was heartbroken and in a foul temper. We knew nothing of his plans or that even worse scattering had happened to our own battalion, especially to "C" Company at Varaville.

Colonel Otway asked the lieutenant: "How many men have you got with you?"

"Six of my own. And I've brought two Canadians." Otway's next question came in a haughty English accent like a bolt from the blue.

"What good are they?"

"They seem very good to me, Sir. In fact, there are times the corporal seems to think he knows more than I do."

"They don't know a damn thing and I say again, what good are they?"

The Lieutenant began in a careful tone: "For God's sake, Sir." It was obvious he could see a terrible misunderstanding coming up.

He was interrupted by the hardrock miner from Kirkland Lake. "We're just as good as any goddamn cotton-pickin' limey!" Eddie Mallon blurted out

There was sudden, ominous silence. Colonel Otway was thunder-struck, speechless and nonplussed at the impudence of a simple private soldier lipping-off a colonel in the British Army. The words he did manage to utter were largely unintelligible. Finally the lieutenant tested: "Well, Sir, what shall I do with the two Canadians, Sir?"

Otway shouted as though his lungs were about to burst. "Send the blighters back to where they bloody well came from."

Incidentally, a rumour has emanated from some 9th Battalion soldiers that there was a confrontation between two Frenchmen and Colonel Otway. When asked by a lieutenant "What shall we do with them, Sir?" he is said to have replied: "Lock them in the barn over there and then shoot them!" This is likely to be a distorted exaggeration of what really happened between the colonel, Mallon and me.

It is only fair to place this story in the context of what was happening to Colonel Otway at the time. It was years after the war before I understood what the frustrated colonel was really saying to his lieutenant by the concertina wire at the Merville Battery that night.

When training in England Colonel Otway built a life-sized replica of the Merville Battery on Salisbury Plain. For weeks his men were put through drills in how they would cut the wire, lay tapes of approach through a mine-field and make their final assault. Practice runs were created for each of the teams of soldiers who would attack different features of the gun battery. They rehearsed the assault over and over again until they could have gone through it blindfolded. What the colonel really meant when he appeared to insult us with "What good are they?" and "They don't know a damn thing!" was that Mallon and I knew nothing about his actual plans. We'd had no exposure to the layout of the fortress or the tactics he had repeatedly drilled into his troops. So what good were we to him? And, by implication, he probably meant that we could even be a hindrance.

But why was the colonel's language with us so short and sharp? Look at his circumstances. By the time we arrived he was supposed to have roughly seven hundred men in place - his own 9th Battalion plus "A" Company of the 1st Canadian Parachute Battalion. At that point he had no more than one hundred and eighty men lined-up on the two units' start-lines. His case was somewhat like Major MacLeod's at Varaville and Colonel Bradbrooke's at the rendezvous in the copse by the Varaville highway: all valorous commanders pushing on with their duty while bereft of most of their troops and equipment. It truly was a night to make "Gentlemen in England now abed think themselves accursed they were not here" - Shakespeare's words as broadcast by General Gale to his troops within earshot on the battlefield that night.

After our stormy meeting with Colonel Otway the lieutenant took us back to the road, took out his map and went over the route we should follow to Varaville. He was more than apologetic about the misunderstanding with the colonel. He was embarrassed about his original insistence that seven men were too few to go "mucking about" in Hitler's Atlantic Wall. Now without any choice he was sending only two of us back down the same route!

We and the young lieutenant were now on good terms and said mutually friendly goodbyes. We went a short way south, then covered quite a long stretch west to Gonneville-sur-Merville. After going directly through the main street of the village we reached a curiously right-angled turn in the road below Gonneville. There we halted and held a two-man conference.

On 6 June 1974, the 30th Anniversary of D-Day, my wife Rosalie and I stood on that same absurd-looking turn. While standing there reminiscing I felt a great weight I had carried around for thirty years, which I could never understand, fall from my shoulders.

For Mallon and I the road leading away from the right-angled turn posed a problem. It led to Varaville all right, but we knew from the briefings that it also passed through open country. That spelled danger. The alternative was a pathway, heavily hedged on both sides, running down to the east of the J-shaped hedge - our original rendezvous. Which route should we take? Mallon left the decision to me, "Since you're the corporal." Without much hesitation I picked the pathway.

On that return visit thirty years later I related the story to Laura Hiervieux's brother Rene. He told me I had made the right decision because there were two checkpoints along the open road, manned every night by Germans with light machine guns. He then threw his head back, raised his glass of Calvados, laughed heartily and said: "I've always claimed life is funny! Isn't life funny?"

After going a considerable distance on the path between the hedges as the first dim streaks of light began to appear on the horizon, we lay peering across a field at Le Grand Château de Varaville. It was almost obscured in the haze of early dawn. Part way across the field we suddenly perceived that soldiers were coming towards us. In the gloom we could not tell whether they were ours or the enemy's. If the latter we were caught in the open, trapped. We lay flat in some debris and knew there was no going back. Any movement would give us away. As they headed straight towards us we prepared to halt them at close range.

When the time came we went through the "Punch and Judy" routine. To our relief they answered "Judy." We were faced by a substantial group of British paratroopers from our own Brigade Headquarters. What a relief! Some of them told us that, as it had appeared to them, the village of Varaville was in Canadian hands and the battle there was over.

With further reassurances from the paratroopers, we confidently slung our rifles on our shoulders and walked into the village. By the time we passed the château it was daylight and we ambled down the concrete promenade as though we were out for a walk. What we did not know was that we were parading directly in front of the high calibre artillery gun which had already caused so much damage and that the enemy machine guns on the trench system were all still in action.

In the end of the antitank ditch closest to the château were several men from 7 Platoon. They began shouting, "Get down!" Were they kidding? We were told the battle in Varaville had been won! But we dove headfirst into the ditch - to the accompaniment of a savage volley of enemy machine-gun fire. Our survival was measured in split seconds. Obviously the British lads we had just met in the field did not understand the Canadians' position in Varaville any better than we understood Colonel Otway's at the Merville Battery.

We were saddened and shocked to hear of the deaths of Major MacLeod, Lieutenant Walker, Corporal Oikle, Private Neufeld and several more. No less stunning was the news that more than two-thirds of our company's personnel were missing. Especially hard hitting was the absence of so many officers, sergeants and equipment resources to finish the job.

By now the general mood of those who had suffered such devastating disappointments and casualties during the night seemed to be one of resignation, waiting for something to happen. We were told that Captain Hanson was negotiating with the enemy to compel their surrender, and that one man had been dispatched to cross the Drop Zone and, if necessary, go on to Le Mesnil to look for a seventeen pounder antitank gun or some 3-inch mortars to bolster our scanty firepower.

Without knowing the full details of our company's situation, I became irascible over the stalemate at Varaville. Unjustly, as I later saw, I launched into a noisy dispute with other NCOs, some of them my superiors, in the antitank ditch. What impelled me I'm not sure. Maybe it was that I had seen first-hand how Colonel Otway, lacking seventy percent of his force, was still pushing on with his plan to destroy the Merville Battery. Hell, did we want that peppery but gutsy Otway to grab his objective but we not ours? Or maybe it was sheer frustration over the "wait and see" mood.

Our only officer not killed or missing, Captain Hanson, was busy out of earshot but our senior sergeant, Mosher MacPhee, heard the ruckus. He double-timed over from the gatehouse and ordered quiet. He dressed me down but heard me out.

I said that, as I saw things, it wasn't enough to keep the immediate enemy pinned down in their gun and trench positions. It had been daylight for more than half an hour. The quite well-armed Germans beyond the village would soon counterattack to relieve their besieged comrades. Where would we be then? Caught between the attackers and the fixed enemy positions.

Right or wrong, I also dragged in inter-allied rivalry. Suppose, for instance, we waited too long and the commandos from Sword Beach who were supposed to relieve us showed up. What a pretty picture that would make: Green Berets bailing out Red Berets, especially Canadian Red Berets!

MacPhee acknowledged such eventualities. But he also knew Hanson's fibre and backed the captain's plan to regain the initiative by inducing the immediate enemy to surrender. MacPhee was a sergeant much admired: authoritative, collected and cool. Who, I asked myself, am I, impulsive bloody Hartigan, to argue about it with him?

Although the battle was not at the moment a furious weapons competition, continuous individual actions occurred. Swim and Rudko were back downstairs, still clinging to their on-guard positions on the lower floor of the gatehouse. A stray soldier from "B" Company, Private Esko Makela, a Bren machine gunner, arrived out of the flooding shortly after daylight. On his own initiative he quickly installed himself in a hidden position in a room adjacent to the one where MacLeod and his companions were killed on the top floor of the gatehouse. A small aperture opened through the outside wall directly onto the field gun and trench system positions. From there, but back a few feet where his muzzle flashes would not be detected, he began to take a toll upon the enemy, using his machine gun on single shot like a sniper's rifle. When the enemy showed themselves from time to time he gave them no respite. A lone soldier subjecting himself to great risk, and doing it for an extended period of time.

Probably the most exposed and dangerous job in the whole action went to Sergeant Dick MacLean after Captain Hanson ordered him to get right up into the church spire to observe and assess the enemy's activity. His tower position was about two hundred and fifty yards from the deadly gun. It was also fully exposed to the enemy machine guns. He spent about five hours there reporting on nearly everything the enemy did, while fully expecting his tower and himself to be blown to hell. It has been often said by those who were there that he deserved official recognition for distinguished conduct. Things don't always go the way they should.

As the struggle continued Hanson, with help from Laura Hiervieux, continued to parley for a surrender by the enemy, while everyone else concentrated on hurting them at every opportunity.

Half an hour after my first conversation with Sergeant MacPhee the subject of breaking into the wired-in position came up again. The opinion was given that we must find a way through the wire and make an assault. The idea got little support from the antitank ditch and one or two men thought that it would be foolhardy. But MacPhee felt the idea had some merit and said he would talk to Captain Hanson soon, so the sergeant's permission was sought to do a personal reconnaissance to see if there was another way to make an approach that would stand a good chance of success. We still had too few Bangalore torpedoes to blow the wire, and clearing the ground of mines up to the wire was out of the question. Now that it was daylight such an attempt in the face of the enemy machine guns would be suicidal.

However, we now had my 2-inch mortar and Makela's extra machine gun, and there were a little over thirty paratroopers in the village. The supply of machine-gun ammunition, shrapnel type 2-inch mortar bombs and smoke shells was increasing as more men came in from the flooded swamps. Some soldiers felt that this additional firepower would give us a new chance.

MacPhee reluctantly gave permission for the solo reconnaissance but gave strict orders to use caution. Yet taking extra risks did not seem out of place because, as the situation developed, the possibility of a German counterattack from outside the village became visibly greater. The present danger in the set-up was so extreme for all of us that it needed resolution as soon as possible. It seemed safer to take risks than to wait for the dreaded counterattack.

When I got the go-ahead to reconnoitre I cautiously stood up behind a Lombardy poplar by our antitank ditch and peered around its trunk for an overall view of the position. I sank down again into the ditch and not too soon. With a deafening crash an armour-piercing shell tore a slab like a railroad tie off the tree I had used for cover. Jagged chunks and shards of wood splayed around the ditch. None of us was seriously injured but some were badly bruised. The most unforgettable reaction came from Bill Chaddock, who doubled over with laughter. In their turn Eddie Mallon and Jack Church laughed at him. Red-faced at having brought the enemy fire down on us, I got on with the reconnaissance.

Hugging the ground, I made my way as ordered to the gatehouse and went in through the lower floor where Swim and Rudko were still on guard. Swim was worried about a report that his closest friend, Peter Bismutka, was dying. When I reached the top of the stairway there was Esko Makela with his Bren machine gun levelled, using some stacked-up furniture as an aiming rest. He was sighting through the small aperture in the outside wall, but was still a good distance back from the opening: a well-trained soldier making it harder for the enemy to pick out his exact firing position. When Esko saw me heading for the room where Major MacLeod and his group were killed he warned me not to go in. I soon saw why. The room was a shambles, but more. A pair of legs hanging by the crotch of the trousers over part of a wrecked bunk bed. A torso - no arms, head, legs or hips - lying on a pile of brick and covered in brick mortar dust; simply an insignificant little remnant clothed in a dirty tee-shirt. It was something which had been a young man a few minutes earlier. And then there were the others! Distorted and twisted, the product of man's greed for power and frivolous values.

Makela was insistent about my safety. Having had a clear look at the German gun and trench positions he shouted, "Go for cover!" His was a sniper's job and called for concealment and smart finesse. My job was to observe and assess, to get a close view of the enemy. I must admit that it was good to get out of there, for I did not envy Makela in his dangerous position.

After crossing the street between the concrete bunker and the mutually supporting gun and trench positions, I used some sparse weed cover as an observation point. Here I had a fairly clear view of the side of the field gun, but only for a moment. A single rifle bullet snapped past my left ear into the turf ahead. An enemy rifleman at the stone and concrete bunker, directly to the rear, had missed. But at that range he would probably correct his aim on the next shot. I did not take long to reach the protection of the gatehouse again and then headed back to Sergeant MacPhee.

He had kept track of the reconnaissance and was not pleased with the last part of it, so gave a direct order to proceed cautiously around the remainder of the position. In reply to his questions I had to admit I'd learned nothing about an effective way to get to and through the enemy barbed wire; but what I had seen could help pinpoint the locations and ranges of the gun and trench positions. Surely, I said, something could be done about both positions using the two-inch mortar from the antitank ditch.

Time crept by as Sergeant MacLean made his continuing reports from the church tower. Suddenly we heard a great explosion from the bridge on the Divette canal. Sergeant Gordon Davies and two other soldiers had been there through the night, waiting for the assigned Royal Engineers demolition team to arrive, then with their help had blown the bridge sky-high. It was an hour before the deadline stated in Operation Order Number 1. "H"-hour plus two!

During the next hour Captain Hanson, with effective help from Laura Hiervieux, kept up communication with the enemy in the trench system. They seemed to be poorly trained or indifferent to their situation, for despite their elaborate cover they sporadically exposed themselves to our fire without good reason. Our case was different from theirs. We had to take chances which at times may have looked foolhardy. If Captain Hanson's efforts to make the Germans show the white flag failed it would still be necessary to charge their trench. Information obtained at risk had to be available when that time came. The key to solving our problems was to keep on punishing the enemy while working out effective measures to take the trench.

There was not a lot of firing during this time, but we knew our enemies were feeling the effect of our punishment. Abruptly, things changed. It became obvious to Captain Hanson that someone new was in charge of their situation. About 09:00 hours Sergeant MacLean reported from the church tower that a column of enemy armour was on the move north from the Colombelles steel plant towards the Airborne lodgement area. Even worse, it was apparently heading for Escoville-Herouvillette. The counter-attack was evidently brewing.

The column consisted of Panther V tanks, which carried 75-mm guns, interspersed with 88-mm self-propelled dual purpose guns that could knock out aircraft or tanks. They were already on our side of the Orne waterways. This could be an oncoming threat to our perilous position, but there were some things in our favour. We expected the Varaville-Caen highway to be blocked by the 1st Canadian Parachute Battalion at Le Mesnil and by the British 8th Parachute Battalion near Escoville and Herouvillette. The enemy armoured column would probably be forced to try to come across Drop Zones K and N by way of large open fields between Herouvillette and Ste. Honorine la Chardonnerette, to retake the Orne bridges. Or it could try to get to the Varaville-Le Mesnil highway where it could turn either northeast to Varaville or southwest to Le Mesnil. Also, if it were successful at the Ranville-Benouville bridges, it could cross over to the west bank of the waterways and act against British Sword Beach. Then again, the column could move along the right shoulder of the Orne estuary to reinforce their troops at Cabourg - Dives-sur-Mer, or to open up the coastal road to Caen, as far as Le Mesnil, by turning on Varaville. This latter move, if successful, would leave the Le Mesnil Ridge vulnerable.

To come across Drop Zones K and N would entangle the enemy armoured column with battalions of the 5th Parachute Brigade. Also, we knew that if these Germans reached the coast and turned inland to relieve their garrison at Varaville they'd find the little bridge on the Divette blown up. They would not be able to get their armour across the canal without stopping to bridge it. The canal was only about six metres wide but in the flooded conditions its water was several metres deep: a totally impassable antitank ditch with a soggy bottom. This knowledge gave us short-handed Canadians considerable comfort - even though the armoured column's 75-mm guns and powerful 88-mm guns would be able to wreak havoc on the village from across the Divette.

Suddenly, to everyone's vast relief, MacLean reported that the enemy tank column had reversed itself and was now proceeding southward towards Caen. What a break! That good news was followed by more. The counterattack threat had no sooner vanished than a white flag appeared at the trench system. By whatever means of communication our Company Headquarters had with the Germans there, two emissaries were allowed to come forward to confer with Captain Hanson.

One was a German sergeant who seemed to be presently in charge of the troops he represented. Hanson questioned him about the major who had been in command. The sergeant was evasive but soon admitted that his major had been wounded. When asked why he wanted a truce the German said he had a considerable number of wounded soldiers but no medical supplies. "In that case," Hanson advised him, "you would be wise to surrender with your men." The sergeant claimed he was unable to surrender at the time, and said the humane thing for the Canadians to do would be to share any medical supplies they had.

At this point in the stand-off Laura Hiervieux approached the German sergeant, whom she knew. Firmly, she told him Captain Hanson was being tolerant but would soon overrun his position if they did not surrender. He and the other emissary would be derelict in their duty if they did not impress the facts upon their friends back in the trench.

Rather than give them supplies, Hanson provided them with a fairly large two-wheel cart from the wagon house. "Here," he growled, "take this and bring your wounded men to our medical aid station in the grounds of the Grand Château."

While this exchange took place I saw an advantage in the lull and asked Sergeant MacPhee to let me complete a further reconnaissance of the château end of the wired-in perimeter. After going a short distance what did I come across but a shallow trench beginning at our antitank ditch and running at an angle towards the enemy trench and gun positions!

Why had this new trench gone undiscovered? Because it was smothered with dead weeds and hay right up to the level of the surrounding field. At the antitank ditch end this "hidden" trench was about a metre deep. It ran for about six metres out into the field, sloping upwards until it petered out at ground level. At that end it should provide a much better firing position than we had in our antitank ditch. I promptly returned to the shattered Lombardy poplar and asked Sergeant MacPhee for permission to make an approach up the sloping ditch to try a shot at the field gun with my 2-inch mortar. "OK," he said, "but I'm coming with you to make any judgment about calling it off if things become too hazardous." Captain Hanson's orders were that every effort must be made to prevent further casualties among our men. The number of troops who had already reached the Le Mesnil crossroads was unknown, but every soldier would be needed when we got there. Extra 2-inch mortar shells, both shrapnel and smoke-type, were gathered from those who had them. Meanwhile, everyone waited for Hanson's truce to end.

Suddenly the two-wheel wagon he had given to the German sergeant came around the gatehouse and through the passageway between it and the wagon house. With it came three or four walking enemy wounded and what appeared to be a healthy German sergeant in charge. He pushed the cart. As they came up the promenade on their way to our medical aid station, we saw the wagon was covered with a tarpaulin. Those of us in the antitank ditch by the splintered Lombardy poplar had no way of knowing how these enemy soldiers had been cleared on the other side of the gatehouse. Therefore, Sergeant Harry Wright halted the wagon party.

Wright and his men began to move out of our antitank ditch to inspect the cart's interior. Then, without rhyme, reason or warning, an enemy machine gunner at their trench system opened fire on their own wagon. The apparently senseless act shattered one or two spokes on the near wheel and three or four enemy bullets went through the box of their cart.

For obvious reasons none of us got up on the promenade, but we motioned to the German sergeant with our weapons and forced him to remove the tarpaulin. There were three or four bodies in the cart. We knew they had been dead all along or some would have cried out when their fellow soldier fired through the box. The reason for this strange behaviour still remains a puzzle. The German wagon party was allowed to continue to the medical aid station, but the errant machine gunner's burst of fire ended the truce. None of the enemy soldiers, including the emissaries, were allowed to go back to their trench position.

Now Sergeant MacPhee and I began a slow crawl up the sloping ditch. The care we took to slowly crush any weeds which had grown above ground level made our progress painfully slow. MacPhee showed such concern for my safety that he almost called our foray off more than once. When the tapering of the ditch caused the ground cover to disappear, and we lay in the open field making use of a half-buried rock for partial cover, the view of the gun became clear. MacPhee guessed the mortar should be fired at nearly flat trajectory, which was possible with the small Airborne 2-inch mortar. After all, it had only a two-by-six-inch base plate and no bipod.

Once the mortar was loaded I lowered its muzzle with one hand until the barrel made an angle with the ground of only a couple of degrees. Then, with its base plate buttressed against the half-buried rock, it was aimed by sighting along the side of its barrel. Handled this way it acted much like a small infantry antitank gun and was surprisingly accurate. I fired two or three shrapnel shells at the enemy field gun, followed by a couple of smoke shells to help conceal our getaway.

Our nerves were stretched to the limit because we expected the big gun to return our fire. I went out of control as we scurried down the sloping ditch on our hands and knees. Without realizing it, I overtook MacPhee by clawing my way right over him and landed in our deep antitank ditch ahead of him.

By that time Captain Hanson's efforts to negotiate with the enemy were reaching a climax. We think the little 2-inch mortar gave the enemy a big nudge, for within a few minutes their white flag was raised again. With admiration we watched our Company Medical Corporal R.C. Hall, wearing his Red Cross armband and carrying his own flag of truce, walk out, accept their surrender and offer to give medical aid to any more of their wounded.

The prisoners were taken to the gatehouse, searched and put under guard. Forty-seven were counted. Two or three more from the stone and concrete bunker then surrendered, giving up Lieutenant Ken Arril and one other Canadian prisoner of war. Sergeant Joe Middleton, who had landed inside the wire on the drop and been held in their trench position, came out with the enemy prisoners. Lieutenant Arril was seriously injured. He and the other wounded were taken to our medical aid station in a two-wheel cart like the one we had let the Germans use.

When the action was finished we advanced into the enemy positions and readied ourselves to defend against any counterattack as we waited for two platoons of Number 6 Commando to relieve us when they got through by way of Sword Beach and the Orne bridges. When we got into the enemy's positions we learned several more things.

The antitank gun turned out to be a French 75-mm field gun produced at the end of World War I. It was adapted by the ingenious Germans as a dual-purpose field gun and antitank gun. They had put it on a swivel base and protected it with a cupola-style cabin. Its telescopic gunsight, so accurate when it tore the huge slab off the Lombardy poplar, was now useless. It was bent beyond repair, almost certainly by the little mortar we had fired directly at it.

One of the gun crew lay dead beside the cupola. The exposed part of his corpse and his clothing were severely scorched - an indication that one of the 2-inch, high explosive mortar shells must have gone through the front opening of the cupola housing. The urgency of the battle now passed, I took the time to survey the trench system and counted twenty-seven automatic small arms weapons left on the parapets - machine guns and submachine guns - plus dozens of rifles. The reinforced dugout had plentiful land mines, grenades and small arms ammunition. Private Swim and Corporal Saunders confirmed the count in case somebody wanted to write about the action some day. It was reconfirmed with Swim several times over the years, and with Saunders in England and Varaville in 1989.

We think that from twenty to thirty enemy soldiers from the Varaville position were on patrol or manoeuvres when our advance party for Drop Zone V landed. They crossed paths with a group of "C" Company previously scattered paratroopers heading for the village. That force, led by Lieutenant Sam McGowan, had emerged from the flooded Dives. McGowan, a gung-ho officer with lots of initiative and guts, is reported to have routed these Germans in quick time. He had them marched off under guard by British paratroopers to 3rd Brigade Headquarters south of Manoir du Monts on the Le Mesnil Ridge, while he and his men pushed on to the Varaville position.

Within an hour after the seizure of Varaville a count of the enemy was made. The count included the fifty who surrendered in the village itself; the approximately seven dead men and walking wounded brought over by their sergeant to our medical aid station; the scorched body found alongside the damaged field gun; and the Varaville-based contingent routed near the village by McGowan's group of scattered paratroopers. In short, a total of roughly eighty prisoners and casualties - two enemy soldiers for every Canadian paratrooper who fought for Varaville.

They had the plentiful weapons, the heavy gun, the trench system, the pillbox and the strength of numbers in their favour. We, the paratroopers, had the determination and the Airborne mystique on our side.

Chapter X
The Men in
the Plateau Country

L. E. O'Leary

None of the Canadian paratroopers who dropped into Normandy on D-Day expected to be dropped into the "plateau country" of France's Channel coast. But as we have seen many were. As a result - even if there had been no enemy troops there, and there were plenty! - these paratroopers stood no more chance of reaching their rendezvous or D-Day objectives than if they had been dropped on the moon.

What was the "plateau country"? It was not where the main D-Day seaborne invasion of Normandy took place. With the exception of Omaha Beach that whole action went ashore on upward sloping flatlands immediately behind long, wide shallow-grade beaches between the River Douve estuary in the west and the River Orne estuary to the east.

As is plain from the Airborne briefings the main British 6th Airborne Division's invasion was to take place between the Rivers Orne and Dives. Going eastward from the left flank of the Allied bridgehead, the coastal topography to the Seine River below Paris and the great port of Le Havre is quite different than that of the area where most of the seaborne and Airborne forces landed.

East of the Dives there is high ground behind the beaches from the east bank of that small river, all the way to Le Havre and beyond to Dieppe, except where three other rivers – the Touques, the Risle and the Seine – exit into the Channel. Yet even in this stretch there is an exception. From Deauville-Trouville to Honfleur, on the left shoulder of the Seine estuary, the ground remains low behind the beaches. But this stretch of coastline is quite short compared to the overall distance from the River Dives to Octeville-Montivilliers, where Lieutenant Cote's stick landed. The Octeville airport is about ten kilometres northeast of Le Havre.

The predominance of high country topped by flat lands in the extended stretch broken up by the three rivers merits the description "plateau country," as some of the soldiers later described it. The sticks from the 1st Canadian Parachute Battalion which landed there were Lieutenant Marcel Cote's, Sergeants Hiram Smith and Jack Hetherington's, Sergeant G. Kroesing's and Lieutenant Philippe Rousseau's; plus a stick from Battalion Headquarters, from which at least one man, Sergeant G. R. Lacroix, was killed near St. Vaast-en-Auge, three or four kilometres south of Villers-sur-Mer on the Channel coast.

To complicate matters for these Canadian paratroop sticks, the steeply sloping edges of the plateaus between the rivers are often gullied and serrated

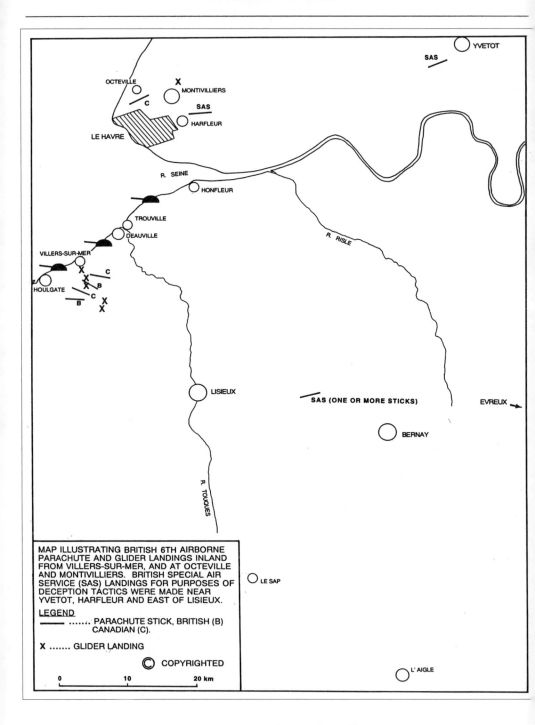

Troops from Villers to Octeville.

into sharp-sloped east-west ravines where ancient rivers ran down to the main rivers which still flow out to the Channel. The many rough features of the area make tough going for foot travel on any east-west axis. Especially difficult are the gullied ravines and wide estuaries. At night they are nearly impossible to cross. In combination with these uneven ground features the addition of a winding railroad and its cuttings, dirt tracks, highways and patchy forested countryside gave the enemy an unlimited number of possibilities for ambush as well as defence. It was inconceivable for the paratroopers, scattered in the coastal plateaus between the rivers, to make headway to the west. Especially at night and - worst of all - at morning and evening twilight.

When Private George Robertson returned from the dawn reconnaissance patrol where Sergeants Beaudoin and Trenholm became casualties, and reported to the other seven survivors from the southwest part of Lieutenant Rousseau's stick, it was obvious that some positive action had to be taken. They decided to move into a nearby ditch. It was connected to the one in which Beaudoin had positioned them early that morning. The move was made because it was now daylight and they judged that the new position would make a much better defensive bulwark against the enemy. Time was needed to plan how to get through the day.

Robertson writes: "A short time after taking up this new position, someone mentioned it was about time the first wave of the seaborne forces hit the beaches west of the Orne. We thought we should be able to get directions from the noise of battle. Yet everything remained quiet for us. Ours was a lonely outpost. Soon a German soldier from one of their patrols came up the trench we had vacated, poked his head around the corner and peered into our new trench position. Private Pledger was ready for this and fired at him. Some of the men who were close to the exchange said the German soldier dropped dead in his tracks. A further exchange of fire followed, part of which was through underbrush as the enemy patrol moved along, making it difficult to see what was happening."

This third contact with the enemy greatly boosted the small group's confidence. Driving the enemy off in quick time showed them what a few men could do, even in exceptionally poor circumstances, when they were determined and prepared to fight.

A conversation between Corporal Gordon McWilliams and George Robertson convinced the group that, although they had "put it onto" the German patrol, its survivors would report the details of the Canadian defensive position to their superiors without delay. Robertson and his friends would soon find themselves surrounded and under a weight of attack they did not have the means to withstand. They had to move again - in broad daylight - and fast. Luck was on their side as, despite the lack of ground cover, they ascended a ravine. At the top they were elated to find a vacant but prepared enemy trench on the edge of a plateau. The location made an excellent defensive position and the paratroopers hunkered down to wait for the enemy to put in an uphill attack.

Robertson adds: "A half mile to the east we saw an old motor car heading along a road north towards the coast. We could hear the low rumbling of big guns or bombing off to the northwest, but could gain no knowledge from it because it was so distant. It sounded like some barely audible grumbling beyond the horizon. At times the rustling of the wind in the tall grass along the top of the bluff made us certain the enemy was crawling up on us. Otherwise the day remained quiet - absolutely no sounds of war at all

"The attack we were expecting did not materialize and darkness on D-Day finally closed in. It was quite late because of the wartime double daylight saving time. About 22:45 hours on D-Day we set off to the east, figuring we'd shortly swing south to outflank the coastal belt of enemy defences and the north-south section of the railway cut obstructing our path to the west. This move completed, and now farther in from the coast, we'd then make quick time west to the River Dives and the Le Mesnil Ridge, where we'd meet the remainder of our battalion. Or so we thought.

"Covered by semi-darkness because of subdued moonlight, we moved in open box formation, which was the attack mode for moving infantry on foot. We crossed the south-north highway where we had seen the old car in the morning, then onward for another mile or so. In the latter stages of this move we came upon the gun pit where the four-barrelled *Flakvierling* had been firing when we dropped. We had been on the go now for over forty gruelling hours since reveille on 5 June in England. The pain of excruciating fatigue, because of lack of sleep, over-exertion and uncertainty, was hitting us hard.

"Later, towards 01:00 on 7 June, we came upon another deep and broad ditch which made a good fighting position. Our earlier plans were now necessarily changed. We were forced to rest because we were totally licked, even if it meant meeting the enemy on the worst of terms the following day. We piled into the new ditch position and flung our heavy equipment to the ground. Some men took portions of their emergency rations and water. We established a sentry rotation and got some sleep. The night passed without disturbance and when we awakened it was dawn.

"We were now somewhat refreshed, but naturally aggrieved because we had missed our opportunity to move south at night. Shortly, we became aware of some movement nearby. We jumped into firing position and got ready for a fight. It turned out to be a French farmer and his son, who was a fifteen-year-old. They were wearing the perennial black berets the French are famous for and were leading about fifteen parachutists, among whom were Privates Broadfoot and MacPherson from our stick. The others were British, of whom the senior rank was a sergeant-major.

"The Frenchman indicated, through the sergeant-major, that we should follow him to his farm, which we did. I was now number-one man in a long line of twenty-five paratroopers, and as the Frenchman led us into the approaches to one of his pastures I could see Corporal Boyd Anderson and Private Morris Ellefson sitting by a hedge in front of his house. What a welcome sight that was! There were now twenty-seven of us, and we now had another machine gun plus a second 2-inch mortar.

"The farmer's wife came out to the pasture and offered to fill our water bottles. I gave her mine, since I was dying for fresh water. Moments later I found I had a bottle full of excellent hard cider.

"The farmer informed the British sergeant-major, who as the top ranker took charge, that he would go to a town which we would have to pass through if we were to reach the invasion area north of Caen. His idea was to see if it was clear of the enemy. It would take him three hours or more to get there and back on foot. Then after dark, if the town were free of Germans, we could head for the Dives. I'm sure the name of the town, three miles away, was either Dozule or Douville. Although the farmer seemed sincere, this seemed to me to be a poor plan. The defended section of north-south railway would still be an impossible obstacle.

"It was at this point that I seriously began to lose confidence in the sergeant-major. I thought to myself: This is ridiculous. We Canadians were certainly already aware that, if we were to follow the route he was considering, we would have to infiltrate enemy positions we had previously made contact with before we could get to Varaville or Le Mesnil. And, in any case, we would not take a chance on going through a town. We would circumvent any town such as Dozule, for we knew before we left England that one battalion of the German 711 Infantry Division was garrisoned there. In my mind I kept going over defenses we had arranged during the past two years, while in England, and comparing them to what the enemy might be doing here. This convinced me the sergeant-major was naive in adopting the farmer's suggestion."

As hour after hour passed without the farmer returning, Robertson's mind began to take charge of him. The farmer's intentions were probably more than sincere, but Robertson became even more fearful of the sergeant-major's plan. The farmer had left his family behind and many things could go wrong which would cause the loss of their lives.

The sergeant major, taking Canadian Private Gordon Conneghan with him, positioned most of his British paratroopers along a hedge on the north side of the pasture, facing the farmer's house. Private Morris Ellefson with his Bren machine gun and Riflemen K. M. Pledger, Jim Broadfoot, Bert Isley and George Robertson formed a covering-fire group and a firm firebase in a shallow depression along the hedge on the west side of the pasture. Corporals Boyd Anderson and Gordon McWilliams, joined by Private Jim MacPherson, hunkered down in a ditch in front of a mounded hedge on the south side of the field, ready to fire over the heads of the sergeant-major's men. The defensive position was completed by Privates Arthur Schillemore, who also possessed a Bren machine gun, V.S. Willsey and J.G.H. Moffatt. Ammunition was laid out and a vigil begun. It was known that lots of enemy soldiers were stationed along the coast, so any attack would probably come through the farm buildings to the north.

"All was quiet," continues Robertson, "until a Focke Wulf 190 fighter screamed over our heads on a north-south heading. I thought, 'Well, he's had a good look at us and has gone back to add his report to what the enemy already knows about us.'

"More quiet time passed with everyone checking the progress of the sun continuously - hoping it would drop over the rim of the horizon and allow us to get out of there. Suddenly, well into the afternoon, battle noises came from among the farm buildings. An attack was coming through. When the oncoming enemy soldiers were close and in plain view Private Gordon Conneghan stood up straight, shot the leading enemy soldier and ordered the remainder to surrender. However, there were too many of them and he in turn was shot dead by a burst from an enemy submachine gun."

Immediately, the sergeant-major ordered his men facing the farmhouse to retreat from the field under covering fire from George Robertson's and Arthur Schillemore's groups. Corporal Boyd Anderson, who had knocked down a couple of enemy soldiers, had his rifle blasted from his hands by machine-gun fire and suffered a painful wound from one of the bullets, which took off the knuckle of his right thumb. Quickly, when he saw there was no way to stop the enemy, he ordered Jim MacPherson to follow him. They crawled to an out-building they had already reconnoitred and hid in a large cider barrel from which someone had cut a square hatch-opening in one end, leaving the barrel lying on its side.

By now the battle in the pasture was reaching a crisis. Privates Ellefson, Broadfoot, Isley, Pledger and Robertson were still firing on the enemy from their firm firebase in the shallow ditch by the hedge on the west side of the area. Soon all the withdrawing paratroopers were gone and the covering-fire group was left to its own devices, having given the others a chance to get away.

George Robertson says: "There seemed nothing for us to do except keep up the battle to an inevitable end. I had a strange calm come over me, convinced of a very short future. Ellefson snapped me out of it when he shouted, 'George, let's get out of here!' I, in turn, shouted the same message to the others, and we tried to break it off with the Germans. Too late.

"We began a fast crawl for the exit at the southwest corner of the field but soon found that Ellefson had remained behind, blazing away with his machine gun to get us out of the field. Suddenly I saw Broadfoot had stopped crawling. I caught up to him and shook the heel of his boot and said: 'Broadfoot, let's go!' I soon realized he was dead. Ellefson's Bren gun stopped firing, and when I looked back he was lying on his back looking over the tips of his boots at me. Then his head slowly lowered and his life was at an end. While this was happening, all in a few short seconds, Pledger was crawling up to Ellefson, so I shouted to him to bring the dead machine gunner's Bren, but the Germans had taken advantage of the lull in the firing to set up a position to the north of us, in our own shallow depression, and were firing straight down its length at us. The situation was hopeless and when Pledger collapsed he was also dead. There was no going back for the machine gun. It would have been certain death. I went like the devil for the exit from the field. Somehow Isley had made it out by another route. Then I finally made it through the exit in the hedges, God only knows how, with snapping bullets everywhere, and an enemy mortar shell bursting close to me in the opening at the corner of the pasture. It was like a nightmare. Once through, I met Private Willsey and a British sergeant who had also remained behind and used the mound of a hedge as a parapet from which to slow the Germans down, and consequently had helped us out from there.

"We wasted no time making it to a sunken lane which ran southward along another mounded hedge from the site of our battle. Unfortunately the field which this new hedge bordered was a very long one, and I could not see how we could make it to the next cross hedge without being shot down. I was not wrong in this, for immediately the sound of enemy soldiers running in hot pursuit could be heard behind us, but on the other side of the thick hedge.

"We went to ground on our side and by worst luck the enemy soldiers stopped exactly opposite us on theirs. We could tell they had begun a search because one of them had a loose heel cleat on his boot which went clink-clink-clink as he walked. Eventually, when we heard hedge saplings crackling, before everything became quiet, we knew they were lying on top of the hedge mound, only two or three feet above us. They were peering out over us, not knowing we were within a few feet of them right under their noses.

"We lay there, absolutely motionless, for about another hour until we heard more crackling of the saplings, followed by more clinking and then silence. This made us think the Germans had moved elsewhere and we might be able to remain undetected until darkness fell. Facing west, I never took my eyes off the horizon, measuring the blue sky between it and the sun and thinking the day would never end.

"Presently I heard something whispered near me. Thinking it was Willsey telling me something, I whispered back: 'What do you want?' When he didn't answer I looked around and saw a German soldier wearing thick glasses. He was above and behind me but didn't appear to see me, so I lowered my head, pushing the front of my helmet hard into the ground with my forehead. Then it happened. I felt like I had been hit on the head with a sledgehammer. Barely conscious, I heard a second shot then a burst of *Schmeisser* sub-machine gun fire. The jig was up. As I recovered full consciousness I realized the Germans were now amongst us and were screaming and yelling threats at us.

"I was staggering about, my head still reeling, when I realized some Germans were looking at me in a strange way. Blood was dripping from the right side of my helmet and was soaking the right sleeve of my camouflaged jacket. Willsey helped me take my helmet off and it was obvious what the German soldiers had been so amazed about. One of the bullets the German with the thick glasses had fired had gone up between my right ear and the inside of the rim of my helmet. The bullet then careened over the top of my head, met steel at a certain angle and raised a jagged tear in the helmet, above my left eye, as it exited into the surrounding countryside. In the process, since paratrooper helmets had especially buckled chin straps, the sledgehammer effect of the bullet had been devastating. Also, the bullet tore a small chunk out of my right ear, and hence the blood on my sleeve."

To get Boyd Anderson and Jim MacPherson's views of what took place, we go back to the time when the Frenchman and his son led the Canadian and British groups into the pasture. Anderson and Ellefson were already there and great relief was felt by all the Canadians. Now, for the first time, everyone from the southwest part of Lieutenant Rousseau's stick, except Sergeants Beaudoin and Trenholm and Private Shulist (now casualties), were together in one place. It was about noon on D-Day Plus One. After Anderson and MacPherson studied the positions the various soldiers had taken up, they became uneasy about their defensive position and about their presence in that pasture.

Anderson writes: "With this new group I felt an added uneasiness. We seemed to be a group without leadership. The sergeant-major had taken command but didn't really make any sensible decisions. He just waited for fate to intervene, which would not give the whole group a chance to survive a fight. I was hoping desperately to get past the day and perhaps have a meeting in the evening with the members of my own platoon.

"On the west side of the field, around the corner from my position on the south side, were Broadfoot, Ellefson and Isley. A little distance farther north from them Robertson and Pledger lay in firing positions and were watching their field of fire. Jim MacPherson was on my right.... He and I were in front of a few old farm buildings, not unlike old buildings from homestead times on the prairie back home. I could feel the friendliness of old-time activity there as I looked at them. It struck me to have a look round for a possible out if things suddenly went badly. It always had been my intention, if I found myself alone and in deep trouble, to escape my predicament and live to fight another day. I said: 'Come on MacPherson, lets have a look.'

"In the main part of a barn we saw several old barrels, six feet long by three to four feet in diameter, lying on their sides. One of them had a square hatch about a foot wide and two feet high cut out of one end. There was also a keg of cider fitted with a wooden spigot, positioned on a stand, ready to pour. We each had a pull from the keg before climbing a ladder to a hayloft, which gave a good view of the surrounding countryside. The door of the loft faced north while the main doors to the building, on the ground level, faced south, with a further opening to the west. The view from the loft door gave us a good look at the pasture where our troops had taken up positions and beyond. It also gave a good view of the land and features to the east of our position, and of the other outbuildings. Just beyond the most easterly outbuilding a road running north and south was concealed by a treed hedge.

"Up there in the loft I noticed MacPherson was as restless and uneasy as I was. All was deadly quiet. Like the old saying: 'It's always calmest before a storm.' We were moving down from the loft when a shot rang out. Quickly, we raced around the outside of the barn to our positions in the ditch, north of the southernmost hedge of the pasture. All hell broke loose and, as a big enemy soldier came through the northeast corner of the pasture land, I saw Gordon Conneghan stand up and cut loose at him. The big German toppled over as though stone dead. As Conneghan shouted something to those following the big man he had shot he, in turn, fell flat on his face, never to move again. I heard Ellefson and Arthur Schillemore opening up with their Bren machine guns and saw enemy dropping to the ground as my friends' fire struck home.

"Moments later I had a perfect aim on an enemy soldier coming down the opposite side of the hedge towards Schillemore, but never got the chance to squeeze my trigger. A German soldier obviously had me in his sights and a hot searing stab of excruciating pain ripped its way up my right arm.

"A bullet had passed through the magazine of my rifle and ripped the top off my right thumb knuckle. I dropped to the ground, wrapped MacPherson's field dressing around my thumb and began to crawl back to my previous firing position. I don't know why, because my rifle was now useless. However, once there, I witnessed the deaths of Broadfoot, Ellefson and Pledger, and the desperate efforts of George Robertson and Isley to continue with their covering fire and then get out of their positions after they and the dead men had covered the retreat of the sergeant-major and his men from the field.

"Ellefson and I had been in the same ten-man section for two years. We never exchanged a mean word. His money was my money and mine was his. The previous night, when the French farmer had buried us in the wheat sheaves in a barn, Ellefson made it known that together we'd do whatever it took to make things work out. Only four months previously he had been the section corporal and I was the machine gunner. He didn't like being a non-commissioned officer and asked me if I would trade positions with him. I agreed and it was arranged through Lieutenant Rousseau. Now he had just fought a machine-gun duel to his death with God knows how many Germans. And I was the corporal responsible for him.

"Everything in the battle area was now total confusion. George Robertson was the last one to get out alive. Every man from our platoon fought to the bitter end, but even after that I could still hear Arthur Schillemore's Bren gun chugging away from a position beyond the southeastern corner of the pasture. It was obvious he was going to make the enemy pay to the last round before he scampered away.

"Added to the enemy machine-gun and rifle fire, their mortar fire erupted over the whole pasture and a hot piece of shrapnel seared the surface flesh of my right leg without doing much damage. We were totally finished as a fighting force by now and enemy soldiers were beginning to come into plain view. In a flash, with no chance to escape down the hedges to the south, I made it to the barn with Jim MacPherson. Like two rats, searching for self preservation, I believe we both at the same time got the idea of squirming into the cider barrel with the open hatch. We were both skinny yet had to take off our equipment to get in. First, in went the equipment and then we, by lying sideways, squeezed through.

"Once in we sat crossways in the barrel as far to the closed end as we could get. Right away the enemy soldiers came closer and closer, shouting and cursing and firing as they came. Suddenly it all stopped and we thought the battle was over.

"MacPherson and I just looked at one another as we didn't even dare whisper. About five minutes later we could hear them at the main door of our building, and then the barrel and the barn shook with bedlam. First grenades and then submachine-gun fire riddled the barn and our barrel did not escape. Later, when MacPherson and I talked it over, we found that the same thought had occurred to us when the enemy search was over. It certainly seemed to us that 7 June 1944 was simply not our day to die. Not only did the enemy bullets which thudded through our barrel miss us, but we both had several grenades in our possession. What's more, we each had a 75 Hawkins antitank mine fully charged with its detonator in place. Our Gammon bombs, primed with mercury detonators, and a length of coiled-up flexible Bangalore torpedo, fully loaded with malleable plastic explosive and armed the same way, were also with us. An enemy bullet striking any one of those weapons would have blown us, the barrel, the barn and the Germans to hell and gone. We also carried several phosphorous smoke grenades which, if hit or torn, would have burned both of us to death instantly in the confines of the barrel. Later, as many enemy soldiers stood around drinking cider, I could have reached out and grabbed a couple of them by the ankles without moving more than two feet down the barrel.

"After an hour or so they vacated the barn. It went without saying that, when counting the dead and prisoners of war, they'd be aware they had not collected all of us from the pasture. They obviously had done such a detailed reconnaissance during the afternoon that they knew exactly where each of us was. That idea is supported by the information from those who had witnessed the deaths of Broadfoot, Ellefson and Pledger. They claimed the whole thing looked more like an execution than the occurrence of incidental deaths from normal military combat. They were not executions of course, the enemy were simply smart enough to get lined up on us before they began their attack."

What the Germans didn't know was what Anderson and MacPherson had learned from their own reconnaissance of the barn and its surroundings earlier in the day. Still, it was expected that the enemy would post listening patrols in the area that night.

After the Germans left the barn Anderson and MacPherson were able to stretch out. It was a huge relief to get the cramps out of their legs, but Anderson's chopped-off knuckle and the nicked cord behind MacPherson's knee were both extremely painful. The latter's injury had been aggravated by his having to squat sideways in the barrel. In Anderson's case the numbness had gone from his hand, and the chopped bone in the injured knuckle was being chafed by the field dressing.

Anderson explains further: "I truly believed that, at this point, we were the only survivors of the battle. I had seen Ellefson, Broadfoot, Pledger and Conneghan die and I had no reason to believe that those who got out of the pasture alive would have survived the moving skirmishes we heard receding from the area.

"When darkness fell we felt a little safer, but a strange unavoidable feeling took hold of me. I began to build a guilt trip. God knows, we had done everything possible to do our duty and prevent so many deaths, but there it was. I could not get the question 'Why us?' out of my mind. Why should all the others die but Jim and I live? Was there something I could have done to give more help? It was foolish, but I had to get out there and look around again. I'd be asking for a bullet, but I had to know something, I knew not what. I looked at the luminous dial on my military wristwatch which said 01:00. It was 8 June. As I squeezed out of the barrel I could hear Jim MacPherson stifling a painful moan under his breath. He was suffering terribly.

"The sky was clouded over and the night dark as pitch. It made no sense, but I thought of the countless nights I had moved around the lowing cattle or sheep, listening for predators, out on the rangelands in southern Saskatchewan. Pictures of my family raced through my mind. I began to crawl. I made it around the barn to the hedge where I had been positioned throughout the fight. I crawled in a slow, careful manner around the corner to the stretch where Ellefson, Broadfoot, Pledger, Isley and Robertson had so valiantly fought. I crawled onward to the hedge facing the farmhouse, to where Conneghan had ordered the enemy to surrender and then met his death. As I progressed I knew what I was doing, but wasn't sure why. Each time, when I came to where the bodies of the dead men had been, they were gone.... I slithered down the hedge on the eastern side to where I knew Arthur Schillemore and Willsey had fought to the end. There was nothing except piles of spent cartridges, empty Bren gun magazines and the smell of cordite. Complete darkness wrapped me, my thoughts and my relics in solemn silence.

"As I crawled back to join MacPherson in the barrel I sensed there were enemy in the area but outside the pasture. I had no real evidence of it, but a definite strong feeling of human presence was overpowering. When I got back with Jim it was 02:00. I felt better but didn't know why. The result of my effort was, I had picked up one English cookie from a backpack I found along the way."

It was October 1989, forty-five years later, before I was able to track down Jim MacPherson for his recollections of what happened to him and Boyd Anderson immediately after the battle in the pasture. The gist of what he told me, and later sent to me in written form, is:

"There was a keg of cider just outside the opening in our barrel. As one German bent down to turn on the spigot to fill a mug, a girl he had with him stood between him and our barrel with her legs partially covering the hatch opening. The sun was setting and was visible through the opening, and was glinting on the sight of a rifle I had in the barrel with me. I remembered a small basket lying up against the vat just outside the opening. I reached out, grabbed the basket and covered the glinting rifle sight with it. Within seconds the German soldier's mug was full and when he stood up they left the barn. I have often wondered whether the girl had noticed the rifle barrel glinting and took up her position on purpose to hide it.

"We stayed in the barrel for two days except to get out at night for cider and for other necessary reasons. We had left our small packs at the position we held during the fight, with our names inside the flaps. When the enemy found these they would know we were not on their list of dead and prisoners but were still in the area. We therefore decided to stay where we were until they became sick and tired of looking for us. On the third evening, when darkness fell, we headed south. There was a long road ahead to reach the Le Mesnil Ridge."

To return to Morris Zakaluk: He had settled down in a long ditch between a double hedge close to where he landed. He dragged his equipment there from his deflated parachute and, with a certain fear in his heart, examined his injured ankle. He gave himself a sharp talking-to about keeping his courage up and then dozed off. But he didn't sleep long. The pain in his ankle was too great.

When he awoke the first streaks of the grey dawn of D-Day illuminated the horizon. He could hear thunderous noises in the distance, which magnified the need to get to the planned rendezvous as soon as possible. But where? Which way? And, how? With pain shooting up his leg his chances of moving far, even had he known which way to go, were not good.

As the light increased he observed the countryside. His position bordered on a small apple orchard. He saw two other parachutes left behind by jumpers who had moved on.

All was quiet so he examined his throbbing foot again. Once stripped down to the skin his ankle looked a mess - black and blue, swollen to an unrecognizable mass of flesh. He wrapped his camouflaged scarf around it and secured it tightly with pins from his first-aid package. He got his sock back on by slitting it from ankle to instep, hoping the pain would diminish with time.

Leaving the bulk of his equipment under cover inside the hedge, Zakaluk took his rifle, his land mine and his grenades with him and hobbled slowly down the long ditch which became his highway. Observing as he went along, he made the best of his predicament and hoped to find some other soldier from his battalion. It was not to be. He was isolated. He was alone. Taking great care not to be spotted by the enemy, he finally saw German troops for the first time in his life.

They were occupying some farm buildings which his long ditch came quite close to. Zakaluk was impressed by how similar they looked to our own troops on manoeuvres back in England. He bypassed this danger zone and reached a second farm, where he saw a farmer walking past what looked like an army transport truck towards his cow in a field. Moving to a different vantage point, he saw a large number of German soldiers digging in around the farm buildings. Hugging the cover of his ditch, he went a little farther but still found no evidence of his own troops. He painfully retraced his route to the bundle of equipment he had stashed when he first landed. There in the field, making for the two parachutes, in single file and in full battle order, were six German soldiers with rifles, submachine guns and stick grenades. One man carried a radio. When the lead enemy soldier reached Zakaluk's parachute he tried the harness on for size but was too big for it. He could not buckle it up. Throwing it to the ground, he came straight towards Zakaluk's position.

Morris Zakaluk writes: "When the leading enemy soldier was less than fifty yards from my position I asked myself: 'OK, Zak, what the hell are you going to do? Are you going to crawl out of here on your belly and give yourself up?' My answer to myself was: 'Not very likely. But still, I can't use my grenades because the hedges are thick and if I wait until the enemy is close enough and then throw them, the grenades are only going to bounce back down from the hedge saplings into my ditch and kill me, not them. If I use my rifle I'll only get one or two of them before they have me dead to rights.'

"I made up my mind. I'd take the second course and let the devil take the hindmost. Thinking that maybe it would be such a surprise to them I'd get them all, I took a bead on the leading man and readied my mind for rapid single bolt-action rifle fire. I was going to let them come close because I wanted the last man to be within easy range of my sights. When I was about to squeeze my trigger the lead man wheeled to his left and the whole patrol followed him along the hedge and through a gap at the far end of the field, to my right. I lay there with a prayer of thanksgiving on my lips while sweat ran down the crevices of my neck and ass. Within seconds three enemy soldiers came into view where the first members of the patrol had appeared. One man was carrying an MG-34 machine gun, ready to fire from the hip, while the other two were loaded down with ammunition. If I had opened fire at the first group I would have been a dead duck by now. I had survived the lethal weapons of a covering fire party.

"My brain was now in high gear. Something within it was screaming at me: 'Zak, plan your moves carefully. You must be most careful. You got away with it this time, but it may be not so easy next time.' They might have observation posts covering all the fields and hedges in the area. After all, our stick probably was dispersed in numerous fields nearby.

"Soon, other German soldiers showed up and dug in around the farm yard. It had previously come to me that I would have to settle down somewhere to allow my ankle to recover. I realized I could go nowhere until it completely recovered. Having had no previous experience with this, I didn't know how long it would take. Maybe one or two days or maybe a week. The enemy didn't appear to be too disturbed by the parachutes which were lying around their area so I began to think again. It came to me like a bolt from the blue; where else would I find a safer place to be than in the lion's den with the lion himself? As evening twilight fell on D-Day, I made a firm decision to hunker down right there amongst the enemy."

Meanwhile, where was A. J. (Scotty) MacInnis? No one who managed to rendezvous with other troops has ever been able to claim that he saw a sign of Scotty since the jump.

Chapter XI

The Robehomme Bridge

Sam McGowan   *Melvin Oxtoby*

When Lieutenant Norman Toseland of "B" Company reached the area of the bridge on the Dives River at Robehomme, having been guided by the young French girl who had come out of the night on her bicycle, he did not find Captain Peter Griffin's Trowbridge party there as he expected. It was approximately 02:30 hours on D-Day. That his stick had been dropped two or three miles from Drop Zone V at Varaville did not shake him or worry him. He, like all the others who found themselves in a similar predicament, automatically assumed theirs was the only stick it could have happened to, and since he had already collected several of his jumpers, all of whom had actually come down closer to the objective at Robehomme than they would have if they had been put down on the correct Drop Zone, all seemed well. He never even considered that most of the battalion had been scattered.

He confidently waited for the first of his platoon to come in from some area close by. But, as in the case of all the initial objectives, individuals or small groups who eventually reached the right vicinity assumed - sometimes wrongly - that they were the first soldiers to arrive. Finding themselves alone, or in little groups that were too small to deal with enemy activity effectively, they remained at reasonable distances away from their actual objectives. This was to avoid discovery by the enemy before more of their own soldiers arrived. They'd hunker down in the plentiful hedgerows, take up firing positions and wait.

One positive result of this was that they'd begin to get a feel for the area in which they found themselves; an important step in the early stages of any stubborn defence or determined assault. But the next man or small group to arrive in the vicinity would likewise think they were the first to come on the scene. It happened at Le Mesnil, Varaville and Gonneville-sur-Merville as well as at Robehomme.

Fortunately for Lieutenant Toseland the process soon corrected itself, for as numbers increased individuals and groups began to discover each other. New arrivals would automatically come up against the settled-in troops and get the "Punch and Judy" password challenge.

Toseland was not long in the area when he challenged a newly arrived soldier and, upon recognition, found him to be from a stick other than his own. Minutes later he was joined by a few British soldiers from the 8th Parachute Battalion, followed by some men from his own battalion's Headquarters Company who were supposed to be nowhere close by. He suddenly became aware that the drop had been a general screwup.

Perplexed and angry, he ordered two or three soldiers to come with him to reconnoitre the entire area of Robehomme and Bricqueville. In about half an hour he found six more men, which brought the total number at the Robehomme Bridge to about twenty-five soldiers. Most of them were stalwarts like Sergeant John Kemp, Private Mark Lockyer, Sergeant Tom Pasquill, Sergeant Joe Lacasse and others.

Toseland deployed most of those present as a firm firebase on the high ground at Robehomme village under the leadership of Sergeant Pasquill. The others, Sergeant Kemp, Private Lockyer, Lance-Corporal O.M. Bastien and Corporal Nickerson, were formed into a demolition party.

Sergeant R. Outhwaite's stick, another from Toseland's platoon, had landed in "Satan's Quadrangle" but west of the Dives between Robehomnme and Bures, near Basseneville. They struggled furiously to extricate themselves from the flooding and the entanglements of the area. They eventually made rendezvous on each other, but took a long time to identify their exact location. Finally, when the whole stick was gathered in, they figured they were well south of the bridge. They headed north towards the Channel and got to the bridge about two hours after Toseland and his party.

The problem Lieutenant Toseland now faced, besides the lack of troops and weapons, was that the Royal Engineers assigned to the job of placing the demolition charges on the girders under the bridge were missing. By now they should have wheeled up the explosives some four kilometres from Drop Zone V at Varaville in a small handcart, but where were they? With proof that the drop was a total mess staring him in the face, Toseland knew he had no reason to expect the engineers to show up at any time soon. He ordered Sergeant John Kemp to collect all the plastic explosive the soldiers present had on their persons and bring it to the demolition party. Kemp did the job quickly, making a collection of about thirty pounds, which was extracted from disarmed Gamon bombs and number 75 Hawkins antitank grenades. Also, number 808 plastic explosive was taken from the space between the shock-harness and the metal roofs in the tops of their steel helmets - the fatalistic way in which paratroopers toted sensitive high explosives!

The demolition party set off to the objective bridge. When they examined the girders, as they had been trained to do in a pinch, they placed the plastic explosive on the bridge girders and taped all their other primed explosive objects tightly to it. That done, the party retreated to a safe distance. Then Mark Lockyer pushed the plunger.

There was indeed a fine explosion which greatly weakened the bridge, but it did not cut the girders sufficiently to dump the small structure into the river. This was an equally huge disappointment and worry for Lieutenant Toseland, because this part of the operation was specifically assigned to him in Operation Order No.1, the official order for D-Day. He felt a deep commitment to getting his job done.

But for now all he could do was make sure that his defensive positions would not let the enemy intrude upon his plans. He ordered Sergeant Kemp to

147

set up a defensive outpost with a few men on a small jut of land south of the bridge. The chosen position was close by the west bank of the Dives on what appeared to be something like a three-plank levee. There were a few logs piled up immediately west of the planks. These gave reasonable cover from possible enemy activity on the upward sloping ground east of the river towards Goustranville, which was a little over two kilometres away. Should the enemy come down the slope to retake the bridge, the small force in the outpost would be right in the teeth of their advance.

Toseland returned to the firm firebase with the remainder of the demolition party. He positioned them half way up the slope towards the Robehomme church so that if the enemy did launch an overwhelming attack, they could help get Kemp and his men out by giving covering fire.

The night became quiet and uncertain for a short time. Then, about 04:30, Captain Peter Griffin arrived leading a number of soldiers, including the Brigade Intelligence Officer, several 224 Field Ambulance personnel and a British Vickers machine-gun crew. About thirty in all. The Vickers machine-gun was a welcome addition, and its crew had a full complement of ammunition.

This new injection of personnel and equipment added to and widened the general defensive position. Griffin established a machine-gun post on the edge of Bricqueville facing the open ground up each side of the Bavent road in the direction of the Cabourg-Troarn highway. Under the covering fire of this latest outpost, the British intelligence officer and the medics moved down through Bricqueville and then two kilometres, generally northwest, to Bavent. From there they went on to the main Cabourg-Troarn highway and turned south to Le Mesnil, now only a few hundred metres away.

Griffin established his bridge-party headquarters in a shed near the Robehomme church. The original task of his Trowbridge party was to reconnoitre the route from the Drop Zone at Varaville to the Robehomme bridge and to the smaller bridge on the farm canal at Le Hoin. It worried him that nobody had yet paid any attention to Le Hoin. He agreed it was reasonable that no one had gone there so far because, until the engineers could arrive with sufficient explosives, the second bridge could not be destroyed anyhow.

Now that Griffin had finally arrived at the objective he was supposed to reach to begin with, he saw no reason why he should not at least carry out a reconnaissance of Le Hoin as part of his original duty. He took two men and made his way to the small bridge at Le Hoin by going down a track from the Bricqueville-Bavent road towards Periers-en-Auge. The ancient unused farm canal, although narrow, made a first-class tank trap - deep and soggy.

The bridge, originally made for oxen teams, was rotten and under two feet of floodwater. It would not bear the weight of tanks, half-tracks or even scout cars, and the width of the canal would be no obstacle to foot soldiers even if the bridge were destroyed. Griffin therefore wrote it off as a non-essential objective and returned to his headquarters. On arrival he made the rounds of his and Toseland's defensive positions and was satisfied everything was as well worked out as it could be with the resources at hand.

By 05:00 Royal Engineers Captain Jack showed up at the Robehomme Bridge with a few of his men, pulling the two-wheel cart with the explosives on board. In less than twenty minutes he turned to Captain Peter Griffin and said, "It's your bridge. Would you like to light the fuse?" Griffin did and a great explosion ripped the little bridge apart. Relief coursed through the fast-beating hearts of the "B" Company personnel who were on the spot. During the briefings in England it had become a point of honour for every officer and man to achieve his initial objectives.

Actually, "whose bridge" was it? Historically, Captain Jack completed a seizure of an important objective by laying the charges. Captain Peter Griffin was in overall charge of the collective group of Canadian troops at the Robehomme operation because of his rank as second-in-command of "B" Company. Major Clayton Fuller had passed through Robehomme as he made his way from his misplaced parachute descent to Le Mesnil to organize the "B" Company positions at the crossroads. But there is no doubt that the actual destruction of the bridge at Robehomme, as an objective, was assigned to Lieutenant Toseland.

Shortly after 06:30 hours the "B" Company troops facing up the slopes toward the Goustranville-Troarn highway saw some activity they could not identify. What they saw is explained in a letter dated March 1988 from Major Harry Reid (retd.). At the time of the drop he was Corporal Harry Reid of "B" Company.

He relates: "The names of the men in my stick, listed on the back of an old photo taken the evening of 5 June 1944, are: Yank, Snipe, and Pete (nicknames), followed by other soldiers' names: Trenfield, Boardman, Shwaluk, Don Paynter, Jim, L.D. Ross, Dray, C.H. Reid, Doc O'Leary, Bill Noval, Sergeant Jones, Kivinen, Sergeant Bill Irvine, Sangster, Sergeant Slipp and Harrington. The emotions and thoughts I'm recording in this letter are as they affected me then, and have remained with me over the years. Some things never leave us.

"'Stand up and hook up' came the order out of the dark. I slam my snap fastener onto the anchor cable of the aircraft. I pull and tug on it to make certain, but the anchor line is jumping up and down because everyone else is pulling and tugging on their snap fasteners too. This never happened on practice jumps in England. My God, it's dark out there. Check equipment - oh, oh! a diversion. What the hell are all those pretty coloured lights out there, snaking up slowly at us in slow curves and then flashing past and upwards like small rockets?

"Oh Jesus, we're in a war. The aircraft is rocking left and right. I'm checking the equipment of the man in front of me and I can feel Boardman behind me checking mine - hope he does it right - wish to hell we had some light. Turmoil in my mind now, the last four years in the army have been simply an interlude in my life. The Germans? Something to sing funny songs about and to make jokes about their leaders - it all floods in! The people on the ground want to see me dead and buried!

"Two-minute red warning light is on. Everyone pushes like hell to be as close as possible to the door. The aircraft is descending noticeably now - we must have been flying way too high - and still zigzagging. It seems to be bucking as it levels out - must be the German anti-aircraft shells exploding close by. The red light was supposed to switch to green after only two minutes. Someone falling down, Christ... help him up! This red is just too long and the ride is too rough - what the hell is the pilot doing? Oh God, my static line has caught under my arm. Phew! Oh no it's not. Thoughts running away with me, tumbling over one another - France, night jumps, German soldiers, don't screw up, damn it quit shoving, check snap fastener again. What if I'm wounded and alone - possible execution. German doctors are good though. Remember the Drop Zone colour codes. Green on! Go-go-go. Can feel chute coming out of its sack followed by the heavenly tug - the ride down is far too long - Jesus! Whump! Flat on my ass in France. I'm now exultant. Let's get at it! Let's get on with the job.

"Soon I can hear other troopers talking in low voices, cussing the hell out of the aircrews for jumping us so high. Where the hell are the others? The rush of activity on the Drop Zone, after a mass drop, is absent. There's hardly anyone about. I find my Bren machine gun and it's completely smashed. There are no rendezvous code flares visible. The few of us who got together are in a tiny field with high hedges all around. It's not like our Drop Zone at Varaville at all. We've moved through the high hedges only to find other high hedges fifty yards away, and so it goes. Hedge after hedge after hedge. We now know we are not only off the Drop Zone, we are a long way off. The topography simply does not match the Varaville area - Christ-aw-mighty! The group I'm with, six or seven men, finally finds a road and we come to a house. We set up a defensive position in a ditch. We do not know we're not the only stick dropped off the mark and we worry unmercifully because we'll be letting the other men in our platoon down, as far as taking our objectives is concerned.

"At dawn we begin a map search by comparing landmarks we can see with our own eyes to features on our map. Finally we are flabbergasted, for we realize we are in the vicinity of Goustranville two miles or more east of the Dives and about four to five miles east of the Drop Zone.

"A large middle-aged French woman comes out of her house, and when she realizes we are the invasion troops, she becomes ecstatic. She hugs and kisses us and wants us to come into her house for refreshments. On our polite refusal she agrees to take care of a jumper with a broken leg.

"After moving across country, around Goustranville, we took the main road from there to Robehomme. Before doing this we had to make some special decisions, one of which was to go directly down the highway instead of infiltrating through the countryside using hedges, shrubbery, topographical features and ditches for cover. In retrospect this decision might seem to have been based on desperation or foolhardiness, but it was not. It was based on our absolute need to be where we were supposed to be.

"Infiltration might have been more militarily sound and safer but those two attributes of conduct would not satisfy our crucial needs. We needed to be at Robehomme four hours earlier than it now was, so it is easily seen our main problem was time, which had run out much earlier during the hours of darkness. Now what was needed was courage, speed and quick-wittedness.

"The decision made, we set out with great trepidation. We were on high ground, exposed to observation by whoever wished to survey our route with the naked eye or telescopic sights - absolutely vulnerable. A couple of things in our favour were deep ditches and eight to ten-foot high hedges on either side of the route. As we rounded a bend in the road some soldiers up ahead came into view. It was difficult to identify them as friend or foe. Both opinions were expressed in our group. In any event they fired on us, but as soon as we hit the turf and returned their fire they disappeared into some depression. The last we saw of them they were scampering into some woods far off to our left.

"About half way to the bridge the highway passed between some farm buildings - a house and a number of sheds. As we approached a farmer came out with his hands up. He led us to a spot behind one of the sheds and showed us the dead bodies of three of our British comrades who had been surprised by a detachment of Germans.

"Due to the briefings in England we had very definite ideas about territory. The ground west of the Dives, in our minds, was ours - east of the Dives, the enemy's. Although all the territory belonged to the Germans, who occupied the entire countryside both east and west of the river, to us that made no difference. We looked upon the west of the river as ours, and that was it. In our minds the ground between the Orne River and the Dives was home to us.

"Since we now knew we were within a kilometre of the bridge at Robehomme we decided to take the dead British lads home for burial, showing the extent to which civilian values still dominated our lives - the harsh values of prolonged combat still waiting to impose themselves within our persons.

"We borrowed a wheelbarrow and loaded the grotesquely stiffened bodies, and went on our way with our cartoon-like order of battle. The sweat from exertion soon convinced us we were doing a hard and difficult thing. But now we could see the village of Robehomme and knew the river was half way between us and it, so we kept on forcing our pace. We finally made it to the east bank of the Dives which looked like you could jump across it, but not quite. Like the Divette at Varaville it was deep and with the bridge now destroyed made a complete obstruction to tanks and motorized infantry.

"The troops who were already there in defence with Lieutenant Toseland, mostly our own "B" Company soldiers except for stragglers from other units, had us under observation for the last thousand yards to the bridge and now advised us we would have to swim the river.

"On doing a little reconnoitring we found another way. There was a huge deciduous tree leaning out over the river bank on our side, so we packed explosives we were carrying around its trunk, and dropped it. It made a difficult but passable foot-bridge and we soon got everyone across, including our rigormortised British corpses. As soon as we were home we got to work to bury them, thinking their saddened British parents would be comforted. We began to dig a common grave with our entrenching tools.

"As I got to work with my inefficient equipment, together with a few other friends, I couldn't help glancing over at the three body-deformed British troopers. The hardness of the ground, yielding slowly to the puny entrenching tools, like life slowly giving way to the new disgusting violence of combat, started me off on a thinking process which brought me to a grim realization. I was now in a situation where none of the niceties of living mattered a damn. The act of burying three human beings, under such deplorable conditions, created a scenario in my mind which was to live continuously in my thoughts every day until the end of the war. And yet this was only the beginning. From now on all my thinking must constantly tell me to do my duty completely and honourably, but in a way to let me survive. We had taken the proper precautions to ensure guaranteed identification of the men we had buried. We then turned to the task of playing our part in the defence of Robehomme."

The Germans were quite slow to react to the Canadian intrusion at Robehomme. They did, however send out patrols into "Satan's Quadrangle," an area that comprised the flooded farm canals south of Goustranville and east of Troarn, almost to Cambremer, and all the way back towards the Channel to Periers-en-Auge and Varaville. The area east of Troarn towards Cambremer, although only partially flooded, was one of the worst sections of "Satan's Quadrangle." It was crisscrossed by myriads of ancient farm canals and thick hedges. Although the enemy efforts were scattered and mainly ineffective, they did cost several Canadian and British paratroopers who had landed east of the River Dives their freedom or their lives.

During the afternoon of D-Day the enemy began some serious reconnaissance work to identify and delineate the Canadian defensive positions at the village.

Private W.J. Brady reports: "I was in Lieutenant Toseland's Number 5 Platoon and landed in the River Dives about a hundred yards south of the bridge at Robehomme. Due to the night clouds and partially dimmed-down half-moonlight, I thought the River Dives was a highway and never bothered preparing for a water landing by getting out of my harness a foot or two before I hit the world. I made it to the river's edge but could not get up the bank, and if Private V.W. Hodge had not come along and rescued me I surely would have drowned.

"After daybreak we had our first battle. Three enemy motor transport trucks loaded with enemy troops came down toward the east side of the destroyed Robehomme bridge where they captured Doc O'Leary and L. D. Ross on the wrong side of the river.

"Most of the enemy soldiers soon deployed in the thick shrubbery and rugged terrain on their side of the Dives. They withdrew one of the trucks up the slopes toward Goustranville and put Doc O'Leary and L.D. Ross on the engine hoods of the other two, creating as they thought a reason for the Canadians not to fire on their vehicles.

"We could not let them get away with that," Brady says, "and a weapons exchange ensued. When Ross was killed, O'Leary escaped and swam to safety on our side of the river. We made up a lot of the weapons we lost on the drop from that skirmish, together with ammunition to match. I was given a German sniper's rifle with lots of ammunition, telescope and cheek rest - the best!"

The afternoon of D-Day was one of quick action - especially in response to probing by the enemy. Their mortaring, medium machine-gun fire from a long way off, and occasional artillery shells from the east left everyone wary.

An influx of soldiers from other units due to the scattered landings became almost a continuous stream by late afternoon on D-Day. Mostly, they were passed along from Robehomme through Bricqueville and up the Bavent road under the protection of the Bricqueville outpost manned by a British medium-weight machine gun.

Perhaps inadvertently the small Griffin-Toseland force performed an invaluable service to scattered members of the 6th Airborne that day and the subsequent night. The distinctive "chug-chug-chug" of the force's Bren guns - which sounded like no other machine guns in the war - guided numerous misplaced soldiers from the flooded areas to the Robehomme position. They were passed on to the Canadian battalion at Le Mesnil and, from there, back to their own units. All this made the nights of 6 and 7 June extremely tense.

Enemy patrols were probing as the Airborne stragglers entered the area. For the Canadian defenders at Robehomme and for the mixed group of defenders of the whole Robehomme-Bricqueville position, it was a nightmarish task to identify which were which: German patrols or small groups of misplaced Airborne troops. Most men were red-eyed but relieved when dawn broke with a bright sun.

On the morning of 7 June it was obvious that the enemy were tightening a loose perimeter around the isolated Canadian position at Robehomme. From the observation post the Canadians had established in the church tower on D-Day they could observe a continuous stream of German infantry and support weapons proceeding west on the Pont de Varaville highway at Periers-en-Auge. Unfortunately the equipment lost on the drop included essential radio transmitter receivers. The enemy, having strengthened their positions at Bavent, had stopped Canadian foot traffic to Le Mesnil by the Bavent route. There was no way our troops at Robehomme could communicate with their brigade, battalion or division. Thus a glorious opportunity to bring down artillery fire on the enemy forces entering the Airborne lodgement area by the restricted Periers-en-Auge route was lost.

At approximately 10:00 hours it was reported that an enemy scout car was approaching from the vicinity of the Periers-en-Auge road. It came up the track by way of the Le Hoin culvert. Lieutenant Toseland immediately organized an antitank party with one PIAT rocket launcher, two soldiers designated as ammunition carriers and a few riflemen. They lost no time in cutting across country until they met the Le Hoin track, slightly north of where it meets the Bricqueville-Bavent road. From there they followed the unpaved track towards the Channel.

At Le Hoin they found no sign of the scout car and assumed it must have turned around at the submerged culvert and gone back to wherever it came from. What did happen, though - which Toseland and his men found quite amusing - was that while zigzagging through the underbrush on their return journey they unexpectedly surprised two enemy soldiers equipped with a light machine gun. They were either scouts or a standing patrol. The Canadians came across them so suddenly, and at such close range, that there was no time to think as the pair bolted into the underbrush and raced away in the direction of Bavent.

When Toseland and his patrol got back to Robehomme enemy counter activity was becoming more severe. Toseland and Captain Griffin decided to try to reach Le Mesnil. Private W.J. Brady writes: "On D-Day Plus One we tried to move on to Le Mesnil but found the highway, which was flooded on both sides, blocked by the enemy near Bavent. We were forced back to the high ground."

But at twilight some heartening news arrived. It was brought by a small patrol of "A" Company soldiers who got through from Le Mesnil itself. Their Lieutenant, Bob Mitchell, reported that they had reconnoitred a feasible route through the Bavent Forest.

Therefore in the darkness of that night the move was made to Le Mesnil by a circuitous route that avoided Bavent. There were now about one hundred and fifty of all ranks in the party including scattered paratroopers from various Canadian and British sticks. The "B" Company personnel were at their strongest since the landing had taken place during the early hours of D-Day. Considering the tragedy of the drop, Griffin and Toseland had been fortunate to gather up as many of their own men as they did. There were now up to thirty "B" Company privates and corporals as well as Sergeants Lacasse, Outhwaite, Pasquill and Kemp. Also present were Sergeant Hiram Smith of the Vickers machine gun platoon and several officers and sergeants who had come in from the flooding during 7 June.

By 23:30 hours the whole force was ready to move. All ranks lined up in column of route, single file, with the officers and sergeants spread fairly evenly throughout its length. "B" Company personnel were in the lead. The trick was to keep the column together and not lose anybody; in the darkness it was all too easy for different sections to diverge and stray away.

The first leg of the route to Le Mesnil was to be through Bricqueville to the Bavent road. This would be followed by a swing southward across flooded fields to the Bavent Forest, then along Lieutenant Mitchell's reconnoitred route back to the battalion positions. The wounded would be taken in a car donated by the priest at Robehomme and on a horse and wagon provided by a farmer. With some pushing and shoving by the paratroopers this was accomplished even in the flooded areas.

The Battalion War Diary reported that on 7 June: "While proceeding just beyond Bricqueville, the head of the column was challenged by an enemy outpost. In a flash, seven of the enemy lay dead and one was taken prisoner. Suddenly an automobile with headlights dimmed down to the usual narrow slits, and which therefore appeared ghostly, was perceived sliding along the Bavent road towards the column. When it was quite close it met a fierce volley of well aimed fire from our column. It careened into a ditch and upon examination was found to contain the dead bodies of four German officers. The way was now clear to get on through the Bavent forest."

The column advanced along the planned route and, at 03:30 hours on 8 June, reached Battalion Headquarters in the brick and pottery plant at Le Mesnil. The operation to destroy the Robehomme bridge had, in spite of the paratroops' landing having been screwed-up, succeeded beyond anyone's wildest expectations. Brigadier Hill and Colonel Bradbrooke later expressed their admiration of the skill displayed under such harrowing circumstances.

Morris Ellefson

Chapter XII
Consolidation of
the Le Mesnil Crossroads

Gordon Conneghan

While endeavours at Robehomme, Varaville, "Satan's Quadrangle," Gonneville-sur-Merville and the plateau country were developing during the night and throughout the daylight hours of D-Day, every scrap of individual soldierly willpower in all the separate scattered troop locations was directed towards reaching and seizing the Le Mesnil crossroads position.

Why was the Le Mesnil crossroads position so important to the 6th British Airborne Division's overriding objective, as laid down by the British 2nd Army?

Remember, the 6th Airborne Division under General Sir Richard Gale had been ordered no less a task than to prevent the German Army from success-fully breaching the left flank of the entire D-Day Allied bridgehead.

To carry this out was a huge undertaking. It called for the interdiction of all highways, secondary roads, tracks and open fields which provided access to the Orne waterways (the River Orne and the Canal de Caen) between Colom-belles and the Channel. A further demand by the British 2nd Army Head-quarters was the defence and retention of two of the 6th Airborne's initial objectives - the Orne bridges at Benouville and Ranville. It was decided to use the Le Mesnil Ridge - which ran from just above Sallenelles on the coast to Troarn, opposite the city of Caen - as one of the two main defensive features for the interdictions. The second feature was the area of open fields south of the Herouvillette-Ste.Honorine-Longueval face of the Airborne perimeter.

Additional troops placed under General Gale's command included a reserve of three battalions from the famous and combat experienced 51st High-land Division (5th Battalion Black Watch plus the 4th and 5th Battalions Gordon Highlanders). Also, as active D-Day invaders and participants for the duration of the battle, were the commandos of Brigadier Lord Lovat's 1st Special Service Brigade: Numbers 3, 4 and 6 Commandos plus Number 45 Royal Marine Commando. Serving with the marines were commandos of the famous Dutch Royal Netherlands Brigade (Princess Irene's) and Belgian commando regiments.

It was the defensive positions of the different Airborne battalions' interdiction points which ultimately formed the perimeter protecting the Orne bridges. These points were established mainly east of the Orne waterways. They ran along a front from the western shoulder of the Canal de Caen, by Ouistreham, to beyond the eastern shoulder of the River Orne at Sallenelles, leaving points along the coast east of Sallenelles - the villages of Les Marmiers, Merville and Le Grand Homme - for Lord Lovat's Number 3 Commando to

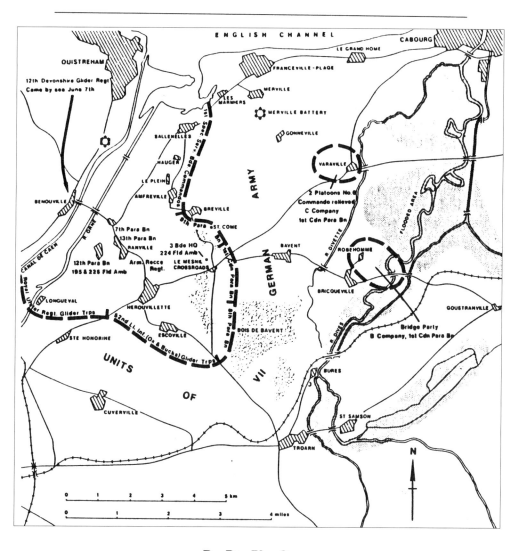

D – Day Plus One.

This map shows the perimeter of Airborne Bridgehead
on the morning of D-Day Plus One.

deal with. But the perimeter per se ran southward from Sallenelles up steep open fields to Hauger, at the northwest end of the Le Mesnil Ridge. From there it continued south through Le Plein-Longuemare past Breville, then southeast through Le Château St. Côme Forest to the vital crossroads at the centre of the Le Mesnil Ridge.

It next paralleled the Cabourg-Varaville-Herouvillette-Caen highway, south again, descending through the western edge of Le Bois de Bavent to the

157

Herouvillette-Escoville area. There it right-angled to the west across Butte de la Hogue, the 8th British Parachute Battalion's Drop Zone K, to Ste. Honorine and continued west to Longueval on the River Orne. That southern side of the Airborne lodgement area covered the open ground (tank country and no-man's land) that lay between it and the Germans' northern thrust. Beginning at the Orne waterways, this enemy front extended eastward past the Colombelles steel plant to Cuverville and Touffreville, then took a left hook up to Escoville.

By noon on D-Day General Gale' forces had taken all their initial objectives. Moreover, by mid-afternoon, strong elements from his six parachute battalions plus the two commando brigades under command had already occupied their planned perimeter positions. Three regular infantry battalions plus a special armoured-artillery reconnaissance regiment would also arrive in place on the evening of D-Day.

Two of the additional infantry battalions would fly in by glider as part of the British 6th Airlanding Brigade. They were the 1st Battalion Royal Ulster Rifles and the remainder of the 52nd Light Infantry - namely, the 2nd Battalion Oxfordshire and Buckinghamshire Light Infantry, familiarly called the Ox and Bucks. The third one was the 12th Battalion Devonshire Regiment (not to be confused with the 12th British Parachute Battalion of the 5th Parachute Brigade). The 12th Devons, although part of the 6th Airlanding Brigade, would actually arrive by sea in landing craft in the early afternoon of D-Day Plus One.

The special armoured artillery reconnaissance regiment was made up of light tanks of the Worcestershire Yeomanry Regiment - together with the 112th Antitank Battery manning our heaviest British-Canadian antitank gun, the seventeen pounder. The regiment also carried a number of 75-mm pack howitzers and reconnaissance scout cars. Known as "Parker Force," it was under the command of Colonel R. G. Parker. It was flown to the perimeter by huge Hamilcar gliders at the same time as the Ulsters and the Ox and Bucks.

These more than remarkable four thousand glider-men, with heavier equipment than the parachutists could carry, would immediately upon landing reinforce the southern part of the lodgement area: The Ox and Bucks taking over from elements of the 8th Parachute Battalion at Escoville, and the Royal Ulsters at Ste. Honorine la Chardonnerette. The British 13th Parachute Battalion entered the fray south of Le Bas de Ranville between Ste.Honorine and Longueval. Parker harboured his heavier equipment at about the middle of the lodgement area behind the 3rd Parachute Brigade below Breville. All of this was to satisfy the vision of General Gale that a long, hard battle would ensue.

Without question the initial objectives of the 6th Airborne Division were important. To recapitulate, those for the 3rd Parachute Brigade were:

(a) The taking of the Varaville positions and the destruction of the bridge on the Divette Canal in that village covering Drop Zone V - landing point of the 3rd Brigade Headquarters and two of its infantry battalions.
(b) The British 9th Parachute Battalion's silencing of the Merville coastal battery, relying on the 1st Canadian's "A" Company for flank and rear cover.

(c) The 1st Canadian Parachute Battalion's "B" Company seizure, destruction and indefinite holding of the Robehomme bridge on the River Dives, and a culvert bridge on a track going south from Periers-en-Auge to a soggy-bottomed crossing at Le Hoin.

(d) The 1st Canadian's Headquarters Company keeping open the Varaville-Herouvillette highway until all the different battalions were dug in on their defensive perimeter positions.

(e) The British 8th Parachute Battalion's seizure and destruction of the bridges at Troarn and Bures on the River Dives south of Robehomme.

(f) The 1st Canadian Battalion's "A" Company destruction of a signals exchange close to the Cabourg-Herouvillette highway opposite Le Bas de Breville. Also their destruction of an enemy sentry box outside the concertina wire on the western side of the Merville Battery.

These and all the other initial objectives were crucial, but they were only the beginning of the Airborne saga. They merely represented the action on part of the first day. It was the battle of the "Perimeter" that told the tale! The tale that showed the stuff the D-Day paratroopers and commandos were made of !

By the evening of D-Day it was almost as though the enemy soldiers within a large part of the Airborne lodgement area had melted away. The 3rd Parachute Brigade controlled the ground as far south as Herouvillette, eight kilometres inland; also for nine and a half kilometres west to east behind the Channel coast, including all the ground east of the Le Mesnil Ridge to the River Dives. In total an area of about fifty square kilometres. By the same time the 5th Parachute Brigade, together with the 1st Special Service Commando Brigade, controlled a similar area west of the ridge. The commandos and the 3rd Parachute Brigade controlled the ground of the ridge per se.

The above objectives were the most vital of the brigade's first-stage goals. But writers have over-emphasized them almost to the point of obscuring the real purpose of their cumulative aim: the interdiction of German Army movement throughout the lodgement area and, by extension, the abortion of any plans the enemy might have hatched to stab the combined Allied invasion forces in their left flank. The over-emphasis placed on the D-Day activities has resulted in the recognition of only a minority of the valiant efforts expended by the sub-units of the infantry brigades involved and of many of the men who filled their ranks.

At the briefings back in England the individual plans revealed for the taking of the many separate initial objectives were directed at meeting that overall goal. Those plans had become mentally and dramatically connected to the excitement aroused by a continuous stream of exultant news that was, day after day for more than a week, released to the troops. The newly divulged, detailed plans, so secret, and so unusual because they were to be carried out by relatively small groups of special infantry soldiers rather than by large forma-tions with heavy equipment, were exhilarating in the extreme. No doubts were left in the troops' minds that this was the beginning of the end of five years of vicious warfare. That the initial objectives were to be seized and consolidated between midnight and dawn was the stuff of old melodrama, bequeathed to twentieth-century soldiers by centuries of military history.

No soldier involved could ask for more: exciting challenges, tests of ingenuity, matching of wits with a clever and dedicated enemy. More adventure in one night than most men live in a lifetime. Yet the reality came through that this was no "stage" with actors portraying some sort of fantasy. They were dealing with a battlefield blueprint, and militarily the real goal was to form an impregnable bulwark which would frustrate any and every attempt the Germans might make to force their way into the newly formed left flank of the Allied invasion bridgehead.

In reality the combined combat of the nearly three-month battle which followed eclipsed the taking of the initial objectives.

The sum total of General Gale's command, with the additions of the brigade from the 51st Highland Division and two brigades of commando troops, plus all the fighting elements of the numerous headquarters units - all under command of the 6th Airborne Division - made a specialized infantry force equivalent to twenty infantry battalions.

When this force's own close support weapons, brought in by sea and by the Hamilcar gliders, were added to the power of the field artillery regiments of the 3rd Canadian Infantry Division, backed up by the big guns of the allotted Royal Navy ships and the power of the Royal and Royal Canadian Air Forces, General Gale's Paratrooper-Commando-Infantry corps was something for the German Army to reckon with!

The occupation of the Le Mesnil crossroads was so important to the Canadians - and to the whole Allied left flank - because it was right in the middle of the intended perimeter, astride the main coastal highway that ran east of the Orne bridges but turned inland to Caen at the port of Cabourg - Dives-sur-Mer. The fact that this highway, which went smack through the crossroads, was the major coastal road leading west from the Seine River estuary to the city of Caen made Le Mesnil decidedly important! Also, the fact that the 1st Canadian Parachute Battalion was ordered to set up its headquarters here, just across the same highway from 3rd Brigade Headquarters, reflects the confidence of the British High Command in the soldiers whom Winston Churchill described as "those formidable Canadians."

Because the troops, Canadian and British, of Brigadier James Hill's 3rd Parachute Brigade had been so widely scattered their first priority was to get onto their perimeter positions. No part of any command could do anything about the scattering. It was now a fact of life which had to be lived with. So, to avoid losing everything, it became urgent for a characteristic to develop within the personalities of the individual soldiers which would spur on a rising of courage and lead them to the all important crossroads.

The scattering, the flooding, the natural and man-made obstacles, the darkness, the weight of equipment that now had to be carried over extended distances, the shortage of time and the stress associated with disappointment, confusion and uncertainty over things gone wrong, all tended to frustrate the soldiers' best efforts. Many of the planned approach routes to the Le Mesnil position became redundant and had to be abandoned altogether. But against all odds they made progress and showed an outstanding display of willpower. Although every feature of their separate predicaments portended failure, they knew individually that something positive had to be done.

In the mind of the individual soldier who had been impressed in the briefings with the absolute necessity of reaching first his rendezvous, and then his immediate objective, there was a motivating urge: "Get your butt in gear and get it done!" The new conditions, which looked like paths to doomsday, were turned around by the soldiers themselves into a formula for hope which made success inevitable. Soon the almost superhuman effort restored something like a skeleton of the original plan.

Two or three sticks of paratroops were dropped in the area of Breville and the St. Côme Forest, both approximately parallel to the northern arm of the Le Mesnil crossroads. A few more landed on Drop Zone K - the British 8th Parachute Battalion's Drop Zone between Herouvillette and Touffreville, five kilometres south of Le Mesnil and nine south of Drop Zone V at Varaville. One or two sticks landed between Bavent and the flooded Dives on a line Duval-St. Laurent-Rocheville, and another along Petiville-Le Prieur. The last two of these were northeast and east of Le Mesnil.

By some fortune of war, with more than four hundred of the five hundred and fifty Canadians dropped that night scattered hither and yon around Normandy, about a hundred landed in all four quadrants of the Le Mesnil crossroads and were within a kilometre or two from it. This was particularly fortunate because the defences to be set up there were planned to become the northeast bulwark against the use of the Cabourg-Caen highway by the German Army. Just as the British 8th Parachute Battalion was to set up as the southeast bulwark three to four kilometres to the south at Herouvillette on the same highway.

As for the Canadians who descended in parachute harness relatively close to Le Mesnil, what were their odds on finding their perimeter positions, without prolonged delay, after being scattered in rough, German-occupied territory in the darkness of early D-Day?

If you can imagine yourself in that situation as a young, fit, highly trained soldier, drilled to move fully equipped over rugged countryside, here's how you might have made out. Even if, like many, you had not the slightest idea of where in Normandy you were.

If despite your confusion after the scattered drop you were "quick to get your butt in gear" and get moving - as most men did - and decided to make a positive move in a fairly straight line, you'd have a seventy-five percent chance of encountering one of the four arms of the Le Mesnil crossroads. Even if your starting point was a kilometre or two from it.

As a paratrooper, you would know that the desired crossroads was close to the highest point on the Le Mesnil Ridge. Although the ridge was a low one and its approaches rose very gradually, walking uphill when you reached a road would most likely bring you directly to Le Mesnil. Once there, you could recognize the crossroads as being the correct one by sighting, in the dim moonlight, the towering smokestack of the close-by brick and pottery plant.

Some survivors have written about the adventures they experienced when getting from their scattered-drop locations to Le Mesnil. In some cases they even elaborate on what took place when they did get there. Private Ray Newman says:

"I dropped in semi-moonlight, on dry ground but off the Drop Zone near Varaville. Alone in the dim shadows and darkness for about two hours, I tried to straighten out the confusion in my mind and to find a recognizable feature which would set me on a correct course.

"Moving along a hedge by a road I came upon an enemy tank. I got going the other way in a hurry. A few days later we found out the tank was a hand-constructed dummy made of wood.

"Soon after I took off from the tank I met up with Jim Ballingall and a few other chaps from my own sub-unit, 'A' Company; then two English soldiers. Not one of us could figure out where we were in relation to the Drop Zone or our objectives - a disaster, in our minds.

"We spent the night lost and then met a larger group from our company. Lieutenant R.J. Mitchell was in charge, coming in from some point probably four or five kilometres south of Escoville. He knew where he was going, and because I was carrying a submachine gun he sent me out ahead as scout.

"Shortly, we managed to get on to Le Mesnil crossroads. Once there we met Colonel Bradbrooke. He appeared to be alone so he was glad to see us. We must have been about the first men in."

A letter from Private Tom Jackson picks up the story: "As my C-47 approached the coast of France at close to one o'clock in the morning, about six hours before the assault divisions came in from the sea, we were on our feet, hooked up and ready to jump. By ducking down slightly, we were able to look out the windows and watch coloured anti-aircraft fire rising up from the enemy batteries behind the beaches.

"I, Louie Goulet and Charlie Johnson were numbers one, two and three in a PIAT antitank squad. We knew from the briefings in England that the 21st Panzer Division was based only seven or eight kilometres from where we were about to land and that the 12th SS Panzer Division was within two or three hours drive by tank from there too. It had been made clear to us that both these divisions were among the strongest and best-equipped panzer divisions in the entire German Army and totalled about thirty-five thousand all ranks of the enemy's best soldiers.

"We were also aware that the River Dives was the dividing line between Field Marshal von Rundstedt's 15th and 7th Armies, commanded by Field Marshal Rommel. Further, it was common knowledge that we were about to descend on Drop Zone V at Varaville less than three kilometres from the Channel, in the defences of Hitler's *Atlantikwall*, amongst the defended villages of the 716th and 711th German Infantry Divisions. We knew these were not ranked among the enemy's best. But the 716th did distinguish itself in the D-Day battle. Also, it became known later that the 711th Division, as early as D-Day Plus One, began to replace 'ground-up' regiments of the 716th in the Airborne lodgement area.

"Our antitank gun, the PIAT, was a hand-held weapon somewhat inferior to the American Bazooka. It could only be effective against Mark IV German tanks, German self-propelled 88-mm guns, which all four enemy divisions would have plenty of, or lighter armoured vehicles. We also knew we were expected to be exceptionally vulnerable and busy for the next few days, until the heavier infantry and armoured units of the 2nd Army could come to our assistance after they were well enough established ashore. The 2nd Army would include large elements of the Canadian Army: the 3rd Canadian Infantry Division and later the 4th Canadian Armoured Division and 2nd Canadian Infantry Division, together with their corps troops.

"Over the coast our plane became unstable, which we thought to be caused by enemy fire and the unbelievable risks involved in getting more than a hundred-twenty-five C-47 transports to drop about twenty-two hundred parachutists on a small field in the middle of the night - all to be done in a matter of thirty to forty minutes with no navigation lights switched on.

"The tilting and jerking up and down made it difficult to keep our balance as we pushed for the door, and slowed us down immeasurably during our exit from the aircraft. Goulet and I landed in water in a location which was to us God knows where, and we did not see Charlie Johnson until several days later when we spotted him in a chow line. Gus lost his leg kit-bag in the flooding during the drop. It contained his rifle so I gave him an old Ivor Johnson pistol I had.

"We made our way to a cemetery on high ground where we found a house nearby. I knocked on the door and soon a man opened it to enquire about what was going on at such a late hour. As soon as he saw our camouflaged helmets tied up with burlap rags, our blackened faces and hands and our weapons, he tried to slam the door. I was too quick for him, seized him by the front of his pyjamas and yanked him out into the yard. Goulet spoke to him in French and obtained directions on how to get to Le Mesnil crossroads. He became ecstatic when he found out we were Canadian, and we left him that way as we got going again in a hurry.

"We soon found our progress to be slow. We were fired upon by some German troops and hit the ditch. When the firing stopped I poked my head up and there, in the half moonlight, I could see an enemy artillery gun with a crowd of their soldiers around it. We put all our training skills in silent movement to work, skirted the enemy gun position and got out of that locality. We then cut back onto the road we had been following. After dawn, as we came close to Le Mesnil, we could see the tall smokestack of the brick and pottery plant located there, but had to get off the road again because we were being constantly strafed by Spitfires.

"When we arrived at the crossroads an officer, Lieutenant Richard Hilborn I believe, directed us to take up positions in a hedge on the south side of the road that led to Breville and which eventually became the 'A' Company position. Battalion Headquarters and 3rd Brigade Headquarters were established about three hundred yards south of this road a few hours later. Some of the men already in position were Privates Frank Goodall, A. Pearson, Clifford Funston and Joe Roberts, Corporal Howard Holloway and Sergeant George Capraru. The sergeant was in charge for a while until his own 'B' Company position was established northeast of the crossroads, a few hundred yards down the Varaville road. All during the morning we were strafed by friendly aircraft and Holloway, with Pearson, had a very close call from a bomb dropped by a fighter-bomber."

The difficulties surrounding the initial establishment of the Le Mesnil crossroads position are indicated by these accounts and others. It should be remembered that during the "C" Company drop several sticks of paratroops went missing: Sergeant G. Kroesing's in the plateau country; Sergeant Willard Minard's back to England; Sergeant Earl Rice's near Colleville-sur-Orne west of the Canal de Caen, right in front of the invasion from the sea; Lieutenant John Madden's near Hermanville west of the Orne close to Rice; Lieutenant Sam (Speedy) McGowan's near Bures; and Captain John Hanson's near Longueval on the River Orne. As for the sticks commanded by Sergeants R.O. (Dick) MacLean, Tom Keel, Harvey Morgan and W.R. Kelly, the last five or six men from each went into the drink. A number of them wallowed in the flooded canals of the Dives until dawn. Then, in the slow gathering period, they picked up men from other companies of their own battalion and from the 8th and 9th British Battalions, who joined them for the trek to the crossroads position. It was easier to rendezvous with Le Mesnil in daylight because they could see the tall smokestack towering over the surrounding countryside.

Like the rendezvous at Robehomme and in the plateau country, movement during the hours of darkness towards the Le Mesnil crossroads had been very slow. Paratroopers arrived there either alone or in small groups. And, as at Robehomme, most who arrived and recognized the position hunkered down thinking they were the first ones on the scene. There were enemy troops in the areas of the brickworks, Breville and the St. Côme Forest, and at the nearby junction where the Varaville-Caen highway meets the Bavent road leading to the Bricqueville-Robehomme area. The enemy consisted of detachments except at Bavent. There, it appeared later, a company of German infantry was dug in.

Once dawn came things speeded up. Troops from Headquarters Company platoons and "A" Company came in rapidly. This was a godsend to Colonel Bradbrooke and his second-in-command Major Jeff Nicklin, for until noon on D-Day ten to fifteen sticks of paratroopers - up to two hundred and fifty men - were so far away that no word of them had reached Le Mesnil. They were simply missing!

164

Among those who did arrive one deficiency caused enormous disappointment: the loss of weapons and other equipment had been horrific. Men carrying parts of heavy weapons were unable to retrieve them when they landed in deep water, including flooded farm canals with mucky bottoms. Vickers medium machine guns, 3-inch mortars, PIAT antitank guns, heavy radio communication sets and kit-bags with up to a hundred pounds of ammunition had to be sacrificed. It was the only way the troopers could avoid drowning or evade dangerous obstacles lurking in the mush of the flooded ground.

By mid-afternoon enough soldiers from all four companies had persevered and arrived in time to allow Colonel Bradbrooke, Major Nicklin and some Headquarters Company lieutenants to lay out the general battalion positions on all four quadrants of the crossroads. The troops began to dig in with a purpose. The Headquarters Company platoon commanders – Lieutenants Hilborn (Vickers machine-gun), Simpson (Signals) and Croxford (PIAT), and Platoon Sergeant Blagborne in place of the missing Lieutenant Cote (Mortars) - organized their areas.

Then, around 16:00 hours, Lieutenant John Clancy and about twenty-five "A" Company personnel arrived, having completed their duties in support of the British 9th Parachute Battalion during its assault on the Merville Battery. These men and their "A" Company comrades who had filtered in during the past fifteen hours, added to several "A" Company sticks that came out of the flooding after midday and to the individuals and small groups still coming in, brought the company close to full strength. Meanwhile "B" and "C" Companies were continuing to build.

As the afternoon of D-Day passed into early evening things did look better, but not great. At 18:00 hours the "C" Company soldiers who had secured the Drop Zone arrived from their battle at Varaville. They brought along two enemy prisoners for every Canadian who had fought there. An hour later Sergeant Minard returned from England in a Horsa glider with his ten-man section intact. Then came Lieutenant John Madden and his stick, followed by Sergeant Earl Rice with his men, both from west of the Orne waterways. When we consider how almost continuous combat raged over much of the territory they had traversed - shelling, machine-gun fire and enemy patrols - it is to their credit that they ever got their missing sticks to Le Mesnil at all.

It was time for the battalion commander to take stock. With a nearly full picture of what had gone wrong on the drop the night before, Colonel Bradbrooke was thankful and somewhat amazed that his battalion was cohesive at all. He could certainly thank the gods of war for the ingenuity and determination of his soldiers. As the sun went down on D-Day it was, considering all the adverse conditions that had to be overcome, remarkable that every single one of the battalion's objectives had been seized, as had the objectives of the whole division.

The best news was that Bradbrooke could count three-hundred-ninety of his soldiers on his planned positions at Le Mesnil. Before twilight that evening troops from other battalions, misplaced near Robehomme, who had been put on course to the Le Mesnil position by Lieutenant Toseland's Bridge Party, reported that thirty to forty men from "B" Company were holding out there after dealing with their bridge objectives.

There was also bad news. First, as the sun sank and the paratroopers dug in feverishly, they gave up over half the ground they had loosely controlled in favour of continuing to establish their planned perimeter. It was their discipline and training that boosted the paratroopers through the nightmare of the first night.

Due to the shortage of men and equipment most companies of the various 6th Airborne battalions were unusually thin on the ground. In the case of the 1st Canadian Parachute Battalion the enemy, when they got over their initial shock, reorganized after dark and began to delineate our Canadian positions. As a result their patrols were able to infiltrate between our companies. This meant full alert all night for everybody.

The paratroops were determined not to give away the exact locations of their positions unless they were forced to. No flares were used to expose the enemy to aimed fire, and no weapons were fired unless it was absolutely necessary for self-defence. The self-control it took not to fire when the men knew that enemy soldiers were close, or were crawling up on their positions, was nerve-wracking. The thing to do was let them get in and out again, hopefully without giving your position away. They would then have less information to report back to their artillery gunners or planning staff. The 6th Airborne Division units were there to hold the chosen ground and not, at this time, to liquidate every German soldier who bothered them.

Once the Division and its troops under command had established their perimeter positions on D-Day, they lined up this way:

Beginning at Sword Beach, at Ouistreham, Number 45 Royal Marine Commando occupied the ground from there to the shoulders of the River Orne and the Canal de Caen. Brigadier Lord Lovat's Numbers 3 , 4 and 6 Commandos were positioned eastward to Sallenelles-Les Marmiers and up the open slopes to Merville and Hauger at the seaward end of the Le Mesnil Ridge. From Hauger parts of the same commando units, their positions along the coast being consolidated, occupied the line up to and including Amfreville. Then there was a space, open fields, between them and the British 9th Parachute Battalion, which was located at Château St. Côme, Le Forêt St. Côme and Longuemare - the left wing of Brigadier James Hill's 3rd Brigade. The 1st Canadian Parachute Battalion covered from Le Forêt St. Côme through the Le Mesnil crossroads, marking as noted the centre of the Le Mesnil Ridge. The perimeter then proceeded onward to the south through the western edge of the Bois de Bavent.

From the right flank of the Canadian battalion, the British 8th Parachute Battalion faced east along the highway through the western edge of Le Bois de Bavent down to the town of Herouvillette and formed the right wing of Hill's 3rd Parachute Brigade. As we have seen they, like the Canadians at Le Mesnil, interdicted the main coastal highway from Cabourg to Caen.

Brigadier Nigel Poett's 5th Parachute Brigade held positions from Drop Zone K near Touffreville on the open fields of Butte de la Hogue through Ste. Honorine and westward to Longueval on the Orne waterways.

With these positions established, there were three wide open areas within the initial D-Day perimeter.

1. The open fields between Lord Lovat's commandos at Amfreville and the British 9th Parachute Battalion at Château St.Côme, with the town of Breville to the west in the background.

2. The open fields between Herouvillette and Ste. Honorine.

3. Some of the open ground north and south of the Orne bridges.

All three of these areas were covered by medium machine guns, 3-inch mortars, roving fighting patrols, and supporting artillery provided by the various battalions located on the open flanks.

In the early going Brigadier Nigel Poett's 5th Parachute Brigade, in conjunction with the right wing of Hill's 3rd Brigade, covered part of open space number 2 - the stretch across Butte de La Hogue to Ste. Honorine. The area from there to Longueval on the Orne Canal, and the stretch from Longueval to well north of the Orne bridges, were covered by battalions of the 5th Parachute Brigade alone.

When D-Day drew towards its close the number of 6th Airborne Division soldiers killed, wounded or missing was heavy for one day of combat. In the 1st Canadian Parachute Battalion, for example, one hundred and thirty men were still unaccounted for; the only way they could be counted at all was as killed or missing in action. Further, the loss of officers from the Canadian battalion was excessive. Killed were "C" Company's commander, the valiant Major Murray MacLeod; our popular and courageous padre Captain George Harris; "A" Company's second-in-command Captain D.S. MacLean; Lieutenant L.H. Adams of the same company; Lieutenant Charles Walker of Number 8 Platoon, "C" Company; and Lieutenant Philippe Rousseau of Number 4 Platoon, "B" Company. Wounded were our Battalion Medical Officer, Captain Colin N. Brebner, and Lieutenant Ken Arril. Missing were Major E.T. Munro, Captain J.M. Girvan and Lieutenant Marcel Cote. Out of twenty-seven officers who jumped into Normandy more than forty percent were killed, wounded or missing in action.

The loss of equipment - more than fifty percent - also appeared disastrous. The commanders had no way of knowing how soon their missing weapons, ammunition, explosives and other tools of war could be replaced. So, all in all, the first full night following D-Day was something of a nightmare.

The enemy troops who had faced all the scattered and organized Airborne troops in the 6th Airborne Division lodgement area - soldiers from the 716th and 711th German infantry divisions and 21st Panzer Division - fought well during this initial stage. They proved themselves tough provided they were in fortified positions, or on the defensive, in small towns or villages like Benouville, Varaville, Merville, Bavent, Herouvillette-Escoville and Longueval. But out in the open in the small fields, and the bocage-country hedges, they were no match for the paratroopers. An interesting thing occurred where small enemy detachments were dug in near woods or farms. They simply melted away as soon as they were attacked! It seemed that they quietly withdrew and probably returned to their parent units. So for several hours the 6th Airbornes' paratroops controlled an area much larger than the planned lodgement area, which was eventually enclosed by the perimeter.

As D-Day wore on the scattered paratroopers attacked or fired on the enemy from many points. The more this happened up until the evening, the more elbow room the 6th Airborne Division was given. This was so except at Escoville, Ste. Honorine and Longueval, where the enemy were able to employ heavy tanks, 88-mm guns and panzer troops. By early evening the 6th Airborne Division completely controlled the ground between the River Dives to the Canal de Caen, and from the coast to nearly as far south as the Colombelles steelworks in the northern suburbs of Caen itself. So in spite of the enemy propaganda concerning their vaunted *Atlantikwall* and the paratroopers' losses of men, equipment and stores during the drop, a mere five thousand paratroops controlled this area of nearly seventy square kilometres within striking distance of about sixty thousand enemy armoured and infantry troops.

They did so while still awaiting the arrival of the 1st Special Service Brigade (3, 4 and 6 Commandos) and the 6th Air Landing (Glider) Brigade. Quite a remarkable accomplishment!

The story of the entire 6th Airborne Division in Normandy is not for this book, except to say this. For every battalion in the five brigades there lay ahead nothing but crises and fierce fighting. One challenge after another, followed by one success after another, filled the days to come. The division's perimeter could be said to personify what a Crimea War report called the "thin red line tipped with steel."

Suffice to say, a raging battle developed on 7 June and lasted in crisis until the night of 12 June when it reached its peak. Small vicious spoiling attacks by the Germans went on around the perimeter until the afternoon of 16 June, when "A" Company forcefully repelled their Panzer Grenadiers who came up the northwest quadrant of the crossroads between the Varaville highway and the St. Côme Forest. Their tanks were turned around by shoulder-fired PIATS, 2-inch and 3-inch mortars, hand-thrown Gammon bombs and Bren machine guns. The Airborne had won its battle but had not finished its work in Normandy. But the enemy never seriously challenged the Airborne's bridgehead flank protection again.

For the Germans a break-in to the main Allied bridgehead was not to be. The soldiers of the 6th Airborne Division - the Canadians included - and the commandos under command were too tough, too determined and simply too bloody minded.

The D-Day actions at the Benouville and Ranville bridges, at Longueval, Varaville, Robehomme, Herouvillette, Escoville and the Merville Battery, as astonishing as they were, became yesterday's news as the more spectacular battles of the perimeter stormed on throughout the following ten

168

days.

For the 1st Canadian Parachute Battalion the main battle began on D-Day Plus Two. All companies, the Battalion Headquarters and the sub-units were hammered by German heavy mortars and artillery. The stretcher-bearers from Battalion Headquarters and from the British 224 Field Ambulance were as always busy, helpful and brave. The men in the slit trenches learned a lot. They suffered unnecessary casualties because they had not dug deep enough, and had failed to put half-roofs on their slit-trenches. They quickly learned to remedy those shortfalls!

The enemy also sent in probing attacks from outside the perimeter. These attacks by one or two tanks and accompanying infantry were made on all the approaches to the Le Mesnil crossroads. It was obvious they were meant to confirm the Germans' delineations from their infiltrating patrols of the previous night.

But that day, with all its action, did not produce any serious threat of overwhelming power. Colonel Bradbrooke took the opportunity to tidy up his battalion. Some sub-units were moved to more advantageous defensive positions and, because of a perceived threat to his "B" Company troops still outside the perimeter at Robehomme, he organized a means of getting them back. There had been no real communication with the Griffin-Toseland force since the drop, thirty-six hours earlier.

Private Ray Newman continues: "In the early afternoon of 7 June, I became part of a planned patrol of four men. Private Schroeder (who spoke German), Private Jones (who spoke fluent French) and I were led by Lieutenant Bob Mitchell of Number 2 Platoon, 'A' Company. We left Le Mesnil after supper (of which there was none) to go to Robehomme. The idea was to reconnoitre a route through the Bois de Bavent in order to bring back the Lieutenant Toseland-Captain Griffin bridge parties, who were still holding out against the enemy at the destroyed Robehomme bridge and at Bricqueville on the Bavent-Goustranville highway.

"On the way, still before darkness fell, we spotted a character skulking along the edge of the Bois de Bavent. He was wearing a black beret, a civilian coat and airforce blue pants. He didn't fool us for a minute. We lined him up in our sights and ordered him to advance toward us. Sure enough, he turned out to be a Canadian Typhoon pilot who had been shot down on D-Day and who was now very relieved. We explained to him how to behave in the kind of territory we were in, and sent him on his way to Le Mesnil.

"The most remarkable thing about the whole route Lieutenant Mitchell chose for our three-mile cross-country patrol was that the shot-down pilot was the only human being we saw on the whole trip. We saw no civilians or enemy soldiers. It seemed miraculous. We perceived the Robehomme position as being surrounded by the enemy, yet forty-eight hours after the drop we were able to walk three miles through what was now enemy territory without being confronted. Upon reflection it appeared that the enemy that had been in no-man's-land gave the parachutists between the Le Mesnil Ridge and the River

Dives a wide berth. In our view, the 6th Airborne Division's 3rd Brigade paratroops must have certainly gained the enemy's respect, which was exceptionally good for morale among our own troops.

"When we arrived at Robehomme, Lieutenant Mitchell reported to Captain Griffin, relaying Colonel Bradbrooke's orders for the entire Robehomme force to return to the Le Mesnil crossroads position. There were a few sharp fire fights that night. The entire Robehomme affair had produced a remarkable result, for they returned to Le Mesnil that night with more than thirty-five soldiers from 'B' Company and approximately one hundred others from practically every unit in the 6th British Airborne Division, who had been dropped into 'Satan's Quadrangle' or somewhere east of the River Dives.

"The next morning 'A' Company was ordered to prepare to support 'B' Company while it attacked some houses along the Varaville-Le Mesnil highway, just south of the junction with the Bavent road. 'A' Company was pulled back towards Brigade Headquarters, leaving only a skeletal defensive screen to keep the Germans from crossing the Le Mesnil-Breville arm of the crossroads, where the enemy might come down from the slightly higher ground at the St. Côme Forest.

"I was a little slow getting off the mark when we started out because of some equipment problem I was trying to right. I was still somewhat disturbed and in a hell of a rush. Private F.N. Roy came racing up to me and said, 'C'mon! We're going to be cut off if we don't get going.'

"We started out in a hurry. By now, our 'A' Company had disappeared. This made us rush even more and, before we knew it, the two of us charged across the Breville arm of the Le Mesnil crossroads and on into a thicket on the other side. All in a rush we suddenly ran smack into 'B' Company's Captain Griffin. When we explained our mistake he said, 'Never mind going back to 'A' Company, you can come with us, we need all the men we can get.' With that he shouted out, 'Who needs a couple of extra men?' Everywhere retorts came back from the 'B' Company section sergeants: 'I do.' 'I do.' 'I do.' In no time we were in a strange section, charging the Germans.

"Men were falling all around us from enemy fire, with me worrying that if Roy and I got killed nobody would know who we were, since we were strangers to this group. As men fell dead and wounded Roy and I made it through an apple orchard and across a field to a hedge by a road. Exhausted, we took up firing positions using the hedge for cover. At that exact moment the 'B' Company commander, Major Clayton Fuller, decided to call off the attack.

"This whole thing had been an horrendous experience for me - charging through enemy machine-gun and rifle fire, with enemy mortar shells bursting and maiming all around. Men dying, and the imminence of death or mutilation testing one's courage and stamina continuously. When it was over I said to myself, 'What the hell am I doing here?' 'A' Company, in support, did get mixed up in the affair and had a few men wounded, Private Gordon Naylor being one of them. Again, I thought to myself: 'On two occasions now I've been through seriously dangerous actions to help out 'B' Company, the patrol to Robehomme and this attack. Probably most of them don't even know who I am. Oh well, the life of an infantryman! We're here only to do our job. Whether we're recognized for our efforts or not doesn't matter.' "

This simple statement of Newman's echoes General Sir Richard Gale's statement in an address at the security transit camp two days before D-Day.

"Men," he said, "What you gain by stealth and guts you must hold with skill and determination!" The message is the same - just do it and never mind the credits.

"After the attack," Newman continues, " 'A' Company went back to its semi-permanent positions in the hedgerows close to the crossroads along the Breville road to block any southward intrusion by the enemy through the scrub-ground between the St. Côme Forest and the Le Mesnil-Varaville highway. From there, as in the other companies, patrols were carried out in enemy territory almost continually to disrupt whatever the enemy were trying to do. Sometimes when our mortars shelled their positions our patrols would be out adding to their misery. At night, the thing to do was keep them awake. If the enemy were organizing for an attack our shelling and our patrols would shake up their plans and schedules - allowing time for the paratroops to shift forces to newly threatened sectors. It was tough, dangerous work but it had to be done - was part of the job - and was effective. This particular battleground strategy was known as the 'static offensive.' Sub-units were dug in on fixed positions from which they repelled enemy attacks, but spent much of their time on patrol, harassing the enemy - never letting their soldiers sleep or rest or be free from fear."

One can imagine the physical and mental stress the paratroopers had endured by the morning of 8 June, when the Germans made their first major attack on the Le Mesnil crossroads. Having arisen in England at 06:00 on the morning of 5 June, they had gone through the rigours of dealing with the day before the invasion, including the move to the Down Ampney and Harwell airports and the flight into combat. Next came the chaos of the drop and their struggle to rendezvous - fought mostly in the swamps of "Satan's Quadrangle" and in the forests - plus the conflicts involved in taking their initial objectives.

Then followed the night after D-Day, when they strained all night to control the enemy's attempts to delineate their actual positions. Hour after hour the paratroopers peered into the darkness in an attempt to differentiate between fact and fiction, as conditions for mirage activity set in: thirst, lack of sleep that was even worse than thirst, fear, dehydration and grief for killed or missing friends. These conditions at night created silhouettes - seemingly buildings or villages, which in fact were outlines of clumps of trees. Tired eyes made fields appear like lakes and lowing animals like advancing enemy boats. As the buildings moved up close and the water faded away, the animals became enemy vehicles or groups of enemy soldiers. In the imagery towns moved away, the lakes re-appeared, and the forming dew made the grass begin to flow so the lake was now a river alongside which a cow became a parked scout car.

When the paratroopers who defended the Le Mesnil position that night tried to adjust their bleary, unblinking eyes and stared at the risen morning sun of 8 June, it was more than seventy-two hours after their reveille in England: three days and three nights of continuous wakeful duty and exertion. The depth of exhaustion was as cruel as physical pain and still there was no end in sight.

Twenty-four hours before, on the early morning of 7 June, Number 7 Platoon of "C" Company began its series of three important patrols into the right flank of the area in which "B" Company's direct bayonet assault would take place the following day. Soon they would be as fully awake as though they had just had a good night's sleep.

The first patrol, a platoon fighting patrol, would approach the German-held village of Bavent, about a kilometre and a half east of the junction of the roads to Varaville and Goustranville. Once there, Sergeant Harvey Morgan's Number 1 Section would charge right into the village, guns blazing, to wrack up the enemy's otherwise peaceful atmosphere. The plan was to push right into some houses or other buildings and kill any German soldiers who were inside. We suspected that there was a fairly substantial enemy force at Bavent, since a patrol had discovered during the night of 6-7 June that the area was being reinforced by their troops coming west over the Periers-en-Auge crossing. The crossing was close to the Channel, behind Cabourg and Dives-sur-Mer, and was the only bridge on the Dives between the Channel and Troarn, east of Caen, that was not an initial objective on D-Day. The goal of this first patrol was to make the enemy fire as many of their weapons as possible, and so give the Canadians an estimate of their strength in the village.

Following Morgan's direct assault into the streets of Bavent with his already somewhat depleted ten-man section, three men would run across the open fields in front of the village, where most of the enemy weapon positions were expected to be. We thought these two actions would certainly make them fire whatever they possessed on that side of the village - including suspected machine guns and light mortars or the six-barrelled artillery mortars known as "moaning minnies."

I was Sergeant Morgan's section corporal and my Bren machine gunner was Colin (Wild Bill) Morrison from Innisfail, Alberta. Bill and I were to do a right flanking dogleg uphill to the top of a low rise at two o'clock from the direction in which we had approached the village. We would give covering fire as Sergeant Morgan led the remainder of the section - Privates Gilbert Comeau, Bill Chaddock, Clifford Douglas, M. M. (Pop) Clark, Eddie Mallon and Jack Church (we'd already lost Willie Middleton on the drop) - on a furious charge right up the main street of Bavent. Nine men, with no artillery support or heavy mortar fire in advance, dashing up the street firing wildly from their hips until, at Morgan's command "Take up positions!" all but two would seek out advantageous sniping locations.

The two exceptions were Morgan himself and Chaddock, who were to charge into a two-storey building. It didn't matter which one. Just any two-storey building. The idea was to do a standard enter and search procedure.

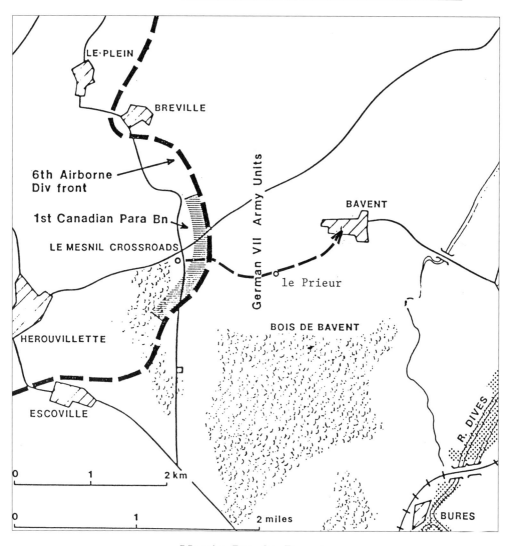

Morning Patrol to Bavent.

Lieutenant Sam McGowan's early morning platoon fighting patrol to Bavent.
Sergeant Morgan led #1 section into house to house confrontation,
himself taking two Schmeisser bullets in his gut.
G. A. Comeau killed charging up main street.
Corporal and machine-gunner work way to vacant lot in
upper town and give support fire.
Three hand-picked men race across enemy's open sights.
A number of enemy company left dead.
Covering fire from firebase was excellent.

They would search for enemy snipers or machine-gun nests on the upper floor or on the village rooftops. We knew how good the Germans were at establishing such positions. The fact had been drummed into us by wounded veterans repatriated to England from Italy.

I took off on that beautiful sunny morning with my 2-inch mortar, my rifle, two bandoliers of rifle ammunition and all the mortar bombs I could carry, together with grenades, a Gammon bomb and antitank mine. Morrison, also heavily burdened, had no trouble keeping up with me; he was a huge raw-boned farm lad of twenty-one, as strong as a horse and wiry as a Tasmanian devil. Sergeant Morgan gave us just enough time to get close to the two o'clock position at the top of the rise, then began his charge.

As they raced up the main street Morgan and his six soldiers met heavy small-arms fire from the opposite end of the street. Meanwhile, up on our rise, Morrison and I dove behind a pile of stones grown over with weeds and wild grass. There were numerous live targets, and while he hammered away with his Bren machine gun my little 2-inch mortar did its stuff. It put down smoke bombs close to the main street between our men and the enemy firing positions, but to no avail for Private Comeau. He was stitched across his chest by a machine gun before he managed to respond to Morgan's "Take up positions!" command. Good old Comeau, probably dead before he hit the ground.

Morgan and Chaddock did their standard entry drill; through the door almost simultaneously, one sweeping the first room to the left, the other to the right, where they killed two German soldiers. Then, after exploding a hand grenade on the space above the hall stairway, up they went and cleared the upper floor. They did their rapid search and, within seconds, Morgan led Chaddock to another building, tossing grenades in as chunks of concrete and brick flew everywhere from enemy machine-gun fire. The bullets sprayed nearby as they stepped aside to let their lobbed-in grenades explode. Another standard-drill entry brought them face to face with a big German sergeant. He and Morgan must have fired at the same instant, for the German fell to the floor and Morgan was wounded. He had two *Schmeisser* rounds in his abdomen on his right side.

Morgan called for a retreat from the village, which took him a few minutes to get organized. Morrison and I had hit on the enemy with a few quick machine-gun bursts and shrapnel-type mortar shells. Some of them were now coming out of upper floor windows and scampering along small ledges to escape over the roofs. One or two other enemy machine gunners had zeroed in on our position on the rise, so we put down two smoke grenades and went like hell down the slope to our firm firebase. Our firing time, it seemed, had lasted only a few minutes. The results of both parties' efforts had already shown that there were a large number of well-equipped enemy in the village.

As we raced towards the firm firebase, made up of Platoon Headquarters and Sergeants Dick MacLean's and Harry Wright's sections, we could hear Morgan yelling orders to his men not to go here or to go there. When he came tumbling over a low stone wall, which had marked our jumping off point to begin with, he was clasping his bleeding abdomen.

He went straight to surgery at 224 Field Ambulance under his own steam. After field treatment he was evacuated to England where he survived.

Most of the platoon members felt the reaction from the enemy in Bavent had been sufficient to gauge their strength. Lieutenant Sam McGowan, an exuberant, tough-minded and highly likable officer, was still not satisfied. Nobody can remember him taking them on a patrol that he did not press to the limit. He complimented the patrol on their achievement but now called for his three man decoy brigade. By coincidence, their names all began with an S: Corporal Saunders and Privates Sauder and Swim.

The "three S's" lit out and headed for a small evergreen copse some hundred and fifty yards away. At roughly the same distance, along the edge of Bavent, were further enemy positions as Lieutenant McGowan had guessed.

The enemy let the three Canadians get almost half way across the field, then opened up with three machine guns and rifle fire. The field had been ploughed recently and seemed to boil around their feet as they ran through the storm of bullets. Amazingly, they covered the distance without taking a hit. Once into the copse they took cover and recovered their breath. They then crawled to the enemy side of the copse and observed the German positions. Soon we saw them reappear on the firm-firebase side of their treed cover. From there Corporal Saunders signalled with his arms that they were ready to come back, and the race was on again. It may be true that miracles happen in combat, but watching them recross the field through an even more concentrated volley of fire than before left us feeling stunned. But McGowan had the information he was after. Now we knew for sure that the enemy had at least a full company of troops in the village of Bavent.

There were a couple of interesting side results. When Morgan's section assaulted the village at its southeastern tip the enemy quickly retreated to its northwestern outskirts. They gave up nearly the whole village to occupy a fringe on its northwest side. The Canadians, who had been green troops until two days before, found the whole thing to be a great morale builder. They now knew their enemies were, like themselves, subject to human frailty. They had done it all, and the enemy, though well armed and in good positions, had managed to kill only one of them.

During the action Sergeant Mosher MacPhee, Corporal Murray and Private Mokelki had moved up beside a thick hedge on the south edge of Bavent and were about half way to the village's west end. They had captured a German infantry mortar with a large supply of ammunition. Shrapnel had punched a hole in the mortar's barrel a few centimetres below its muzzle, but the weapon still had about three quarters of its thrust. The three men lobbed a continuous stream of shrapnel bombs into the northwest quadrant of the village during the whole action.

When the patrol got back to Le Mesnil its troops were both sad and elated. The killing of Comeau and the severe wounding of Morgan weighed heavily upon them. Yet knowing that they could shake up a much larger body of enemy soldiers boosted their confidence. Even so, everyone was happy to be well out of it and figured it would be some time before they'd have to do something as crack-brained again. Nine men with light but well-organized support from a firm firebase had assaulted a considerably greater enemy force, killed four to six of them and wounded others, and got away with it. They wondered when the Germans would try to do something like that to them. Everyone dug a little deeper and resumed a full alert at 09:30 hours.

The illusion that there would be a spell of freedom from extreme risks like those they took in the morning attack on Bavent didn't last long. By 11:00 hours, less than two hours after they got back, Sergeant MacPhee came round again. Sergeants Dick MacLean and Harry Wright, and Corporal Hartigan, were ordered to bring their sections into "C" Company Headquarters in an old house just a few metres from the Le Mesnil crossroads. There, at an orders group, Major Hanson disclosed that MacLean's section would lead a group of Royal Engineers and Forward Observation Artillery Officers (known as FOOS) part way back to where MacLean and Wright had established their firm firebase a few hours earlier.

The objectives were twofold. Two engineers would familiarize themselves with the route to be followed by a patrol that night into the rear of the enemy position at Bavent. There, they and four other engineers would place booby traps and antipersonnel mines among enemy vehicles and heavy mortars. There would be fourteen Canadian paratroopers and six Royal Engineers on the night patrol. The seven survivors of our ten-man section were to remain behind and defend the platoon's position on the Airborne perimeter.

While the two engineers were getting to know the night route to the rear of Bavent, the two FOOS would position themselves to observe a large group of enemy soldiers. These Germans had moved onto a field a short distance west of Le Plain (not to be confused with Le Plein). They were dug in not far across the Bavent road, on the right flank of the planned assault that "B" Company would make the next morning down the Varaville road.

In a taped conversation with "Sinkor" Swim and Willard Minard in the early 1960s, Swim told us how the men found it totally incredible that they were slated for three hair-raising patrols - one in darkness and all three over the same route - in one day. When they considered the numbers of enemy at Le Plain and Bavent, they felt that taking the same route - a long stretch of which was down a straight farm canal and under the shadows of arching trees - was certain suicide. Eventually, all the enemy would need to do was place an MG-42 machine gun on the edge of the canal and fire straight down its length, and the whole patrol would be obliterated. Or the enemy could let the night patrol actually enter Bavent, then ambush them after they passed into the village's rear. In either event, it seemed their fate would be sealed.

By high noon Sergeant MacLean was leading his own section, plus two FOOS and two engineers, out of the Le Mesnil position. They moved through some apple orchards to the nearest point on the Le Prieur irrigation canal. The sun was high but a sharp afternoon breeze had sprung up. The rustling of the early summer foliage and the shushing of the tall grass outside the archway of trees brought everyone's nerves to the snapping point. It was like that on every patrol into enemy territory or into their side of no-man's-land. Careful! Careful! Careful! Every step of the way might be the last you would ever take.

MacLean and Swim were together up front, one watching forward and left, the other forward and right, both sweeping the upper reaches of the treed arches. Sergeant MacPhee took up the rear but passed up and down the line fostering courage in every soldier.

They went under the temporary bridge at Le Prieur to a point opposite to where they thought the main dug-in concentration of enemy would be in the sparsely treed fields between Le Plein and the T-junction of the Bavent and Varaville-Le Mesnil roads. They turned west and crossed into some trees north-west of the Bavent road. There, they hunkered down and waited while the two engineers and two Canadians completed their reconnaissance of the water route to Bavent.

By the time the reconnaissance group returned the unsuspecting German soldiers, having dug in, were lying around on the grass out in front of the watching patrol. They appeared to be enjoying the afternoon breeze and sun, even when a shell exploded at some distance to the east of them. One of the FOOS talked some corrections into his radio. Then another lone shell exploded a similar distance to their west, and the FOO talked to his dummy friend again. All was quiet for a few minutes. The relaxing German soldiers paid no attention to the two shell explosions which had occurred at a safe distance on either side of them. Then the ground on which they sprawled began to boil. Deafening blasts turned their locality into a roaring hell. The artillery had caught the enemy right on target.

Swim told me later that, although they were our enemies, it was agonizing to watch their awful fate - dead bodies lying everywhere as the living squirmed along the ground trying to reach their slit trenches.

The patrol was back at Le Mesnil by 15.30 hours, settling down to try to get some sleep in the old house that was Major Hanson's Company Head-quarters. They were the first "C" Company soldiers officially allowed to sleep since reveille in England on the morning of 5 June. It was now mid-afternoon on 7 June.

Even then the tense soldiers slated for the night patrol could not sleep. How could it be, they wondered, that after the early morning ruckus they'd kicked up at Bavent, and the artillery barrage after noonhour, the enemy would not wise up to their route and would let them get away with it a third time that night? Surely, by then, the enemy must realize that the artillery had been directed from close by and that the Canadians in the morning raid had made it up to the village by a concealed route. How could they not now recognize the canal as the route, and not shut it off with machine guns? It seemed insane to rely on the same ploy a third time.

177

Finally one man snapped and began to urge the others not to go. Swim shoved him up against the wall, shouted at him and shook him so hard the others thought he'd fall apart. When the man still persisted Swim called in Sergeant MacLean, who in a rage reported to the company commander. Big, blustery, raw-boned John Hanson was nobody to trifle with when it came to doing one's duty. He ordered them all outside and read the riot act. This hurt most of the men's feelings deeply, for Hanson threatened fire and brimstone as though they were all guilty. The feats they had performed in the last sixty hours were nothing short of heroic. Yet the commander they knew and admired was apparently tarring them with the same brush as the weakling. It seemed cruel, unfair and, tough though Hanson was, out of character. Sergeant MacPhee promptly assured them that Hanson's tirade was not meant for them individually. Suddenly they witnessed what they had expected - Hanson grabbing the troublemaker, slapping him around and leaving him in no doubt about what would become of him if he ever showed signs of disloyalty again. Back inside the farmhouse they tried once more to get some sleep. To a man, it eluded them. The risks of the night ahead still seemed like certain suicide.

At 19:00 they were called up and issued food from 24-hour ration packs taken from the equipment of the evacuated wounded or the dead. There had been no ration resupply since the drop. After eating they were searched for any identifying or informative scraps of paper. They were given fresh makeup to blacken their already dirty hands and faces. Their killing knives, firearms and ammunition were inspected. For the next hour they studied the countryside they would be operating in from maps and aerial photographs. Then they were ready to go.

It was now 22:00 hours. The fresh breeze of the afternoon had become a moderate evening gale. Thunder rolled and lightning flashed. It could also be seen in the distant sky over the Channel - a fairly widespread summer storm. The patrol members looked like devilish apparitions as they slipped out of the crossroads position again. As before, they advanced through the orchards towards the upper reaches of the small farm canal and headed down the waterway to Bavent.

This time Swim was out front by a good thirty metres as taskman and scout. Then came Sergeant Dick MacLean with the platoon runner; Lieutenant Sam McGowan with his batman; Sergeant Mosher MacPhee with most of the other Canadians; and the six Royal Engineers. Behind them, securing the rear, came Privates Bill Chaddock, Ralph Mokelki and Andy McNally.

Alone in the darkness, feeling caught in the grip of almost certain death, Swim went on cautiously. They passed beneath the Le Prieur bridge, something he'd had a good look at on the FOO patrol earlier in the day. It looked like a German Army temporary replacement that would withstand tank traffic.

Now they were in the deadly straight section of the canal, breathlessly expecting an enemy magnesium flare and the violence of machine-gun fire lacing down the canal at them. The lightning had ceased and the night was

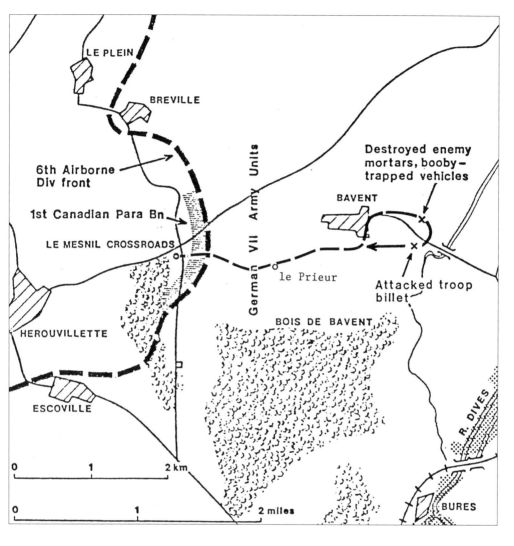

Lieutenant McGowan's Night Patrol to Bavent.

Followed same route as morning patrol.
Passed into enemy rear, split into three groups, booby trapped enemy vehicles,
destroyed enemy mortars, attacked enemy billets and fought way out.
Private Swim's confrontation with open sewage pit was devastating.
(Historically Correct.)

black. Soon Swim judged they were getting close to Bavent. He was about to pass down the word to halt, because he knew everyone else would have frayed nerves like his own and could use a short respite, when he heard a noise ahead of him. It sounded like a rifle bolt being eased home. He stopped and let Mac-Lean catch up. They sent a runner back to pass the word for assured silence and were soon joined by Lieutenant McGowan and Sergeant MacPhee.

The four men peered into the blackness. Swim quickly explained in a strained whisper what kind of noise he had heard and the lieutenant guessed right. What Swim had really heard was an enemy guard quietly unloading his rifle, not easing home a bullet. He passed back an order for Private Mokelki, who spoke German, to come forward. When Mokelki caught up McGowan told MacLean and Swim to go ahead.

The two men eased forward and encountered the guard who, on seeing them in the dark murky night, was stupefied with terror. He stood there as if frozen, leaning forward on his unloaded rifle. McGowan removed the rifle from the guard's frozen grip and told Mokelki not to bother talking to the man. He decided that the guard would not dare tell his fellow soldiers what had happened. The runner was ordered to go down the line and tell everyone: "You'll see a German guard ahead. Just ignore him and pass him by."

Soon the patrol was through the enemy defences and continued through the village, where they formed a firm firebase in the upper section. The Canadians helped the Royal Engineers find enemy equipment and haunts to booby trap. Now that they had not met the expected storm of machine-gun fire in the canal, and had been reassured by the somewhat giddy encounter with the slack German guard, they almost began to feel they were having some fun. The engineers set their charges in fine fashion - under the seats of trucks, in out-buildings and even down the barrels of some enemy heavy mortars. As they were completing their rendezvous back at the pitch-dark firm firebase, at approximately 04:00, their presence was discovered by the enemy and the jig was up.

There was shouting from both sides. Tracers raced across the night through the apple orchards on the fringes of Bavent. Wild firing of hand-held weapons ripped the area as bullets snapped past and added to the ruckus. Soldiers and bullets careened through the dark streets of the village which neither side had known for long. The wind howled, seemingly at the now cascading rain. Ricocheting steel whined, snapped and moaned on the night, feet scurried, men called out for help, the devil danced to his own tune and blind combat in lovely Normandy took its toll.

At one point, to escape enemy fire, "Sinkor" Swim jumped into a depression he could barely see in the shadows when enemy flares slipped earth-ward on their small parachutes - simply a blacker patch on a black landscape. He landed in an open cesspool. MacPhee called to him and came back to help. Swim says that except for the valiant act of his platoon sergeant his life would have ended right there.

A mixed group of Canadians and British engineers managed to gather in the canal. Swim soaked himself to clean off the sewage as best he could; gagging, retching, puking, swearing and looking for more help. Most of the patrol arrived back at Le Mesnil in ones and twos up to 07:00 hours with strained distortions on their faces.

The enemy at Bavent had been given another good shaking-up and, after feeling the impact of the three patrols, they became uncertain of themselves. This was confirmed two days later. A German soldier, ostensibly sent to draw maps of the Canadian positions but really, we thought, being sacrificed as a decoy to satisfy the needs of an enemy observer, rode his bicycle right into 7 Platoon's position. He was literally grabbed by Corporal Myles Saunders. When questioned he described how at night the men in his group were jittery and uncertain, not knowing when they might be attacked as they were trying to rest in their slit trenches. He claimed that he and his friends were so impressed by the courage of the Canadians who had attacked them at Bavent in the early morning of 7 June, that they gave Gilbert Comeau an honours burial - a firing party and the works.

It was mid-morning of 8 June when "B" Company formed up behind "A" Company's positions along the Breville arm of the Le Mesnil crossroads. They were preparing for a return to their own company positions along both sides of the Varaville-Le Mesnil road. These would be their jumping-off positions for an attack down the road towards Varaville. The idea was to push the enemy back from a bold advance they had made into a group of small bungalows on the northwest side of the road and into the yard of a large farmhouse, with outbuildings, on the southeast side. They were not far from the junction the Robehomme-Bavent road makes with the main highway to Varaville.

The small bungalows reminded us of temporary wartime housing we had seen in Canada. With shrubbery and defensive earthworks dug here and there among the buildings, the location was ready-made for defence and the enemy had not failed to take advantage of it. The large house was set in apple orchards and was surrounded by a stone wall. The Germans were very good at superimposing their own defensive capabilities upon such natural bulwarks.

As Ray Newman says in his letter, "'A' Company was providing flank protection for this frontal attack, as it had done for the 9th Battalion's assault on the Merville Battery two nights earlier. It was quite a bit better off for personnel than 'B' Company was. Two whole platoons of 'B' Company had been dropped into 'Satan's Quadrangle' on 6 June, and Lieutenant Rousseau's stick (most of Number 4 Platoon) were missing - killed or captured in one of the side-battles in the plateau country far to the east of the River Dives."

The forming-up Canadian troops had no illusions about the importance of their imminent attack on the enemy. The Germans had advanced into strong defensive positions dangerously close to "B" Company's ground. It was decided by Brigade Headquarters, in consultation with Colonel Bradbrooke and Major Fuller, that "B" Company must attack first - and fast. The officers' order-group also decided that they'd have to attack with no artillery support from outside the Airborne perimeter! Any such long-range artillery fire was liable to overshoot such a short no man's land and would then be bound to fall on Major Fuller's assault force.

When Airborne units are encircled by the enemy, as they usually are, any substantial artillery support must come from outside the perimeter. In this case, it would have to be from either the 3rd Canadian Infantry Division's support brigade, across the River Orne to the west beyond the British 3rd Infantry Division or from the cruiser HMS *Arethusa* keeping station out in the Channel to the north. With the Canadian paratroops and the German infantry so close together in the Airborne lodgement area, and support fire so far away, there was no margin for error. Instead of artillery, Major Fuller would have to rely on the battalion's own 3-inch mortars for support.

Fuller, with his sixty or so remaining men, was about to order an assault on a superior enemy force. The Canadian paratroopers, like the other parachutists on the Le Mesnil Ridge, had not slept since reveille in England on the morning of 5 June - nearly eighty hours earlier. They were sweaty, tired and hungry and were fighting sorrow over the loss of so many comrades. But their morale was high. They were eager for the coming showdown with an enemy they had sworn to each other to defeat.

As always before facing machine-gun fire, which each of them knew would be inevitable, most of them prayed. Lieutenant Toseland and Sergeants Pasquill, Capraru, Huard and Lacasse reassured their men. The men, quiet, were favourably responsive and the reassurances became reversed - it was the leaders who gained confidence from their troops when the latter fixed their bayonets. The soldiers signalled to each other with an upward motion of their rifles. It meant: "Up the enemy's arse!"

Captain Griffin, across the road to the southeast, gave Sergeants R. M. McIsaac and Arthur Stammers a final briefing. They both commanded their platoons, Lieutenant Arril having been severely wounded and Lieutenant Rousseau killed. The men confidently opened the pouch tops of their bandoliers, anticipating reloading requirements. The seconds ticked away until Major Fuller nodded to Griffin and waved a signal to Toseland across the highway. Both parties began to advance.

Fuller's company, made up of Number 6 Platoon, a few men from Company Headquarters and the remnants of Numbers 4 and 5 Platoons, proceeded through the apple orchards towards the large farmhouse. Toseland's force passed through the bramble bushes on the open ground east of the St. Côme Forest. Both parties moved parallel to the Le Mesnil-Varaville highway. They were no sooner out of their jumping-off positions than their own battalion's 3-inch mortars and the 2-inch mortars from their platoons rained down on their objectives. A line of enemy machine guns outside the stone wall encircling the farmhouse was quickly abandoned by the Germans in the face of the firepower of the advancing paratroops. But return enemy mortar and machine-gun fire farther back began to cut down the Canadians.

In Lieutenant Toseland's group Sergeant C.E. Huard, Corporal O.M. Bastien, and Privates W.W. Shwaluk and M. Lanthier dropped in their tracks, dead. Privates H.W. Hughes, M. H. Lockyer and several others lay wounded. Across the highway Sergeants George Slipp, Joe Lacasse, Bill Irving, R. Outhwaite and R. M. McIsaac led their men with distinction. The men performed willingly for their sergeants under Major Fuller, Captain Griffin and Lieutenant Toseland, and also for the two platoon sergeants whose officers were dead or out of combat. Several other soldiers were cut down as the assault progressed, but the remainder kept going until they were actually beyond the stone wall, right in the yard of the big farmhouse.

In relation to the number of men who had started out casualties were high at this point. Now conditions had changed and to go further would have meant tackling even larger enemy forces and suffering still higher casualties. Captain Griffin decided to halt the advance, feeling that further loss of life was to be avoided. Major Fuller could not fight battles yet to come with a decimated company. Their present gains were enough.

The "B" Company troops who made the direct frontal assault, and those of "A" Company who protected their flank, behaved in an exemplary way but paid a heavy price for the goals they achieved.

This was one action fought on the third day of a vicious larger battle which lasted for ten days on the Le Mesnil Ridge, until the enemy gave up mounting one concerted effort after another to defeat the paratroopers of the British 3rd Parachute Brigade and 1st Special Service Brigade.

The first night, 6 and 7 June, had seen the delineation of the Airborne positions by the Germans. On the second day, 7 June, the 6th Airborne's consolidation of the perimeter was completed by the 6th Airlanding Brigade's glider regiments.

Now, on the third day, the enemy tried to break into the lodgement area by driving across the Airborne's northeastern face - the fields between Amfreville and Château St. Côme in front of Breville. This was the weakest point on the 6th Airborne's all too thin bridgehead perimeter. The enemy thought that if they could break through there and drive southwest to meet their own forces driving northwest towards the Orne bridges from the open tank country north of Herouvillette, Ste. Honorine or Longueval, they could cut the 6th Airborne Division in two. Or even into three "pieces of pie" if they could actually reach the coveted Orne bridges.

The consolidation of Breville on the northeast side of the perimeter would have been a clever move on their part. It was a logical step in the tactics they thought would finally destroy the 6th Airborne Division piecemeal. If allowed to continue, their drive would have converted the inward bend on the northeast quarter of the lodgement area into a permanent corridor through to the Orne bridges. And if that corridor were joined by a thrust across Butte de la Hogue towards the main bridges it would have left the 3rd Parachute Brigade on the central and southern Le Mesnil Ridge, Lord Lovat's commandos on the northern part of it and the 5th Parachute Brigade to the west of it all ripe for picking!

As seen by the enemy, the 1st Canadian Parachute Battalion at Le

Mesnil formed the left shoulder of the inward bend, while Lovat's Number 6 Commando formed the right shoulder and the British 9th Parachute Battalion formed the apex. All of the units defending the ridge were fighting hard to stem separate enemy assaults which severely tested the strength of the Airborne positions.

Then "B" Company's attack came down on the Germans and achieved several purposes. It pushed their forces back from the company's forward trenches to their own side of the temporary housing project and the big farm-house, both of which had been vexatious vantage points for the enemy. Even more importantly, the attack served notice on them that the paratroopers on the bend's left shoulder were not about to wait to be attacked and then just fade away. Let them try to push the Canadians to the southeast at their own peril!

Over the next few days the enemy rammed one attack after another up the northeast quadrant of the Le Mesnil crossroads, trying to dislodge the 1st Canadian Parachute Battalion from its positions. They were rewarded with failure every time.

Chapter XIII
Paratroopers Still Loose
in the Plateau Country

Philippe Rousseau

James Broadfoot

By 9 June "B" Company's paratroops from Robehomme, "C" Company's from Varaville, most of those dropped west of the River Dives in "Satan's Quadrangle" but not in the plateau country, together with "A" Company's and Headquarters Company's, were concentrated at Le Mesnil. Only the men in the plateau country and those in the southeast corner of "Satan's Quadrangle," east of the River Dives, were still missing. Some had been drowned in their efforts to get out of the flooding or were killed or captured by the enemy. Those who had survived but had not made it back to the west side of the river, were still on the go and game, even now, to outwit their potential captors. The almost matching Nazi line which had formed to oppose the Airborne perimeter had been thickened up by the enemy. It now formed a solid line which confronted the entire 6th Airborne Division and the troops under its command.

There was a very slim chance that any of the remaining misplaced Airborne soldiers east of the River Dives could infiltrate from the enemy rear to reach their own lines, even if they could move west to the right bank of the river. The approaches to the rear of the beefed-up enemy positions were almost impenetrable.

They could only fight to the finish or surrender. There is no evidence that the latter choice was made except where men were seriously injured, out of ammunition or caught dead to rights in the sights of enemy small arms at close range. All along the coast - from Regimental Sergeant-Major (Knobby) Clark in the eastern Dives section of "Satan's Quadrangle" to Lieutenant Marcel Cote's stick at Montivilliers-Octiville, northeast of Le Havre - there is evidence of fighting from D-Day to the evening of 8 June, D-Day Plus Two. And, as we shall see, even after that there were Canadian paratroopers on the loose amongst the enemy for the next seventy-five days or so.

After the stubborn action in the pasture between the rear of Villers-sur-Mer and the lower western slopes of Mont Canisy near Deauville, the Germans apparently took care of the bodies of the Canadians who died there. The remainder, most of whom were wounded, were captured and finally removed from the area. The Germans also took away their own dead and wounded plus the paraphernalia of battle, especially the Canadian equipment and weapons.

Six of the twenty men from Lieutenant Rousseau's stick were now known to be dead. Privates A. J. (Scotty) MacInnis, Colin MacKenzie and A. Moffatt were missing. Boyd Anderson and Jim MacPherson were still in the barrel. The other nine men who also stood and fought to cover the majority out of the battle area were eventually captured, six of them wounded. This small sub-unit had been stranded in unfamiliar territory with no heavy weapons to support them and, most of the time, with no commander above corporal. They had no way to determine the strength of the forces stacked against them yet parried the enemy for more than forty hours. Those captured were moved into a sunken lane to be searched and tied up by their wrists with binder-twine with their hands behind their backs. They counted their captors as having the equivalent of four forty-man infantry platoons. The Germans, supported by medium machine guns, 3-inch mortars and smoke canisters, had ambulances, medics and signallers. They behaved reasonably well as far as the Geneva Convention was concerned - except for the binder-twine.

Anderson and MacPherson, still hidden in the barrel, knew the enemy would find their small backpacks in the depression along the north side of the hedge. Their personal regimental numbers, stencilled inside their pack-flaps, could easily tell the Germans that these two Canadian paratroopers were still on the loose somewhere close by.

They decided to wait right there in the barn to allow time for the Germans to lose interest in the area. Surely, they told themselves, the enemy would not come back to the battle site after that length of time. They waited two nights, leaving the barn only during darkness.

Anderson continues in the written description he sent to me: "When a few hours went by we began to change our thinking. It came to us our situation was extremely dangerous and we could easily believe the enemy had dug in around us. If the Germans really combed the area looking for men they knew to be on the loose, and did not find any who matched our regimental numbers, they might quite reasonably decide to come back to the shed or set up a permanent watch for us. Sure enough, on D-Day Plus Two (8 June) French civilians and German soldiers came in from time to time to refresh themselves with cider. We decided we had better get out of there that night to look for safer accommodation. Besides, we had eaten the English tea-biscuit and only had one emergency-ration supercharged chocolate bar left for the two of us.

"Thinking that most of our comrades were dead, we made up our minds we would move only after we had used our brains. Then we would move slowly and carefully away from the coast, directly to the south. Our heads told us that, since we had heard tracked vehicle movement going west during the nights, we'd need to be very careful crossing any byways or highways. The aim was to get deeper into France before swinging west toward the original division lodgement area.

"Close to midnight on 8 June we departed from our protective barrel for good. We crawled slowly and carefully for a long time to the south, and we really did do what we had planned. We moved like the old North American Natives we had heard about in Ontario and the Wood Mountain Hills of southern Saskatchewan as youngsters - stealth, brains and discipline - eyes and ears wide open - with cover always at hand. Sometimes we'd recognize enemy activity in our path, then we'd back up and try again. When the first grey streaks of dawn showed up to the west on the morning of 10 June we felt good, but naked because we had made the difficult decision to leave our weapons behind in the barrel. Our mission had solely one purpose, to get to Le Mesnil where we could join the fight to free France.

"We found a dense copse of evergreen trees and sacked out for the day on some green moss. When darkness came we got on our way again cautiously and silently, especially when crossing highways. That night we followed the same pattern and the following morning we hunkered down on a high ridge looking down a long valley. The traffic through its winding road was largely French civilians going to church with horses and wagons for transportation. That afternoon the horse-drawn wagon trains of the *Wehrmacht* started rolling again. We thought, 'For cripes' sake, if they're down to this there can't be much room for this war to continue.' How wrong we were! We had dropped at midnight Monday, 5 June, and the sixth, D-Day, was Tuesday. It was now midday the following Sunday, 11 June.

"When the sun was low in the west we watched horse-drawn artillery and wagons filled with supplies heading into the sunset. We had never seen horses being used in our army and so were completely mesmerized by the show. The horses were well taken care of and we could see the glint of the sun sparkling off their brushed rumps. As the sun went down we thought it would be easy to get across the highway but then we waited too long and the enemy moved the wagons up close to each other, so we had to wait until the whole wagon train passed us by close to midnight. Next afternoon, starving, we were about to approach a house we had been watching all day when some German officers came out of it. We were less than a hundred yards from them - a close call.

"We followed a pattern now of going cross-country at night, never on roads. We discovered that potatoes were forming on the spring plantings, golf ball size, so we lived off them whenever we could find them - raw. If we had not been in such top-notch condition when we left England we would not have been able to go on. About 14 June, after an all night rain which continued into the next afternoon, we knocked upon a doorway.

"A young housewife came to the door. After some explanations, using our English-French phrase book, she called to her twelve-year-old son who took us to the upper loft of their barn and hid us there. Before dark a thirty-year-old man, a school teacher who was the lady's husband I suppose, came to the barn with some delicious loaves of French bread, smoked sausage and lots of cheese with a bottle of cider. What a feast!

"When we had eaten he asked us how it felt to be eating German officers' food. He reassured us we need not worry, we would be safe in the loft and should be prepared to move the next afternoon. When we awoke in the morning we were confident. We had slept with a roof over our heads for the first time in nearly a week, and on full stomachs. Our plan was going well. We were now fairly deep into France, well south of the Rouen-Caen highway, somewhere southwest of Lisieux.

"The next afternoon the school teacher came and led us about six miles farther south to a farmyard that was hidden away in a heavily forested big valley. The farmhouse was a huge one and some British paratroops were gathered there. The lady of the house was a nurse from Caen. She was home on vacation when the invasion came and could not get back. One of the British paratroopers had a sprained ankle and as yet could not be moved. The others had a Vickers medium machine gun set up to cover the valley, and told us they were seven miles from any other travelled highway.

"There had been little food in the house when they arrived and now it was gone. With MacPherson and I present there were now over twenty soldiers and the lady of the house to feed. There was bickering going on among the British lads so we didn't like the set-up. Neither did a shot down American pilot who was with them. We two and the pilot asked a Frenchman who came by to get us some civilian clothing so we could proceed further south and make a proper attempt to contact the French Resistance to help us get to the Le Mesnil Ridge. This he did and we planned to strike out on our own, just the three of us, the next day.

"The British lads were planning to go out to forage for food so I, having seen a great flock of sheep about three miles back as we were being led in by the school teacher, and having had lots of experience in catching and slaughtering sheep back home on the ranch, volunteered to do the job for them. The nurse had soaked and rebandaged my now infected and swollen hand, and I was in relatively decent shape. I timed it so we would get to the sheep a little before dark, which we did. I was peering through a hedge, picking out a likely victim, when I heard one of the British lads say, 'We've had it, mate.' I turned my head and stared straight into eight German rifles and submachine guns. I was stunned and felt like every one of the weapons was especially pointed at me. It was now the 16/17th of June.

"The enemy had come upon us on bicycles and we'd never heard a sound. I felt pretty strongly we'd be shot, as some insinuated we would be. However, we were taken in enemy staff cars to a guarded building. When we were escorted inside I received a most pleasant surprise. There in front of me were several of the soldiers from my D-Day stick, men from the battle in the pasture whom I figured were all dead. The Battle of Normandy was over for us. We had done our best!"

The reason Jim MacPherson did not go with Boyd Anderson on the sheep butchering foray was that a schedule had been set up to man the Vickers machine gun outside the house in the forested valley. It was now time for Jim's scheduled turn on the gun. He had volunteered to take Boyd's place so that Boyd could carry on with his plans.

When Boyd didn't come back, Jim and the American Thunderbolt fighter pilot discussed striking out on their own. When more time went by and

Boyd still did not return from his sheep foray the American decided to leave. But Jim, the only remaining Canadian, persuaded him to wait.

"With my experience as a deep woodsman in northern Ontario, I felt I should help the others out before we left," Jim MacPherson says.

"The nurse had doctored the wound behind my knee and with a few days rest while we were there it felt much better. I took two of the British lads and, like Boyd had done, went on a foraging patrol. After a long time we came upon a herd of cattle. We rounded up a young steer and I led it into some woods and butchered it.

"The American pilot's name was Richard Savage Carlton Reed. We called him Dick. He came with us on the meat patrol but took no part in the foul deed of rustling the steer except to give us some pointers on how to skin it. It was a long heavy haul to carry the beef quarters back, but by the late afternoon I was roasting beef for the lot and stuffed some into a metal container so Dick and I could push on that night.

"Dick had received a leg wound in the dogfight in which he was shot down. The first couple of days out we did not make good time. He had been given some bandages and ointment from the big house before we left. At the end of the second day we came upon a trail which ran southwest, a direction we did not wish to take, so we set ourselves a course across country to the south. Immediately, we ran into rough country, thick with forest and underbrush which didn't do much for Dick's leg or our pace of advance. It did not take long until we were feeling travel weary and trail worn, but we persevered and by morning broke out onto some farmland. Our roast beef was already gone so we decided it was time to take a chance and contact some civilians.

"When the farmer opened his door he appeared as though he was looking at an apparition. But with Dick using my phrase book and with the few words of French I knew we convinced the farmer we were not Germans in disguise. It was not long until we were devouring a super-hearty breakfast. Between bites we were able to make the people understand we really needed to get in touch with the French Resistance. If there were any in the area this family was not about to reveal them to us. I needed more civilian clothing and was presented with a pair of pants, a shirt and a nondescript jacket. Our red berets had black linings in them so I was wearing mine inside out to look like a Frenchman. The clothing was from some huge man, twice my size. That was great, as I did not want to get caught without my uniform on. I just pulled everything on over it - hot but effective.

"As we left we thanked the people profusely. In fact we could not thank them enough. Our stomachs were full. We had clothing for a reasonable disguise and could now follow side-roads instead of going cross-country. It certainly felt good to travel in daylight where we could identify trouble before trouble found us. We now made good time, for we had entered a part of Normandy where apple orchards stretched for miles and miles. Up until now we had been changing course a lot due to the forest and thick underbrush. Now it was much easier going but very warm with all the extra clothing.

"By evening on the first day in the orchard country we came upon an old shack - no windows, no doors, no maid service, no indoor plumbing, but lots of air conditioning through the roof. We hit the floor and went to sleep. The night became cold and we were glad for the extra clothing that caused us to heat up in the daytime. We twisted and turned all night and when I sat up in the morning there on the wall was an old calendar. What do you suppose was the feature above the date sheets? Nothing less than a map of the Department of Orne. At last we were able to locate ourselves on a map of Normandy and could steer a course to or from any town we choose.

"After a washup in a little creek we stopped at another farm and had breakfast, which as usual in that part of France consisted of bacon and eggs, some kind of vegetable, lots of bread and cheese and coffee made of roast barley - rank! The food was good though and the people, especially under such conditions, were exceptionally generous.

"One evening we came upon a huge, run-down red brick building with turrets and a brick wall around it - a once elegant château whose time had faded into obscurity long ago. As we entered a high arched gate, admiring the tall arched windows and doors and thinking the place was vacant, a pair of shutters opened on the third floor and a veritable old hag, white-haired and squawky voiced, lashed out at us in the proverbial witch's tone. Without understanding a word she said we knew we had better get to hell out of there. She wanted nothing to do with us and we figured she would turn us in without hesitating. I'll tell you, we put some distance between her and us before the evening turned to night, and even then we kept on going for quite a while before settling down for the night.

"The next day we were proceeding along a lonely side road when we met a man who could speak English quite well. After telling us he was from Belgium he asked us if we had eaten yet that day. Since we had not, and it was getting on into the late afternoon, he offered to go and get us some food if we would remain where we were. After he had gone Dick became quite uneasy. He hadn't liked the guy. It didn't take us long to get out of there and within twenty minutes or so we heard the baying of a bevy of dogs. We will never know the answer to the obvious question.

"There is no question that while we were slowly yet successfully achieving what we wanted to do many things were working against us. Our lack of normal rest, continuously living off the land, unable to cook food and averaging only one meal every two or three days were bad enough. Exposure to heavy rains meant wearing dirty wet clothing. Frustration over impediments to progress as we moved across forests and rough soggy ground, and fear of becoming trapped, also took a toll on our physical well being. We had to consciously make our wits stay sharp as we watched the wearing down of our physical systems, which fed off our own body fat.

"Three days after our brush with the old hag in the run-down château we came upon a large two-storey concrete structure with no apparent windows and only one boarded up door at ground level, and one vacant square opening on each floor to let the daylight in - no windows or shutters on them to keep the weather out. We entered to reconnoitre and found it absolutely empty with a cement floor. There was an opening for a stairway to the second level, but no stairway in place and no ladder to get up by. Using a system of leg-up combined with a shoulder stand, I arm-pulled my way up and then reached down and pulled Dick up beside me. We found nothing except a mound of straw in one corner. The structure looked totally unused and seemed to be a perfect place to hide in safety. We checked out the square opening at the back and the surrounding countryside. There was an escape route there because of the sloped roof of a shed attached to the ground floor which ran out close to the forest. We hunkered down on the straw and fell asleep.

"Suddenly we were awakened by a rifle shot close by and, even with all the stiffness in our joints, snapped to our feet. Nerves frayed, we controlled our movements with great difficulty. Squinting through a crack in the concrete wall we saw a German soldier carrying a dead rabbit. He was heading in the direction we had come from, but we had not come across any sign of an enemy encampment. Was he lost or had we missed something? The soldier went on his way and exhaustion put us into a deep sleep once again. When we came to the sound of excited voices came from the lower floor. Peering over the edge of the vacant stairwell we saw, there below, two men butchering beef. Besides the two men, as if this was a black-market operation, there were a half-dozen customers, some of them with great wads of money in their hands.

"We knew we were now in mortal peril, for death was the penalty for black marketeering. The only reason these people were here was that, like us, they thought there was no one else around. If they became aware of us there was no chance that they'd let us live. Witnesses meant certain death for them and they'd never take the trouble to hear our reasons for being there. Dick put it together that there might be a connection between the German with the rabbit and these men. Maybe he was part of a group searching for these black-market people. If he brought his fellow soldiers back to search this place, and the Germans found us, they would lump us right in with them and we'd be goners anyhow.

"Dick caught me by the collar, eased me back from the stairwell opening and motioned for me to take off my shoes as he was doing. We then tiptoed to the square opening at the back and slipped down onto the shallow sloping roof of the extension to the main building. Quietly, we walked across the roof, dropped to the ground at the back and took off into the forest. We moved as fast as we could but it was a long time before we breathed full drags of air. We now headed south by southwest."

Morris Zakaluk was still on the loose too. When last mentioned he was trying to recover from having given his ankle a bad sprain on the drop just after midnight on 5/6 June. He had holed up between the two rows of thick bushes of a double hedge, had several close calls with the enemy, and heaved himself along between the hedges as he tried to reconnoitre his surroundings to pin down where he might be. With enemy troops everywhere he decided to hunker down right among them. He was still close to the position he first took up after getting out of his parachute. It was now D-Day Plus Two and his ankle, though still painful, was feeling somewhat better.

On the third day his problem was still how to contact a farmer who might help him link up with the French Resistance.

Morris says: "Unexpectedly, I saw some movement in one of my hedges. It turned out to be two men from my own stick. They had a Vickers machine gun and belts of ammunition. We had a conference and decided that, since I was hurt, I would stay with the machine gun and they would leave to try to make contact.

"I was alone again and could have easily lashed out at the enemy still dug in around the farm, but it would have meant death or capture after my ammunition ran out. In the long run it would have been useless. In any case, by remaining quiet I suddenly observed an unexpected benefit. The enemy was moving out. When they had gone I kept the farmyard under observation. I learned the farmer knew I was there all the time, for he came towards me, examining and talking to his apple trees continually. Finally he beckoned to me to follow him. It was difficult to walk but I hobbled along behind him and was soon sitting on a little bench in his barn. I tried to get him to bring a doctor but he let me know that it was impossible. He took my boot off, looked at the bruising and swelling, soaked it in hot water and bound it with bandages his wife brought from the house. He then got me to climb a ladder, mainly with the use of my good foot and the strength of my arms, to the rafter area of his barn where a few boards lay on the vacant ceiling joists. He then indicated that I should get some sleep. First though he made certain I had eaten lots of good food.

"I had brought my rifle and grenades with me, could see the entrance-way to the barn and could defend myself from my position if I had to. Before I went to sleep I tried to get information from him about where I now was but he'd have none of it. I was no better off in that regard than before but one of the Vickers men, who had gone to contact the Resistance, had said he thought we were somewhere a long way east of the Dives. The farmer would not confirm this for me either and could not understand my fragmentary French or much of my sign language. It was now late in the day and when he and his wife left the barn I flaked out.

"The next morning he helped me down from the loft and gave me boiled eggs, bread and milk. He then took me outside to a horse and wagon. The wagon was loaded with hay and he hid me there. It was a long ride but eventually, in the afternoon, we came to a farm where I got out of the hay and met some people who took me in. I took out my silk map of northern France and my phrase book. The new people made me understand that there was no doctor and no way for me to get west to Le Mesnil. I was able to let them know that I had either sprained or cracked some bones in my ankle, and they convinced me the condition would slow down the process of connecting up with the Resistance. Later I devoured large amounts of bread, cheese and milk and was thankful for that!

"The next day a young Frenchman comes by who can talk broken English. He leads me patiently and ever so slowly to another farm. We travel all night, stopping frequently to rest my ankle. Finally we get to the edge of a wood where he makes some bird-call imitations with his mouth which are followed by some cow mooing from the farmyard. 'C'est bon,' he says and we proceed to the farmhouse.

"This farm looked like our own back home, mixed farmers as we were. For the first time I turned nostalgic and worried about my parents and family, wishing I were there instead of here. That did not last long, though, because a young teenager who could speak good English began to interrogate me. He wanted to know how many of us had landed, where and how. I could not tell him these things and wondered how to solve the problem, since it was now obvious they thought I might be a Gestapo infiltrator.

"I still had my uniform on, my rifle and ammo, my Canadian cigarettes, my silk map and my dog-tags, What more proof did I need? 'Well,' he says to me, 'the Gestapo have all that equipment from dead Canadians, and they're now out there trying to trap us.'

"I explain that I'm sorry about that, but that I'm no goddam Gestapo officer. We're in a dilemma and I can tell my broken Canadian-Ukrainian accent is causing a lot of the trouble. They are armed with automatic weapons and have not bumped me off just yet. So I say, 'Someone mentioned that you have other Canadian parachute soldiers in hiding. Bring them here, or blindfold me and take me to them, so they can confirm who I am.'

"The English speaker says, 'We have to keep moving. The enemy has whole battalions of Gestapo spread out over Normandy now. The whole countryside is being searched. We'll move fast at night and with great care.' A few days pass and my ankle is getting better now. I can walk and even run a little. It crosses my mind I should break away from them and strike out on my own, since they really won't give up the thought I might be an enemy infiltrator.

"But I have to be careful about that, for if I do break away, and they catch up to me later, they'll be convinced I am an agent and will shoot me for sure. There's no doubt they are a courageous group and, after all, we are fighting the same enemy. They get ready to move. The plan is for me to travel on the handlebars of a bicycle. Now there's a problem, I'm still in uniform. They solve it by getting a piece of burlap large enough to cover up my camouflaged smock and equipment, Sten gun and grenades; my rifle is now taken from me. Before I have time to appreciate what is going on we're coursing along back roads and trails, with me still sitting on the handlebars of a bicycle.

"We are now in an area where the signs of war are everywhere. Dogfights in the sky, droves of bombers rumbling overhead, the dull thuds of bomb explosions in the distance. As we pass along the evidence is that railyards and bridges are going up in smoke. In another location we come upon more Canadian parachutists mixed in with the Resistance fighters. My two buddies that visited me for a short while in my double hedge position, a couple of weeks back, are here. Among this group there is also a middle-aged Resistance fighter. He seems to be a man of authority and really gives me a grilling: 'Who are you, where did you come from, why are you here?' It appears that he's eventually satisfied that my story matches with what he's been told by the other parachutists. I'm finally in. They accept me! We are now friends and allies."

In our discussions Morris Zakaluk's information confirmed statements from other Normandy veterans, such as Jim MacPherson. No immediate close friendship was possible with the members of the Resistance. If you were lucky enough to make contact with a good group, then more luck was needed to find a way to prove you were genuine. The enemy constantly tried to infiltrate these groups before the invasion.

The French freedom fighters had every reason to be sceptical. If detected, their resistance to their country's occupiers would be ended. And in the hands of the Gestapo their treatment would not be as merciful as a mere bullet in the head. But Morris Zakaluk was now, as he put it, "in!" He felt he had now made it in life. His ankle was feeling more normal and he was ready to fight a new war - the war of the Resistance.

Among the prisoners in the area there was still no word from anyone that they'd seen or knew anything of the fate of A. J. (Scotty) MacInnis.

Chapter XIV
Enigmas Surrounding the
D-Day Scattered Drop

Kenneth Pledger   *Bill Chaddock*

Ever since 6 June 1944 a vexing question has confounded some former soldiers who took part in the 6th Airborne Division's entry into Normandy that night. How could the aircrews who flew the transports have gone so far wrong?

They were supposed to drop the nearly six hundred paratroops of the 1st Canadian Parachute Battalion on some adjoining fields which together made up hardly more than 1.5 kilometres square - what one might describe as a specific pinpoint of Normandy countryside. Instead they dropped them along fifty-five to sixty-five kilometres of the Normandy coastline as the crow flies, and almost 105 kilometres if one travelled by road from the most easterly point of the drop to the most westerly.

Given the claimed record of the RAF during that period of World War II, it did seem incomprehensible. But was it? Some don't think so. Probably, the word "why?" as it applies here will always remain a moot question unless British Intelligence releases more secret information from its files. However, even without new sources of information there is much circumstantial evidence concerning features of the Airborne operation which bear analysis today. The evidence leans two ways to support both sides of the question: were certain parts of the scattered drop accidental, or were they engineered for a good tactical reason?

Was there human error on the part of the paratroops as well as on that of the aircrews? Were some occurrences which appeared to be caused by human error in fact based on clandestine orders to the aircrews? Was Drop Zone V chosen and later, during the operation, found to be too difficult to achieve? Was the joint Army-RAF equipment up to the tasks assigned for it? Were the soldiers who operated it capable of handling all aspects of it? And were well-meaning paratroopers partially responsible for stretching out the length of some sticks by having added too much weight to the loads they were each ordered to carry - thereby greatly increasing their individual weight and reducing personal mobility at exit time because of what they actually stuffed into their equipment? Extra ammunition, grenades, antitank mines and explosives.

It is now more than fifty-five years since the Normandy operation took place, during which it has become ranked as one of the most influential events in military history. The 1944 re-entry of the Western Allies into northwest Europe - so powerful in its magnitude - was the harbinger of the complete collapse of Nazism and Hitler's Third Reich.

For the benefit of those generations who were not even born at the time, it's now appropriate to review some of the technical language used then. It is of course self-evident that in wartime anything to do with military matters, and consequently everything planned by any country's armed forces, must be kept in strict secrecy and the summation of these secrets adds up, in the parlance of the new language, to "National Security." As a consequence, every added operation needs a new vocabulary - code names the enemy do not understand and will not be able to understand or decipher until he picks up slipped bits of information from the other side.

For the battle of Normandy, some of the new words or symbols which affected the Allied troops who went ashore on D-Day were:

OVERLORD: All the Allies' strategy-related military plans for northwest Europe.

NEPTUNE: The cover name for the entire assault force which landed on Normandy on 6 June 1944.

FUSAG: The "1st United States Army Group" - a fictitious skeletal mock-up of two fake United States armies in southeast England. Ostensibly, these two armies were poised to strike the French coast along the narrow part of the English Channel, defended by the German 15th Army. This fake 1st U.S. Army Group should not be confused with General Bradley's 1st United States Army, and it is more easily identified as a stage in the career of real-life General George S. Patton, its play-acting commander. Patton was chosen for his skills as a real commander, and for his flamboyance, to add credibility to the hoax.

QUICKSILVER: The cover word for various operations designed to increase the enemy's belief in FUSAG, especially operations Glimmer, Taxable and Titanic.

GLIMMER, TAXABLE: Code names used to cover a combined RAF/Navy effort. The Royal Air Force dropped bomber loads of tinfoil strips into the atmosphere above flotillas of small naval ships towing barrage balloons along the French side of the Channel. On the night before D-Day this was done off the French port of Boulogne, near Dunkirk, and off Cap d'Antifer, a short way north of Le Havre. Putting Glimmer (the dropping of the hundreds of tonnes of tinfoil strips from four-engined bombers) and Taxable (the Navy's towing of the barrage balloons) together gave the enemy a radar picture of two huge invasion armadas heading for the Channel ports of Le Havre and Boulogne, with the left wing possibly heading for Dunkirk.

TONGA: The code name cover for all the Airborne elements of the assault forces that landed during darkness on the early morning of D-Day.

FLASHLAMP: A planned series of actual bombing raids on ten chosen targets along the invasion coast between midnight 5/6 June 1944 and dawn on D-Day. The Merville Battery, the Houlgate Artillery Battery close to the right shoulder of the Dives estuary, and other important points were included.

MALLARD: An operational cover word for huge Glider brigades of the same Airborne divisions as the paratroops who had landed during the night.

These new arrivals landed on the late afternoon of D-Day before the sun went down.

TITANIC: This code word covered operations of the British Special Air Service (SAS), which went relatively deep at twenty-five to forty-five kilometres inland from the coast. They operated imitation battle-noise machinery and other misleading devices. Their hoaxes also included flare activity, dummy paratroops, mock machine-gun fire and mock artillery flashes. Some of these small SAS teams also carried relatively powerful field radio transmitter sets which could communicate from France with FUSAG in England, thereby adding to the "reality" of Patton's phantom army group and falsifying the threat of an invasion coming across the narrow part of the Channel. They were dropped at or near Harfleur, a suburb of Le Havre, and at Yvetot, both east of the Seine. Yvetot is on the eastern route to Rouen, which also leads to Paris. Additional SAS small teams were dropped at one or two points along the Rouen-Lisieux-Caen highway, with others close to the junction of the British 2nd and 1st U.S. Armies near St. Lô. These drops took place shortly after the 3rd Parachute Brigade's Advance Party from the 1st Canadian Parachute Battalion landed at Varaville, which represents the actual beginning of the landing of the assault troops in the Neptune operation.

To understand the scattering of the paratroops and of some gliders of the 6th Airborne Division, why and how it happened, and why it affected events the way it did, it is necessary to look deeper than was done in the early years after World War II. We need to know whether it was a case of miscarried plans having beneficial results for the Allies, or whether it was something which simply caused hardship for, and had poor effects upon, the operations of the 6th Airborne Division. This relates especially to Brigadier James Hill's 3rd Parachute Brigade, since most of the scattered troops were meant to be put down on Drop Zone V, which was the landing point for Hill's Brigade Headquarters together with two of his three parachute battalions. Most critical were the impacts upon one of these units, the 1st Canadian Parachute Battalion, because its soldiers were scattered more widely than those of any other battalion from the 6th Airborne Division.

Before discussing how these various intelligence operations apply to the 1st Canadian Parachute Battalion, we should recall what was supposed to have happened. "C" Company of that battalion was to begin its drop at 00:05 on 6 June. There were 19 Albemarle bombers to carry the overall Advance Party - twelve bombers for the Canadian "C" Company, one bomber for the British 9th Parachute Battalion's ten-man reconnaissance patrol to the Merville Battery, and six bombers for Britain's 22nd Independent Parachute Pathfinder Company (two for each Drop Zone: V, K and N).

All of the Advance Party units would be on the ground in Normandy by 00:20 hours (twenty minutes after midnight) on D-Day. "C" Company's mission was to secure Drop Zone V. This meant clearing the Drop Zone of the enemy's immediate defensive positions, of which there were three: An enemy signals exchange located on its southeast side, some defended houses near its southern end, and a fortified village called Varaville on the Drop Zone's southeast corner. The village objective included all the strongholds within it, which represented the enemy's main strength within the area.

It will be remembered that Drop Zone V was a small one, and was surrounded by flooding on its two ends and its east side. The force landing there after the "C" Company drop required one hundred and fifty C-47 Dakota transports. All of these were to fly down the length (less than two kilometres) of the narrow strip during a period of about fifteen minutes. This was to happen in the darkness of a partly clouded though somewhat moonlit night sky. The transports used no navigation lights, but were supposed to follow ground light markers laid out by the 22nd Independent Parachute Company group, which had flown with "C" Company in the Albemarle bomber stream.

Once beyond the south end of Drop Zone, and having discharged their paratroops, the transports were to fly on the same heading to a point a bit north and east of Troarn. Here they were to turn left 90 degrees, and fly northeast past Cambremer on their right and the Channel coast on their left, across the Seine estuary below Paris but behind Le Havre. Then nearly another 90 degrees left to the north, out over the Channel coast in the vicinity of Fecamp, and so back empty to England.

When the 3rd and 5th Parachute Brigades (six parachute battalions, with their two Brigade Headquarters under the two already famous Brigadiers James Hill and Sir Nigel Poett, and the glider-borne General Sir Richard Gale with his Division Headquarters - all in nearly four hundred and fifty heavily loaded C-47 Dakota transports) strained up into the sky above the Berkshire-Hampshire hills and meadows southwest of London that night, they formed up into three air-streams at about fifteen hundred feet. They were carrying the Drop Zone V paratroops as well as those for Drop Zones N, D and K. Beginning about an hour later, 74 Hamilcar and Horsa gliders took off. They carried everything from light tanks to elements of the 53rd Antitank Battery, reconnaissance cars, jeeps, medical supply trailers, water-tank trailers and ammunition trailers together with their operations personnel. The gliders boosted the total number of British 6th Airborne troops on the ground to nearly ten thousand.

These were the men who potentially would face sixty thousand enemy soldiers, whom they either landed in the midst of or who were within a few hours' striking distance of the Airborne lodgement area. The four enemy divisions which were either in the area or within twelve hours' striking distance of it were, in order of proximity: 716th Infantry Division (8,000 men), 21st Panzer Division (18,000), 711th Infantry Division (9,000) and 12th SS Panzer Division (20,000). When we add the enemy's coastal artillery troops, plus his engineering, anti-aircraft and German service corps troops, a total of sixty thousand within striking range is not an exaggerated figure.

In case this seems like a David and Goliath scenario, it is acknowledged here that there was never a chance the enemy would move all these forces against reported Allied Airborne landings early in the battle. Also, there is good evidence that they did some awkward decision-making and some severe bungling in the transmission of orders for the two most powerful of these divisions - 12th SS and 21st Panzer - when our paratroops intruded during the dark hours of D-Day. But because of the location of the lodgement area and the scattering of the drop, the parachutists were heavily involved with the enemy's 716th and 711th Infantry Divisions right from the start.

Collectively, the paratroops and their support elements would be alone until the more heavily supported Glider Brigade and the seaborne Commando Brigade could reach them on the afternoon and evening of D-Day. When that happened, it would mean the completion of Operation Mallard in the pre-twilight evening of D-Day. If the gliders landed as planned, directly upon their designated Zones, every operation should go like clockwork. The paratroopers knew there would be fierce opposition everywhere, but precision flying was expected to allow them to win the day.

As the low-flying armada approached the south coast of England the three air-streams aligned with three exit points from east to west - Worthing, Littlehampton and, twenty-four kilometres to the west of that, Bognor Regis - directly south of Brigadier James Hill's home town of Chichester. Once over the Channel, they continued on headings which took them to a point a little over half way between their exit on England's coast and the beaches between the Rivers Orne and Dives in France. That point in the Channel was fifty-five kilometres almost straight north of Le Havre. The air-streams now took a twenty to thirty degree swing southwest, which allowed them to slip down between the enemy's heavy Le Havre anti-aircraft batteries and the main concentration of Neptune ships: The ships now pressing inexorably for the Normandy shore between lines directed at Caen in the east and the eastern base of the Cherbourg peninsula in the west.

The streams of aircraft were expected to hit the crossing points of the French beaches with pinpoint accuracy, by which time they would be able to pick up the pathfinder lights laid out on Drop Zones V, N and K, only 1.5 to 9.5 kilometres from the coast. However, the old Robert Burns truism "The best laid schemes o'mice and men gang aft a-gley" had now been operating for some time.

Several air transports had wandered from the stream and hit the French coast far from their designated points. Consequently they could not find Drop Zone V. What's more, the tail end of the big Atlantic storm which had caused the twenty-four hour postponement of D-Day was still running in the Channel. There was now a somewhat moderate wind blowing which infantrymen call "a fresh breeze" when adjusting their sights. The military weather people called it Force 6 and it may be also described as the point at which a flag flies steadily at right angles to the flagpole. There was close to a half moon along with two types of cloud. Scattered cloud blew in on the breeze coming from the western approaches to the Channel. Far off, in the southeast sky, light cirrus cloud cover, broken into large patches, let some moonlight filter through, making the night into dimmed-down half moonlight, but moonlight bright when the fresh breeze shoved the clouds aside. These weather factors help us understand one reason for the scattering of the paratroops.

Personally, I have always seized opportunities to be a natural observer. For instance, when we travelled in army trucks, which were usually covered with tarpaulins except at the back end, my choice of seat was always at the tailgate. This provided the best view there was. So, as stated earlier, when "C" Company got airborne from Harwell Airport that night I immediately went aft across the exit aperture in the floor of the Albemarle bomber and took up a position in the Plexiglas tail section, where the tail guns had been removed or never installed. From there, since the Plexiglas ran some way forward along the sides of the fuselage, I had a perfect view of the night, the clouds and the sea with its moon path racing along beside us. Especially, I could view the sky's reaction to the tail end of the big storm we had experienced the afternoon of the fourth.

Generally, the scattered cloud was drifting across our bows as we headed a few degrees off east or south, depending on which dogleg of the flightpath we were flying before and after the adjustment away from Le Havre, half way to our destination - Varaville. As late as 1991 a member of my stick, William Middleton, reminded me of the detailed running report I gave them on the way across. Within minutes of our landing, one of the big bombs meant for the Merville Battery landed on the opposite side of one of Normandy's famous built up hedgerows and caused considerable shock. Owing to the resulting delay, I was still crossing the Drop Zone on foot when the main force of paratroops arrived.

In my mind there is no question that the Drop Zone at the time was obscured by a mixture of light cloud, dust from the bombing of the Merville Battery, and light rain. In addition to the dust kicked up by the huge bombs, a sizable rain cloud also crossed the area at the time the main force came in. On the fresh breeze it could have passed out of the area before the fly-in was complete, resulting in disagreement about the weather conditions at the time of the drop. Some men would have been dropped in the moonlight and others in the cloudy dark. In any case, it seems obvious that there was a short period when the aircrews could not see Drop Zone V or its lights, whether the bombing had occurred or not.

While interviewing veterans from the 1st Canadian Parachute Battalion over a period of thirty years, I found strong evidence that many of them jumped a short time before they reached the Drop Zone or while the aircraft made their planned turns over "Satan's Quadrangle." The turns occurred a short way north of the line Troarn-Caen, extending east but north of Cambremer, which put large numbers of them in the worst part of "Satan's Quadrangle." All it would have taken to cause this was one or two simple conditions. If the paratroops were late getting out or the aircrews were a kilometre or two off to the east of the actual flightpath to begin with, it would have placed the paratroops where the submerged irrigation canals were most numerous. This would explain the extraordinary number of Canadians who landed in the flooded ground astride the Dives, and in the awful submerged canals from

Bures, southeast towards Cambremer and a long way from Drop Zone V.

Visibility was not the only problem the aircrews encountered. There was nervousness resulting from the number of transports crowded into such a small area, in such a short period of time, with no running lights. Fear of collisions caused some to hit the coast in the wrong place, and when they missed Drop Zone V they circled and had to re-enter the flightstream under blacked-out conditions. The pressure on the aircrews must have been devastating, especially when they had to drop their troops without positively identifying their target Drop Zones or faced other uncertainties. It was not lost on them either that, along with the twelve small bombs each aircraft carried, hundreds of grenades and dozens of light antitank mines, Bangalore torpedoes and other explosive devices were carried by the troops in the aircraft - all with primed detonators which made lethal targets for shrapnel from light anti-aircraft fire while the planes were at point-blank range, only five to seven hundred feet above the enemy guns. The flight crews almost had to be wizards to achieve success on that night of nights.

These explanations by no means exhaust the possible reasons for scattering on the British-Canadian portion of the D-Day Airborne operation. In the case of the "C" Company drop - which was made without the aid of ground lighting from obsolete two-engined Albemarle bombers which arrived during much better visibility and in fewer stress-related situations - the scattering of the paratroops and equipment was also severe. It will be remembered that the Albemarle bombers were flying line-astern, three quarters of a minute apart, so by comparison there was little crowding. The Drop Zone was more visible because the moon was in a period of relative clear. But this group too suffered great scattering, and their short-term loss of men and equipment was even worse than it was for the main force. Obviously we must look for other reasons for their scattered drop. Why did the scattering continue far up the coast, all the way to Octeville-Montivilliers, northeast and east of Le Havre beyond the Seine? In short, thirty-five kilometres away as the crow flies.

Among Canada's Airborne veterans there has been a lot of discussion about whether or not organizations of command close to the Supreme Command had access to decision-making that affected the deployment of troops from regular units, without the knowledge of their lower-ranked generals such as corps and divisional commanders. The same point has been raised about the Dieppe raid. For D-Day we can only put forth for-and-against possibilities as seen from research and common sense.

From years of reading, interviewing, listening and rationalizing, I believe there are sound arguments for suspicions and biases for both points of view on why certain 6th Airborne paratroops were scattered that night. These pages deal with the possibility that some paratroop sticks from regular parachute battalions were used as decoys on D-Day, and, alternately, that every weird happening simply fits the model for Murphy's Law: "Anything that can go wrong will go wrong."

To consider the possibility of deliberate tinkering with the assault forces, it is necessary to examine suspicions that there was collusion between the top intelligence branches, the High Command, and the top political prosecutors of the war effort. And further that this went on without the knowledge of the lower-ranked army generals.

The British considered intelligence and deception to be a most important operations tool in the prosecution of the war. They undoubtedly allowed the various branches of their Intelligence Services to spend great amounts of money, and lives, to lead the Germans astray with regard to Allied war plans - and with good reason. In the long run it was efficient and economical to spend money and lives. It appears now, looking back, that the expenditure of the lives of a relatively small percentage of armed services and intelligence personnel paid handsome dividends in lives saved in the later operations. Nowhere was the expenditure of these assets greater than it was to expedite the invasion on D-Day and the ongoing battle for Normandy.

Following the creation and expansion of FUSAG, General Patton's phantom army, many of its tentacles and ramifications reached deep into France, the Low Countries and Germany. One of several which directly affected Neptune was Titanic, as described early in this chapter. The most important of the Titanic deceptions was the simulated radio communications with FUSAG's phony infantry and armoured divisions. In this the SAS parachutists in France might have been quite influental in deepening the Germans' belief in the fictitious "1st United States Army Group."

However, there was nothing phony about the sticks of Canadian paratroops spread along the coast, most of whom were fighting right in the Atlantic Wall. Although Lieutenant Cote and part of his stick were taken as prisoners of war when they landed by the Le Havre (Octeville) airport, this landing could easily have served to convince the enemy that the Allies were most interested in the Bay of the Seine, the Seine estuary and the flat land behind the long beaches all the way from Villers-sur-Mer – Deauville to Honfleur. This is especially true since Lieutenant Rousseau's and other Canadian paratroop sticks were in and behind the coast defences in that area.

Whether they were put in those locations by accident or design, if one combines the enigma of the placement of these Canadian sticks with the planned placement of Titanic's special SAS squads at Harfleur, and along the Evreux-Lisieux highway, it is easily seen that either British Intelligence or the gods of war would have created a blatant conundrum for German Intelligence. Generally, their belief was that the Allies would invade where they could get their armoured divisions onto the open plains behind the narrow part of the Channel, and secure a good port from which to unload their supplies. It was easy for the Germans to visualize that the port of Le Havre would be a colossal asset to the Allies' supply lines.

In the case of Lieutenant Cote, caught at the Le Havre (Octeville) airport, it is known that elements of his stick were still fighting, firing Bren machine guns in the wheat fields north of the Le Havre-Yvetot road, when the sun went down on the late evening of D-Day. Similarly, as we have seen,

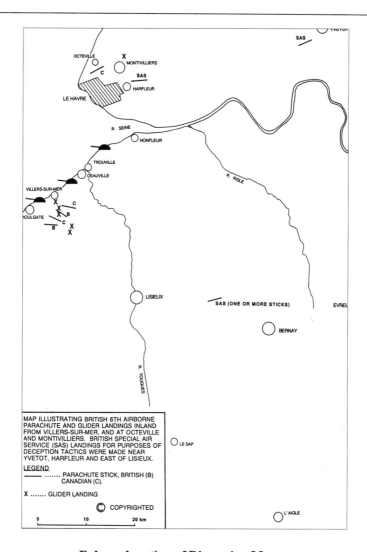

Enlarged section of Dispersion Map.

Enlarged from the map on page 134, the map emphasizes (from a German point of view) the threat of invasion through the Bay of the Seine.

Lieutenant Rousseau's stick ran a hit-and-move operation against the enemy for over forty hours, with at least fourteen of the twenty-man stick either killed or wounded by the morning of 8 June.

Before Private Colin MacKenzie of that stick was wounded, he almost certainly shot two high-ranking German officers somewhere between St. Vaast-en-Auge and Gonneville-sur-Mer. Sergeant G. R. Lacroix of the 1st Canadian Parachute Battalion Headquarters was killed up on the plateau above St. Vaast-en-Auge. In addition to the Canadians fighting against troops of the German

15th Army in the plateau country east of the Dives, there were some British glider troops under the command of senior Airborne NCOs in the area. The Canadian Sergeant Lacroix may have joined them, since he and some of their soldiers are buried together in the little church yard at St. Vaast-en-Auge. These troops (and probably two hundred and fifty others), mostly from Hill's 3rd Brigade but, on a per capital basis, more from the 1st Canadian Parachute Battalion than from other units, surely made a great contribution to the success of D-Day and the subsequent battle of Normandy. At this late date that claim might seem exaggerated, but it is not.

The Supreme Commander of all German Armed Forces was of course Hitler. The High Command (OKH) of his army was led by Colonel-General Jodl, Hitler's close associate, and by Field Marshal Keitel. The Commander in Chief West was Field Marshal Gerd von Rundstedt. Field Marshal Rommel was his Army Group Commander during the latter months leading up to D-Day until he was seriously wounded in the Battle of Normandy in July 1944.

These German supreme and high commanders, together with their staff of myriads of high-ranked subordinates, experienced very difficult problems during 1943 and early 1944 as to how they were going to defend their *Atlantikwall* against what they knew would be an eventual massive onslaught of combined Allied forces. They struggled with great differences of opinion about whether to allow the Allied forces ashore, and then defeat them in open battle upon the territory of their choosing, or whether to meet the Allies on the beaches wherever they landed and quickly throw them back into the sea.

Two hugely effective results of these sober deliberations were: Field Marshal Rommel would see to it that the *Atlantikwall* was beefed up, so that Herr Goebbel's propaganda claims would become valid and the "Wall" would truly become impregnable. In the meantime three super-powerful mobile Panzer divisions would be built up and stationed at strategic locations along the "impregnable wall" to serve as von Rundstedt's (after approval by Hitler) mobile reserve. Together with the regular defenders of the "Wall" these powerful reserves, quickly thrown against the Allied invaders coming ashore, were supposed to see the intruders rapidly thrust right back into the Channel.

The enemy did have secret information, supplied by their spies from the Allied side, which allowed them to recognize when the invasion was going to happen. They did get the warning at about 22:00 hours on the eve of D-Day, exactly thirty minutes before the 3rd Parachute Brigade left Harwell airport. Because of the Force-6 weather running in the Channel, the enemy who mattered in this instance did not regard their sources as credible. One Intelligence Colonel at 15th Army Headquarters did put that army on full alert at about 23:00 hours on the eve of D-Day, nearly two hours before the 6th Airborne Division's main drop began, but less than one and a quarter hours after the beginning of the British 6th Airborne Advance Party's entry into its lodgement area. The remainder chose not to put their men on alert.

It is difficult to believe that the enemy troops firing the four-barrelled anti-aircraft gun (*Flakvierling*) which Lieutenant Rousseau's stick straddled, and who would have been part of the 15th Army's fully alerted defence system, would not have reported immediately to their superiors that paratroops were landing near Villers-sur-Mer – Deauville. The *Flakvierling* crew had even lofted three successive flares to locate downed parachutists after the German guns stopped firing, all within minutes of the stick's landing. So it seems impossible that the enemy would not have been warned of signs of invasion by 01:30 at the latest.

Besides all that, the German Army did have specially trained antiparatroop units whose specific task it was to eliminate any Allied paratroop landings as soon as they received reports of them. It seems unthinkable, in the light of the urgency with which matters such as these would have been handled by the Canadian or British Armies on the south coast of England if the situation had been reversed, that the enemy could have ignored warnings about such crucial events.

What is more, George Robertson and others saw a British Horsa glider with its headlight on pass low over their locations two or three kilometres west of Deauville, to land a kilometre or two behind Mont Canisy near Danestal. In addition, one of the 1st Canadian Parachute Battalion's Headquarters Company sticks - a Vickers machine-gun stick - was strung out on the ground in the same general area from Heuland all the way to behind Honfleur on the west bank of the Seine estuary.

These troops may have had a definite and important effect on the performance of the German Army on D-Day, an effect far above what might be expected of a mere handful of infantry soldiers. It can be seen from the actions of Field Marshal Gerd von Rundstedt. At about 04:30 hours von Rundstedt did make a move; but he also went badly off track! He rightly ordered General Fritz Witt's 12th SS Panzer Division plus the SS Panzer Lehr Division to the Calvados coast. His error was to order about twenty-five percent of Witt's forces, under the 25th SS Panzer Grenadier Regiment's commander Colonel Kurt Meyer, to the coast north of Lisieux. Why? To react against reported Allied paratroops and to confront a seaborne landing that von Rundstedt reasoned would likely follow. In short, much to Kurt Meyer's annoyance, the *Feldmarschall* shoved a large force of SS Panzers off in the wrong direction!

Who were the paratroops that distracted von Rundstedt into diverting Meyer's troops from the Allies' real planned invasion area? They were almost certainly the scattered sticks, largely Canadian, from James Hill's 3rd Parachute Brigade who ended up in the plateau country. Other misplaced 6th Airborne Division soldiers including some glider troops were also there.

Owing to the time wasted at Lisieux, SS Colonel Meyer did not mount an attack against the Canadian 3rd Infantry Division until the afternoon of the following day, 7 June. Whether planned or by accident, the scattering of paratroops had contributed to von Rundstedt's mistaken redirection of Meyer's panzer forces. It was probably Lieutenant Marcel Cote's stick - which landed next to the Luftwaffe-controlled Octeville airport and south towards Montivilliers on the eastern outskirts of Le Havre - together with the Battalion Headquarters stick behind Honfleur, and Lieutenant Philippe Rousseau's stick in the Mont Canisy - Villers-sur-Mer region - that had the greatest effect on German reaction.

If the state of affairs during the night of 5/6 June is examined we find (with all due respect to damage done by bombing, saboteurs, and all non-regular Allied forces in northern France that night) that telephone and other communications between von Rundstedt's headquarters at St. Germain en Laye and Rommel's headquarters at La Roche Guyon, with all important enemy corps and divisional headquarters, were in good working order. This is proved by records of extensive voice communication and interplay between all those locations. In addition, the enemy unmasked the ruse of the Allied dummy parachutists very early in the game and there is no evidence of formal invasion units, big or small, located close to Deauville.

There were only the scattered paratroops. The closest SAS teams were at least twenty-five kilometres farther inland than von Rundstedt's order was concerned with. It appears that planned naval and RAF deceptions including the Glimmer-Taxable hoax - plus real Airborne troops scattered in the plateau country and fighting it out with real rifles and machine guns - caused Field Marshal von Rundstedt to act the way he did. Another indicator is that the Canadian sticks at Le Havre and in the plateau country were in action very early on D-Day, probably by 01:15 hours - less than an hour and a half after "C" Company was on the ground. Canadian paratroops and Germans soldiers were fighting, dying, being wounded and captured, not in some remote forest or pasture land as later happened deep in France, including the Evreux-Lisieux highway, miles from the enemy's fixed defensive positions, but right in the Atlantic Wall close to the enemy's huge concrete coastal bunkers. The same was true of the British 9th Parachute Battalion at Merville. It therefore seems reasonable that Lieutenants Rousseau's and Cote's sticks, as well as three or four other Canadian sticks and some 9th Battalion troops also misplaced in the vicinity, probably had the greatest influence upon von Rundstedt and prompted his misdirection of Kurt Meyer's 25th SS Panzer Grenadier Regiment. The espionage and hence deception department of British Military Intelligence was admirably served if, indeed, the scattered paratroops were dropped near and in the Deauville and Octeville-Montivilliers locations by accident. It would seem rather too co-operative on the part of fate to ordain all this beneficial placement without a reason. It all appears too coincidental for the scattering to have fallen in with operational intelligence intentions the way it did by accident!

There were other misplaced Canadian paratroop sticks besides those in the plateau country. If the stretch from Heuland westward past the River Dives to the middle of Sword Beach is examined, it is found that several other drops were conveniently placed to mislead the enemy. This can be seen if one plots a graph on a reasonably large-scale map, using light lines to represent the thinnest of thin red lines. First connect Sergeant Earl Rice's drop at Colleville-sur-Orne to Lieutenant John Madden's at Hermanville in front of Ouistreham, both in front of Sword Beach. Next continue the line to Sergeant D. R. Christianson's stick, now situated between Caen and Falaise close to Bellengreville. (Uncomfortably close, for this was the headquarters of Colonel Hans von Luck, who commanded the 125th Regiment of the 21st Panzer Division.) Now the line should move on to another landing point (thought to be Sergeant G. Kroesing's) very near Heuland to the southwest. The line should next link these points up to the Canadians in the plateau country, all the way to Octeville-Montivilliers. The picture one now sees is an extremely thin red line forming a perimeter outside the Airborne lodgement area perimeter, connected to a similar line up the coast to beyond Le Havre. That this could happen accidentally seems rather far-fetched!

It is highly interesting to speculate about what purpose such a distribution served. We do not have to look hard to come up with some intriguing possibilities. When Sergeant Rice's and Lieutenant Maden's locations are looked at, it is natural to think about opportunities relative to the defence of the Orne bridges after they had been captured by Major John Howard's reinforced company of 52nd Light Infantry (Ox and Bucks) glider troops.

There were enemy strongpoints between Carpiquet airport, west of Caen, and Benouville off the west end of the Orne bridges. It is elementary, in assessing the intended bridgehead area, to conclude that any attempt by the enemy to recover Major Howard's captured bridges would make Benouville a stiff battleground. Which it did.

Whether by accident or by design, Rice's and Madden's sticks, strung out southward from Hermanville-sur-Orne and Colleville-sur-Orne, created a conundrum for the enemy.

The proofs of such a conundrum were reports coming in to the many German headquarters during the night. Colonel C.P. Stacey says in his Official History of the Canadian Army in the Second World War, Volume 3, *The Victory Campaign*, page 123: "A peculiar feature of the German story is a report recorded as made by the 736th Grenadier Regiment's 2nd Battalion at 5:10 a.m. of parachute landings having taken place [during the night] between the battalion headquarters at Tailleville and Bernieres."

This is near the coast, in front of the intended junction of Juno and Sword Beaches. Headquartered at Tailleville, the 2nd Battalion of the 736th Grenadier Regiment could easily have had sub-units stationed in the area of Colleville and Hermanville-sur-Orne, where Madden's and Rice's sticks were. Stacey's history says next about the enemy report: "It is stated that the [2nd Battalion, 736th Grenadier Regiment] sent out one company plus one platoon against these paratroopers." In the German Army that was five platoons of about forty men each, or 200 men if they were up to strength, against the twenty paratroopers.

"But," Stacey continues, "none of the [German] troops committed returned. One may perhaps assume that the report originated in the presence of parachutists dropped in this area by mistake, and that the German troops dispatched to encounter them became involved in fighting which followed the seaborne landings."

207

Although Rice's and Madden's sticks did not directly encounter the enemy at that time, Stacey's statement fits in with the conundrum effect caused by the Canadian paratroop landings. For the German battalion at Tailleville reacted quickly against the misplaced paratroops when they might just as easily have acted against the Airborne's capture of the vital Orne bridges near Benouville. Their decision not to do so may well have resulted from a perplexity initiated by the scattered drop.

It is not difficult to imagine such wrong decision-making at the various German headquarters stationed northwest, south, southeast and east of Caen. For there were accidentally or deliberately dropped Canadian paratroops in three of the four quadrants of the Airborne lodgement area.

The 21st Panzer Division headquarters was based in Falaise. Its 125th Grenadier Regiment under Colonel von Luck was east and south of Caen in the area Troarn-Vimont, most particularly at Bellengreville. However, elements of its first and second battalions were as far forward as Escoville. It was inevitable that it would clash with Brigadier James Hill's 8th (British) Parachute Battalion under Colonel Alistair Pearson, an often-decorated colonel from several battles while serving in the 1st Airborne Division (of Arnhem fame) in the Mediterranean theatre. He is in the Guinness Book of Records as having been the only officer in the British Army ever to have won the Distinguished Service Order four times. Also, von Luck's regiment would automatically clash with the 52nd Light Infantry (Ox and Bucks) on the morning of 7 June.

Elements of the 192nd Grenadier Regiment of the 21st Panzer Division were not only northwest of Caen but north of Carpiquet on a level with the Colombelles steel plant. Their support regiments, panzer artillery and other divisional units were on Bourguebus Ridge, east of the Caen-Falaise highway. In this case, the scattered drop could have easily continued to pile up decision-making problems for the enemy, especially when reports came in to different German headquarters that invading paratroops had landed along some of the same roads that some of their own troops were positioned on. These paratroops were from Sergeant D.R. Christianson's stick from "A" Company of the 1st Canadian Parachute Battalion.

Then there was the "C" Company stick which landed at Heuland. It was probably Sergeant Kroesing's stick from the Advance Party, out of an Albemarle bomber. In a clandestine plan it would form a junction with the continuing spotted landings up the Calvados-Eure shore. Heuland was only slightly east of where a good many misplaced paratroops had landed - beneath the exit-turn of the transport planes, in the southeast section of "Satan's Quadrangle." That occurrence had to be accidental, since there could be no rational motive for it in any positive military plan. It might seem to follow that the Munro stick was another accidental drop; but that's not necessarily so, because of the differences in weather conditions between the time of the Advance Party and the time of the main drop. It's reasonable to conclude that both occurrences came to the attention of the enemy early on and contributed to the belief by von Luck's Regimental Headquarters that the invasion was taking place east of the Dives. This would impose on the Germans a further conundrum about how their formations should be moved to deal with the Airborne landings west of the Orne.

To continue with the argument that the scattering, with the exception of those who landed in "Satan's Quadrangle," was part of an overall plan, it might be said: If the gods of war ordained this whole affair - scattering the paratroops by means of a series of accidental coincidences - then the gods of war made better senior staff strategists than did the actual deception planners! The latter sent only small teams of special forces, with measly dummy parachutists made of straw and with fire and phony battle noises into the hinterland of the Calvados coast; but the gods of war were far more realistic. They sent armed Canadian paratroopers and other Airborne combatants to fight hard in the German's Atlantic Wall defences. There the troops from all the scattered units would spark fighting-patrol battles with enemy units, who would quickly report to their senior headquarters that invaders were at hand, and so help mislead the Germans about where the real invasion was to happen.

Maybe another factor was involved in the wild scattering - a mismatching of developing technologies. As one example, it is true that winged aviation had made remarkable strides in less than five decades, yet by World War II it was still a youthful science. The types of aircraft used as D-Day paratroop transports, some of which were known to be out of date even then, would not pass muster today even for short-distance intercity travel. The concept of airborne forces was even younger. The Russians pioneered the world's first airborne division in 1934, but the program faltered after the Stalinist execution (on trumped-up charges) of its main proponent, Marshal Tukhachevsky, in 1937. So the Red Army's paratroops were hardly used as such during the war. It is true that Germany's first major airborne operations were used with devastating success in their invasions of Belgium and Holland, and were prominent in the capture of Crete in May 1941 - but in the latter campaign the loss of their *Fallschirmjager* (paratroops) was so extreme that Hitler ruled out any more use of airborne forces in such offensive roles. The more flexible Allies, despite their own similar experience in the taking of Sicily in June 1943, refused to be discouraged, and we have seen that in the massive Normandy invasion the 6th Airborne parachute forces - incredibly weakened as they were by getting scattered far and wide - took all their D-Day objectives on time. And also - by that very scattering - they may have unwittingly taken part in the great deception plan of Operation Fortitude!

As we have seen, conditions over Drop Zone V were poor for part of the night of 5/6 June, and many writers have accepted this as an adequate explanation for the widespread scattering of the paratroops. My own research, including the study of unpublished accounts and interviews with fellow veterans, confirm my on-the-spot observations and memories. Weather conditions at the time of the "C" Company Advance Party drop were reasonably good, but three quarters of an hour later when the main paratroop forces landed they were mixed from reasonable to horrific. At many other locations, beyond a kilometre or two away, the scattered thunder clouds and wind resulted in conditions of visibility that were continually changing. For many soldiers it was a moonlight night, as it was generally reported to be. For others it was dark.

The fresh breeze was influential in various ways. A wind is never good for night jumps - you can too easily slam into solid objects when you have a horizontal drift-speed added to the vertical speed of your descent. At Drop Zone V that night the descent speed overall must have been close to forty-five kilometres per hour. The wind also spread the dust raised by the bombing of the Merville Battery hither and yon, largely in the direction of Cambremer. This caused a condition that, in a continually moving localized area, left the night moonlit initially but caused a completely dark period later on. Moreover the wind from northwest by west was forcing broken cloud across the landscape. Together with the battle dust, the wind vastly affected the laid down flight plans of the aircrews during the final crucial minutes of their run-in from the Channel.

It may be recalled that there were observers of the main drop who were already on the Drop Zone. They were men from the Advance Parties: the 22nd Independent Parachute Company, the 1st Canadian Parachute Battalion Advance Party and the ten-man British Advance Patrol from the 9th Parachute Battalion. For them there is no question about whether Drop Zone V was obscured from the air. At least the north end of it was, north of a line from Gonneville-sur-Merville to Varaville, and although the fresh breeze was slackening it was still blowing. Added to this there was a moderate rain shower for a time. But the most serious happening was that the C-47 transports were crossing over the Drop Zone on various headings, most flying southeast, some flying southwest and others at all points in between. At least one flew from west to east directly across the flightpaths of the incoming stream. Yet you may remember what had been stressed in the briefings: The transports would be flying from north to south and the men already on the ground who needed directions could get their bearings from the sound of the flightstream, they had been told.

To bring home the reality caused by such a predicament, think back to the British officer who took six of his own men and two Canadians to Colonel Otway at the 9th Battalion's start-line positions. When this small British-Canadian group first met somewhere close to the Drop Zone they certainly needed direction and could not get it from the "listening" method suggested in the briefings. Most of the C-47s were approaching from an arc between 11:00 hours and 13:00 hours and were exiting through a similar arc towards the south.

They were not flying from north to south but only generally on that heading. Most of the soldiers who were already on the ground firmly believe that, when the main force arrived, it would not have been possible for the aircrews to see whatever landmarks they planned to use for orientation - even if they had arrived over the Drop Zone on time, and even if the pathfinder lights had been present. Of course, many of them did not arrive on time. Owing to misplaced arrival at their coastal landfall in the first place they had to go round again, causing them to be late. Most of the pathfinder lights were not in place because they, too, were wrongly dropped.

In any event, after nearly three quarters of an hour - the elapsed time between the end of the bombing and the beginning of the main drop - the wind at an estimated speed of fifteen to twenty kilometres per hour would have extended the dust clouds southeast from the Merville Battery and over "Satan's Quadrangle" towards Cambremer. That area also coincided with the planned left-turn exit of the flight streams eastward towards the Seine, the turn itself being slightly north of, but nearly opposite, Troarn.

To further complicate the drop, the rocking and jockeying of their transports caused many soldiers to fall down after they had stood up, hooked up, and crowded up against one another for a fast push to their exits. Most blamed their upset on anti-aircraft fire. Actually, as noted earlier, there were over a hundred and fifty C-47s, without navigation lights, all seeking the small Drop Zone V - little more than 1.5 kilometres square - in an extremely short ten to fifteen minute period. Even though there was bothersome anti-aircraft fire at point-blank range, the instability of the planes was likely caused as much by fear of collision as by enemy guns.

Another thing that lessens the blame laid at the door of the aircrews was the earlier-mentioned behaviour of the paratroops themselves. Many of them even sewed extra pockets on their clothing and took other measures to stuff extra ammunition into every place they could think of. Most carried thirty to forty extra pounds so were not as nimble on their feet as they would have been with only the prescribed amount of supplies. In addition, many of those who jumped with kit-bags strapped to their right legs had packed in excess ammunition until they could barely lift their loads. This added burden seemed great even before they experienced the flight to France. But when the aircraft became unstable over enemy territory, and their heavy loads got out of control, it took some time to wrestle them into line again. The time wasted in freeing themselves from paratrooper-to-paratrooper entanglements was in some cases excessive.

Normally in training a stick of twenty men in battle gear bailed out in about thirty seconds, or in about a kilometre at the plane's jumping speed of 145 to 160 kilometres per hour. Now some sticks were being spread out over as much as three to six kilometres and in one case perhaps more than fifteen. The point is that in such cases not all the blame could be laid on the aircrews. One thing is certain: when it came time for the largest mass drop in a single lift - the drop on the Rhine, 24 March 1945 - there was nowhere near as much overloading of personal equipment on the persons of the paratroops. A real lesson had been learned - quietly, without much said.

Some aircraft which flew southeasterly, and accidentally crossed over the Drop Zone without releasing their paratroops because they could not recognize it due to poor visibility, realized their mistake as little as two or three minutes later. They then gave their paratroops the green light, not realizing they were still directly over "Satan's Quadrangle" or were making their left turn up the Channel coast past Cambremer. Those who flew on a heading slightly southwest by south would undoubtedly run into anti-aircraft fire from the flak battalion of the 21st Panzer Division's 192nd Panzer Regiment on the west side of the River Orne on the northwestern edge of Caen. The transport planes would be, by then, out in the subdued moonlight and flying down the western edge of the city. The smartest thing the pilots could do was to hightail it out of there to the south, then make their turns to the east, once past Caen, and head up the Channel as originally planned. This may be how one stick was dropped south of Caen near the Falaise road. The Merville bombing, the northwest by west wind, the dust, the aircrews' fears of collision, the scattered clouds, the coincidence of the Merville Battery dust cloud drifting between Drop Zone V and Cambremer, and the planned exit turn out of the area might all account for the large and disproportionate number of Canadians dropped into "Satan's Quadrangle" and farther eastward, up the plateau country towards Octeville.

When considering the question, "How could they have been so far off their targets?" it is also worth looking at the facts of geography and the intended flightpaths. It has been explained that the adjustment-to-the-right point in the flight plan for crossing the Channel was about fifty-five kilometres north of Le Havre. The adjustment automatically directed the most easterly flight-stream, the Worthing one, to within about fifteen kilometres of Le Havre. As they crossed the Bay of the Seine, heading for the Varaville Drop Zone V, the aircrews probably were, with good reason, concerned about the closeness of the heavy anti-aircraft guns at Le Havre. Understandable nervousness on their part might have affected the landfall points of the aircraft involved.

As for the degree of divergence from the planned flightpaths, the most important would be the divergence which occurred from the adjustment-to-the-right point to landfall along the Channel coast. Actually, the three air-streams approached the Orne-Dives section of the coast at roughly 45 degrees. The effect of this, only a few degrees off the planned flightpath, spread over the distance from the adjustment-to-the-right point to Drop Zone V, could cause an error of five or six kilometres by drop time. Added to this, a six kilometre divergence in the air translated to nearly ten kilometres on the ground because of the 45-degree approach. A few degrees off course were quite significant when it came to calculating how far troopers landed from their Drop Zone targets. The point here is that, although strong arguments exist in favour of deliberate decoy action, there is room for other rational argument about why the scattering occurred over such distances.

For Lieutenant Marcel Cote's stick, which landed at Octeville-Montivilliers, the explanation for a deliberate occurrence is even more simple. Again, if the flightpaths are considered, the heading used after coming out over Worthing - if continued past the adjustment-to-the-right point without any deviance at all - would carry the flight directly over Octeville-Montivilliers. All that would be necessary would be to simply overlook the adjustment to the right. It seems impossible to contemplate experienced aircrews making such an omission without dire, last minute orders from some High Command source.

If this happened, and if the aircrews switched on the red light (to warn of the coming green) at the same distance from the coast as they would have done for a drop at Varaville, then the green would come on at the point almost directly over the Le Havre (Octeville) airport. What is even more startling is this: It will be recalled that there were strangers in Cote's C-47. They were a British captain, a lieutenant and two other ranks who carried a large radio transmitter and some automatic weapons - and who knows what was really in the parachute containers under the wings? Did the containers hold SAS battle-noise makers? Were these soldiers an SAS small team? If they were the team put down at Harfleur, or even more probably the one at Yvetot, it was exceptionally convenient for the planners of Titanic. A small adjustment to the right, after dropping Cote's men, would put an SAS team over Harfleur, a few kilometres beyond Montivilliers. Even less of an adjustment could drop them at Yvetot, not far ahead. It is known that SAS teams did operate at both locations.

To believe that an aircrew captain, co-pilot or trained navigator could simply forget to follow a flight plan seems a little ridiculous. Further, to believe this could happen by accident to one of the few 1st Canadian Parachute Battalion sticks that carried strangers to the right place, at the right time, to serve some masterplan so conveniently, is like asking one to believe the moon is flat. But we should remember there probably were other radio teams, besides the SAS, who landed in France that night. They could have been forward observation officer teams, meant for Drop Zone V, to direct naval gunfire onto areas close to the Le Mesnil Ridge or other perimeter positions after D-Day. Or they could have been artillery officers attached to the 6th Airborne Division to direct regular army shelling of enemy positions or military movements. Teams such as these could network with the phony signallers of FUSAG. So perhaps the strangers in Cote's plane had nothing to with the SAS small teams, but were specialists heading behind the Atlantic Wall for some other function.

In 1989, when revisiting Normandy, I made a point of walking the beach at Deauville at about midnight. It happened to be a similar night to the one before D-Day, and it was 6 June. As mentioned earlier, it was possible to see across the Bay of the Seine. I could see the outline of the promontory at Le Havre and the silhouettes of the oil refineries near Harfleur on that night of high cirrus cloud penetrated by the half moon. Except for the occasional dark cloudbank and rain shower on D-Day, it was remarkably like the night of the drop in June 1944. For experienced aircrews it would be impossible not to know where they were. The city of Le Havre and the Seine estuary would be unmistakable. Nothing along the coast is even remotely similar.

However, there is one area close by which supports the theory that the misplaced drop could have been accidental. After a meeting with George Robertson and his wife Betty at the Beach Hotel in Deauville in 1989, we decided to go into the area between Mont Canisy and Villers-sur-Mer, where Robertson, Bert Isley, Jim MacPherson, Stan Shulist and Boyd Anderson (all in Lieutenant Rousseau's stick) landed. If you drive from Deauville to the high ground on the west side of Mont Canisy, about half way down the far western side, there is a turn off to the south. As we progressed along the side of the hill, it was difficult not to believe that we were looking at the huge open fields between Breville on the Le Mesnil Ridge and Ranville near the Orne bridges. It is easy enough to visualize some aircrews - say possibly the crew of Lieutenant Rousseau's C-47 transport - coming down between the main D-Day flotillas and Le Havre, suddenly realizing they were off to the east a little, then making an adjustment to the right (west) and, coming in over the River Touques, thinking it was the Dives (Deauville and Trouville representing Cabourg and Dives-sur-Mer). And then, not being able to find Drop Zone V, deciding to let their troops out on what they thought was Drop Zone N.

Another accidental scenario might be this: They came in over Drop Zone V all right, but because it was obscured they missed it and began to go round again. When they came back out into the half-moonlight north of Cambremer, flying on for a few minutes to get some distance between themselves and the mass of transports making their turns over "Satan's Quadrangle," they'd suddenly see several outstanding features on the French landscape. They'd see the big open fields southeast of Villers-sur-Mer which looked like Drop Zone V; they'd also see Mont Canisy, which at night, with impaired depth perception, looked like the rise where the Merville Battery was located; and then, to confirm it all, they'd see Deauville-Trouville straddling the Touques, which looked a lot like Cabourg - Dives-sur-Mer straddling the Dives. They'd then decide that they had hit the coast at the wrong place to begin with, and would let their troops out between Villers-sur-Mer and Mont Canisy, thinking they were over Drop Zone V. From the air at night, even in moonlight, the third dimension is not easy to discern. Although Mont Canisy is quite a lot higher than the Merville hill it would be easy to confuse them, and even more so the Breville hill with the Merville hill and their relationships to Drop Zone N.

On the morning of 6 June 1944, a Tuesday, the Calgary Herald announced the following under the headline LATEST INVASION NEWS: "LONDON June 6 (CP). Trans Ocean News Agency in a Berlin broadcast today said the Allies had established a 15-mile front from a half mile to a mile deep between Villers-sur-Mer and Trouville (Deauville's twin city straddling the River Touques) .... This area is south of the big port of Le Havre where trans Atlantic liners docked in prewar days and takes in the beach resort area of Deauville."

"BARCELONA, Spain. June 6 (AP). German reports received here today said Allied forces were in full possession of Honfleur on (the south side of) the mouth of the Seine."

Of course it was generally known within a few days that both reports were erroneous. Why were the reports so widespread and so readily accepted over the whole world? The British and Americans were very circumspect and non-committal about this, with Churchill on the same morning making an especially low-key announcement in parliament at the end of a long, laudatory speech about the fall of Rome two days earlier.

There are various possibilities. Perhaps the Germans were so steeped in their belief that the Allies would invade at or close to the Pas de Calais area that they did believe the deceptions of Glimmer, Taxable, Titanic, and especially the intentional or accidental scattering of the 3rd Brigade, 6th Airborne Division. Perhaps the fighting in the Atlantic Wall near Deauville and Villerssur-Mer near Honfleur, or at Octeville, did add a reality which convinced them in the early stages - absolutely!

Against such a possibility we must ask: Since they had paratroop prisoners in the early morning of 6 June, a few of whom were unlucky enough to land directly within the enemy's barbed wire at some of their fortifications in the Caen area as early as 01:00 hours, why did they still consider the wrong location to be the right one? The answer is that Taxable and Glimmer must have turned the tables. Or that MI6 was responsible by working with unfaithful elements of the German Intelligence Service, the *Abwehr*, in arranging the Berlin releases through Berlin and Barcelona. That could be quite possible and realistic if Admiral Canaris were involved.

There is a second possibility. The Germans knew the truth, but fostered a belief in the wrong place to fool the Allies into thinking they had been taken in. This would tend to give the Germans more freedom in moving their troops to the west of Caen in Normandy, which they did later in the morning.

A third and more interesting possibility is that the reports were influenced by British Intelligence agents in both Berlin and Barcelona, or in London. It is widely known that the British double agent Garbo, broadcasting through his German controller Kuhlenthal in Madrid, could have had spurious material sent from Britain placed on Hitler's or Jodl's desk within an hour of its transmission from London. British Intelligence could have had Kuhlenthal or his co-workers in Spain, or collaborators in German Intelligence in Berlin, release the bogus news items printed in the western press the following morning.

Anyway, the whole deception plan and the logistical paraphernalia used to carry it out, right from FUSAG through Taxable, Glimmer, Titanic and the Neptune paratroops scattered deep in the coastal plateau country - of whom such a great number were 1st Canadian Parachute Battalion soldiers, who often fought to the bitter end - greatly affected both the German Army and the enemy's Supreme Command. There is no doubt, whichever scenario is accepted, that man for man the misplaced Canadian paratroops made an outstanding contribution to the Allied war effort, and deserve to be remembered for their part. At the time, and for many years after the war, their efforts and circumstances were not known. The soldiers involved have largely remained unsung heroes of nameless triumphs. It is hoped that they will be accorded at last the fame the free world owes them for the accomplishments they unwittingly achieved.

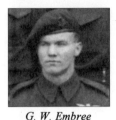

G. W. Embree

Chapter XV
The Defence of
the Le Mesnil Crossroads

H. M. Walker

The true defensive struggle for the Le Mesnil crossroads began on D-Day Plus Two with "B" Company's attack down the Varaville highway towards the Bavent junction. As we saw in Chapter XII, "A" Company provided flank protection for "B" Company, as it had done for the British 9th Parachute Battalion during the attack on the Merville Battery in the early hours of 6 June. The reason for this attack was that the Germans had taken advantage of a number of houses on the St. Côme Forest side of the Varaville highway, advancing their front too close to the "B" Company positions.

The period between dawn on D-Day, when the seaborne forces came over the beaches, and the morning of D-Day Plus Two was taken up by digging in, preparing other measures for defence and jockeying with the enemy. They delineated our positions and we mapped out theirs. Reconnaissance patrols carried out by our paratroops not only provided new information about the enemy, but sharpened our skills in the use of stealth, accurate observation and swift evasion tactics. Fighting patrols, carried out as small but violent punishing attacks upon the enemy, kept them disturbed and constantly uncertain, which let them know that if they expected to drive the paratroopers off the highways in the bridgehead they were in for a fight. For the ordinary soldier these were not long-practiced training manual activities. They were a front-line learning experience which hardened his will and determination, or limited his stay in combat.

An example was Number 7 Platoon's fighting patrol to Bavent, which forcibly informed the Germans that they were facing paratroops who were willing to take on their infantry plus their supporting tanks, self-propelled artillery, and 75-mm and 88-mm guns, together with their heavy mortars and field artillery.

In the case of the 3rd Parachute Brigade it is interesting to consider the conduct of its soldiers, which brought victory to the more lightly armed Airborne side. Certainly, without the excellent physical conditioning built up in the personnel of the 6th Airborne Division during the preceding months, the paratroops' offensive ability might not have been so great. Considering the scarcity of their rations, and especially their prolonged lack of sleep, it's doubtful they could have been effective beyond day three or four unless they had been in top shape. It's also unlikely that without their detailed briefings under ideal conditions in England, rendezvousing could have occurred in the beneficial way it did. Moreover, if Airborne activities had been any less efficient than they were, the formation of the solid fighting perimeter so crucial to holding the lodgement area and the main Orne bridges would have been impossible. This could have - and probably would have - prevented the seizure of some of the other initial objectives. As a result, the interdiction points on the routes through the entire Airborne lodgement area might never have been set up. If objectives such as these had been unachievable, it would have been pointless to attempt a protracted defence of the most important initial objectives: the Orne bridges. The critical high ground at the Le Mesnil Ridge and the open country from Herouvillette to Longueval on the Orne (the southern face of the perimeter) could have been left only partially defended. The main Orne bridges would then have been vulnerable; their protective perimeter too weak to withstand the strong enemy assaults of 7 and 8 June.

In reality, much of the intended military action the original briefings planned for did not take place. Only mere fractions of the planned troop concentrations were in the right places at the required times. Still, in every case the under-strength paratroops did find ways to do their jobs and took all their initial objectives. The stress the briefings laid on personal initiative in any situation - planned or not - paid off.

Brigadier James Hill had forewarned his troops that uncontrollable or unforeseen conditions would undoubtedly produce some chaos. No one expected the potential chaos to reign to the extent that it did, so personal speculations on the matter during the hours before the drop were ambivalent. The men were certain of their aircrews' abilities to drop them in the right place. Yet, paradoxically, they were apprehensive about possible scattering. They knew that it had happened during the invasion of Sicily and again during the drop into the deep, flat-bottomed mountain valleys in front of Salerno. But surely, they reasoned, the rapid advances in airborne technology since 1943 would forestall the repetition of such "snafus" when they parachuted into Normandy.

Well, okay, suppose some scattering of sub-units should occur in the vicinity of the Drop Zone? It would simply give them more scope to prove their mettle. They were equally confident that even if some overpowering enemy actions drove them into chaotic disorganization when on the ground in France, they would reassess themselves, seek new solutions, and restructure to achieve the planned goals. They judged themselves well trained to handle almost any contingency. Let the unexpected happen! Let the enemy do what he damn well pleased. Adjustments would be made at the 1st Canadian Parachute Battalion's interdiction points (Robehomme, Gonneville-sur-Merville and the paths westward to the Orne estuary, Varaville, the Bavent junction and the Le Mesnil crossroads) to keep the enemy out of the Airborne lodgement area at the centre of the Le Mesnil Ridge. If the perimeter held up at the other interdiction points around the perimeter, General Montgomery's Orne bridges would be safe - that was that!

In the following days the perimeter came under almost continuous attack, but hold up it did. The ferocity of the fighting came as a shock to the enemy at various headquarters levels farther back. To them it seemed self-evident that their heavy panzer divisions could easily kick around lightly armed Airborne units. Therefore, by the evening of 7 June, they were forced to say to themselves, "We've had enough for now." They stopped fighting, issued new orders and took 8 June (D-Day Plus Two) to reorganize and clear the severe casualties they had suffered. The 6th Airborne Division did likewise on the remainder of the southern face of the perimeter: Herouvillette, Escoville, Butte de la Hogue, and on to Longueval on the River Orne.

The 6th Airborne's indefatigable adversary Colonel Hans von Luck writes on page 163 of his 1989 book *Panzer Commander*: "An order came from division [21st Panzer Division, commanded by General Edgar Feuchtinger]: 'Von Luck's battle group will assemble on the morning of 9 June for a decisive attack on Escoville, advance on Ranville, and take possession of the Orne bridges. Assigned to it for this purpose will be: Panzer Reconnaissance Battalion 21, No. 4 Company of Panzer Regiment 22, three batteries of Major Becker's Assault-gun Battalion 200, and one company of Antitank Battalion 220 with [88-mm all-purpose guns]. The division's artillery will support the attack within the limits of its supply of ammunition.' "

All this was in addition to Numbers I and II Panzer Grenadier Battalions and other regimental troops.

Before dawn on 9 June, with the enemy artillery, massive "moaning minnie" heavy mortars and medium machine guns entrenched on top of a hill south of the village of Escoville, the German grenadiers and tanks soon forced their way into the village. But the 6th Airborne's troops were ready for them and called in heavy bombers and naval gunfire on the reinforced and self-assured 125th German Regiment. As von Luck puts it (p.164): "During the night we had been plastered with heavy naval fire and bombs. Our preparations had evidently been spotted."

Von Luck adds (p.164): "6th Airborne Division put up fierce resistance. When it became light, heavy fire from the navy began to fall on the centre of the village [Escoville] and its southern edge. We could make no progress." On his next page he cites tank commander Werner Kortenhaus: "On the evening of that 9 June we realized that we could no longer drive the British back into the sea" - which they had hoped to do by breaking through the bridgehead that included the 1st Canadian Parachute Battalion.

That same evening, following four gruelling, sleepless nights and days which would have exhausted many units beyond any kind of reasonable performance level, the reserves of stamina and energy were still there in the paratroops. If it had not been so the battle for the Le Mesnil Ridge, the other key objectives of the German Army in the Airborne bridgehead, would have gone in favour of the enemy.

The massive attack by von Luck's battle group on the southern face of the perimeter had been frustrated. This caused his division commander Feuchtinger to go over to the defensive on that sector. Indications were that the

Germans had reviewed their plans. They were still determined to eliminate the Airborne troops east of the River Orne, regain the Le Mesnil Ridge, and thereby recapture the Orne bridges. But their re-assessment of the situation resulted in new strategy.

They had battered away on 8 and 9 June at the southern face of the Airborne perimeter without success. They were turned back from the villages spanning Butte de la Hogue time after time by the 8th Parachute Battalion of the 3rd Brigade, the armoured troops and antitank artillery of "Parker Force" and the glider battalions of the 6th Airlanding Brigade. To the west, on the open ground from Ste. Honorine to Longueval (by the Orne), the 12th, 13th and 7th Parachute Battalions of the 5th Parachute Brigade frustrated their every move in front of Colombelles. These were tough, vicious battles.

Most of the enemy troops involved were from Colonel von Luck's heavily reinforced 125th Regiment of the 21st Panzer Division, supported by the several other units just detailed in the quotation from his book. The new task given to von Luck by General Feuchtinger was to "crush" the 6th Airborne Division. The Germans soon found out that this was not a task they could achieve in response to a simple one-line order.

Their new, clever re-assessment of the battlefield situation was that they should take advantage of an inward bend on the Airborne's defensive perimeter at its north-east side at Breville. In the first days after D-Day this bend appeared innocuous. Originally, it had shown up there almost by chance. As we have seen, on D-Day the huge number of initial objectives and the scattering of the paratroops on the drop put large elements of Brigadier Hill's 3rd Parachute Brigade far outside the perimeter during the hours it was being formed.

In the early hours of D-Day the British 9th Parachute Battalion was engrossed in seizing and silencing the Merville Battery. Consequently it was one of the units temporarily absent from the eventual perimeter. So was Lord Lovat's Marine Commando Brigade, which came over Sword Beach and could not arrive in the perimeter until the late afternoon of D-Day.

Similarly, "C" Company of the 1st Canadian Parachute Battalion was involved most of the day at Varaville. Although it had captured the village (and met all its other initial objectives) by dawn on D-Day, the company's orders were to defend it and wait to be relieved by commandos on bicycles in mid-afternoon. "C" Company, therefore, did not come into its perimeter location - two kilometres southwest of Varaville at Le Mesnil - until about 18:00 hours.

A large part of the Canadian battalion's "B" Company was absent from the perimeter altogether. It was at Robehomme for two days defending the site around the bridge it had destroyed - thereby blocking one of the branch roads from the Seine River into the lodgement area.

All these otherwise engaged troops left the whole stretch of ground from Le Mesnil up through the Château St. Côme Forest, and past Breville to

Amfreville, almost devoid of Brigadier Hill's troops until the evening of D-Day.

When the British 9th Parachute Battalion did arrive from the Merville Battery and the Canadian "C" Company from Varaville, the 9th occupied the space between Château St. Côme and Le Plein, below Amfreville. "C" Company dug in on the actual Le Mesnil crossroads and Lord Lovat's commandos occupied Amfreville and Hauger above Sallenelles.

The enemy on 9 June fixed their eyes and effort on the inward bend at Breville. If they could seize Breville and force a crushing drive from there across the open ground to the vicinity of Ste. Honorine they could slice off the now reinforced 3rd Brigade and, with a side thrust to Benouville, split the 6th Airborne Division in three. Then they could deal with the chunks of the pie piecemeal. The commandos would be held in place at Amfreville on the right shoulder of the inward bend, while the Canadians would be held where they were at the Le Mesnil crossroads on the left shoulder.

The tip of the perimeter's inward bend was tenuously secured by the battered, depleted, casualty-ridden British 9th Parachute Battalion. The Germans took it for granted that they would run over this lightly armed unit without much trouble, the brunt of their spearhead causing the 9th to crumble under the weight of their new southwest drive. As for the British Airborne battalions on the southeast corners of the perimeter (Herouvillette, Escoville, Ste. Honorine), von Luck's battle group would surely hold them at a standstill.

To some extent the Germans were right. The British 9th Parachute Battalion under its redoubtable commander Colonel Terence Otway, now of Merville Battery fame, had been weakened by its losses in the scattered drop and in its seizure of the battery. Since taking its place in the perimeter, in front of Breville, on the late afternoon of D-Day it had been further weakened in hard fighting at Le Plein, Longuemare and Château St. Côme.

Now the battle for a decision - whether the German Army or the Airborne soldiers were to control the open ground, the swamp and the high forested ground of the Le Mesnil Ridge, east of the Orne waterways - was about to take on a new urgency. The new enemy drive was meant to cause a violent shake-up of the Airborne, and to determine the main aims of the German plans one way or the other.

The night of the 9th was warm and the activity on the perimeter, by both sides, was desultory. Flares coursed into the sky, indicating that frequent patrols were active throughout the whole perimeter. The crump-crump-crump of sporadic artillery fire chilled the lonely, sleepless senses of the infantrymen. The angry rattle of machine guns from every direction, some far away, some close, from both sides, sliced across the battlefield with the geometrically determined aim of fixed lines of fire. The ones close by produced a wrathful, threatening cacophony. The distant ones, barely audible, gave off a series of telling mutters which created sympathy for dead or wounded members of the patrols which had drawn their fire to begin with. Each gun sound had its own message for the restless night watchers. The fast-firing enemy *Maschinengewehr* sounded impatient and lethal; the slower-firing paratroopers' automatic machine gun more determined. The chug-chug-chug of the British-Canadian Bren gun and the roaring sputter of the enemy MG-42 were never to be forgotten.

Late on 10 June, noise and explosive punishment within the bend mounted to a new clamour! Escalated mortar fire by the enemy and counter fire by the Airborne and intensive machine-gunning and artillery from both sides. The sharp squealing of tank tracks, with sporadic fire by the grenadiers' tank guns, intensified the terrifying racket as did more "moaning minnies" and shattering shellbursts from the big naval guns out on the Channel. In the Canadian positions at the Le Mesnil crossroads the lethal disturbances floating across the landscape from the Château St. Côme Forest fell on sympathetic ears - even as we ourselves fought the lesser battle to contain the attacking Germans. God, how easy it was for us to feel sorry for the men of the 9th Battalion and the Black Watch, how guilty for hoping the melee and the horror would not come our way - when certain that it would. If not now then this afternoon, this evening, tonight or tomorrow.

Out of the Clouds (second edition, 1995) by John A. Willes, the official history of the 1st Canadian Parachute Battalion, says on page 91: "At this point, Brigadier Hill realized that his Brigade was confronted by 346 Division, a first class German [infantry] Division, and that the 21 Panzer Division was [again] very active in the bridgehead area."

While attempting to push their heaviest thrust through the 9th Battalion, the Germans did not neglect Amfreville or the crossroads at the centre of the Le Mesnil Ridge. Throughout the day, right up until twilight, they continued to hammer the ridge. In addition to artillery barrages they sent out probing patrols and stepped up their sniper offensive. This took a toll on the holding battalions while the enemy prepared their main effort for the following day, 11 June. Meanwhile the 9th Battalion was still courageously hanging on. In the case of the Canadians, we knew we were containing a holding action and were suffering a less concentrated enemy effort on our section of the perimeter. We did suffer casualties on the 9th-10th, but our battalion was able to reorganize and lick its wounds after the "B" and "A" Company attack down the Varaville highway towards the Bavent junction on 8 June. Even so, the days of the holding action were treacherous. Men were killed and wounded from every company of the 1st Canadian Parachute Battalion on those days of enemy preparation.

Privates A. R. Archibald, A. E. W. Blair, M. Lanthier, D. A. Race, W. W. Shwaluck and D. G. Turner were all killed. Also several were wounded including Sergeant E.W. Page, together with men from "C" Company, in an after-dawn barrage. The 1st Canadian Parachute Battalion suffered sixteen casualties during two strictly defensive days.

This number of casualties over only two days of holding action - four percent of the total number of Canadian paratroops now in the bridgehead -

meant that these were victorious days for the enemy units opposing them. It also indicated just how severe the results could be when a methodical, calculating and efficient enemy put their long experience to work. On an attack day casualties were to be expected. On a defensive day they seemed less necessary and so all the sadder.

At the Le Mesnil crossroads, by the time the sun came up on 11 June, the enemy had closed up. Their snipers were for the first time well placed in trees and other vantage points. As is always the case with sniper activity, a man here and a man there has one or more close calls or almost silently drops stone dead. When someone dies from sniper fire anger builds rapidly in the minds of his fellow soldiers and an increasing toll of revenge is exacted upon the snipers.

That day, after a period of such activity, enemy artillery ranging shells began to drop. For the first time accurate, highly concentrated enemy mortar and artillery fire screamed onto the paratroops' position on the actual crossroads. The slit trenches were slammed with a vengeance.

Up to this time many of the paratroopers were green, untried and somewhat naive infantry soldiers who had not dug deep enough. Also, none of their L-shaped trenches had half-roofs covering one arm of the "L" to make them more shrapnel-proof. So several good men were needlessly lost: Sergeant Tom Keel; my own trench-mate Colin (Wild Bill) Morrison, who was also our section machine gunner, J. E. Gillespie and more. J. P. Thomas (the superb pianist who had entertained so elegantly back in the security camp) had his hands mutilated by shrapnel. Hard lessons, quickly remedied by experience.

By mid-afternoon Lieutenant Norman Toseland, somewhat harried following his prolonged defence of the destroyed Robehomme bridge position and the previous morning's attack towards the Bavant junction, was put on notice to lead what he knew would be a hair-raising patrol back to Varaville that night. The objective of the patrol was to check the bridge "C" Company had destroyed there on D-Day. The reason was that the bridge on the Dives at Periers-en-Auge provided a crossing into Varaville four kilometres behind the Channel beaches at Cabourg. Like Varaville, it was deep in the German Atlantic Wall outer defences. Oddly, unlike all the bridges that were destroyed as initial D-Day objectives, it had not been slated for ruin. It was the only bridge between Troarn and the Channel so favoured. Perhaps as early as the morning of 7 June, after the commandos had relieved "C" Company at Varaville, the enemy began using the route through Periers-en-Auge to move troops and armaments onto the vacated glider landing zones southwest of the Cabourg-Varaville-Herouvillette highway. These enemy troops were now all set to recapture the Orne bridges. If they could establish a solid firm base northwest of the Varaville-Le Mesnil highway they could probably expand the distance between the shoulders of the inward bend in front of Breville and make more room for a bigger drive between the 6th Airborne's northeastern positions. The discovery of these troop concentrations created a strong suspicion that the enemy had replaced the bridge, blown up on D-Day, on the Divette Canal at

Varaville. It was Toseland's hazardous task to get verification.

At evening twilight came a fresh wind, noisy and nerve-wracking for men crossing enemy lines and beyond into their logistical support areas. The moon, nearly full but obscured by cloud, gave no relief to the blackness of that 10/11 June night. Conditions were somewhat similar to those during Lieutenant McGowan's booby-trap patrol to Bavent a couple of nights earlier: wind and thick black cloud but no rain this night.

The patrol advanced parallel to the Varaville highway, which swerved northeast towards the original Drop Zone V. The enemy and their support troops were concentrated in the fields and hedges. Their flares coursed into the black night and left the patrol's soldiers bathed in anaemic greenish light as they froze in their tracks before the flare-shells reached the apex of their various trajectories. The urge to hit the ground had to be forcefully resisted since any movement would be a dead give-away. The men had to close their eyes as long as the brilliance lasted. If not, they would retain no night-vision once the flares went out - even shadows would be blocked out when the brilliance was over. Inevitably the mad clatter of machine guns, mixed with the piercing snap-crack of streaking tracer bullets, followed as the enemy rent the night with pre-planned fixed lines of fire, a tactic which their soldiers were more than good at.

The concentration of enemy troops made progress so impossibly slow for most of the night that Lieutenant Toseland knew that he must return to Le Mesnil without completing his patrol. Otherwise he and his men would be caught by the dawn and could be wiped out in thickly defended enemy territory.

Getting out was nearly as slow as getting in. The Germans were just as good at dealing with fleeting shadows as were our paratroopers. On the return route, quite close to our own lines, in the dimness of false dawn, the patrol heard an enemy vehicle barrelling up the Varaville highway. It was heading straight for "B" Company's road block, with which it would collide in less than thirty seconds. The patrol sprang into firing positions by the road and opened fire. The vehicle careened into the opposite ditch and rolled over.

It was a reconnaissance car from the 21st Panzer Division. It had been properly subjected to a fusillade of small-arms fire, plus a Gammon bomb, and was almost torn apart. It seemed impossible that anyone could be left alive inside it. But soon a plaintive voice came from the wreck: "Kamerad! Kamerad! Nicht schiessen! (Don't shoot!)." Toseland stepped forward with his Sten sub-machine gun at the ready to accept, he thought, the surrender of an obviously wounded enemy soldier in need of help.

The man continued to sob and beg for aid. But suddenly, without warning, he snapped to his feet, stepped out of the wreck looking perfectly fit and put a burst of 9-mm *Schmeisser* submachine gun fire into Toseland's abdomen at point-blank range. Within seconds he paid the supreme price for his treachery. Toseland was one of the most critically wounded soldiers to survive in the entire 1st Canadian Parachute Battalion during the battle of Normandy. Angry paratroopers dealt with the other occupants of the car with sub-machine gun fire. Two members of the patrol raced for their own lines to get medical aid and stretcher bearers for Toseland. All-round defensive firing positions were taken up by the remainder of the patrol to protect their smitten officer and the medics. A section of the British 224 Field Ambulance was regularly attached to the 1st Canadian Parachute Battalion. A corporal accompanied by Private Jock Hendrie from this unit, plus two of the Canadian battalion's medical orderlies, hurried down the Varaville highway under fierce enemy fire in the brightening morning. They carried Toseland to the battalion medical aid station in an old garage across the highway from the Le Mesnil brickworks and pottery plant.

The brigade doctors decided that Toseland could not be moved until his condition reached - if ever - an acceptable level of stability. He remained there for several days while verbal bulletins on his state of recovery were passed from soldier to soldier around the various battalion positions. Finally word came down the line that he had been evacuated to hospital in England.

Toseland's patrol is but one more example of the spate of actions carried out by the Airborne battalions. Everywhere along the perimeter's front line the enemy were tested and dogged throughout periods of darkness. Still, their infiltration across the coastal highway at Periers-en-Auge proceeded onward to Varaville, only about two kilometres away. They used this route to clog Drop Zone V and the rising land across the fronts of the 1st Canadian Parachute Battalion, the 9th Parachute Battalion and Lord Lovat's commandos with reinforcements for their drive within the Breville bend.

During the night that Toseland's patrol tried to get through to Varaville, a patrol from the 12th Parachute Battalion of the 5th Parachute Brigade discovered a large number of enemy soldiers being concentrated on the western edge of the huge fields of the glider Landing Zone between Breville and Ranville - close to the 6th Airborne Divisions Headquarters. They were not far from the Orne estuary near a large gravel pit, which on D-Day had been the rendezvous point of the 5th Parachute Brigade's 13th Battalion. The enemy troops were to form a strong assault force and were ordered to conceal themselves by using the numerous wrecked Horsa and Hamilcar gliders as forming-up points - the gliders having been abandoned on the huge Drop Zones near the Orne River by the 6th Airlanding Brigade after their landing on D-Day. About a thousand Panzer Grenadiers were involved. A mixed force of the 1st and 2nd Battalions, 858th Regiment, and some companies of the 744th Regiment, 711th Infantry Division, brought over from east of the Dives, made up the German force.

The 6th Airborne Division Headquarters reacted quickly and decisively to this latest threat. Acting in co-operation its three brigades repositioned many of their Vickers medium machine guns and their 3-inch mortars in an effective defence arrangement which brought all the possible enemy assault positions under a new, tight fire-plan grid.

The enemy move would undoubtedly be co-ordinated with an attack northwest by the 21st Panzer Division from Escoville and Ste. Honorine into the same glider Landing Zones. If successful the joint effort would split the 6th Airborne Division, and its commando brigades under command, into two. That would probably enable them to make a further drive west to recapture the Orne bridges, which would slice the 6th Airborne into three chunks.

Once the combined weight of the 6th Airborne's medium machine guns and 3-inch mortars had been repositioned, the biggest worry was that the enemy might *not* attack. The trap was now set: a great concentric basin of machine-gun and heavy mortar fire would cascade upon the Panzer Grenadiers when they advanced from the gliders.

Close to noon the enemy obliged. A media eyewitness of their attack, war correspondent Leonard Mosley, described the confidence with which the paratroops were ready to turn it into a rout. In his article dated two days later Mosley related:

"Paratroop Captain Charles Bliss [12th Parachute Battalion] had that grin on his face that always means something brewing. 'This,' said Charles, 'is going to be good....We have a report of at least six hundred panzer grenadiers advancing through the woods and believe they're going to try to drive through Ranville to break our line and gain the east bank of the river. Well, what we are going to do to those Jerries should make a nice little story for you. Look.' "

Even if he understated the " Jerries'" numerical strength, the captain's self-assurance was not misplaced. The enemy formations were under heavy pressure from their high commands to kick the Airborne forces out of the troublesome bridgehead across the Orne from the main Allied invasion front. The Panzer Grenadiers started out at the double from their jumping-off positions in the Horsa gliders strewn around Drop Zone N. As they came forward they shifted to a slow, deliberate advance towards the Airborne lines across the great open crescent prepared for them. About three hundred metres out they flopped on their bellies, hidden in the corn and wheat to rest. Minutes later they charged.

The Airborne soldiers held their fire and let the over-confident grenadiers race onward, full of the scent of victory. When their range was down to about a hundred metres from the concealed Airborne machine guns, and the Germans were a long way into the crescent – shaped trap, a common signal alerted the paratroopers and the glider men to unleash the full weight of their crossfire and mortars. Said Mosley, "The corn went down as if under a flail." So did the German grenadiers.

The scene was horrifying. Good soldiers that they were, small groups of grenadiers managed to rendezvous and to continue their charge. This time the carnage was even worse. The now broken enemy tried to go back but they were helpless and few got away.

This was not specifically a 1st Canadian Parachute Battalion action, but it did demonstrate how effectively support elements of the battalion could be co-ordinated with other divisional units. The Canadian battalion's Vickers platoon and mortar men added their expertise and weapons to the devastation of a major effort by the enemy.

After more than fifty years I still have a clear vision of big Sergeant Herbie Archer from Sydney Mines, Nova Scotia, ploughing across "C" Company's positions at the Le Mesnil crossroads with his head shoved through the heavy leg assembly of a Vickers machine-gun pod, which sat on his shoulders as he rushed his men carrying the gun barrels and belts of ammunition towards the 9th Parachute Battalion and commando positions near Breville-Amfreville.

There, they were dispersed to their firing points for the battle. After it was over, the enemy's senior commanders were shocked by the determination of what they had regarded as an almost wiped-out Airborne division. The estimate at the time was that the enemy suffered about four hundred soldiers killed and many more wounded.

Now the fat was really in the fire. The Germans decided to attack again and would blast the paratroopers and glider men east of the Orne out of there once and for all. The losses suffered by General Feuchtinger's Panzer Division (the Grenadier Division together with a vast number of corps troops) were severe. The deficiencies were partially made up by drafting in fresh troops from the 346th Infantry Division southwest of Caen, and others from the 711th Infantry Division in the Deauville-Trouville area on the River Touques. Both of these divisions contained first class infantry units of the *Wehrmacht*.

The perimeter became quiet again while the enemy cleared the battlefield of casualties. Patrols were out in force once more, and General Gale determined that the enemy formations were building too great a force to be withstood by what was now, in effect, the equivalent of one and a half brigades of Airborne troops with half a brigade of commandos. All his original brigades in the line had been cut down to approximately half strength - now a total of five thousand men at the most.

Strong elements of three German divisions were now pressing hard on the Airborne perimeter, plus remnants of the 716th Infantry Division which was almost destroyed by both the Airborne assault and the assault from the sea on D-Day. The units now regrouping in what would be their final assault on the 6th Airborne Division were:

- Colonel von Luck's 125th Regiment plus all the special strong support units he had utilized during his attack on Escoville-Ste. Honorine on the morning of 9 June.

Large elements of that division's armoured battalions and battle groups from the 346th Infantry Division.

- Other troops from the 21st Panzer's support units, such as antitank, anti-aircraft artillery and medics - together with the 744th Infantry Regiment drawn from the 711th Infantry Division, brought across the Dives from the 15th German Army.

General Gale's corps commander, Lieutenant-General J. T. Crocker, decided to reinforce the 6th Airborne Division with three battalions of regular infantry. Each battalion was nearly twice the size of an Airborne battalion. For a change, quiet activity began to permeate the night of 10/11 June, while the 153rd Brigade of the 51st Highland Division (former 8th Army desert troops) moved in.

That night also saw the assignment to Brigadier James Hill of two battalions of Gordon Highlanders, Numbers 5 & 7, and the 5th Battalion Black Watch. He assigned the Gordons to the general area of the British 8th Parachute Battalion, west of the Canadians near Herouvillette, and the Black Watch to the British 9th Parachute Battalion, which was still on the Canadians' left to the north. This was to let the Gordons oppose the right wing of von Luck's sector while the Black Watch joined the 9th Battalion at the most southern point of the inward bend at Breville. The 9th was by this time desperately low in personnel due to its losses during the enemy's former tries at splitting the Airborne bridgehead.

The German 346th Division was to attempt the drive from the northeast, between the Canadian battalion's front on their left and the Commando Brigade's front on their right, then onward through the remnants of the 9th Parachute Battalion, past Breville through Château St. Côme and on towards Ranville and the Orne bridges.

They still hoped that success in breaking up the 6th Airborne Division would open the way for them to drive across the Orne bridges into the east flank of the Allied bridgehead; then across the plain between Caen-Carpiquet and the D-Day beaches - rolling up the tails of the 3rd British and 3rd Canadian Infantry Divisions in turn. This would wipe out the effects of the Allied landings at both Sword and Juno Beaches.

The double purpose of the reinforcement plan by the 6th Airborne's senior commanders was to buttress the perimeter in the areas of the 8th Parachute Battalion and the left wing of the 5th Parachute Brigade in the vicinity of Escoville-Herouvillette-Butte de la Hogue, up against the 21st Panzer Division; and to reinforce the 9th Parachute Battalion in holding the perimeter in front of the strong German position at Breville. The Black Watch, placed on the 9th's right before Breville, should spoil the enemy's plans and stabilize the Airborne lodgement area and the perimeter in one stroke by seizing Breville.

Early on 10 June the first trucks of the convoy carrying the lead elements of the 5th Battalion, Black Watch, appeared in front of Number 7 Platoon of "C" Company, 1st Canadian Parachute Battalion. The platoon interdicted the arm of the crossroads which swings straight down the western edge of the Bois de Bavent from Breville to its junction with the Escoville-Troarn highway, one kilometre southeast of Escoville and the same distance northeast of Touffreville.

The troops of Number 7 Platoon's roadblock were dug in less than fifty metres from the Le Mesnil crossroads. Early on the morning of 10 June the paratroops there were aghast to see the string of huge troop-carrying trucks, with their canvas tarpaulins rolled up like China-rigged transport trucks in Vancouver, jammed full of Black Watch infantrymen who appeared to think the convoy's leaders knew what they were doing. The convoy was driving along the Airborne side of no-man's-land and was in imminent danger of being shelled or machine-gunned into oblivion.

It is true that the highway they were on would have taken them through the crossroads and on to the 9th Battalion before reaching their destination, the German positions at Breville. But the risk of their slaughter was enormous.

After a fast conference with Major John Hanson, "C" Company Commander, the convoy did an awkward U-turn through 7 Platoon's field of fire and headed back, with instructions to take a right onto a dirt track a short distance below Number 7 Platoon's roadblock. This would take them just south of 3rd Brigade Headquarters and on to the 9th Battalion by a safer route. It was wondrous to hear their soldiers innocently wisecracking and laughing as the trucks turned around, while the paratroopers held their collective breath and waited for hell to arrive from the other side of no-man's-land. Miraculously, it didn't happen.

By mid-morning on 11 June the soldiers of 7 Platoon had given the Airborne perimeter's inward bend at Breville the nickname "Bomb Alley," because somebody was always shelling it. By that afternoon, with "moaning minnies," tank activity, artillery fire from both sides, shelling of the Breville and St Côme areas by British warships from the Channel, and shelling of the Breville and St. Côme areas, explosions were so concentrated it almost seemed as though everybody was shelling the place simply for the hell of it.

Some of the guns involved from both sides were the 3rd British Division field artillery from west of the Orne, huge guns of the Royal Navy, German self-propelled 88-mm antitank guns and the "moaning minnies," German field and coastal artillery from east of the Dives and, of course, the 6th Airborne Division's own heavy mortars. Allied fighter bombers and strafing fighters added to the din. "Bomb Alley" was living up to its name.

With prospects of the war going on for another year the future for the paratroops in the line did not look too rosy!

The 10 June battle at "Bomb Alley," together with its violent resumption at dawn on the next day, left no doubt that ferocious action was in the works. The big battle building up would be unprecedented in the Airborne bridgehead.

Now the 5th Battalion Black Watch was to counterattack and hopefully clean up the bend as a problem.

As the afternoon of the 11th wore on the shelling and counter-shelling continued to saturate "Bomb Alley." By 13:00 hours the pounding became so severe that we wondered how anyone could exist on that hellish part of the perimeter. Suddenly, in the early evening, the shelling stopped. It sounded as though the Black Watch was on a bayonet assault - lots of German machine-gun fire but no artillery barrages. It was hoped they would push the Germans back and so eliminate the pesky bend. But such hopes were stymied. The enemy counterattacked and a seesaw battle lasted into the late evening as the Germans and British continued to clash in head-on drives which were going nowhere. When darkness fell the exhausted adversaries laid low to regroup and take care of their wounded.

On the morning of 12 June the enemy attacked early and by 07:00 the battle was well underway. This time we Canadians at the Le Mesnil crossroads could hear action which came from east of Breville. This meant that the right shoulder of the German drive - Lord Lovat's commandos at Amfreville - was now heavily engaged.

Soon afterwards we saw two Mark IV tanks come towards us up the northwest quadrant of the Le Mesnil crossroads, accompanied by a concentration of German infantry. Simultaneously a heavy mortar attack on our battalion's defensive positions fell on us. The previously heard shelling in the vicinity of Amfreville and the barrage hitting our positions, plus the appearance of these attackers, told us that the Germans were again attempting to widen the shoulders of the "Bend" - or at the very least were trying to hold us, the Canadians, and our commando allies in place.

The attack on the Canadian positions did not seem to be too determined, so the latter purpose appeared to be the case. With some resistance by the Canadians the enemy withdrew to their own defensive positions. Before long we could tell from the direction of the noise of the burgeoning battle that the Germans had shifted the main weight of their drive to the Black Watch and the remnants of the 9th Battalion, who like the Canadians and the commandos were holding steady. By 11:00 hours the tide of battle was still at a standstill and everything quieted down. The Canadians wondered if the enemy were "out of gas," too exhausted to carry on their drive, and had decided to call it off.

Suddenly, at about 14:00, all hell broke loose again and the Germans laid on the most concentrated artillery and mortar attack so far experienced by the two resisting battalions at Château St. Côme-Breville. The shelling went on with undiminished ferocity for about forty-five minutes. Then the squealing of tracked vehicles, the sporadic firing of single shot antitank weapons and the back and forth action of medium machine guns could be heard. Soon the concentration of fire began to move west.

The portent of the battle noise did not take long to sink in. The perimeter was being stretched inward. The enemy were achieving what they had set out to do and had at least reached the Breville-Le Mesnil road. They had either crossed or were about to cross it, only about one kilometre north of the Le Mesnil crossroads.

The midnight oil had been burned on the night of 11/12 June into the "wee" hours by the four brigade commanders - James Hill, Nigel Poett, Sir

Hugh Kindersley and Lord Lovat - but most of all at General Gale's 6th Airborne Division Headquarters. Far reaching, effective decisions were reached. General Gale's final decisions were: The Black Watch would have another go at taking Breville on 12 June to drive the enemy back and finally straighten out the pesky "bend" in the perimeter. If that didn't work, he would loose an attack by the 5th Parachute Brigade's 12th Parachute Battalion, supported by strong elements of "Parker Force" - the jeepborne armed reconnaissance company of the 12th Devons and the Hussars' 53rd Antitank Battery. There would be a massive stonk by field artillery. Advance preparation would come from 51st Highland Division artillery. The guns of the Royal Navy battleships on the Channel would also do battle. All this would smash the Germans in the Breville bend once and for all!

At General Feuchtinger's headquarters the Germans were certain they'd defeat the Airborne perimeter forces and would drive through and beyond Ranville-Benouville. One more head-on clash, they thought, would do it. They'd put it all in the pot - destroy the Airborne defences totally. The bridgehead would be cut into two or three chunks. That would shorten the German front on its right flank northeast of Caen and set up conditions to cut through the rear of the British and Canadian assault divisions west of the Orne River. On the Airborne side the plan was that the British 9th Parachute Battalion would protect the western flank of the Black Watch in the attack. Meanwhile the Canadian paratroops and the commandos would continue to hold the southeast and northeast shoulders of the inward bend respectively, not letting the enemy gain more elbow room. The "one more time" attack by the Black Watch would go in at mid-afternoon. If it didn't work, Gale's night attack at 22:00 hours by the mixed force of the 12th Battalion and its support units, would shove through between the commandos and the 9th Battalion to seize Breville and cut off the enemy at Château St. Côme. If successful the troublesome inward bend would vanish before midnight, 12 June.

The plans of both sides pointed to a deadly combination. Two reinforced, determined and powerful entities were planning for a head-on collision rather than an offensive-defensive action - both sides with skilled infantry plus heavy armoured and artillery support.

In the late afternoon of 12 June it became obvious to Brigadier Hill that the Black Watch battalion was taking another savage mauling as it attacked towards Breville. But so were the Germans, still trying to force their drive from northeast to southwest. Eventually the Black Watch was ordered to shift over to the defensive.

Next would come the night attack on Breville. General Gale reasoned that the enemy would not expect an attack when they had just forced the reinforced Airborne over to the defensive. Gale counted on the attack - striking at the enemy out of nowhere in the dark - to hit home and create a big advantage as a total surprise.

The troops from both sides contesting the Le Mesnil Ridge had been fighting hard for three days. German units from the 21st Panzer Division, 711th Infantry Division and 346th Infantry Division had all taken severe losses. Most Germans losses had resulted from the 6th Airborne's mortars and machine guns on the glider landing zone on 10 June, a mauling from the Black Watch on the 10th and 11th, and fierce fighting against the Canadians at Le Mesnil and the commandos at Amfreville. So on the afternoon of 12 June Gale relied on his earlier idea that the Germans would now be far weaker than they were before the three-day battle had begun. Therefore he gave the job of seizing Breville to the 12th Parachute Battalion and supporting forces according to his original plan. Gale organized his assault units in the early hours of the evening and moved them up to their start-line between Amfreville and Breville in only a few hours, which in itself was a remarkable performance. The die was cast for a final showdown for the village of Breville and the inward bend on the Airborne perimeter.

In the late afternoon, when the Black Watch went over to the defensive, the enemy had no intention of slowing down their drive for the banks of the River Orne. Now that our side had backed off, and the Germans had all but broken through into the clear, they brought up more Mark IV tanks, self-propelled 88-mm antitank guns and fresh troops. They then set out to hammer the Black Watch and the remnants of the 9th Battalion again.

The rumble and rattle of the battle at the most southerly part of the inward bend were again starkly audible to the Canadians at the Le Mesnil crossroads. As before, we felt deeply for our fellow soldiers to the north, obviously suffering the hellfire of "Bomb Alley" one more time.

By 18:00 hours on 12 June it was possible to ascertain from our positions that the enemy were making progress. The realization was shocking. Sure, we in the 1st Canadian Parachute Battalion were up against a rough holding attack, but that seemed mild compared to the onslaught happening on our left.

By 18:30 hours Colonel Otway of the 9th Parachute Battalion knew that his decimated unit could not withstand the pressure being put upon his sector. The writing was also on the wall concerning the Black Watch being able to hold their sector on his right. So he warned Brigadier Hill about the probability of an imminent collapse in the whole Breville-Château St. Côme area. That could kibosh General Gale's plans for a night attack.

James Hill was an astute brigade commander. He recognized that although his own troops were somewhat exhausted, so were the enemy's. He had faith that Gale's plan would do the job if the present positions could be held for the few hours until 22:00.

The brigadier approached Colonel Bradbrooke of the 1st Canadian Parachute Battalion and asked for the use of "C" Company to help Colonel Otway out. Bradbrooke was himself pressed but he agreed, and replaced "C" Company on the crossroads positions at Le Mesnil with Headquarters Company soldiers.

Although a pragmatic commander and a stickler for discipline, Hill was close to his soldiers. He would not order Major John Hanson and his men into the lop-sided conditions "C" Company was heading for without he, himself, going into the fray with them - a soldiers' soldier! Here was a brigadier who'd had most of his left buttock blasted off by bomb fragments six days earlier on D-Day. And he'd already had a lung shot away during his first battalion command in the Tunisian campaign.

"C" Company, after six days in the bridgehead, had been cut down to about sixty soldiers, so an additional ten or twelve were scrounged from Battalion Headquarters. Now Major Hanson's force was a weak, lightly reinforced Canadian Parachute infantry company of about seventy men - barely more than two platoons.

The move to "Bomb Alley" was executed on the double. By 19:30 hours, led by Major Hanson, the Canadians were lined up behind the Black Watch to the right of the Germans on the tip of the inward bend. We were west of the Château St. Côme in a German-dug trench on the immediate west side of the Le Mesnil-Breville road, with our right wing anchored to the driveway to the Château St. Côme property; exactly where the 9th British Parachute Battalion stele is today.

Our left wing was situated about ninety metres to the north towards Breville, which was some three hundred and fifty metres away. The inside of the prepared infantry trench dug by the Germans, perhaps three years earlier, was now overgrown with mossy grass. We used the trench as a jumping-off position to make a sweep through the St. Côme Forest and drive the Germans back from the road into the Château's grounds. Then we were to stay put and never surrender one inch of the ground we had recaptured. And although we ordinary soldiers had not been informed of General Gale's planned attack, there we would stand our ground.

It had been decided to withdraw the Black Watch from the line since they were now almost totally without officers and were exhausted. They pulled back to the west edge of the St. Côme Forest as "C" Company began to pass through their ranks. It was not exactly reassuring to witness their number, some 350 soldiers, and compare that to the number of our now advancing "C" Company personnel. They made no bones about their feelings. They were glad to see the takeover and kept repeating, "Here come the Canadians!" A number of them kept saying, "You chaps should not be going into that forest."

Our fight with the Germans began immediately. But as soon as they recognized that they were faced with paratroops - whom they thought were freshly rested - they backed out of the woods completely. They withdrew across a horseshoe-shaped field into the Château and its grounds.

In this assault the Canadian Army's policy of selecting trained soldiers as paratrooper recruits from other army units, initiated when the battalion was formed back in 1942, really paid off.

Several soldiers present in "C" Company had come from the Saint John Fusiliers, which was a Vickers machine gun battalion. The Black Watch had left behind two or three Vickers medium machine guns, which were ideal for defence and very good for support during an attack. Plentiful belted ammunition was also left behind. Even before our exchange with the Black Watch was completed, while we were still in the long trench by the Breville road, Sergeant Earl Rice of 8 Platoon and Private C.A. Allen of 9 Platoon, both former Saint John Fusiliers, had spotted two of these guns standing silent and now had them hammering away at the enemy.

A number of the company's soldiers had once served in the Royal Canadian Coastal Artillery. They knew how to range, fire and act as effective spotters for heavy artillery guns similar to naval guns - up to 9.2 and even 14-inch calibre. Sergeant Willard Minard of 8 Platoon now teamed up with a British forward observation officer, Captain Paul Greenway, and by radio link brought down devastating Royal Navy artillery fire within the area of the inward bend from battleships out on the Channel. This helped to prepare the way for the Airborne soldiers' counterattacks which followed during that evening. After "C" Company made its fixed bayonet assault into the St. Côme Forest, forcing the enemy to retreat back to the Château, they laid out their defensive positions on the open ground. The orders were to go no further but to make a "bloody-minded" stand so the enemy would know they could forget the St. Côme Forest forever!

"C" Company passed over the forward slit trenches which had been the Black Watch's most advanced positions and proceeded to the north and east edges of the forest.

Number 8 Platoon and half of Number 9 positioned themselves along the driveway to the Château, facing north across the 350-metre wide fields to Breville.

The other half of Number 9 Platoon plus 7 Platoon positioned themselves along the east edge of the St. Côme Forest. They faced across a 100-metre wide, horseshoe-shaped field towards the Château itself.

So far there was only one casualty. He was C. A. Allen, whose abdomen was ripped open by a return volley of fire from a German MG-42 machine gun. He suffered hell during his subsequent fight with "Old Deadly" but eventually recovered in Number 9 Canadian General Hospital at Horsham, England. I know this because for some weeks he was in the next hospital bed to mine. His fight with the German machine gunners displayed his monumental courage. But his battle with gangrenous infection and excruciating pain was even more admirable.

After "C" Company drove them out of the St. Côme Forest it was only a few minutes before the enemy counterattacked. From Breville they came at Number 8 Platoon and the part of 9 Platoon facing north. From the Château St. Côme grounds they drove for Number 7 Platoon and the remainder of Number 9 Platoon.

Their Panzer units brought up Mark IV Panzer tanks, self-propelled 88-mm guns and infantry with numerous MG-42 fast-firing machine guns. Their "moaning minnies" and regular heavy mortars were already in position to the east of the Château.

The paratroops had answered the emergency in such haste that they had neglected to bring entrenching shovels or earth picks. So we could not dig in! It seems that no one really thought we would get beyond the Black Watch forward diggings. And now, rather than pull back to those slit trenches, we stood pat on the edges of the forest. From there we had a clear view of the attacking enemy across the fields to Breville and to the Chateau St. Côme's once serene landscaped grounds.

The enemy's field artillery and the accurate large calibre, flat-trajectory shellfire from their tanks and self-propelled guns, together with their heavy mortars and "moaning minnie" concentrations, raised a wicked storm of weapons fire. All this - plus machine-gun fire spewing from tank turrets and from infantry positions across the fields - inflicted injuries right, left and centre.

One Panzer tank stood on a sharp slope out of range of our PIATS. It must have had one of its 9-mm machine guns lowered as far as it could go, for it swept back and forth several times, chopping off bramble bushes where we lay on the open ground. We pressed our cheeks into the turf and rolled our eyes upward to watch the brambles being mowed down as though by a scythe about a foot above our faces. Several of our men were killed or wounded by the enemy tank fire.

Private Cliff Douglas from Courtney, B. C., the third man on my right and now my machine gunner, blasted away at tanks with his Bren gun, hoping to spray a few bullets through one of their machine-gun ports. At the same time Bill Chaddock, next to me on my left and equipped with a sniper's rifle, was trying to achieve the same thing with his telescopic sight. Cliff Douglas and Ralph Mokelki were ripped through their thighs by the tanks' medium machine guns. They were helped and patched up with tourniquets by Private Eddie Mallon, our section taskman.

By now the enemy had become co-ordinated in their efforts. Most of their offensive weapons zeroed in on the north and east edges of the forest. With no protection from the fierce concentration of shrapnel or from the machine-gun fire, both of which were now continuous, we were sure our jig was up.

But the enemy, contrary to their standard practice, never sent their heavy equipment forward during the colossal blistering they inflicted in this action. They did try to send their infantry across several times. The paratroops turned them back every time.

That's where the company's soldiers earned their greatest credit. With no way to effectively attack the enemy's superior numbers or heavy equipment, and with no trenches in which to protect themselves, the paratroopers refused to give up an inch of ground. They held their positions and fought back from the edge of the forest floor with their machine guns, their shoulder-fired PIAT anti-tank guns and their little 2-inch airborne mortars.

An example of how vicious the enemy fire had become is what happened to the seven men, including me, in my own Number 1 Section of Number 7 Platoon.

At the forest's east edge by the horseshoe-shaped field, I was ordered to form the right flank of the platoon, facing the Château. But also my section was to guard the ground beyond the bottom of the field, looking back towards the Le Mesnil crossroads. As we reached our position we spotted a fairly deep infantry trench, obviously dug by the Germans sometime before D-Day.

It looked like a godsend because it was exactly where we wanted to set up our defensive position. But on closer examination its bottom consisted of sloppy muck which looked like quicksand. The original diggers had struck ground water. Taskman Eddie Mallon was ordered to examine the trench in detail while the remainder of the section spread out along the edge of the forest. Eddie soon reported that the muck was at least five feet deep as measured with a long stick he picked up, and that its banks were unstable - totally useless to us! The sides had crumbled away, so the trench was about as wide as it was deep instead of having its original two-foot width. With no time to waste we crossed it by backing up and taking a running leap.

The bramble bushes along the forest edge were no more than four or five feet high. They formed a belt ten feet wide along the edge of the horseshoe-shaped field. So not much room was left when we dropped into the brambles with our light infantry weapons.

About this time the crescendo of the enemy's combined fire reached its peak and our situation seemed totally hopeless.

The heavy mortar shells especially terrorized our position. One struck a tree above and behind Bill Chaddock and me - lying two or three feet apart. Bill was hit in numerous places and was fatally wounded. I was hit with five steel chunks; later it was determined that my wounds were inflicted by fragments from three different shells, not just the one which struck the tree.

By that time, besides the five of us wounded in my section - for Malcolm (Pop) Clark was also a casualty - eight others from our depleted platoon needed to be bound up and made ready for some kind of evacuation. Six or seven more from Numbers 8 and 9 Platoons were calling for medical help too. This was an impossible situation for our company medics, some of whom were themselves wounded.

Our section was way down the line on the right flank, so there could be no prompt aid from the medics for us. Their position was close to the corner of the forest, at Major Hanson's Company Headquarters. Naturally they helped the wounded in turn as they reached them on the way down the line.

Chaddock, Douglas and Mokelki were my most severely wounded. Mallon, my only unscathed soldier, took care of Douglas and Mokelki with whatever help he could get until the medics arrived. I, still able to walk and not bleeding profusely, did my best for my dying friend Bill Chaddock.

I slit open his camouflaged battle smock and his trousers and pulled off his boots. He was terribly injured from head to foot. I gave him an ampoule of morphine, which we all carried in our first-aid kits, and put a tourniquet and sling on his upper left arm. By now the tank with the fully depressed machine gun had stopped sweeping our position, but the shells were still unrelenting. The enemy were able to get the range of our exact position when we had to get on our feet to help the most seriously wounded. Three successive mortar shells plunged into the deep sloppy muck of the trench, only six feet from us. We could hear them getting sucked down into the slop like someone slurping soup. They were each missiles of death for at least four of us, but God intervened. They did not explode!

My section was a shambles. Only Mallon was left. I wanted to cry but had no time. Nine out of the ten of us who landed six days earlier, on D-Day, were now dead or wounded. Lieutenant Sam McGowan came and examined my right foot, hit by four of the five shell fragments my body had taken. He ordered me off the battle-line immediately. "In ten to fifteen minutes you'll be of no more use here," he said. "You won't be able to walk."

During the most devastating part of the shelling H. B. (Sinkor) Swim probably had the strangest experience. He found a shallow depression, about the length of a man, close to the edge of the forest. It was not deep enough to prevent death from shellfire but was better than flat ground. He stretched out in it and hugged the bottom as only a praying infantryman can. Soon his legs began to tremble beyond his control, but he dared not raise his head to look back and see why. When the tanks stopped firing and the mortars slackened he asked his sergeant, Dick MacLean, to help him up, for he thought his legs were now useless. He then found the real cause of his problem. A huge rat was there shaking like an automatic paint mixer. It had crawled to Swim's legs to save its life. Typically infantry! The soldier and the rat reduced to the same status.

Once patched up, Ralph Mokelki could just about hobble. With help from Corporal W.D. Murray, also wounded, and from Corporal Miles Saunders' Bren-gun group on our left, we set about getting Bill Chaddock and the other wounded across the treacherous, sloppy-bottomed trench. We had a hell of a time but we succeeded.

Two walking wounded from another part of the platoon took C. N. Douglas. Corporal Murray and I took turns carrying Bill Chaddock on our backs. Mokelki and Clark hobbled along with others as we made our way back to the Le Mesnil-Breville road.

Eddie Mallon, our sixth soldier, was left behind to defend about sixty metres of the St. Côme Forest's edge of the horseshoe-shaped field. All by himself like Horatio at the Bridge. Our section "taskman" was now, in effect, a one-man section!

As we bore Chaddock through the forest, Murray and I also guided a psychologically injured friend on a tether made from our toggle ropes. He repeatedly shouted to the world that we had blinded him and were going to bury him alive. His problem stemmed in part from the fact that he had jumped onto what he thought was a chunk of old windfallen tree covered with fallen leaves from the days of shelling; but it was a three-day-old German corpse, swollen to the size of a cow. When our friend's boots landed the corpse broke open and saturated him with an unbearably sickening stench. The reality that he could not rid himself of the filthy smell, plus the immense stress he had suffered from the continuous shelling and machine gunning, had destroyed his will to see his world the way it was. In reality he could see, but he was blind. Mentally blind!

On our way out of the forest we came across our Brigadier James Hill, who was still on his feet after going through the whole raging enemy assault. The brigadier, seeing that Private Mokelki was played out from pain and loss of blood, handed him his shepherd's crook, even though he himself badly needed it due to his severe wound on D-Day. Mokelki returned it to him at a reunion in Edmonton in 1973 - twenty-nine years later.

Private J. A. Anderson from Number 7 Platoon, who had insisted on being the brigadier's personal bodyguard on the way into the forest, lay wounded at the latter's feet. After the war they became mutually respected friends.

When finally we reached the Le Mesnil-Breville road (about seventeen of us, for we were forced to leave our dead behind in the care of the soldiers still fighting it out with the enemy) we were somehow guided into a hedged-in area which held the day's wounded, about a quarter-mile behind our new front line. When we had first arrived in the vicinity of the St. Côme Forest on our way up from the Le Mesnil crossroads, a German officer stood on the ground between a Panther V tank and his armoured scout car. He was waving his closest troops forward to occupy the medical compound near Bois du Mont. On seeing us approach with our bayonets fixed he quickly changed his mind and disappeared with his troops into the forest amidst the devastated, and orderly withdrawing, Black Watch.

A wounded British sergeant who had been in the first-aid compound for some time told me that he thought there were five to six hundred men on the grounds. But he did not stay long to talk, because of the stench my tethered friend gave off.

There were wounded from different units - the Black Watch, the 9th Parachute Battalion, medical orderlies, 3rd and 5th Brigade Headquarters personnel, tank men, artillery gunners, transport drivers, Canadian paratroopers and Germans - with every kind of wound imaginable. Men with missing legs or arms or both. Men hit in the lungs, bleeding from their mouths. Men groaning, gurgling or crying because they were in unbearable pain or suffering from the battle exhaustion called "shell shock." Men vomiting, others chewing on bread, others dying or dead.

My friend on the tether still shouted every few seconds, "They're going to bury me alive! Alive! Alive! So they blinded me." After a while some of the terribly wounded began to shout with sobbing voices, "For God's sake shut that guy up," which was impossible.

In about half an hour a 224 Field Ambulance attendant pulled up in a jeep with some stretchers on it. He walked over to me and said, "How badly wounded are you Canada?" I replied, "Not too badly but I'm useless to my platoon." He numbered my wounds on a ticket, tied it to my dog-tags and said, "Can you still walk?" My foot was still numb so I said I thought I could. He directed me to the nearest medical-aid station, about half a mile away, and asked if I thought I could make it there with my raving friend. I told him, "I guess so."

As the two of us headed down the path I began to understand mental blindness. The enemy heavy artillery was now shelling our rearward areas - "crump! crump! crump!" - big stuff. I had to get my friend down into ditches several times, but he looked at the ditches and thought they were pre-dug graves. That started him sobbing again, still abusing me with accusations of trying to bury him alive. I could tell that he actually saw the ditches - at least as black depressions. But mentally he saw only graves. That was enough to keep him crying out that I was a son of a bitch for wanting to bury him, a "blind man," alive.

At last we made it to the treatment tents of the field aid station. There they shot up my friend with a calming injection and took him off my hands. He remained mentally blind in hospital in England. After prolonged treatment he was sent back to Canada and honourably released from the Army, but was left with a permanent stutter. In a few years he became frail and died suddenly from no apparent cause. Such can be the severity of shock from the horrors of combat.

I was turned over to a captured German sergeant medic. He was competent, like most German soldiers, and was concerned. I could tell, as we dragged on our Canadian smokes, that he felt the same as I did: "We're both out of battle now, so why hold any malice?"

While in the firm but agreeable care of the empathetic enemy sergeant, well within earshot of the continuing struggle, I had time to reflect on some of my experiences in the embattled forest. My foot throbbed but I counted myself well off when I thought of the soldiers with limbs torn off by great chunks of shrapnel or abdomens torn open by machine-gun fire. In the midst of the turmoil there had been personal moments too. Just before I was hit I felt some-one shake the heel of my boot. I squirmed around and came face to face with a man from my section who had avoided church parades back in Carter Barracks by officially declaring himself an atheist. He shouted in my ear, "Will you teach me the Lord's Prayer?" I yelled back, "I can't teach it to you in this racket but we can do it like the vows at a wedding. Repeat the words after me." After-wards, when he dragged himself back to his own position, I offered up my side of the prayer to St. Anthony, as we always did at home when we needed to find something important. I asked him to help me to find a road home. Within min-utes the three enemy missiles with our names on them got sucked into the sloppy-bottomed trench without exploding.

I hope I also offered up thanks for the battalion medical orderlies: men like Corporal R. C. Hall, Private J. R. Elston and others who scurried back and forth amid the flying shrapnel and bullets, never once putting them-selves first when seeking cover. Not surprisingly a number of them lost their own lives in their dedicated but devil-may-care attention to duty. And I trust that I included a prayer for our taskman Eddie Mallon, still battling it out as the only soldier left in our section.

It was a victorious but badly decimated "C" Company that returned to the Le Mesnil crossroads the next day. Even before setting foot in the St. Côme Forest the company had lost forty percent of its personnel - killed, wounded or literally lost in flooded rural Normandy since our midnight jump into the darkness of early D-Day. In the just concluded battle twenty-three more were killed or wounded. From Number 7 Platoon alone Privates Sauder and Chaddock lay dying; Privates Mokelki, Carver, Hogarth, Pilon, Douglas, Croft, Anderson and Guenther, and Corporals Murray and Hartigan - with my mentally blinded friend - needed evacuation to hospitals in England. From Number 8 and 9 Platoons twelve more were added - Sergeant Davies was killed, and ten others evacuated to England. Sergeant MacLean and Private McNally were also wounded but were able to return to the line after treatment by 224 Field Ambulance.

Château St. Côme after the Battle.

The greatly reduced company that remained was saddened by its losses but elated by its success! The German Army had been driven from the Château St. Côme Forest and, more importantly, it was held fast until General Gale's 22:00 hour Airborne attack on Breville went in. In recognition of the 1st Canadian Parachute Battalion's achievement we were handsomely commended by the general in a letter to our "C" Company commander, Major John Hanson.

General Gale summarizes the Breville assault that night in his autobiography: "We had to clean up this festering sore... and the assault went in at 10 p.m. Under cover of artillery fire from the 51st Highland Division the troops moved forward. German reaction was sharp, their defensive fire was heavy though indiscriminate. Before the troops crossed the start line the 12th [Parachute] Battalion, who, with a company of the Devons and the remains of my Independent Parachute Company and two tanks from the 13/18 Hussars, were to carry out the attack, lost their commanding officer, Lieutenant-Colonel Johnson. [Brigadier] Hugh Kindersley and [Lord] Lovat were both seriously wounded. [Le Plein] was like an inferno, alight with burning houses, and Breville, too, was in flames. Breville was taken at a sad cost to us of eight officers and a hundred and thirty-three other ranks. German dead littered the ground; but Breville was taken." (*Call to Arms*. London: Hutchinson, 1968, pp. 141-142.) The Canadians had stabilized the Château St.Côme part of the perimeter long enough for them to do it.

Many of the casualties sadly noted by General Gale were caused by so-called "friendly fire." Brigadier Hill is quoted as saying in Max Arthur's *Men of the Red Beret* (London: Hutchinson, 1990, p.143) that the attack "was preceded by a monumental artillery bombardment which did considerable havoc to both the Germans and our own troops." But the tide of the battle for the 6th Airborne's bridgehead was turned. The ridge was safe!

Four days after the battles at the Château St. Côme and Breville, it looked as though the enemy were about to revive their quest for the Le Mesnil Ridge. They had been soundly driven off the Breville section and the inward bend had been straightened out; but they gamely formed a new line, with their troops and logistical mass still situated southwest of the Le Mesnil-Varaville highway.

"A" Company patrols discovered that some of the German forces were reorganizing there in the fields and among the hedgerows. Battalion Headquarters Company was quick to react and broke up an impending attack with strong artillery barrages from the Canadian 3rd Infantry Division west of the Orne, and with the big guns of the warships in the Channel, before the Germans could get it under way.

The enemy knew, however, that the forces holding the ridge had suffered severely since D-Day. Also that General Gale would have to let Brigadier Hill hold his two battalions of Gordon Highlanders where the 21st Panzer Division faced the open plains between Escoville, Ste. Honorine and Longueval.

Earlier, before the northeast route through Breville became an option for the enemy, most of the serious pressure on the 6th Airborne Division had come from south of the perimeter. So the Germans decided that now Breville had fallen, Gale must be preoccupied with the south section of his front once again.

Also, the enemy undoubtedly observed the many ambulances and trucks which plied the roads westward through Ranville, carrying the hundreds of Airborne and attached regiments' wounded soldiers from the Breville and other Le Mesnil Ridge battles back to Sword Beach for evacuation to England. They now reasoned that a new try up the Varaville-Herouvillette highway through the Le Mesnil crossroads (the 1st Canadian Parachute Battalion Headquarters and 3rd Brigade Headquarters) and onward to the British 8th Parachute Battalion position at Herouvillette might finally work.

"A heavy enemy attack on 'A' Company positions was launched...on June 16th," says John A Willes in the battalion's official history *Out of the Clouds* (second edition, 1995, p.94). "The attack was preceded by an extensive mortar and artillery barrage, in which tanks and S.P. guns were used to spearhead the advance of the enemy infantry."

"A" Company positions were still in the northwest quadrant of the crossroads. They were along the road towards Breville as far as the eastern edge of the St. Côme Forest - between "C" Company of the 1st Canadian Parachute Battalion and the much more diminished 9th Parachute Battalion. The enemy, if successful in eliminating the "A" Company positions, would be able to launch a much more freewheeling attack on "C" Company aimed at seizing the crossroads itself.

Willes' account continues: "The fighting was especially heavy on the right flank of 'A' Company, particularly when a Mark IV tank and infantry made their way to within 100 yards of 'A' Company defences. A Vickers machine gun opened up on the [enemy] infantry at this point, and dispersed the advancing troops, but had no effect on the tank, which continued to advance towards the corner of the hedgerow. Pte. C.A. Johnson...scored two hits with his PIAT gun, but failed to stop the tank."

Johnson and Lance-Corporal G. Boyd were killed, and Sergeant Dwight Green and Lieutenant Bob Mitchell were seriously wounded as the attack unfolded. The tank fired several rounds of high-explosive shrapnel ammunition into other "A" Company positions. Then, because it now lacked infantry support, the tank was turned back by the determined paratroops. They had shown that although their first two antitank bombs had failed to stop the tank, another one in the right place could be fatal for its crew.

At the same time, while "A" Company troops were heavily under fire from German ground-located medium machine guns, another Mark IV tank broke into the centre of their defences. As the paratroops tried to stop the tank from getting too close to their company headquarters, Corporal James Ballingall (the company clerk, now in the trenches and fighting hard) was wounded. Company Sergeant-Major G.W. Embree was killed right beside him.

The Mark IV swivelled its turret and began to slam away at another camouflaged trench position, occupied by Privates J. H. Roberts, L. S. Henwood and R. Boardman. The position's parapets, built of logs reinforced with earth, were quickly blown away. Roberts and Boardman were instantly killed. Henwood, though severely shocked, did not cower in the trench. In plain view of the tank's crew, and now only fifteen metres from its 75-mm gun, Henwood jumped into the open, walked with his Bren machine-gun pressed hard against his hip and sprayed .303 ammunition at the tank. Slowly, he marched sideways onto the dirt track on which the monstrous machine was parked. He rammed a new magazine into his gun and sprayed again, expecting to die within seconds. Instead, Henwood simply collapsed. He could see that the tank was turning away but did not know why.

Later, to his surprise, he was given the answer. The enemy saw him go down into the dust and thought he was dead. When he awoke, he had been carried to the 224 Field Ambulance medical aid station by battalion medics. He would live, but had one of the most miraculous near-misses in history. When his "lights had gone out," as the tank's machine guns concentrated on him personally, one of the bullets had slammed through his neck muscle about an inch below his left ear. His head snapped to the left and the next bullet did the same thing under his right ear.

Several stubborn, bloody-minded actions on the part of "A" Company's paratroopers signalled to the enemy that the Canadian block at the Le Mesnil crossroads was off limits. Also that any further attempt to proceed up the Caen-Varaville highway was definitely out of the question; the price would be too heavy.

The entire-seven day battle, 9 to 16 June, on the northern side of the perimeter had cost both sides dearly. On our side the 9th Parachute Battalion was practically eliminated and the 5th Battalion Black Watch tremendously damaged. A great toll also had been exacted on Lord Lovat's Royal Marine Commando Brigade.

As for the 1st Canadian Parachute Battalion: of the twenty-eight officers who jumped at midnight 5/6 June, sixteen (fifty-nine percent) were dead, wounded or missing. Nineteen of fifty-seven sergeants (thirty-three percent) were gone. Of the 438 other ranks, 219 were killed, wounded or missing by the evening of 16 June; exactly one out of every two soldiers.

These were heavy casualties for such a short period in the field. Even when you consider the number and type of initial objectives taken and destroyed by the battalion on D-Day, the jeopardies of the subsequent patrols and attacks the individual companies had made, and the extent of the battalion's contribution to the division's most vital objective - establishing and holding the defensive fighting perimeter of the Airborne lodgement area and consequently the Orne waterways and bridges.

A major reason for the success accomplished by so few troops was that during the briefings, in conversations between the rank and file soldiers, expectations before the drop ran as high as fifty or sixty percent casualties on D-Day alone. Enemy propaganda had convinced the world, including the German people, that the Atlantic Wall was tougher than it was. The willingness of the assault units to tackle it included their readiness to accept high casualties.

Now on 17 June, the day after "A" Company rebuffed the enemy's final try to open the coastal highway to Caen by driving through Le Mesnil and Herouvillette - and thereby increase their chances to cut the Airborne bridgehead into isolated groups - Brigadier Hill's 3rd Brigade was withdrawn from the Le Mesnil Ridge. With the rest of the brigade, the 1st Canadian Parachute Battalion was sent back near the invasion beaches for a rest.

During the following days the survivors of our unit could see at first hand the mammoth weight of equipment and logistical support it had taken to breach the enemy's Atlantic Wall - albeit a somewhat weaker wall than had been expected. They learned that "strength" and "weakness" are strictly relative terms. Meanwhile, it was the 6th Airborne Division's own, already rested, 5th Parachute Brigade which relieved the 3rd Parachute Brigade, including the Canadians, on the evening of 17 June.

The ten-day battle for the Orne bridges and their waterways was ended. The enemy were now convinced that, despite its importance to them, the cost of taking the ridge would be too high in relation to their other pressing needs across the Allied invasion bridgehead. They had utterly failed to remove the Airborne and its troops under command from the ridge. We had won the battle for the Le Mesnil Ridge. But the battle for the lodgement area still went on.

The enemy were forced to keep strong opposition in place all along the Airborne perimeter to stop the Allies from using it as a breakout point for an attack towards Paris - which did occur late in July. So the Airborne perimeter again became the static-offensive perimeter - from Longueval, on the River Orne, through Ste. Honorine to Escoville-Herouvillette, Le Mesnil, Château St. Côme, Amfreville-Le Plein and down to Sallenelles, on the right shoulder of the Orne, and so to the Channel beaches. A front six to seven kilometres long.

To keep facing this lengthy perimeter the enemy were forced to tie up nearly half their 21st Panzer Division, a major portion of the 346th Infantry Division, significant formations from the 711th Infantry Division and large elements of many types of support units. These included antitank, anti-aircraft, short-range artillery, and "moaning minnie" battalions which each had 26 multi-barrelled *Nebelwerfer* mortars.

Brigadier Hill's 3rd Parachute Brigade relaxed in the area of the Orne waterways for eight days. While some shells still hit the area, the troops sunbathed, swam in the river and off the beaches near Ouistreham, toured the landing zones of the D-Day seaborne invasion and drank their share of Calvados, beer and wine.

On the night of 25 June the refreshed Canadian paratroopers returned to the Le Mesnil Ridge and relieved men of the 5th Parachute Brigade, who in their turn went back to rest by the Orne.

During the five weeks 25 June to 24 July - from the beginning of the battle for the continued ownership of the Airborne lodgement area to the start of a long rest period, 25 July to 4 August - the style of the battle changed perceptibly. The enemy thickened up their rearward positions east of the River Dives, especially with artillery and air support for their ground forces.

Both sides reinforced their front-line defences, installing roadblocks and wired-in positions behind more concentrated minefields. On the Airborne side, which continually maintained its static-offensive action, patrolling became more continuous and even more difficult and dangerous. The enemy were now doing what the Airborne had done to them since D-Day. They were into the static-offensive concept themselves. Day-to-day casualties on our side from their artillery, fighting patrols and snipers began to increase.

On a rest period in July the Canadian parachutists literally witnessed the reason why Field Marshal Montgomery's British 2nd Army had wanted the Orne bridges, together with the Airborne bridgehead east of the Orne water-ways, kept intact. Caen had fallen to the Canadians and British on 9 July, and St.Lô to the Americans on 18 July. Montgomery now saw a chance to break out into the open country east of Caen and drive towards Paris; or at least to bolster his policy of attracting German armour to the Caen flank of the Allied bridgehead while the Americans got ready for their huge, successful breakout on the western flank near St. Lô.

On 18 July "Monty" mounted a massive armoured offensive code-named Goodwood/Atlantic. There is evidence that he hoped the assault would fully occupy the Bourguebus Ridge south of Caen and even reach Falaise. Its failure to do so was a bitter disappointment. It did - though at tremendous cost in casualties and tanks before it ground to a halt three days later - extend the British-Canadian bridgehead by about nine kilometres. It also met its objective of "tying down as many German panzer divisions as possible to make it easier for the Americans to break out as planned further west." (Von Luck, *Panzer Commander,* p.179.)

While only a partial success, the attack provided a valuable side benefit for the Airborne troops. It was an eye-opener for them to see the buildup to such a huge offensive, adding to their reserves of knowledge for future operations. The Canadian paratroops, in their rest area at the mouth of the Orne, watched wide-eyed as several hundred tanks, innumerable artillery guns, endless truck convoys of ammunition and other supplies crossed over into their Airborne bridgehead.

At the time of the rest period the 1st Canadian Parachute Battalion received seven officers and one hundred other ranks as reinforcements from the Canadian Army's pool of replacement combat soldiers. These excellent infantrymen performed well for the Airborne unit when it returned to the lines, two kilometres down the road from Escoville towards Troarn on 27 July. From then until 16 August, when patrols found the Bois de Bavent free of enemy troops, they fought the same static battle which had become standard since early July - nasty patrol work and the gathering of information about the enemy.

During that three-week period the enemy were alert. But they never took on the 6th Airborne again on a full scale. It was a war of nerves and punishment for both sides, just as it had been in the early days after the invasion. Now, though, in the heat and moisture of July and August, hordes of huge mosquitoes filled the Normandy countryside. The same conditions scourged our divisions and the enemy's. To again quote Colonel von Luck, commander of the 125th regiment of 21st Panzer Division: "July was particularly hot. We all suffered from the mosquitoes; some people had to receive medical treatment for their swollen eyes....During the night of 19/20 July, torrents of rain set in....I shall never forget on our night march to the north the stink of the dead cows lying in the fields. On 20 July, moreover, there was a further heavy thunderstorm, which turned the battlefield into a swamp."

For everyone involved in the battle of Normandy the hot period of the summer went on like that. Not much movement of the front. Casualty lists piling up. Short, wicked encounters between fortified positions and minefields, killing and maiming the soldiers of both sides. Shallow patrols into thick enemy lines, as horrifying as the long flights Bomber Command airmen were experiencing while carrying their weight to Berlin.

Slowly the nights and days of static battle crept towards 16 August. During the three - week period after the 1st Canadian Parachute Battalion returned from their July rest on the banks of the Orne River, the unit lost numerous men, killed and wounded, to the whims of the so-called "static battle."

That night they were ordered to break out to the east and seize the Bois de Bavent. The move would allow them to close up to the west bank of the Dives River. The long, hard seventy-two-day battle of the 6th Airborne Division in the lodgement area between the Orne and Dives rivers was now completely over. The enemy were on the run.

A. J. (Scotty) MacInnis had still not been seen. No one had heard a word from him. If still living he could look back to that day in 1937 when he had remarked, "Jesus, Bye, if we ain't careful that bastard Hitler is going to have us byes from Cape Breton over there fightin' again." For Cape Bretoners and other Canadians from sea to sea, his grass-roots prophecy had come true with a vengeance.

244

W. E. Oikle

Chapter XVI

The Return to Freedom

W. R. Kelly

Although the main battalion had fought its ferocious battle for supremacy at the Le Mesnil Ridge, and through July and most of August was in a continuous struggle with the enemy to maintain the stability of the Airborne's perimeter, several Canadian paratroopers were still displaced, surviving a life and death existence completely away from the Airborne lodgement area. Privates Jim MacPherson and Morris Zakaluk who were continuously on the move, and Private Colin Lewis who worked as a farm labourer during the entire battle of Normandy, were representative of the men in the plateau country on the loose behind the enemy lines. Many others, having fought their personal and small-group battles to the end of their capabilities and supplies, were now in the hands of the Germans as prisoners of war.

Lieutenant Marcel Cote was taken by degrees towards the centre of the continent. He was interrogated time and again by Hitler's security police - the SD - who worked in merger with Himmler's Nazi Secret Police, the detested Gestapo. They repeatedly asked the same question: "Why were you dropped at the Le Havre airport?" Cote always gave the same answer: "I have no idea. I simply don't know." The Nazis wouldn't believe him but he was telling the truth. Like many other scattered paratroopers he continually asked himself why he was dropped so far off target. Nobody ever hinted that he would end up in the vicinity of Le Havre. Even if he had been dropped four to five kilometres off the Drop Zone he and his men might have begun to believe it was an accident; but forty kilometres off - as the crow flies - when they were less than one hundred and twenty-five kilometres from the last check-point in England? If the paratroopers had remained on board all the way from the Drop Zone, up the French coast and across the Seine estuary, and then had swerved northwest behind Le Havre and out towards the Channel before they were dropped, even that might have been entitled to some credence. But they had come across the cliffs at Octeville in a direction opposite from the one they should have taken to reach Varaville, forty kilometres away. It made no sense and just could not be believed. It was convincingly a "set-up" to the paratroops on board. To them they had to have been dropped as decoys!

Privates Joseph Nigh and John Coburn died while resisting the Germans late on the evening of D-Day. It is thought they were the ones heard firing Bren machine guns in the wheat fields near Montivilliers when Lieutenant Cote and Sergeant George Breen were beginning their truck ride, in captivity, to Rouen that same evening.

Privates Warwick, Waddell, Summerhays, Mearow, Dumas and

Dunphy, together with Corporal Miller, were put in prison at Le Havre where they were also interrogated. Harold Miller writes:

"We landed in a field by an airport a few miles from Le Havre ... on the wrong side of the Seine estuary. The Germans surrounded the field with patrols and (throughout the day) killed some and picked up others. They marched those of us who could march to a prison in Le Havre, where they kept us for a few days while they interrogated us by the starvation method. Then they started us on a zig-zag course across the country by train. First to Rouen, then to Beauvais, then Amiens. From there back south to Paris, northeast to Brussels, southeast to Luxembourg, Frankfurt, Obersul and Wetzlar. Obersul was a bad one. All of them brought more interrogations, all wanting to know why we had dropped at Le Havre. But Obersul was especially grim!

"After the Allies crossed the Rhine in March 1945 the Germans started us east on foot. After five days on the road, the U.S. 3rd Army (Patton's tanks) picked us up. We rode on into Germany with them for about two weeks and then were sent off to the Canadian Army for new uniforms and other gear. We were then flown back to England from the same Octeville airport at which we had landed on the night before D-Day."

After Jim MacPherson shook hands with Albert (the Resistance Man with the price on his head) and said goodbye to Albert's wife, he and his friend Dick Reed, the P-38 fighter pilot, moved on to a farm with a large stone house and good outbuildings with lots of implements. "Beyond the house was a fine disused grist mill.. About two hundred yards away was a château which was occupied by the Germans most of the time we remained there. The French family kept a close surveillance on the enemy so we were able to get out into the fields and help the family with their hay-making. Getting a little overconfident one day, I stepped out into the yard at the house and there, with his back to me, was a German soldier. After coming all this way, my heart sank down to my boots. He had come to ask for eggs, and while he was talking to the farmer I gradually backed into the house. The farmer looked over the German's shoulder and never batted an eye. That was the last of the really close calls we experienced. Phew! That was nerve wracking!"

Meanwhile more than thirty days went by before Morris Zakaluk was finally accepted into the French Resistance. It may be recalled that he had to go through a long, arduous process to achieve that - proving himself to French civilians who knew that a wrong decision could cost them their lives. Morris continues his account: "Peter, the English speaker, informs us we are about to raid some kind of a German headquarters building in a nearby village. It was to be an early morning raid. Since the Germans there had a habit of sleeping late, the raid would catch them by surprise - all in a rush: shoot the place up and then run like hell!

"We get into this panel truck and drive to the locality. We have grenades, Sten guns, a rifle or two and lots of ammunition. Peter is the leader -

just a kid. I stay close to him so I'll have some idea of what's going on. 'What do we do about casualties,' I ask? 'Forget about casualties,' says he. The attack goes in. Grenades through the windows followed by wild firing into any opening in the building; then we race like hell for the panel truck and speed away. We get away scot free, no casualties, simply relishing in laying it onto them. As we turn off onto a wood road enemy machine-gun tracers fill the sky overhead. Everybody laughs wildly!

"Next time it's a tobacconist catering to a German Luftwaffe station across the street - guards close by and the works. Three men go in with handguns, clean the shelves, pay with phony French francs - off to our bicycles with a gunny sack of tobacco and rolling paper good for a month."

So it went for Morris Zakaluk during July and August 1944. His ankle mended by now, he ran with the French underground, the Maquis. Their frequent raids were disruptive and injurious to the enemy. The Maquis was good at pre-attack reconnaissance. When attacks went in they were violent with high firepower and generally inflicted severe casualties. On the other hand they were delivered with such sudden surprise that the Maquis were gone by the time the enemy began to get organized. For the Maquis themselves injuries and deaths were comparatively infrequent.

During these weeks and months Jim MacPherson and his U.S. Air Force (Thunderbolt) fighter-pilot friend Dick Reed continued to evade the enemy. They moved farther and farther south, being fed every day or two by French farmers sympathetic to the Allies. Time and again they barely scraped through close encounters with enemy soldiers until they felt like the proverbial "man who always got away!"

They managed to slip into the deep forest after watching through the vacant stairwell while French black marketeers butchered and sold off a rustled steer. From there they moved more cautiously. They estimated that by the first week in August they had worked their way south to a point somewhere between Le Mans and Laval, almost directly south of Caen.

MacPherson continues: "We were getting bits of information - almost rumour type stuff - from time to time. It was pretty certain the American advance was somewhere south of Argentan and heading east towards the Seine. Dick figured we'd stand a pretty good chance of getting through the lines in that area, since word went round that the German front was beginning to show signs of breaking up. We then headed pretty well straight north.

"We reverted to travelling at night again and made straight for Alencon. Since it was fairly open country, and enemy traffic was continuous on the main highways, we took to the fields and pastures again. The number of days and nights it took us to get to our first goal remains a question, even to us, but when we did reach Alencon there were signs that enemy units were digging in, mostly in open country. There were now a lot of French refugees mixed in with the enemy traffic, so we figured it would be better to get mixed up with them. "We decided to get out of the open country and go right through a city. I don't know why, but when we got right inside the city after dark there was not a soul in sight or a sound to be heard. It was at that time I realized the loose cleats on my boots were making a terrible racket. Dick and I both sat down and took our boots off.

"After we proceeded for a short while, I realized I had left a pair of good Canadian kid gloves I had brought to France in my pocket lying on the curb where we had sat. The label, 'Made in Canada,' was still on them as plain as day. We were not about to take a chance on going back for them, but worried a lot about the Germans finding them. Our night progress was favourable and at some time in the early pre-dawn darkness we came to a fork in the street system. We were doubtful about which fork to take. We wanted to get to a place named Sees. I shinnied up a sign post and, sure enough, a sign with Sees on it pointed out the correct direction. Still in our sock feet, we bypassed Sees on what looked like a hiking path, spent a night in a barn and had breakfast with a farmer. Crowds of people were on the highways once more, so we proceeded in daylight again.

"Nearing the area of Argentan, we saw a crowd of people on the highway and were quite close to them when we realized it was a German checkpoint. We were too close to it to back up without arousing suspicion, nor could we cut across the fields without being followed, but Lady Luck was with us. Right there to our left was a road sign pointing to Flers, so we took that road and got away with it. We had just turned the corner when we came face to face with a German patrol coming towards us not two hundred feet away.

"We were stumped, but also on that corner was a large house. We simply changed direction, walked up the path to the front door, opened it, walked straight through the house past a group of gawking French folks, and out the back door. We spoke to no one and no one spoke to us, and the Germans just kept on going to the checkpoint.

"As we got closer to the Allied front we became more edgy about the possibility of getting caught between the Germans and Americans. This in turn caused us to think of the many close calls we had come through before we had reached the Le Mans-Laval area. It seemed unlikely we would experience anything as hair-raising as that again, but couldn't help thinking how terrible it would be to get caught at this late date.

"One day we were looking for a spot to lie low, and upon investigating a log barn we wandered into an enemy signals station. The aerial wire was strung out to a huge tree by the log barn and we didn't see it until we came right up to it. Just as we made a quick right turn out of there a huge German soldier came out and stood looking at us as we walked out of the vicinity.

"The next day we met some French Maquis and they took us to a big farmhouse for a huge meal. The man of the house could speak English, and after we were fed he took us to a village some kilometres away and installed us on the upper floor of some type of workshop. We were given a large pail of water and were then left to our own devices. As they left they padlocked the door from the outside and this gave us a bad night. To be locked up in such a way did not look too promising; especially in the morning when they did not return.

"About mid-morning, though, a truck convoy of Germans showed up and parked all around the building where we were incarcerated. Through some cracks in a boarded-up window we could see the enemy soldiers milling around and shouting blue murder at one another, but could not tell what they were saying. What a spot to be in at this late stage! Were they there to take over the building or what? However, after about three hours they just piled into the trucks and drove away. They must have been hiding from Allied fighter bombers or something, since they did not appear to accomplish anything while they were there.

"About twilight our Maquis friends returned, took us away to another country house and gave us another huge meal. After eating we were moved again and walked some miles to a large estate. There we met an exceptionally dignified and elegant Lady of the Manor. We now knew we had contacted the formal French Underground at last. The lady was very kind to us and, after we were sent to a sumptuous bath with soap to go with the water, we were supplied with fresh robes and socks. Our dirty ragged clothing was taken away to be washed. We were then ushered into a big bedroom. The beds were equipped with overstuffed down mattresses. They were the first soft beds we had slept in for nearly two months.

"We never did see the lovely lady again. Late next morning we were awakened and met by a young man who returned our belongings and introduced himself as Marcel. He did not look too impressive standing there in his worn out clothing and his wooden clogs. His English was not too crisp but better than our French. It soon turned out that this lad really knew how to play the dangerous game he was involved in.

"We found ourselves half sprinting through a deep forest, trying to keep up with Marcel and his wooden shoes. Dick's wound had not completely healed and he had an extremely painful time keeping pace. After about an hour of this we were back on a paved road, passing a hospital which had a large arched entrance with iron gates. A cast-iron picket fence surrounded it. By the iron gates was a mountain of a man, a German sergeant, standing with a Schmeisser sub-machine gun slung on his shoulder. Marcel never turned a hair. The German sergeant descended three steps to the sidewalk and fell in behind us. I can still feel him breathing down my neck for the next two blocks.

"As we came to an intersection, 'Man Mountain Dean' still clomping along behind us, an enemy platoon led by an officer approached from our left. The officer halted his platoon to converse with the big sergeant. Once again we were given a reprieve and were off the hook. How the big man had not seen through our thin disguises we will never know. I think it must have been the clip-clop of Marcel's wooden shoes that covered the sound of the steel cleats on my boots.

"Our greatest concern was that, if caught, Marcel would have been executed on the spot while Dick and myself would have stood a good chance of being taken prisoners. Through all of it Marcel never flinched and one had to wonder where these people found the great courage to do the things they did for us. At the end of his run Marcel turned us over to another man, called Albert, who helped us on our way.

"Albert also had a price on his head and he and his wife were hiding out in a lean-to built into a hillside under some extraordinarily heavy brush. We were told the flat fields at the top of the hill were used as a Drop Zone for RAF arms drops. Albert was the man who distributed the weapons and supplies.

"After a dinner of good old British Army compo rations we crowded into the lean-to with Albert and his wife. It was there we discovered a new meaning for the word discomfort. We never did get the lumps and bumps out of our bodies which the hard, rocky ground of their abode impressed there. It was with rickety bones and tendons that we hobbled away to meet a downed Canadian Spitfire pilot a few days later. His name was George Murray, a Nova Scotian, and he was helped out by a French couple who saw him shot down. We returned to the lean-to and every day or two George Murray was brought to see us. Some time later it was apparent the front was getting nearer to us. We saw aerial dog-fights taking place overhead and planes from both sides were being shot down.

"Suddenly, one day, there was a real commotion on the fields up above - the Drop Zone. Albert investigated and came racing down the hill in a great fluster, he and his wife grabbing everything they could carry. Dick and I copy-catted them. Albert raced for the valley below. When we arrived at a spot where we could rest, his wife explained what it was all about. Albert had spotted the Germans setting up an anti-aircraft battery there. It was decided Dick and I would be sent to a farm somewhere east of Argentan. A man came to lead us there. We shook hands with Albert and his wife and never saw or heard of them again.

"Dick and I moved out of the area with the help of a Resistance cell. The owner of the home we moved into had been a sergeant in WW I. As at the previous large stone house we had lived in, with the grist mill in the backyard, there were German soldiers bivouacked behind the house.

"The beds in our new home were unbelievable for men who had relied on the ground for a mattress for the past few weeks. When you got into them and stretched out on the feather down, it took about five minutes to sink to the bottom. The third evening after we moved in a lot of enemy armoured vehicles began to move east. It was a good sign. The news we were now getting was all good.

"On the seventh a small convoy of U.S. Army light tanks came rumbling up the road. The following morning George Murray, Dick and I shook hands with the family who had so bravely risked their lives to help us and were so good to us. It was an extremely nostalgic moment - again like leaving home for the last time. We caught a Jeep ride to Falaise where we met the Canadian Army. We obliged them by helping Canadian Army Military Police to escort a big crowd of German prisoners of war to a camp somewhere towards the Channel. When we arrived there I sat down and took off my worn out boots and my civilian coveralls, dusted off my parachute wings, turned my red beret right side out and stood there in full Canadian paratrooper uniform. Now standing in front of me were a bunch of bug-eyed Germans. Following a four or five day rest and clean-up in the area of St. Lô, we were flown back to Britain. After seventy-four days behind the German lines we were free, and they were locked up!"

Dr. Colin N. Brebner had been taken to Bon Saveur hospital in Caen and was taken care of by The Little Sisters of the Poor. Dr. Brebner says, "I figured I was the first Canadian in Caen, but not in an approved way."

When the doctor and his three travelling companions settled into the hospital he decided that his injuries mainly required bone healing, which would occur in a couple of months anyhow, so he insisted that the German and French doctors take care of his friends first. Nobody would listen to him, and the hospital medical staff made a great fuss over him. Later he found out why: the RAF had bombed Caen on the night of 6/7 June, trying to eliminate the *Wehrmacht's* headquarters in the city; but they missed and had taken out the residential section, causing seven thousand casualties. "Unfortunately, the poor British wounded were now not very popular," Dr. Brebner says.

"Lieutenant Casares of the 13th Battalion was with me all the time. He was very badly injured on his right side. I was injured on my left wrist and arm, as well as having my broken pelvis. The nurses therefore put my bed on his left so I could hand him things with my good right hand, and he could receive them with his good left hand. He suffered terribly, but never complained. The nurses were good, and through all the bombing and shelling were very brave.

"One day in early July Casares and I were taken away again, to a spa in a beautiful valley southwest of Caen. On my being held up at the door of Bon Saveur Hospital on the way out to an ambulance, one of the sisters slipped me a flask of Calvados brandy. Casares and I decided to save it for a rainy day. Some time later, as we were driven out of Caen amid mortar fire and flaming buildings on both sides of the street, it seemed like a rainy day to us; it was a godsend. Once having arrived at the spa we were carried to the top floor by German paratroop officers who had just come in for a rest after their defence of Monte Casino in Italy. They were quite friendly and sent their senior medical man in to see me. He told me he was sorry to see a doctor, who could very well be used at the front, so badly injured.

"One day near the middle of August we saw an American Jeep driving down a highway. All the walking wounded were hanging out of our spa windows hollering and shouting at the men in the Jeep. In good old U.S. fashion, in no time at all a new field hospital was erected and we were in there having our casts changed and new dressings put our wounds, and were getting penicillin shots all round for those with infections. On 13 August I was airlifted to an airport near Oxford, England."

Later Dr. Brebner was evacuated to Canada by way of the *Isle de*

France, the same ship the Battalion came home on after the war. He arrived in Toronto on 3 October 1944.

Morris Zakaluk was getting weary. It was now just past the middle of August. The primitive lifestyle he had led for more than ten weeks, along with a meagre diet and the wear and tear on his clothing and footwear, had left him dirty, itching and smelly. He had not had a bath since leaving England. Successful airdrops of supplies, for him, simply meant more dirt, as he was the one in his Maquis cell who knew how to degrease submachine guns, grenades and the Airborne-type 2-inch mortars. Everything came packed in grease inside the parachuted containers.

As he says: "Until I trained some of the others how to handle these problems, and how to safely arm everything with the detonators provided, I was in grease up to my armpits.

"Finally rumours reached us that the Allies were moving up and had broken out east of Trun. With great glee the shout goes up: 'Every man for himself!' I head out for Argentan looking for armoured columns. Thousands of civilians do the same. Soon U.S. armoured columns come into view and a continuous stream of fighter and bomber aircraft form a spectacular sight while dogging the enemy to the east.

"Civilians mix with U.S. soldiers who are tossing chocolate bars and chewing gum everywhere, amid dancing and tears of joy. The French haul out their cider, toss flowers and smother everyone with hugs and kisses. Two months of hell on the move, the attacks, the pain and hunger are suddenly over. Life turns into heaven on earth.

"I'm corralled by three young girls, probably in their early twenties, and they're all over me, knocking me down and smothering me with their bodies and flowers - the heat of the cider and their beautiful bodies mingling with the flood of tears running off their faces. Oh God, what a glorious beginning to a lost soldier's freedom! I'm pinned down in a sea of affection and wonder why I'm singled out. I'm in civilian clothes, armed with grenades and carrying an enemy rifle. The girls make it understood they want me to stay in France and go home with them. I want to stay. In showing love and affection, the French girls are unmatched - they know how to make a man feel like a supreme being. To describe it, I can think only of Winston Churchill's rhetoric. Truly, 'this is my finest hour!'

"I'm living beyond my wildest dreams and imagination. The love and passion coursing within my being in response to the tenderness and loving warmth of my new friends is consuming me. Goddamnit all to hell, the world spins and reality floods in. I have to go back. The Army is like a bloody octopus. Its tentacles envelop everything. The war is not over, it's just the end of a battle. A few hours later I get an English-speaking Frenchman to explain it all to my beautiful young lovers. I have to go back. I've lived hell on earth for over seventy days but in the end I had my day in the Sun.

"The following morning, on unsteady legs, smelling of sweat, dirt, and grease, I turn myself in to the Yanks. I'm interrogated by an American major. Astounded by my revelations, he's wide-eyed with interest and admiration. He pats me on the shoulder and tells me to wait on an adjacent chair. 'I just have one more enemy prisoner to interrogate,' he says, 'then I'll look after you personally. Take you where you can get cleaned up and get some new clothing and footgear.'

"The next guy up is a high-ranking German officer. He tries to be coy with the Yank officer - unco-operative and haughty! Speaks excellent English. The U.S. major snaps at the enemy prisoner, 'Look here you son of a bitch, you see that young kid sitting over there on that chair? He's a Canadian paratrooper who's spent the last few months behind your lines and right now he's as mean as a scalded wildcat. If I just give him a flick of my finger pointed at you he'll put a you-know-what right between your goddamned ever-lovin' eyes. The enemy officer looked me over and then began to sing like a humming bird. One continuous melody.

"Shortly the prisoner was whisked away by some U.S. Military Policemen and the interrogation officer took me down a grade to his unit, where I got showered and shaved, and was given a haircut and new clothes. He then saw to it that I was properly fed and drove me to an airdrome where he personally put me on a C-47 for London. There, I spent a few days with British Intelligence, doing the debriefing thing all over again. I must say everyone was very good to me.

"I was put in a Canadian General Hospital at Horsham, Number 9, I believe, for fattening up. At first, when I looked in the mirror, I was surprised that a man could have lost so much weight. By the end of September I was back in my old barrack room at Carter Barracks with the remnants of the occupants who had left there on the morning of 28th May. It was easy to see it was going to take a while for us to get back in shape. It was obvious we'd all been through the mill and came out as coarse grist. As everything whirled in my brain those first few weeks back, my soul automatically paid tribute to the brave French people who helped me to survive so I could rejoin my unit and fight again."

Chapter XVII

The Drive for the Seine

Mosher MacPhee

On the morning of 17 August the advance towards the Seine River began. To quote John A. Willes' history of the battalion, *Out of the Clouds*: "To effect this action, the 6th Airborne Division was ordered to advance to a line joining Cabourg on the left, and Bures on the right, with the 8th and 9th British Parachute Battalions to seize Bures, and the 1st Canadian Parachute Battalion to sweep through the Bois de Bavent once the village had been seized."

This was the first time Brigadier Hill's 3rd Brigade acted in unison, on an attack, in the Normandy campaign. The move by the British was swift because the enemy had withdrawn beyond the river during the night. On the Canadian front, however, in the dense part of the Bois de Bavent, the enemy had left a surprise.

As Willes adds (pp. 97-98): "By this time, the enemy had withdrawn from the woods, but had left behind an incredible number of mines and booby traps, which slowed the Canadian advance, and resulted in a number of casualties to 'B' Company. The woods were eventually cleared, and the Battalion, along with the rest of the 3rd Parachute Brigade, crossed the River Dives on bridges that had been constructed by the 3rd Brigade squadron of Royal Engineers. By 21:00 hours that day, the 1st Canadian Parachute Battalion had advanced a distance of three miles along a railway line running northeast from Bures, to a point where 'A' Company made contact with the enemy at Plain Lugan. At this point, the Battalion stopped its advance, and took up positions for the night. The Brigade's operation, code-named 'Paddle', had been completed."

The next phase of the Airborne's advance, code-named Operation Paddle II, was motivated by the enemy's destruction of the main bridge crossing the St. Samson – Dives-sur-Mer Canal. It was known for certain, prior to Paddle II on 17 August, that the enemy was thick on the ground in defence of the four remaining St. Sampson Canal bridges as part of their withdrawal plan.

The Falaise Pocket had been nearly slammed shut by the 1st Canadian Army's seizure of St. Lambert, south of Caen by Falaise, on 15 August. The great wheeling movement which Montgomery's pre-D-Day plan had envisioned, hinged on the Airborne lodgement's perimeter along the lower Dives, had been slowly turning eastwards as the 1st Canadian and the 2nd British Armies gradually shifted from their original southerly advance towards Falaise to a new southeast advance. This took them towards Les Champeaux and Camembert, flanked by the line St. Lambert-Trun. Now the 6th Airborne with its Special Service Commando Brigades under command were to continue an advance east of the Dives which would carry them on a straight frontal assault all the way to the Seine River. The main bulk of Montgomery's two armies, the 21st Army Group, completed their left wheel to face Antwerp and Brussels.

The 3rd Parachute Brigade attack, as far as the 1st Canadian Parachute Battalion was concerned, was planned with "A" and "C" Companies up, and "B" Company in reserve. Headquarters Company's heavy weapons platoons - Vickers machine guns, and mortars - were in close support, with squads from Signals, Intelligence and PIAT (antitank) platoons attached as needed. Medics were always attached to the various sub-units when the battalion was in the attack phase.

The orders that came down from General Gale's headquarters had been written with a view to the weapons lightness of his forces. He cautioned that his Airborne battalions and brigades were to attack only when they were certain the enemy was already withdrawing. For his money, his troops had suffered enough casualties in Normandy, and although he knew that they would necessarily suffer more he wanted to keep injuries and deaths as low as possible. The 6th Airborne Division was going to need major reinforcement and retraining after the Battle of Normandy was over. He would need a strong cadre of experienced combat soldiers with which to rebuild the division's esprit de corps and effectiveness.

With the "Airborne mystique" always in play and Brigadier Hill's Motto "Speed in Thought and Action" dogging the 3rd Brigade soldiers' footsteps, the General's order to push the Germans only when they were already on the run was bound to founder on the heap of empathetic good intentions. This was especially so in the Canadian paratroopers' collective mind; the "Speed and Action Concept" dominated. To them it had been promoted and had become essential, strung out on huge banners on the walls of their Carter Barracks gymnasiums.

Professor John Willes' work continues (p.98): "Four railway bridges, each separated by distances of about one quarter of a mile were shown on the map, with the most northerly bridge being on the [main] rail line to Troarn crossing the canal not far from Goustranville.

"The attack was set for 21:45 hours on August 18, 1944, and by 22:20 hours 'C' Company had seized the [most northerly] bridge." They also seized a hundred and fifty enemy troops as prisoners of war. "Within an hour and thirty minutes following the seizure of that first bridge, the remaining bridges fell into Canadian hands. The southernmost bridge, which was captured intact by 'A' Company, was named 'Canada Bridge' in honour of the Battalion. In slightly more than two hours the Battalion had wiped out two well-fortified positions, and taken 150 prisoners. Operation Paddle II drew to a close with the 9th Parachute Battalion crossing [one of] the partly demolished railway bridges." That same night they destroyed the remainder of the 744th Grenadier Battalion of the Germans' 711 Infantry Division.

The advance through the Bois de Bavent to the completion of Operation Paddle II cost the 1st Canadian Parachute Battalion twenty three soldiers killed or wounded. These were heavy casualties for such a previously depleted battalion to experience. But one must wonder, when considering the number of enemy soldiers wounded, killed and taken prisoner, plus the difficulty of seizing canal bridges in almost any battle, why the paratroop casualties were comparatively light.

It seems to the paratroop survivors of the war, who experienced many battles where the ratios of enemy prisoners taken were in high contrast to casualties amongst the Canadian paratroops, that their absorption of Brigadier Hill's concept of "Speed in Thought and Action" provides an answer. This same phenomenon proved to be the case over and over again until, by the end of World War II, the battalion had counted more than six times its own strength in prisoners of war. This excludes prisoners gained in any mass surrender such as the thousands who surrendered their weapons during the last two weeks of the war.

In discussions with Sergeant Freddie Rudko of Number 9 Platoon and Sergeant G.J.A Young of Number 8 Platoon, as well as with two consecutive Company Sergeants-Major, Willard Minard and Dick MacLean, it was found that their opinions were similar. To them, the soldiers on the attack who were quick and could keep their heads about them were the most successful. They all gave high praise to the mortar, PIAT antitank and Vickers platoons for their quick support and their obvious adherence to that concept, "Speed in Thought and Action." They were specific about the speed of advance once our troops departed their start-lines. Sergeant Rudko stated: "The speed with which our assaults on the enemy went in was no different than it had been practiced in training - rushing the enemy with our weapons firing from the hip - onward across their positions with numerous of their soldiers slumping in their slit trenches." Disarming them quickly once we had reached the objective was important too. Rudko, especially, was convinced that a lot of credit was due to putting into practice other Airborne field-training ideas. Concepts such as getting good cover before the start-line was crossed and making weapons-fire count before the actual attack began. The separate attacks on all four bridges were completed in exceptionally short time.

"A" Company's Canada Bridge gave many Canadians a special thrill. Almost continuous transport and equipment convoys sped eastward by that route to supply the 21st Army Group during the great battles in Belgium and Holland the following fall and winter.

With the St. Samson Canal bridges secured, quickly replaced and open to traffic, a continuous advance was set in motion by General Gale and his brigadiers. Gale's division now operated with five brigades. They were the 3rd and 5th Parachute Brigades and the 6th Airlanding (glider) Brigade, together with his other units under command: the 1st British Special Service Commando Brigade and the 45th Royal Marine Commando Brigade, with Belgian and Dutch (Princess Irene's) commandos.

Back on 23 July the second-in-command of the 1st Canadian Parachute Battalion, Major Jeff Nicklin, stepped on a mine and was quite severely wounded. Immediately a call went out to the Training Battalion for a replacement major. On 1 August Acting Major G. Fraser Eadie arrived at Le Mesnil and took up the position of temporary second in command of the battalion.

Then, on 23 August, the unit received a visit from Lieutenant-General Ken Stuart, Chief of the General Staff of the Canadian Army. His visit culminated in the promotion of the battalion commander, Lieutenant Colonel G.F.P. Bradbrooke, to General Staff Officer, Class 1, Royal Air Force 38 Group. With Nicklin still in hospital, Brigadier Hill placed the new major, Fraser Eadie, in temporary command. There were only a few weeks left of the combat portion of the Battle of Normandy, as far as the paratroopers' participation was concerned. During the four weeks since he was taken on strength Eadie had gained a reputation as a quite fair and quick-witted officer, with a flair for showing initiative and a habit of displaying a quick temper. The battalion took to him in a way that had not happened with the original commander or with Major Nicklin. Bradbrooke had presented himself as an aloof, not very visible commander, which was his prerogative in choosing a style of leadership; but it did not make for warm human relations with the rank and file. With Nicklin away and Bradbrooke assigned to the RAF, the battalion began to gallop towards the Seine estuary with its new temporary commander, Major Eadie. The over-worked and over-stressed remnants of what had been a superb unit when it had come to France took on an added spirit.

In the Airborne, with regard to exceptional military professionalism and general competence, there seemed to be a level playing field across the Western Allies' Airborne establishment. None of the six Airborne divisions on the Allied side were much more than three years old when they merged into the 1st Allied Airborne Army in the autumn of 1944. To many of the old tried and true infantry divisions from WWI that were reconstituted in WWII, the new Airborne divisions might have seemed somewhat like whipper snappers without much savvy. But everyone had to admit that these new boys on the block did have something exciting about them. Their commanders called it the Airborne mystique. It was freely admitted that even if they were young in experience, they sure as hell could cut the mustard! With elan and with "Speed in Thought and Action," they tore on towards their River Seine objectives, and Major Eadie's style of command certainly fitted that mode.

General Montgomery had placed the 1st British Corps, which included the 6th Airborne Division, under the command of General Crerar of the 1st Canadian Army. At first the general officers of the 1st British Corps did not like the idea of serving under a Canadian general, apparently never giving a thought to the fact that for nine years in the two big wars, up until now, numerous Canadian Corps had fought magnificently under British command. Even right now, the sixty-thousand man 1st Canadian Corps was fighting in the 8th Army under General Alexander in Italy. Up until 23 July the 2nd Canadian Corps had fought in General Dempsey's 2nd British Army. And now the officers and men of the British 6th Airborne Division were proud to serve in the 1st Canadian Army under General Crerar. It is properly recorded in the *Official History of the Canadian Army in the Second World War* (Vol. 3, pp. 196-197) that General Crocker refused the first order that General Crerar had issued to him. Crocker was probably surprised at the alacrity with which the gentleman, Crerar, straightened him out. And it was not long until the troops and officers of the 1st British Corps, who remained with the 1st Canadian Army until March of the following year, felt the same way that the 6th Airborne Division did to begin with. Those were the months when the 1st Canadian Army fought the terribly vicious battles of Holland and the Rhineland through the numbing fall and winter of 1944-45.

Now, in the present situation, the five alternating brigades moved forward, marching on their sore flat feet without transport, and keeping pace with the motorized divisions of the 1st British Corps on their right. One brigade followed the coastal highway and another went along the second main highway in from the coast on an axis Dozule Pont l'Evêque-Beuzeville to Maison Mauger near the Seine. The five brigades alternated from forward on the attack to following in reserve. That way they arrived in the vicinity of the Seine estuary on 25 August. That day, which should have been a happy one, was a sad time for "C" Company, 1st Canadian Parachute Battalion.

The 3rd Parachute Brigade had moved into Beuzeville to rest, but the 1st Canadian Parachute Battalion had one more objective to take - a little job beyond Maison Mauger. Once it was taken the battalion settled down there for the night. Action for the Canadian paratroops in Normandy was over because the enemy at Maison Mauger had merely melted away. The evening twilight was crowding in on the new stillness; then it happened. A little pop on the edge of a small wood, not more than two hundred feet away, sounded the launching of a rifle grenade by a lone enemy soldier who had fallen behind his fleeing comrades. The relaxing Canadians, lounging on the late summer turf, each thankful for having survived the scalding eighty-one day battle of Normandy, hardly gave the subdued "pop" a lift of an eyebrow. The hiss of the grenade's descent gave them warning not to be complacent, but too late. As though by accident it landed beside Sergeant Mosher MacPhee. Every unbelieving eye remaining in Number 7 Platoon was riveted upon the scene, absolutely incredulous. Mosher MacPhee was dead. Killed by a "god-damned fluke."

It is hard to describe the sorrow and anger conjured up by this rotten stroke of fate. Sergeant MacPhee was a favourite because he deserved to be a favourite. He was highly respected because he deserved that too. He was every acquaintance's good friend because he had earned that friendship. And he is terribly missed because he deserves to be missed - even after fifty years! Every man had vivid recall of this "immortal sergeant" in action. Sergeant MacPhee hammering away at the Germans with a captured mortar that had a shrapnel hole in its barrel. Sergeant MacPhee firmly but coolly calming the storm aroused by one rebellious soldier before an impossible night patrol. Sergeant MacPhee, at his own peril, saving Private (Sinkor) Swim from what would have been a filthy death in the cesspool at Bavent. Sergeant MacPhee with great calm directing the attack on Varaville, on D-Day, between the time Major MacLeod and Lieutenant Charles Walker were killed and the time Captain Hanson arrived. Such memories seem endless and are still almost a daily occurrence. Nearly every third man in the platoon had died during the previous eighty days, but Mosher's death seemed the most unjust death of all.

On 28 August orders came down from the 1st Canadian Army for the 6th Airborne Division to move into reserve. The Battle of Normandy was officially closed for the Canadian paratroops.

From an almost certain defeat laid on by a disastrously scattered drop during the midnight hours of 5/6 June - D-Day - the men summoned the courage from the depths of their personal guts to turn almost certain defeat into victory. Of the battalion's five hundred and forty-one paratroops who dropped that night, three hundred and sixty-eight were killed, wounded or missing by the end of the 83-day battle.

They had fought and played a full part in the British 6th Airborne Division's battle for the defence of the Orne bridgehead and its sixty initial D-Day objectives. That meant doing their share in a violent, prolonged and remarkable battle. They had performed their patriotic duty in a superb fashion. Although the main part of the shattered battalion departed for England from the port of Honfleur on the Seine estuary, some who had special rearguard duties departed through the port of Ouistreham. When they marched through the battle-torn hedges, fields and villages surrounding the Le Mesnil Ridge on their way home, more than one soldier could not hold back a tear in his wonderment of the silence there.

But what about A. J. (Scotty) MacInnis from Sydney, Nova Scotia? To this very day fifty-five years later there is still no sign of him. But had he been able to continue with the battalion for its later battling advances in Europe through Belgium to the River Meuse and over the Rhine, followed by the race across Germany to the Baltic Sea, one can predict what Scotty would have said on seeing the starved and brutalized inmates of Belsen along the way. "Thank God we came over and fought this war, eh! The sight of these poor souls tells us again what we knew from the start. We have fought for a just cause!"

Private A. J. (Scotty) MacInnis.
One of the soldiers named on the Monument to the
Unknown Soldier at Bayeux, Normandy.

INDEX

Adams, Bill, 96.
Adams, L. H., 167.
Advance Party, 36, 51, 65, 68, 108, 110, 197, 208-210.
Age, average, of paratroops, 18, 25.
Airborne mystique, 43, 132, 255, 257.
Aircrews, 45, 56, 63, 73, 74, 77, 78, 99, 120, 195, 200, 211, 212.
Albemarle bomber, 37, 38, 45, 50, 63, 65-67, 108-110, 197-201, 208.
Aldershot (NS), 11.
Alencon, 247.
Aleutians, 10, 13.
Alexander, Earl of Tunis, 257.
Alexandria, 13.
Allen, C. A., 233.
Amfreville, 28, 166, 167, 183, 219-221, 226, 229-231, 243.
Amiens, 246.
Anderson, A., 77.
Anderson, Boyd, 2, 3, 7, 8, 10, 14, 74-79, 81, 91, 106, 136-143, 185-189, 191, 213.
Anderson, J. A., 237, 239.
Anti-aircraft fire, 75, 76, 80, 84, 88-90, 107-110, 116, 149, 150, 204, 205, 211.
Antitank ditch, 39, 47-49, 112, 114, 125, 127, 128, 130.
Antitank guns,
  75-mm, enemy, 42, 43, 114, 116, 118, 125-132.
  PIAT, 29, 34, 36, 38, 54, 66, 111, 114, 153, 162, 163, 165, 168, 234, 241, 255, 256.
  6-pounder, 54, 110.
  17-pounder, 54, 110, 125, 158.
Archer, H. 226.
Archibald, A. R., 221.
Arethusa, HMS, 182.
Argentan, 247, 248, 250, 252.
Arnhem, 77.
Arril,Ken, 24, 64, 85, 115, 131, 167, 182.
Atlantic Wall (*Atlantikwall*), 28, 31, 51, 70, 74, 75, 77, 80, 85, 122, 124, 163, 168, 202, 204, 206, 209, 213, 215, 222, 242.
Australia,-ns, 9, 14.
Austria, 12.
Axis, 9, 13, 19, 52.

Baku, 62.
Ball, Mike, 111.
Ballingall, Jim, 162, 241.
Bangalore torpedo, 43, 45, 47, 49, 50, 65, 111, 127, 142, 201.
Barrels,use of, 140-144.
Barrie (ON), 10.
Basseneville, 147.
Bastien, O. M., 147, 182.

Battle of the Atlantic, 9, 13, 14, 69.
Bavent, 22, 24, 42, 43, 82, 83, 148, 153, 155, 164, 167, 169, 170, 172-181.
  Bois de, 99, 117, 154-157, 166, 169, 227, 244, 254-255.
Beachy Head, 69.
Beaudoin, D. N. J., 76, 81, 82, 95, 96, 103-106, 135, 140.
Beauvais, 246.
Begg, Robert **60**
Belgium, 9, 12, 156, 190, 256, 259.
Bellengreville, 28, 207, 208.
Benouville, 108, 129, 156, 167, 168, 207, 208, 220, 230.
Bergen-Belsen, 1, 259.
Bernieres, 207.
Beuzeville, 76, 82, 258.
Bismutka, Peter, 38, 65, 72, **99**, 108-114, 127.
Black marketeers, 191, 247.
Blagborne, B. T., 87, 165.
Blair,A.E., 221.
Blindness, psychological, 236-238.
Bliss, Charles, 225, 256.
Boardman, R., 149, 241.
"Bomb Alley" (See Inward Bend.) 228, 231, 232.
Bombing, 38, 50, 75, 79, 80, 82, 91, 108-110, 116, 121, 136, 200, 212.
Bon Saveur hospital, 251.
Booby-traps, 22, 180.
Boulogne, 196.
Bourguebus, 208, 243.
Boyd, G. R., 241.
Bradbrooke, George, 19, 21, 25, 30, **59**, 85, 86, 124, 155, 162, 164-165, 169, 181, 231, 257.
Bradley, Omar, 196.
Brady, W. J., 152-154.
Bras d'Or Lakes, 5.
Braumberger, H. D., 107.
Bray, Larry, 38, 47, 49, 116.
Brebner, Colin, **60**, 83, 84, 96-97, 167, 251.
Breen, George, 87, 88, 102, 103, 245.
Bren machine gun, 36, 79, 91, 92, 126, 127, 137, 138, 141, 143, 150, 153, 168, 172, 174, 202, 221, 234, 236, 241.
Brenner Pass, 21.
Breville, 28, 33, 34, 43, 157, 158, 164, 170, 171, 183, 214, 219, 220, 222, 224, 226-240.
Brickworks (See also Pottery), 224.
Bricqueville, 22, 24, 32, 147, 148, 153-155, 164, 169.
Bridges,
  Canada, 255, 256.
  Dives, 56, 82, 146, 159, 254.
  Divette, 42, 47, 49, 50, 111, 116, 128, 129,

158. (See also Robehomme.)
Le Hoin, 100, 148.
Orne, 33, 82, 108, 129, 131, 167, 183, 207, 208, 214, 217-219, 222, 225, 227, 242, 243.
Plain Lugan, 254.
St. Samson canal, 254.
Briefings, 19, 21, 22, 24, 26-34, 36-50, 159.
Britain, 8-10, 12, 13, 69.
Battle of, 13, 69.
British Army Units.
21st Army Group, 255, 256.
2nd Army, 156, 163, 197, 243, 254.
8th Army, 257.
1st Airborne Div., 208.
51st Highland Div., 156.
6th Airborne Div., passim.
3rd Infantry Div., 26, 109, 182, 227, 228.
6th Airlanding Bde., 26, 34, 158, 168, 183, 219, 224, 256.
3rd Parachute Bde., passim.
5th Parachute Bde., 26, 82, 108, 158, et al.
8th Parachute Bn., 29, 34, 82, 100, 129, et al.
9th Parachute Bn., 25, 29, 34, 39-42, et al.
12th Parachute Bn., 158, 219, 224, 225, 230, 231, 239.
13th Parachute Bn., 158, 219, 224.
22nd Independent Parachute Coy., 63, 197, 198, 210, 239.
Black Watch, 156, 221, 227-234, 237, 242.
Devonshire Rgt., 158, 230, 239.
Gordon Highlanders, 156, 227, 240.
Ox and Bucks Light Infantry, 108, 109, 158, 207, 208.
Royal Engineers, 22, 31, 49, 100, 110, 128, 147, 149, 176, 178, 180.
Royal Ulster Rifles, 158.
Worcestershire Yeomanry Rgt., 158.
4th Anti-tank Battery, 110.
51st Highland Div., 227, 239.
53rd Anti-tank Battery, 198, 230.
13/18 Hussars, 239.
(see also Commando.)
Broadfoot, James, 34, 76, 80, 81, 93-95, 106, 107, 136-143, **185**.
Brooks, R. R., 107.
Brussels, 246, 255.
Bulford, 14, 34.
Bulgaria, 12.
Bures, 28, 147, 159, 167, 200, 254.
Butte de la Hogue, 158, 167, 183, 218, 219, 227.

Cabourg, 24, 42, 43, 50, 72, 86, 129, 148, 157-160, 166, 172, 214, 222, 254.
Caen, passim.

Canal de, 85, 109, 156, 164, 166, 168.
Caesar,Julius, 69.
Cairo, 13.
Calvados, 99, 124, 205, 208, 209, 243, 251.
Cambremer, 152, 198, 200, 210, 212, 214.
Camembert, 254.
Camp Borden (ON), 10.
Camp Shilo (MB), 10, 11, 14, 101.
Canadian Army Units.
1st Canadian Army, 254, 257-259.
1st Canadian Corps, 65, 257, 258.
2nd Canadian Corps, 257.
Canadian Parachute Corps, 3, 10, 14.
4th Canadian Armoured Div., 163.
2nd Canadian Infantry Div., 163.
3rd Canadian Infantry Div., 73, 160, 163, 182, 205, 227, 240.
1st Special Service Bde. 10, 183, 261.
1st Canadian Parachute Bn., passim.
2nd Canadian Parachute Bn., 10.
Highland Light Infantry, 75.
Regiment de la Chaudiere, 73.
Royal Canadian Coastal Artillery, 13, 233.
Royal 22nd (Vingt-Deux) Rgt., 87.
St. John Fusiliers, 232.
Canals
(See also Caen, Canal de; Divette; St. Samson.), 22, 24, 26, 28, 29, 33, 54, 90, 101, 148, 152, 164, 176, 200.
Canaris, Wilhelm, 215.
Cap d'Antifer, 156.
Cape Breton, 4, 5, 7, 13, 18, 244.
Capraru, George, 52, 164, 182.
Carlton, Bob, 114.
Carpiquet, 102, 207, 208, 227.
Carter Barracks, 14, 19, 20, 36, 51, 253.
Carts, use of. 130, 131, 147, 149, 151.
Carver, Don, 65, 239.
Casares, Lieutenant, 251.
Casualties, 1, 31, 52, 114, 115, 167, 182, 183, 185, 192, 197, 221, 233-238, 239, 241, 242, 245, 256-259.
Caucasus, 12, 62.
Chaddock, Bill, 31, 66, **195**.
Channel, English, 21, 42, 56, 63, 66, 69, 71, 72, 75, 78, 82, 84, 85, 87.
Cherbourg (Cotentin Peninsula.), 199.
Christianson, D. R., 206-208.
Church, Jack, 66, 111, 113, 114, 127, 172.
Churchill, Henry, 15.
Churchill, Winston, 160, 214, 252.
Clancy, John, 24, 165.
Clark, Malcolm, 66.
Clark, W. J. (Knobby), 90, 106, 185.
Coburn, John, 102, 245.
Cody, Buffalo Bill, 2.

Coleville-sur-Orne, 99, 101, 109, 164, 206, 207.

Colombelles, 128, 158, 168, 208, 219.

Commandos, 40, 41, 120, 126, 131, 156-160, 166-168, 183, 184, 199, 219, 220, 224, 225, 229, 242, 256.

Comeau, Gilbert, 66, 70, 71, **73**, 172-175, 181.

Conneghan, Gordon, 81, 137, 138, 141-143, **156**.

Costigan, P. G. **60**.

Cote, Marcel, 34, 86-88, 102, 103, 165, 167, 185, 202, 205, 206, 212, 245.

Cote's plane, soldiers in, 87, 202, 213.

Crerar, Harry, 257, 258.

Crete, 9, 12, 209.

Crocker, J. T., 226, 258.

Croft, H. R. **66**.

Croxford, W.R., 165.

Cuer, Frank 77, 79.

Cuverville, 158.

Czechoslovakia 12.

Dakota, C-47, 56, 63, 64, 73-76, 79, 82, 83, 87, 88-91, 110, 113, 122, 162, 163, 198, 210-214, 253.

Damstrom, E. H. 66.

D-Day, passim.

Danestal, 205.

Davies, Gordon, **1**, 36, 38, 49, 111, 116, 128, 239.

Deauville, 43, 133, 185, 202, 205, 206, 213-215, 226.

Deception, 196, 197, 202, 214.

Delamere, E. J., 38, 47.

Depression, the, 2, 4, 5, 8.

Devil's Brigade, 10.

Dieppe, 62, 65, 69, 103, 133, 202.

Dives, River, passim.

Dives-sur-Mer, 42, 43, 50, 72, 129, 160, 172, 214, 254.

Divette canal, 22, 28, 38, 40, 49, 50, 100, 151, 158, 221.

Dodd, T. A. (Doc.), 52.

Douglas, Clifford, 66, 172, 234, 236.

Douve, River, 133.

Down Ampney, 27, 51, 63, 64, 73, 77, 89, 171.

Dozule, 27, 32, 76, 82, 83, 89, 93, 100, 106, 137, 258.

Dray, F. A. 149.

Drop Zones, passim.

Ducker, Bill, 52, 83.

Dumas, Jean, 102, 245.

Dunphy, Clyde, 102, 245.

Dunkirk, 65, 102, 196.

Dutch Harbor, 10, 13.

Duval, 161.

Eadie, Fraser, **59**, 257.

88-mm guns (enemy, self-propelled), 129, 163, 168, 216, 218, 228, 231, 233, 240.

Eisenhower, Dwight, 18, 62, 93.

El Alemain, 13.

Ellefson, Morris, 81, 91-94, 136-138, 140-143, **156**.

Elston, J. R. 238.

Embree, G. W., 24, 25, **216**, 241.

Equipment, paratroops', 11, 16, 62, 63, 65, 71, 73, 75, 88, 91, 93, 97, 110, 112, 160, 165, 167, 211.

Escape aids, 53.

Escoville, 26, 28, 100, 128, 129, 158, 162, 168, 208, 218, 220, 225-227, 240, 243, 244.

Eure, 208.

Evreux, 202, 206.

Exit Doors, 71, 108-109.

Explosive, plastic, 142, 147.

Falaise, 101, 207, 208, 212, 243, 250, 254.

Farms & farmers, Fr., 95, 106, 120, 136, 151, 154, 163, 181-183, 188, 246-250.

Fecamp, 195.

Feuchtinger, Edgar, 218, 219, 226, 230.

Field Ambulance No. 224: 39, 40, 41, 49, 97, 100, 110, 169, 175, 224, 229, 237, 241.

1st Allied Airborne Army, 257.

Flakvierling, 136, 204, 205.

Flashlamp, Operation, 63, 196.

Flers, 248.

Flexer, Alex, 38, 47, 107.

Flooding, 22, 28, 29, 46, 54, 69, 72, 74, 83, 90, 99, 110, 112-113, 118, 147, 152-155, 160, 165, 185, 198, 200.

Focke-Wulf 190: 137.

FOO (Forward Observation Officer), 176, 177, 178, 213, 233.

Fort Benning (GA), 10, 14, 101.

Fortitude, Operation, 209.

France, passim.

Franceville-Plage, 108.

Frankfurt, 246.

Fuller, Clayton, 21, 22, 24, 29, 64, 149, 170, 181-183.

Funston, Clifford, 164.

FUSAG, Operation, 196, 202, 213, 215.

Gale, Richard, 11, 26, 34, 53, 54, 56, **57**, 124, 156, 158, 171, 198, 226, 229-232, 239, 240, 255, 256.

Gammon bomb, 120, 142, 147, 174, 223.

Garbo, 215.

German Army Units.
7th Army, 162.
15th Army, 107, 109, 162, 196, 204, 205,

226.
Panzer Lehr Division, 205.
346th Infantry Div., 221, 226, 227, 230, 243.
711th Infantry Div., 107, 137, 163, 167, 198, 199, 224, 226, 230, 243, 255.
716th Infantry Div., 163, 167, 198, 199, 226.
12th SS Panzer Div., 198, 199, 205.
21st Panzer Div., 26, 56, 162, 167, 198, 199, 208, 212, 218, 219, 221, 223, 225-227, 230, 240, 243, 244.
21st Panzer Recce Bn., 218.
22nd Panzer Recce Bn., 218.
25th SS Panzer Grenadier Regt., 205, 206.
125th Regiment, 207, 208, 218, 219, 226, 244.
192nd Regiment, 208, 212.
736th Grenadier Rgt., 109, 207.
200th Assault Gun Bn., 218.
220th Antitank Bn., 218.
744th Grenadier Bn., 224-226, 255.
I-II Panzer Grenadier Bns., 218.
858 Regiment., 224.
Germany, 6, 9, 10, 52, 78, 202, 246, 259.
Gestapo, 8, 103, 117, 191, 194, 245.
Gillespie, J. E., 222.
Girvan, J. M., 167.
Glace Bay, 5, 13.
Glimmer, Operation, 196, 206, 215.
"Gods of war", 165, 202.
Goebbels, Josef, 204.
Gonneville-sur-Mer, 203.
Gonneville-sur-Merville, 25, 26, 33, 34, 40, 43, 45, 64, 72, 124, 146, 156, 210, 217.
Goodall,Frank, 164.
Goodwood/Atlantic, Operation, 243.
Goulet, Louie, 162, 163.
Goustranville, 22, 24, 32, 33, 146, 148, 149, 153, 154, 169, 182, 183.
Greece, 9, 12.
Green, Dwight, 241.
Greenway, P., 233.
Grenier, L. C., 38, 66, 112.
Griffin, Peter, 22, 24, 32, 33, 146, 148, 149, 153, 154, 169, 182, 183.
Guenther, H. E., 65, 239.
Gulf of St. Lawrence, 5, 10, 13.

Halifax (NS), 11, 13.
Halifax bomber, 63, 108, 110.
Hall, R. C., 83, 131, 238.
Hallucinations, 92, 93, 171.
Hamilcar glider, 54, 158, 160, 198, 224.
Hanson, John, 36, 38, 47, 49, 109, 115-118, 125-131, 164, 176, 177, 178, 228, 231, 232, 225, 239, 259.
Harwell, 45, 51, 63, 65, 73, 171, 200, 204.

Harfleur, 197, 213.
Harrington, A. E., 149.
Harris, George, 57, 74.
Harrison, Russel, 24.
Hart, R. C., 238.
Hartigan, Dan, 66, 69, 71, 79, 118-128, 130, 131, 176, 232-239.
Hawkins (Antitank Mine), 142, 147, 174.
Hauger, 28, 157, 166, 220.
Hedges, 28, 29, 43, 45, 90, 120, et al.
 "Jackboot hedge," 45, 72, 108.
 J-shaped, 43, 45, 46, 72, 110, 120, 121, 124.
Helena (MT), 10.
Hendrie, (Jock), 102, 224.
Henwood, L. S., 241.
Hermanville, 102, 109, 164, 206, 207.
Herouvillette, 28, 33, 34, 43, 128, 129, 156-159, 161, 166-168, 217, 218, 220, 222, 227, 240-243.
Hetherington, Jack, 88, 133.
Heuland, 109, 205-208.
Hiervieux, Laura, 111, 118, 124, 126, 128, 129.
 Rene, 117, 124.
Hilborn, Richard, 34, 86, 194, 165.
Hill, James, 11, 14,16, 26, 37, 49, 57, 65, 99, 110, 155, 160, 166, 197-199, 204, 205, 208, 217, 219, 221, 227, 229-231, 237, 240, 243, 255, 256.
Hindenberg, P. von, 6, 7.
Hitler, Adolf, 6, 7, 12, 117, 195, 204, 209, 215.
Hodge, V. W., 152.
Hogarth, Andy, 66, 87, 239.
Holland, 9, 12, 21, 256, 258.
Holloway, Howard, 108, 164.
Honfleur, 89, 133, 202, 205, 206, 214, 215, 259.
Hong Kong, 13, 65.
Horsa glider, 39, 54, 94, 95, 102, 110, 165, 198, 205, 224, 225.
Horsham hospital, 233, 253.
Hotchkiss arms factory, 42.
Houlgate, 196.
Howard, John, 207.
Huard, C. E., 182.
Hughes, H. W., 183.
Hungary, 9, 12.
Hutot, 89, 107.
Hyndman, C. F. 60.

Improvisation, 16, 118, 147.
India, 9.
Intelligence, British, 195, 202, 206, 215, 253.
Intelligence, German, 202, 204, 215.
Intelligence Section,
 (1st Cdn. Parachute Bn.), 27-29.
Interdiction points, 156, 217.

Interrogation, 103, 245, 246.
Inward Bend, 219, 220, 228-231, 240.
Irvine, Bill, 149.
Irving, Larry, 31, 32, 183.
Isle de France, the, 250-251.
Isley, Bert, 4, 8,10, 14, 73, 75, 81, 137, 138, 140, 141, 143, 213.
Italy, 9, 21, 52, 65, 69, 174, 251, 257.

Jack, A. J., 149.
Jackson, Tom, 162-164.
Japan, 9, 13, 52.
Jeans, Earnie, 90, 107.
Jodl, A., 204, 215.
Johnson, Charlie, 162, 163, 241.
Johnston, R. F., 37, 38.
Jones, L. S., 149, 169.
Juno Beach, 207, 227.

Keel, Tom, 49, 110, 116, 164, 222.
Keitel, Wilhem, 204.
Kelly, W. R., 49, 110, 113, 164, **245**.
Kemp, John, 31, 32, 147, 148, 154.
Kendry, W. H., 87, 102.
Kindersley, Hugh, 34, 229, 239.
Kit-bag, 16, 19, 20, 75, 84, 89, 90, 163.
Kivinen, H. W., 149.
Kortenhaus, W., 218.
Kristellnacht, 8.
Kroesing, G., 12, 109, 116, 133, 164, 207, 208.
Kuhlenthal, 215.

Labrador, 5, 8, 9.
Lacasse, Joe, 31, 147, 154, 182, 183.
Lacroix, G. R., 133, 203, 204.
Lancaster bomber, 63, 108, 110.
Lanthier, M., 182, 221.
La Riviere, 22, 32, 42.
La Roche Guyon, 206.
Le Bas de Breville, 28, 33, 38, 47, 85.
Le Bas de Ranville, 28.
Le Grand Homme, 64, 156.
Le Havre, 69,75, 79, 99, 102, 103, 133, 185, 196-202, 205-207, 212-214, 245, 246.
Le Hoin, 24, 28, 32, 40, 56, 64, 100, 148, 153, 154, 159.
Le Mans, 247, 248.
Le Mesnil.
  Crossroads, 30, 33, 40, 56, 64, 85, 100, 129, 137, 146, 149, 156, 160-171, 173, 176, 216- 243.
  Ridge, 100, 129, 132, 136, 144, 156, 157, 159, 161, 166, 169, 182, 183, 188, 213, 214, 217, 221, 240, 242, 243, 245, 249, 259.
Leningrad, 12.

Le Plain, 34, 157, 176.
Le Plein, 176, 177, 220, 240, 243.
Le Prieur, 168, 176-178.
Les Boursiers, 110, 118.
Les Champeaux, 254.
Les Champs, 22, 32.
Les Marmiers, 25, 28, 64, 156, 166.
Letters (censored & uncensored), 53.
Lewis, Colin, 89, 245.
Lights, Red/Green, 45, 71, 72, 78, 79, 83, 88, 89, 107, 108, 110, 118, 150, 213.
"Lilli Marlene", 53.
Lisieux, 187, 197, 202, 205, 206.
Littlehampton, 199.
Little Sisters of the Poor, 251.
Lockyer, Mark, 147, 183.
Lodgement area, 24, 29, 54, 82, 102, 128, 153, 158, 159, 163, 168, 183, 198, 204, 217, 219, 242, 243, 245.
Lombardy poplars, 39, 47, 48, 112, 114, 127, 130, 132.
Longuemare, 157, 166, 220.
Longueval, 116, 156, 158, 164, 167, 168, 217-219, 240, 243.
Louisbourg, 5, 13.
Lovat, Lord, 156, 166, 167, 183, 184, 219, 220, 224, 229, 239, 242.
Luck, Hans von, 26, 207, 208, 218, 219, 226, 227, 243, 244.
Luftwaffe, 102, 103.
Luxembourg, 246.
Lynn, Vera, 66.

MacInnis, A. J. (Scotty), 4-8, 10, 16, 18, 35, 72, 73, 81, 104, 106, 145, 185, 194, 244, 259, **260**.
MacKenzie, Colin, 81, 104, 106, 185, 203.
MacLean, D. S., 24, 167.
MacLean, Dick, 38, 47-49, 65, 66, 72, 110-112, 116, 118, 126, 128, 129, 164, 174, 176-178, 180, 236, 239, 256.
MacLeod, Murray, 36-39, 42, 45, 47, 49, 50, **51**, 64, 72, 84, 108, 110-114, 167, 258.
MacPhee, Mosher, 31, 36, 38, 48, 66, 111, 112, 115-117, 124-131, 175-178, 180, **245**.
MacPherson, Jim, 3, 7, 8, 10, 14, 73, 79, 81, 94, 95, 136-138, 140-143, 185-188, 190, 191, 194, 213, 245-250.
Madden, John, 36, 38, 47, 49, 101, 109, 115, 164, 165, 206-208.
Maison Mauger, 258.
Makela, Esko, 126-128.
Mallard, Operation, 196, 199.
Mallon, Eddie, 47, 66, 121-124, 127, 172, 234-238.
Manoir du Monts, 132.

MAPS, 15, 23, 41, 44, 48, 55, 68, 105, 119, 134, 157, 173, 179, 203.
Maquis, 247-249, 252.
Mass Drop, 16, **17**.
McGowan, Sam, 31, 36, 38, 47, 48, 66, 109, 115, 132, **146**, 164, 173, 175, 178-180, 223, 236.
McIsaac, R. M., 182, 183.
McNally, Andrew, **19**, 47, 66, 86, 111, 118, 178, 239.
McWillians, Gordon, 81, 133, 137.
Mearow, Douglas, 102, 243.
Medics, 110, 131, 148, 224, 237, 238.
Merville Battery, passim.
Meyer, Kurt, 205, 206.
Middleton, Joe, 115, 118, 131.
Middleton, Willie, 66, 71, 172, 200.
Midway (battle), 13.
Miller, Harold, 87, 88, 102, 246.
Minard, Willard, 47, 48, 109, 112, 116, 164, 165, 176, 233, 256.
Minor, Harvey, 90, 107.
Mirages, 92.
Mitchell, R. J., 24, 154, **162**, 169, 170, 241.
Moffatt, Joseph, 73, 81, 137, 185.
Mohring, H. S., **108**.
Mokelki, Ralph, 48, 65, 111, 113, 114, 175, 178, 180, 234-237, 239.
Mont Canisy, 185, 205, 206, 213, 214.
Monte Casino, 251.
Montgomery, Bernard, 18, 74, 85, 217, 243, 257.
Montivilliers, 99, 102, 133, 185, 201, 205-207, 212, 213, 245, 254.
Morgan, Harvey, 38, 65, 66, 70, 71, 110, 116, 164, 172-175.
Morrison, Colin, 66, 172, 174, 222.
Mortar,
"Moaning Minnie", 172, 228.
Nebelwerfer, 243.
2" & 3", 34, 36, 47, 111, 116, 125, 127, 128, 130-132, 136, 165, 167, 168, 174, 182, 186, 224, 225, 234, 252.
Moscow, 12.
Mosley, L., 225.
Mosquito fighter-bomber, 38, 50, 63, 108, 109.
Munro, E. T., 107, 167, 208.
Murray, George, 175, 250.
Murray, W. D., **66**, 236, 239.

NAAFI(canteen), 30, 73.
Nanaimo(BC), 10.
Naylor,Gordon, 170.
Nazis,-ism, 7-13, 51, 52, 65, 74, 87, 103, 117, 195, 245.
Neufeld,L. A., 38, 66, 114, 115, 125.

Neptune, Operation, 196, 197, 199, 202, 215.
Neutral countries, 9.
Newfoundland, 8, 9, 13.
Newman,Ray, 162, 169-171, 181.
New Zealand, 9.
Nickerson, C. H., 83, 147.
Nicklin, Jeff, 30, **59**, 64, 85, 86, 164, 165, 256, 257.
Nigh, Joseph, 87, 102, 245.
Normandy, passim.
North Bay, (ON), 3, 73.
North Sydney (NS), 5.
Norway, 9, 10, 12, 21.
Noval, Bill, 149.
Nova Scotia, 4, 11, 13, 18, 73.

Objectives.
Airborne, 19-35, 36-50, 100, 108, 156, 158-160, 217, 229.
Enemy, 183, 218, 219, 224, 226.
O'Connell, T. B. 107.
Octeville, 99, 102, 103, 133, 185, 201, 202, 205-207, 212-215, 245, 246.
Oikle, W. E., 36, 38, 66, 111, 114, 115, 125, **245**.
O'Leary, L. E., **133**, 149, 152, 153.
Omaha Beach, 133.
Operation Order No. 1, 32, 83.
Orne, River, passim.
Otway, Terence, 26, 123-125, 210, 220, 231.
Ouistreham, 40, 43, 109, 156, 166.
Outhwaite, R., 147, 154, 183, 206, 243, 259.
Overlord, Operation, 196.
Owens, Jesse, 7.
Oxtoby, Mel, 76, 81, 95, 104, 106, **146**.

Pacific, the, 9, 10, 13, 14.
Paddle, Operation, 254, 255.
Page, E. W. 221.
Parachute Infantry Training Coy., 10.
Parachute Training Centre, 10, 14.
Paris, 99, 133, 197, 198, 242, 243, 246.
Parker Force, 158, 219, 230.
Parker, R. G., 158, 219.
Pas de Calais, 215.
Pasquill, Tom, 31, 32, 83, 147, 154, 182.
Passwords, 64, 65, 80, 81, 91, 95, 121, 125, 146.
Paterson, W., 87.
Pathfinders, 40, 63, 199.
Patrols, 153, 154, 169, 171, 176, 216, 222, 223, 240, 244.
Patton, George, 196, 202.
Paynter, Don, 149.
Pearl Harbor, 9, 13.
Pearson, A., 164.

Pearson, Alistair, 208.

Periers-en-Auge, 24, 32, 42, 43, 148, 152, 153, 159, 172, 222, 224.

Perimeter, Airborne (See also Inward Bend; "Bomb Alley"), 156-160, 167-169, 176, 181-184, 207, 218, 219, 226, 228, 230, 240, 242, 243.

Petiville, 22, 31, 32, 42, 47, 111, 161, 168.

Pilon, R. E., 66, 239.

Pinay, Edward, 66, 110.

Plain Lugan, 254.

Plateau country, 133-145, 156, 164, 185-194, 204, 207, 212, 245.

Pledger, Kenneth, 81, 135, 137, 138, 140-143, **195**.

Plexiglas, 66, 200.

Poett, Nigel, 34, 82, 167, 198, 229.

Poland, 9, 12, 13, 89.

Pont l'Evêque, 43, 76, 82, 106, 258.

Pottery/brickworks (smokestack), 155, 162-164, 224.

Press, the, 18, 27, 56, 100, 102, 214, 225-227.

Prisoners of War, 53, 102.
  Hands tied, 93, 115, 186.
  See also Escape aids.

Proctor, H. D., **59**.

Provost Section, 27.

Queen Elizabeth, the, 11.

Quicksilver, Operation, 196.

Race, D. A., 221.

Radar (Eureka; Rebecca), 16, 66.

Ranville, 28, 43, 102, 108, 109, 129, 156, 158, 168, 214, 218, 224, 225, 227, 230.

Reed, Dick, 189-191, 246-250.

Reid, Harry, 146.

Resistance, French (See also Maquis), 188, 189, 192-194, 246.
  Albert, 246, 250.
  Marcel, 249, 250.
  Peter, 246, 247.
  Rene, 117.

Rhine, River, 211, 246, 259.

Rice, Earl, 36, 38, 101, 109, 116, 164, 165, 206-208, 233.

Ringway Parachute Training School, 73.

Risle, River, 133.

Robehomme, 22, 24, 28, 32, 40, 56, 64, 82-85, 100, 107, 146-156, 159, 164, 165, 168-171, 181.

Roberts, Joe, 164.

Roberts, John, 241.

Robertson, George, 74, 76, 79, 81, 95, 96, 104, 135-138, 140, 141, 143, 205, 213.

Rommel, Erwin, 13, 51, 162, 204, 206.

Roosevelt, Franklin D., 9.

Ross, John, 38, 66, 110, 112.

Ross, L. D., 149, 152, 153.

Rouen, 82, 103, 106, 187, 197, 246.

Rousseu, Maurice, 32.

Rousseau, Philippe, 24, 32, 64, 73, 75-77, 80, 81, 85, 93, 95, 100, 104, 106, 133, 135, 140, 141, 167, 181, 182, **185**, 202-204, 206, 213, 214.

Roy, F. N., 170.

Royal Air Force, 8, 13, 56, 63, 77, 80, 91, 108, 109, 121, 160, 195, 196.

Royal Canadian Air Force, 8, 72, 109, 160.

Royal Canadian Navy, 8, 13.

Royal Navy, 109, 160, 196, 228, 230, 233.

Rudko, Freddie, 112-114, 126, 256.

Rumania, 9, 12.

Rundstedt, Gerd von, 204-206.

Russell, Fred, 66

Russia, 9, 10, 12, 209,

St. Côme.
  Château, 157, 166, 167, 183, 220, 227-235, 239, 240, 243.
  Forest, 28, 99, 157, 161, 164, 166, 168, 170, 171, 182, 216, 219, 221, 232-239, 241.

St. Germain-en-Laye, 206.

St. Lambert, 254.

St. Lô, 197, 243, 251.

St. Samson canal, 254, 256.

St. Vaast-en-Auge, 133, 203, 204.

Ste. Honorine, 129, 156, 158, 167, 168, 219, 220, 225, 226, 240, 243.

Salerno, 217.

Salisbury Plain, 37, 101.

Sallenelles, 25, 28, 64, 156, 157, 166, 220, 243.

Sangster, W., 149.

"Satan's Quadrangle", 89, 99, 107, 109, 147, 152, 156, 170, 171, 181, 195, 217, 245.

Sauder, L., **36**, 65, 175, 239.

Saunders, Myles, 47, 65, 66, 71, 111, 132, 175, 181, 236.

Scatari Island, 5, 13.

Scattering of paratroops, 85, 86, 90, 91, 99-103, 109-111, 146, 153, 160, 161, 164, 165, 181, 195, 217, 245.
  Enigmas of, 195-215.

Schillemore, Arthur, 81, 137, 138, 141, 143.

Schmeisser submachine gun, 139, 173, 174, 223, 249.

Schroeder, E., 169.

Scotland, 11, 14.

Security transit camp, 19, 20, 27, 34, 37, 40, 51, 62, 94, 101.

Seine-Maritime, 99.

Seine, River, passim.

Shulist, Stanley, 80, 81, 91, 95-98, 106, 140, 213.
Shwaluk, W. W., 149, 182, 221.
Sicily, 209, 217.
Signals station, enemy, 28, 38, 42, 47, 49, 112, 159.
Simpson, John, 85, 165.
Sinclair, J. S., 107.
Sleep, lack of, 93, 171, 216.
Slipp, George, 149, 183.
Sloan, J. G., 66.
Smith, Hiram, 88, 133, 154.
Snipers, 128, 172, 174, 222.
Special Air Service, 197, 202, 206, 213.
Spitfire, 94, 95, 164, 250.
Stacey, C. P. 207, 208.
Stalingrad, 12, 13.
Stammers, Arthur, 182.
Static offensive, 171, 243, 244.
Sten gun, 223, 246.
Sterling bomber, 63.
Sticks (of paratroops), 45, 47, 66, 72, 73, 75, 76, 80, 81, 83, 87-91, 100, 102, 103, 106, 107, 109, 110, 118, 133, 146, 147, 149, 150, 188, 195, 201-208, 211, 212.
Stonehenge, 14, 20.
Strafing, 38, 50, 108, 109, 228.
Stuart, Ken, 257.
Suez Canal, 13.
Sulpha (sulfa), 94.
Summerhays, W. J., 102, 245.
Sweder, W. L., 107.
Swim, H. B., 47-49, 65, 72, 108, 110-115, 126, 127, 132, 175-181, 236, 258.
Sword Beach, 21, 26, 43, 109, 126, 129, 131, 166, 206, 207, 219, 227, 240.
Sydney Harbour, 10.
Sydney (NS), 4, 5, 13, 73, 259.
Sydney Mines, 5, 226.

Tailleville, 109, 207, 208.
Tanks, 24, 34, 54, 129, 163, 168, 169, 229, 231, 233-235, 237, 241.
Taskman, 234.
Taxable, Operation, 196, 206, 215.
Thomas, J. P. 52, 222.
Thompson, G. A., 66, 110, 113, 115.
Timmins (ON), 96.
Titanic, Operation, 196, 197, 202, 213, 215.
Tonga, Operation, 196.
Toseland, Norman, 22, 24, 31-33, 64, 82-85, 107, 146-154, 166, 169, 182, 183, 222-224.
Touffreville, 158, 161, 167, 227.
Touques, River, 106, 133, 215, 226.
"Toys", 46.

Training, 10, 11, 14-19, 36, 46, 123.
Transatlantic Ferry Command, 9.
Trenfield, N. W., 149.
Trenholm, Jack, 81, 95, 96, 104, 106, 135, 140.
Trepanier, R. E., 49, 116.
Troarn, 22, 28, 31-34, 43, 82, 89, 97, 107, 109, 148, 149, 152, 156, 159, 172, 198, 200, 208, 211, 222, 227, 244, 255.
Trouville, 133, 214, 226.
Trowbridge party, 32, 33, 146, 148.
Trun, 252, 254.
Tukhachevsky, Mikhayl, 209.
Turner, D. G., 221.

U-boats, 13.
U. S. A., 9, 10, 12, 14.
U. S. 3rd Army, 246.

Varaville, 22, 30-34, 38-40, 42-50, 181, et al.
    Chateau, 110-112, 115, 120, 124, 125, 130.
    Church Tower, 118, 126, 128.
    Concrete Bunker, 38, 39, 42, 47, 49, 111-113, 115, 118, 128, 131.
    Gatehouse, 112, 114-116, 126-128, 130, 131.
Vernon (BC), 10.
Verriers, 28.
Veterans, Airborne, 209.
Vickers machine gun, 30,34, 86, 88, 148, 154, 165, 188, 192, 224, 226, 232, 241, 255, 256.
Villers-sur-Mer, 106, 133, 185, 202, 205, 206, 213-215.
Vimont, 208.

Waddell, Don, 102, 245.
Walker, H. M., 36, 38, 47-49, 110-115, 125, 167, 216.
Walker, Reginald, 47.
Warwick, Mike, 102, 245.
Weathersbee, R. D. J., 21, 29, 85, 86.
Wetzlar, 246.
Wilkins, Don, 24-26, 29, 64.
Willes, John, 221, 240, 254.
William the Conqueror, 69.
Willsey, V. S., 81, 137, 139, 140, 143.
Wind, Force 6: 199, 204.
Witt, F., 205.
Wood Mountain hills (SK), 2, 73, 77, 92, 186.
Woodward, S. R., 66.
World War One, 1-3, 8, 9, 18, 78, 132, 250.
World War Two, 1, 7-9, 13, 52, 195, 197, 209, 256.
Worthing, 199, 212.
Wright, D. F., 107.
Wright, Harry, 66, 111, 116, 130, 174, 176.